REAL IMAGES
Soviet Cinema and the Thaw

JOSEPHINE WOLL

I.B. Tauris *Publishers*
LONDON · NEW YORK

First published in 2000 by I.B. Tauris & Co Ltd,
Victoria House, Bloomsbury Square, London WC1B 4DZ
175 Fifth Avenue, New York NY 10010
website: http://www.ibtauris.com

In the United States of America and in Canada distributed by
St Martin's Press, 175 Fifth Avenue, New York NY 10010

A full CIP record for this book is available from the British Library
A full CIP record for this book is available from the Library of Congress

ISBN 1 86064 369 8 hardback
ISBN 1 86064 550 X paperback

Library of Congress catalog card number: available

Set in Monotype Calisto by Ewan Smith, London
Printed and bound in Great Britain By WBC Ltd, Bridgend

Contents

Illustrations

KINO: The Russian Cinema Series
General Editor's Preface

Cinema has been the predominant popular art form of the first half of the twentieth century, at least in Europe and North America. Nowhere was this more apparent than in the former Soviet Union, where Lenin's remark that 'of all the arts, for us cinema is the most important' became a cliché and where cinema attendances were until recently still among the highest in the world. In the age of mass politics Soviet cinema developed from a fragile but effective tool to gain support among the overwhelmingly illiterate peasant masses in the civil war that followed the October 1917 Revolution, through a welter of experimentation, into a mass weapon of propaganda through entertainment that shaped the public image of the Soviet Union – both at home and abroad and for both élite and mass audiences – and latterly into an instrument to expose the weaknesses of the past and present in the twin processes of *glasnost* and *perestroika*. Now the national cinemas of the successor republics to the old USSR are encountering the same bewildering array of problems, from the trivial to the terminal, as are all the other ex-Soviet institutions.

Cinema's central position in Russian and Soviet cultural history and its unique combination of mass medium, art form and entertainment industry, have made it a continuing battlefield for conflicts of broader ideological and artistic significance, not only for Russia and the Soviet Union but also for the world outside. The debates that raged in the 1920s about the relative revolutionary merits of documentary as opposed to fiction film, of cinema as opposed to theatre or painting, or of the proper role of cinema in the forging of post-Revolutionary Soviet culture and the shaping of the new Soviet man, have their echoes in current discussions about the role of cinema *vis-à-vis* other art forms in effecting the cultural and psychological revolution in human consciousness necessitated by the processes of economic and political transformation of the former Soviet Union into modern democratic and industrial societies and states governed by the rule of law. Cinema's central position has also made it

General Editor's Preface

a vital instrument for scrutinizing the blank pages of Russian and Soviet history and enabling the present generation to come to terms with its own past.

This series of books intends to examine Russian and Soviet films in the context of Russian and Soviet cinema, and Russian and Soviet cinema in the context of the political and cultural history of Russia, the Soviet Union and the world at large. Within that framework the series, drawing its authors from both East and West, aims to cover a wide variety of topics and to employ a broad range of methodological approaches and presentational formats. Inevitably this will involve ploughing once again over old ground in order to re-examine received opinions but it principally means increasing the breadth and depth of our knowledge, finding new answers to old questions and, above all, raising new questions for further inquiry and new areas for further research.

The continuing aim of the series is to situate Russian and Soviet cinema in their proper historical and aesthetic context, both as a major cultural force in Russian history and Soviet politics and as a crucible for experimentation that is of central significance to the development of world cinema culture. Books in the series strive to combine the best of scholarship, past, present and future, with a style of writing that is accessible to a broad readership, whether that readership's primary interest lies in cinema or in Russian and Soviet political history.

Richard Taylor
Swansea, Wales

Preface

This book deals with Soviet cinema of the 'thaw' years, a period here demarcated as beginning in 1954 and ending in 1967. From the start the designations so confidently proclaimed by the title raise questions. The thaw conventionally denotes a particular period of Soviet history, essentially the years of Khrushchev's rule (1953–64), and the ideas that characterized it, but does that metaphoric designation apply to cinema? In other words, had cinema been frozen, did it melt into new life, did that regeneration falter or die? The subtitle couples Soviet cinema and the thaw. Does Soviet cinema here refer to the movie industry – studios, personnel, censorship, distribution – and its relationship with a political and intellectual phenomenon? Or does it signify the impact of that phenomenon on the movies themselves, images projected onto a screen in a dark room? The thaw's dominant ideological revisions included dethroning Stalin's cult of personality and some of its collateral historical falsifications. To what extent and in what ways did such revisions pertain to film? Finally, the title itself ambiguously juxtaposes reality and image. Do real images constitute a coy denial of actuality, an implication that those images themselves constitute reality, or does the seeming oxymoron conceal compatibility and interdependence?

The first set of questions has relatively straightforward answers. The metaphor of thaw fits cinema reasonably well. Like all the arts in the Soviet Union, cinema suffered acutely during the last years of Stalin's reign, in a variety of ways, and slowly revived afterwards. Throughout Soviet history, thanks largely to the Bolsheviks' recognition of the propaganda possibilities inherent in cinema's technology, the Soviet film industry consistently received substantial state support, even in the post-war years when production languished. Beginning in late 1954, a palpable sense of excitement pervaded the studios, the industry's primary journal *Iskusstvo kino*, and its most important training centre, the State Institute of Cinematography (VGIK). Released from the most onerous political shackles, if not from doctrinaire constraints, film-making took off, and audiences responded with enthusiasm.

Preface

Not that Stalin's death marked an absolute or clear watershed. On the one hand, individuals who had been active in the industry in 1951 and 1952 did not vanish on 6 March 1953, nor did their *modus operandi*; on the other hand, signs of renewal pre-dated Stalin's death, most concretely in Vsevolod Pudovkin's *The Return of Vasilii Bortnikov* [Vozvrashchenie Vasiliia Bortnikova], completed shortly before the director's death in 1953. With its psychological credibility, its lyricism, its treatment of infidelity, and its imaginative use of camera and sound, *Bortnikov*'s portrait of an unhappy veteran's difficult readjustment to civilian and family life anticipates the Soviet films of the late 1950s and early 1960s. But its poetry and imagination reflect Pudovkin's artistry and personality; *Bortnikov* is not a 'typical' film of that period.

The thaw was marked by hesitations and reversals as much as by liberalization and greater candour. Skittish compromises and dogmatic retrenchments hobbled each step forward. Nevertheless, in the years between the Twentieth Party Congress of 1956 and the fiftieth anniversary of the Bolshevik Revolution in 1967, the film industry flourished. The number of full-length features increased dramatically, from fewer than fifty to roughly triple that number. Facilities and personnel expanded proportionately. With the end of Stalinist isolation, Soviet cinema benefited from exposure to a wider world that encompassed West European (and, to a much lesser degree, American) film as well as the cinema of Soviet bloc nations.

Most of the generation of directors and scriptwriters whose careers had flowered in the Stalin years continued to work within the industry, though by and large their films have not endured. Two men were particularly influential. Ivan Pyrev had had a long and successful career as a director before the thaw began, but his prominence during the thaw derived from the high administrative posts he occupied within the industry, and from his willingness to use his stature and his bureaucratic power in the interests of film and, especially, of young film-makers. Mikhail Romm, with an illustrious career behind him, spent much of the 1950s quiescent as a director, although he remained exceedingly active as a teacher and mentor to younger colleagues. Unlike Pyrev, Romm found within himself creative resources that resulted in two of the most significant films of the thaw, *Nine Days of One Year* [Deviat' dnei odnogo goda, 1962] and *Ordinary Fascism* [Obyknovennyi fashizm, 1965].

Two generations of film-makers emerged in one short decade, both of whom studied their craft with their elders. The first wave of young men – nearly all were men – finished their training in the early 1950s, and were entrusted with film projects just as the thaw was beginning in earnest. For the most part these were the men who made the landmark films of the mid-1950s: Grigorii Chukhrai's *The Forty-first* [Sorok-pervyi, 1956], Marlen Khutsiev's *Spring on Zarechnaia Street* [Vesna na Zarechnoi ulitse, 1956], Aleksandr Alov and Vladimir

Real Images

Naumov's *Pavel Korchagin* [1956], Eldar Riazanov's *Carnival Night* [Karnaval'naia noch', 1956].

Within a few years of the first wave of thaw films, a second group of gifted men and women graduated from the State Institute of Cinematography in the early 1960s. They – Andrei Tarkovskii, Kira Muratova, Nikita Mikhalkov, Larisa Shepitko, Elem Klimov, Georgii Danelia and many others – began their careers in the twilight of Khrushchev's reign and the hopeful dawn of Brezhnev's. Brimming with energy and ideas, their youth and professional inexperience made them more vulnerable (if not more victimized) than their older colleagues to the increasing repressions, and their careers suffered, in some cases substantially, in the stultifying atmosphere of 1967 and 1968.

The end of the thaw for cinema was not co-terminous with Khrushchev's reign: it outlasted him by a few years. Nor did it end abruptly, its scope and tolerance abrogated in one action like the invasion of Czechoslovakia. Filmmakers of talent continued to work, and the industry itself prospered, turning out a flood of feature films, documentaries, popular science films, children's movies and cartoons, and movies made for television. But by 1967, the thaw for Soviet cinema was over. Significantly intensified state intervention blocked what might otherwise have appeared on Soviet screens. Censors abounded in different posts and at various levels of the system, and they vetoed potentially innovative projects, aborted interesting scripts, re-edited or shelved imaginative and untraditional films, stifled the creative dialogue that would have evolved naturally among artists.

This book, then, examines the film industry as it revived over a period of a dozen or so years, and its relationship to the structures of power in Soviet society. But those years also witnessed a far more elusive metamorphosis, a revision of concepts integral to Stalinism, and to Stalinist Soviet society. Movies were tremendously popular throughout this era. During the 1950s and 1960s, the average Soviet citizen visited cinemas at least twice a month; regular viewers attended about thirty-five times a year. People spent about as much time at the movies as they spent reading newspapers. Until the late 1960s, when television replaced cinema as the dominant medium of entertainment and information, films had a major impact on the way people thought, fantasized, understood their past and construed their future. Formal ideology, Marxist–Leninist and socialist realist, retained its official primacy: like any revealed truth, it could not be significantly modified. But slippery and amorphous cultural paradigms could and did change.

During the twenty-five years of Stalin's reign, school textbooks and mass-marketed fiction, popular songs and movies, Young Communist League (Komsomol) and factory and Party meetings defined the individual's relationship to the collective, the relationship of public and private, family roles, the nature of heroism and key aspects of national history. The definitions were not uniform

Preface

throughout those years, but they were precise and, at any given time, relatively inflexible.

Thus the Cultural Revolution of 1928–31, with its apotheosis of industry, levelling of human differences, and militancy towards anyone suspected of political ambivalence, chose its heroes from among Komsomol activists and dedicated soldiers of the revolution. Between 1932 and 1936, when socialist realism triumphed as the dominant cultural ideology, its hostility towards stylistic individuality created a unified mass culture. Joyful movies celebrated new heroes: the simple-hearted but shrewd Chapaev, one of the most beloved of Soviet screen protagonists; intellectuals (*Baltic Deputy* [Deputat Baltiki, 1936]); risk-taking aviators (*Valerii Chkalov*, 1941) or their fictional counterparts (the stunt man in *The Circus* [Tsirk, 1936]).

In the frightening and culturally repressive post-war years, resolutely bland and optimistic movies apotheosized leaders both historical and contemporary, all bearing an uncanny resemblance to Stalin, while ordinary men and women more or less vanished from the screen. After 1953, slowly and unsteadily, film-makers reassessed and revised all of these paradigms, leapfrogging over the final years of Stalinism to reclaim some of Soviet cinema's earlier images and values. Cinema was hardly unique in exploiting the expanding opportunities available after Stalin's death to urge reconsideration of such concepts. But because of its power to affect viewers, to impress on them new images, to manipulate how as well as what they saw, cinema may finally have merited the famous description attributed to Lenin as the most important of all the arts.

The films of this period were intimately embedded within the thaw. As part of the cultural machinery of the Soviet state, they reacted to shifts in official policy. Directors recut old films to eliminate scenes with Stalin, and considered the will and whims of powerful individuals as they worked on new ones. More significantly, many film-makers, scriptwriters, cameramen, editors and film critics were active, deliberate and usually eager participants in the transformation of national consciousness signified by the thaw.

Film plots and genres reflected the legitimation of private emotions and lives in an emerging focus on ordinary people living everyday lives. The virtually interchangeable leader-figures of late Stalinist cinema gave way to fallible, puzzled, ambivalent heroes and heroines; villainy lost its cartoon dimensions; schematic black and white shaded, often quite literally, into grey. Films presented critical national icons, Lenin in particular, and the mythologized history of the civil war and the Second World War, with different emphases and from different angles – actual as well as figurative – than had been possible before. Whether they promoted officially-sanctioned attitudes, such as criticism of obstructive bureaucrats, anticipated mandated changes, or defied official strictures, film-makers used the power of their medium to shape the attitudes of their fellow Soviets.

Real Images

For that reason, this book combines chronologically structured cultural history with analysis of individual films. I selected films for various reasons. Between 1954 and about 1960, although production increased every year, the Soviet film industry generated relatively few B-grade movies. The movies of significance declare themselves, as much by their distribution patterns and audience-size as by their substance, critical reception and continuing reputation; it was not difficult to identify influential films for close study, since people were able to see little else. With a few exceptions, almost all of those films came out of the Russian rather than republican studios. Of that body of work, I tried to examine films that most compellingly demonstrate the radical revision of critical themes and values, whether the acceptance of private feeling or the exaltation of labour, rather than leader.

In the early and mid-1960s the situation changed. By then well over a hundred (if probably never the 150 claimed) feature films opened annually, produced by flourishing republican studios as well as Mosfilm, Lenfilm and Moscow's Gorky Studio, nominally specializing in films for children and young adults but in fact producing general features. Despite official resistance to the ideologically unacceptable division between elite and mass cinema, in reality a body of B-grade movies developed, many made for television. I tried to see as many as I could, but they are under-represented in this book; since those I did manage to see generally confirmed the trends discernible in more celebrated work, I concentrated on the latter.

Russian films receive disproportionate prominence over republican films. By the mid-1960s the republican studios released several of the most innovative and provocative films produced in the Soviet Union. The Baltic studios, each of the rapidly developing Central Asian studios, the Georgian, Armenian, Belorussian and Ukrainian studios merit separate attention, for whether or not one can attribute a national style to each, their films are strikingly, visibly distinctive. I scrutinize several that received Soviet-wide distribution, and discuss their relationship to contemporary Russian cinema, but I am neither thorough nor comprehensive. Indeed, they deserve a book of their own.

The majority of films discussed in this book are now, fortunately, available on videocassette, in most cases without English subtitles. While I strove mightily to convey in a verbal medium some sense of film as a visual and aural medium, language is incommensurate with and inadequate to the task. I hope that after reading this book, intrigued readers will want to seek out the films and see – in every sense of the word – for themselves.

I am grateful to many people, institutions and organizations who helped me complete this work. In Moscow, the State Institute for Film Research (NIIK), and its director Liudmila Budiagina, graciously arranged film screenings and access to printed material; its staff, like that of the State Archive for Literature and Art (RGALI), was consistently helpful. I am especially grateful to colleagues at the Museum of the Cinema and to its director, the indefatigable and remarkable Naum Kleiman.

With their overwhelming abundance of cultural signs – from decor to dance fads, hemlines to hairdos, pop songs to political slogans – movies may be the most culturally specific of all media, and no westerner, however knowledgeable, can understand Russian culture the way Russians do. To the extent that I accurately 'read' Russian films and understood them within their historical and societal context, I did so largely thanks to borrowed Russian lenses. I relied on the stimulating work of Russian scholars, in particular Lev Anninskii, Vitalii Troianovskii, Valerii Fomin and Irina Shilova, the last of whom took time out of a frenetic schedule to discuss my project. Maia Turovskaia, doyenne of film scholars, generously shared memories and advice, reminding me of how much I had still to learn without discouraging me from proceeding. Russians living in the West, in particular Konstantin Simis and Dina Kaminskaia, dredged up forty-year-old reactions and deciphered obscure references for me.

I enjoyed the hospitality of the School of Slavonic and East European Studies at the University of London, using its library and exploiting above all the knowledge, taste, judgement and film collection of Julian Graffy. I fruitfully discussed movies and the thaw with Richard Taylor, Ian Christie, Birgit Beumers, Svetlana Carsten, Stanley Forman and James Mann, colleagues and fellow movie-buffs in London and at Oxford.

My sabbatical, during which I drafted most of this book, was funded by a generous grant from the National Endowment for the Humanities. IREX's support enabled me to see films and read archival material in Moscow; in Washington I used the superb holdings of the Library of Congress. I have received unwavering moral support from my mother, Alice Woll, my sisters, Diana Zurer and Judith Woll, friends Caryl Emerson, Al Frost and Carol Hall, and – despite his dislike of Soviet films – from my husband Abe Brumberg.

This manuscript, in parts and as a whole, has benefited incalculably from the counsel and criticism of many, many careful readers, among them Julian Graffy, James Mann, Richard Taylor, Greta Slobin, Raye Farr and my editor Philippa Brewster. Helena Goscilo tried valiantly to thwart my perverse predilection for passive verb constructions, with, it is to be hoped, some success; her every comment sharpened my focus as well as my prose. Denise Youngblood and Peter Kenez have been stalwart readers from the very beginning, nudging me back on track when I wandered, and reminding me of the crucial questions that needed attention. All of these friends and colleagues share the credit for what is good in the book. For its flaws, omissions, errors and inaccuracies, I am alone responsible.

Apart from the accepted English spelling for a few names, I have used a

Real Images

simplified Library of Congress transliteration system in the text, while adhering to a more accurate system in the Notes, Filmography and Bibliography. The first reference to a film includes its Russian title and year of production; thereafter, only the English title appears. All translations from the Russian are mine unless otherwise indicated. Details from films are based on my screening notes.

Part I The Big Sleep, 1953–56

1. The Big Sleep: Introduction

Stalin's demise on 6 March 1953 left rudderless a Soviet Union he had coerced into industrial and military strength and had controlled with despotic cruelty. He designated no successor; he prepared no institutional transition. As a result a power struggle ensued, its main contenders Georgii Malenkov – who initially became both premier of the Soviet Union and, briefly, First Secretary of the Communist Party – and Nikita Khrushchev, who took over as First Secretary in September 1953. (Lavrentii Beria, chief of the secret police, tried to edge out his rivals, who retaliated by arresting and executing him in June 1953.) Within eighteen months Khrushchev had sufficiently consolidated his political support to oust Malenkov, and he held the post of First Secretary for the next nine years.

Cinema was slow to react to Stalin's death, in part because movies require time. Poems and prose can appear in print within months, sometimes within weeks, of their writing. Movies cannot. In any country, the process of making a film, from initial script to final release, is laborious and time-consuming. In Stalin's Soviet Union two rounds of cultural butchery – the 1946 Zhdanovshchina, named after Leningrad party head and chief ideologist Andrei Zhdanov, and the anti-cosmopolitan campaign of 1948–49 – had so complicated an already fraught process that in 1953 the film industry was nearly paralysed.

Movies had suffered in two ways, substantively and procedurally. Post-war Soviet policy reimposed cultural isolation and ideological rigidity on citizens who had experienced a few years of contact with western countries, years relatively free from political indoctrination. As soon as the war ended the Party stepped up both the frequency and the shrillness of its propaganda campaigns, turning to cinema in September 1946. The Central Committee criticized Eisenstein, Pudovkin, and the team of Kozintsev and Trauberg, for specific infractions and more generally for 'formalism', a code word for each filmmaker's individual style. It singled out for opprobrium Leonid Lukov's *A Great Life* [Bolshaia zhizn'], enumerating its egregious errors.[1] Wary scriptwriters and directors took heed: to avoid censure (or worse), they would be wise to concentrate on social issues to the near exclusion of personal concerns, to show the Party's role as pre-eminent in every aspect of Soviet life, and to sanitize dilapidated, dirty reality, burnishing it to a high sheen.[2]

Two years later, the anti-Semitic purge of intellectual and artistic life known as the anti-cosmopolitan campaign further disfigured the film industry. Arrests deprived the studios of talented individuals, and the demonization of foreign influences and accompanying insistence on Russian superiority shrank the range of subjects and the aesthetic choices available to film-makers. As a result, contemporary Soviet life virtually vanished from movie screens in the last years of Stalin's reign, apart from a few formulaic exercises in Cold War rhetoric. Film-makers opted for the relatively safe past, sometimes adding a contemporary gloss. Thus, films about national heroes, whether military (admirals Nakhimov and Ushakov), scientific (Michurin), literary (Zhukovsky, Belinsky, Shevchenko) or artistic (Glinka, Mussorgsky), demonstrated in flat and expository form the duplicity of foreigners, the inspiring example of the masses, and the wisdom of Russian leaders.

Production mechanisms suffered as well. After 1948 individual studios lost the authority to conclude direct contracts with writers. The Ministry of Cinema reserved that right for itself, and burdened scriptwriters with an incapacitating amplitude of political requirements. All organizations and institutions with any relationship to a film, whether the Young Communist League or the Ministries of Education and Defence, had to approve its script, and they continued to safeguard the interests of their constituencies in post-production screenings.

For eight years, from the end of the Second World War until Stalin's death, all of the arts suffered from aggressive Party interference. But as a collective enterprise dependent on state funding for production and distribution, and as a medium whose significance Party spokesmen continually reiterated, cinema was particularly vulnerable. As a result, a once dynamic enterprise became moribund. Between 1945 and 1953 the studios produced only 185 feature films (the number dipped to a startling low of nine in 1951), some of them films of stage productions, and, even then, not all received distribution authorization.[3]

These circumstances help explain film-makers' tardy response to the death of Stalin, compared to that of writers and musicians. In the months following Stalin's death, in major periodicals like *Literaturnaia gazeta*, *Sovetskaia muzyka*, *Komsomolskaia pravda* and *Kommunist*, the publishing organ of the Communist Party itself, prominent writers, critics and composers challenged the dominant artistic ethos of the late Stalin period. Olga Berggolts, a poet whose voice had become familiar to millions thanks to her radio broadcasts from besieged Leningrad, wrote in defence of lyric poetry and the poet's right to artistic autonomy. The composers Aram Khachaturian and Dmitrii Shostakovich assailed the stifling cultural bureaucracy. Ilya Ehrenburg condemned the practice of writing 'to order'.

In the December 1953 issue of the monthly magazine *Novyi mir*, Vladimir Pomerantsev, a young literary critic, criticized the conflation of political and aesthetic categories. While his essay, 'On Sincerity in Literature', did not explicitly attack socialist realism, it was sufficiently radical to elicit a sharp rebuttal the very next day, and for much of 1954 the debate raged on the pages of the literary journals.[4]

Nothing similar happened in the movie industry. In 1953 the largest Soviet studio, Mosfilm, met each week to discuss films underway, films completed, films planned. (Beginning in 1934, ministry-issued plans specified the number of films to be made by each studio, and allocated topics and genres.) For several months before Stalin's death the minutes of these meetings record methodical, indeed plodding, discussions of each week's activities, and for more than a year afterwards such discussions continue with virtually no change in either tone or substance. No lively exchanges, no substantive arguments at all, can be found in the documents of 1953 or indeed 1954, although discontent with the film industry began to brew before Stalin's death; the Nineteenth Party Congress in early October 1952 discussed industry shortcomings, and Malenkov's five-hour speech referred to movies as well as drama and fiction.

Anonymous bureaucrats, none of them involved in any creative aspect of film-making, counted off the number of metres shot for each film. Over-fulfilment of the advance plan pleased them; too little footage dismayed them. At one meeting, for instance, participants were gratified to learn that 1,143 metres had been shot, a figure surpassing the plan by more than 50 per cent.[5]

Week after week, scripts received the brunt of attention, as they had since the early 1930s. Although the great Soviet directors of the 1920s had conceived and imaginatively developed montage as film's primary aesthetic tool, the cultural revolution of 1929–31 castigated montage as 'formalism'. The primacy of montage yielded to a new emphasis on script, in part because scripts were easier to supervise, and throughout the 1930s and 1940s scenarios were privileged over other components of film-making.[6]

The curiously circular logic characteristic of so much Soviet theory recurred to the point of absurdity. One man objected to Nikolai Virta's script for a film about the historical figure of Dmitrii Donskoi, for example, on the grounds that Virta's exposition *could not* be right: had events transpired in the way the script describes, 'Moscow could not have become the centre of Russia'.[7] Since it did, the script was wrong.

Both studio members and official censorship organs scrutinized scripts before shooting ever began; indeed, long before authorization to shoot was given. They carefully examined literary scripts (that is, with dialogue and exposition, but without camera and editing direction) and director's scripts (with camera and editing instructions added), since they could far more easily control a printed text than a crew on a studio set, let alone on location. Studio members therefore articulated criticism and requested radical revisions most often when a film existed only on paper.

Financial prudence also mandated script changes: re-shooting or substantial re-editing of a completed film cost money and time. Once a studio endorsed a script, self-interest dictated approval of the final version, since a rejection would hardly reflect well on its initial assessment. But the whole cumbersome process left studio facilities standing idle while directors scrambled to finish script revisions, choose and rehearse actors, find costumes and staff, and so on.

At the time of Stalin's death about a dozen studios functioned under the control of the Ministry of Cinema. Later the Ministry of Agitation and Propaganda took over, and then the Ministry of Culture. By the mid-1960s Goskino, the central state administrative body for cinema, supervised all studios – Mosfilm, Lenfilm, Gorky Studio, those in the republics and those that produced documentaries, educational films, popular science films, cartoons and children's films. Individual departments managed distribution and advertising; as the Soviet Union emerged from its Stalinist quarantine, a department for international relations oversaw film export and import, co-productions, and dubbing of foreign films, while another ran film festivals and press conferences.

Close ties bound the film industry bureaucracy to the political hierarchy. Throughout the 1950s, and in fact until the demise of the Soviet Union, high-level film industry bureaucrats routinely had connections with the Party Central Committee and often with the KGB. The Minister of Culture in 1955 reported directly to the Central Committee on the achievements and, more often, transgressions of the film industry, frequently basing his reports on information provided by in-house informants and anonymous letters.[8] Aleksei Romanov, who ran the industry from 1963 to 1973 as chairman of Goskino, had previously been deputy chairman of the propaganda department of the Central Committee.

All the studios operated in essentially the same way. 'Script Boards' read and evaluated drafts of scenarios; artistic councils [khudsovety], consisting of directors, editors, writers and other involved personnel, discussed approved scripts and the subsequent projects. 'Creative units' [tvorcheskie ob"edineniia], the basic working teams, actually made the films. In each team the director made artistic decisions, the production manager handled business matters, a group of editors worked together with writers and acted as censors, and a team khudsovet – critics, writers, actors, cameramen and others, plus at least one Party representative[9] – met to assess screen tests, watch rushes and so on. The studio's in-house newspaper contained reports of its discussions.

Each completed and approved film received a classification category, upon which depended the number of authorized copies, and whether copies would be in colour or black and white. A small measure of *de facto* decentralization existed, since municipalities and republics could decide whether or not to accept a film for local distribution. Expanded construction throughout the 1950s – *Iskusstvo kino* regularly reported on the growing number of cinemas, seats and screenings – resulted in thousands of cinemas equipped with 35mm projectors. In addition, films were shown in 'palaces of culture' operated by unions and other organizations, and at film clubs.

The Department of Personnel and Education administered scholarly archives, research institutions and training facilities. Of those, the most significant were the State Institute of Cinematography (VGIK), the nation's most prestigious film school, the Scientific Research Film and Photography Institute (NIKFI), the All-Union Scientific Research Institute for Cinema (VNIIK), and the Archive of Foreign, Pre-revolutionary and Soviet Films (Gosfilmofond).

In 1953 *Iskusstvo kino*, the 'intellectual' journal of film professionals since the mid-1930s, appeared regularly. *Sovetskii ekran*, established in 1925, had ceased publication in 1941, and was revived only in 1957, as a bi-weekly mass-market fan magazine filled with pictures and short, punchy pieces. Its print-run eventually swelled to two million, while *Iskusstvo kino* stabilized at approximately 50,000.

In the summer and autumn of 1953, however, such expansion would have seemed a fantasy, remote from actual circumstances. Apparatchiks at Mosfilm continued to catalogue names and compute metres, as they had for years. *Iskusstvo kino* published articles virtually indistinguishable from those that had appeared a year or two earlier. Its January 1954 editorial begins with accolades to Lenin's 'genius' and Stalin's 'greatness', and concludes with tributes to the perfect conditions which enable Soviet artists to produce 'the richest, most multi-faceted, most brilliant, most impressive' art possible.[10] Eleven months later its December editorial continued to hail Stalin as Lenin's great heir.

For most of 1954, *Iskusstvo kino* published little worth reading. Self-criticism abounded, as it had since the inception of the Soviet film industry. Articles asking 'what's wrong' – with film adaptations of literary classics, with acting, with movie posters – joined demands for satiric and 'educational' films. The Young Communist League loudly requested films that would provide contemporary role-models for young people.

Nearly everyone took for granted cinema's pedagogic-*cum*-propagandistic power. The chairman of a collective farm, whose *kolkhozniks* watched movies avidly, echoed the belief of Bolshevik theorists from the 1920s onward, that cinema was 'one of the most important media for conveying the idea of communism in the village'.[11] The country needed more films about agriculture, so the Party launched a new 'movie magazine', *Agricultural News* [Sel'skokhoziastvennye novosti].

Slowly, new buzzwords – authenticity [*dostovernost'*], unvarnished [*neprikrashennaia*] reality – began to punctuate the stale greyness of articles such as 'Ballet on Screen' and 'About Several Painful Issues in Documentary Film-making'. Someone with an official imprimatur (a worker, kolkhoz chairman or Komsomol secretary) might applaud Italian neo-realist cinema's 'authentic' portrayal of 'real' life. A critic might praise a Soviet documentary about oil workers on the Caspian Sea for its attention to everyday details that may seem insignificant but are not, 'precisely because they create atmosphere and accurate background'.[12]

By the end of 1954 these new cues came straight from the Ministry of Culture, and were reiterated at studio meetings, in *Iskusstvo kino* editorials, and in articles about individual films. Thus, for example, the Ministry of Culture prescribed 'warm' and 'sympathetic' treatment of plausibly complex film characters, whether historical and folkloric figures or contemporary heroes, 'ordinary' Soviet men and women.[13] The next two issues of *Iskusstvo kino* predictably echoed the call for more movies that featured complex portraits of 'ordinary' Soviet men and women as heroes.

Writers, directors and studio administrators needed the skills of expert trapeze artists to balance the conflicting demands issuing from on high.[14] Films were expected to demonstrate the grandeur and dignity of workers, peasants and intellectuals, but they must also be true to life, and therefore acknowledge human weaknesses. They must expose flaws, but not to the detriment of the heroic image. They should reveal the complexity of human emotion, but not at the expense of the larger picture, because 'the people' reject 'grey, cold, unartistic works that are devoid of ideas',[15] and a world limited to narrow personal interests oversimplifies reality and results in too many love stories and the absence of a 'broad canvas'.[16] Films should take pains to avoid naturalism and *bytopisatelstvo*, the depiction of everyday life 'stripped of its larger social … context'.[17]

Despite contradictory demands, despite entrenched resistance, the film industry began, tentatively and creakily, to change. Plans were made and slowly implemented to resurrect the republican studios, quiescent during the last years of Stalin's life. The Party had advocated an increase in film production: the sixth Five-Year Plan, announced in 1955 for the years 1956 to 1960, allocated substantial sums for the repair and expansion of studio facilities and equipment, the enlargement of existing cinemas and the construction of new ones. People flocked to film festivals and enthusiastically responded to questionnaires about their tastes and opinions.

Film-makers replaced bureaucrats in key positions. Ivan Pyrev, whose direct-ing career began in the late 1930s, became director of Mosfilm in October 1954. Pyrev was an enormously energetic, irascible and high-handed man, adroit at manoeuvring within the system. Even colleagues who resented his arrogance recognized his dedication to the interests of the film industry and film art as he perceived them. He took risks for projects he had faith in and he trusted people, especially young people, whom he respected.

Pyrev had plenty of company in his efforts to involve younger cinema professionals. After the end of World War Two, the State Institute of Cinematography (VGIK) had graduated large numbers of competent writers, directors, camera operators, editors and actors. Due to the small number of movies produced during the last Stalin years, many of them ended up in jobs unrelated to cinema. For film production to increase to the levels desired and mandated by the Party, the industry needed new cadres. Pyrev, both as head of Mosfilm and later as the first secretary of the Union of Cinematographers, used his considerable acumen and power to encourage young directors, offering them genuinely interesting projects, and assigning to them, for their own protection, experienced units and crews.[18]

The Twentieth Communist Party Congress, which took place from 14 to 25 February 1956, stimulated the revival of the film industry, as it did the society and economy more generally. The process began in earnest only after Khrushchev's major oration, delivered on the final day, but tremors were felt sooner. The Party secretary of Gorky Studio, for example, castigated studio members for tolerating director Sergei Gerasimov's arrogance: 'We have not yet eradicated our habit of servility toward our masters,' he chided back in 1955.[19]

Khrushchev asserted the Central Committee's 'resolute opposition' to the 'cult of personality alien to the spirit of Marxism–Leninism, which turns one or another leader into a miracle-performing hero and, at the same time, minimizes the role of the Party and the popular masses'.[20] He addressed his speech to the political elite, not the population as a whole, which had no direct access to its text. Nevertheless, Party officials like Suslov and Mikoyan reiterated its themes in their own speeches, and editorials in *Pravda*, *Izvestia* and *Iskusstvo kino* repeated the crucial points. (*Iskusstvo kino* first used the term 'cult of personality' in its March 1956 editorial, repeating virtually verbatim Khrushchev's characterization of it as 'alien' to Marxism–Leninism.) The sense of the speech, if not its actual text, was widely disseminated at regional and local Party meetings, in Komsomol sessions and school auditoriums.[21]

In the months following the Twentieth Party Congress, Party policies did not shift suddenly, radically and in full public view. Nevertheless, modifications incorporating the principles of Khrushchev's speech occurred in every area of life. Harsh laws pertaining to worker status, for instance, relaxed significantly: compulsory transfer of workers, the prohibition on unauthorized job changes and the prosecution of absenteeism were all discontinued. 'Comrades' courts', instead of the more punitive law courts, adjudicated breaches of labour discipline. To deal with the persistent problem of low agricultural productivity, the Party amalgamated collective farms, appropriated substantial resources for the cultivation of new farmland, and granted sizeable price increases for foodstuffs, thereby raising peasant incomes.

A major reshuffle occurred within the Party elite. Newly elected members, many of them previously associated with Nikita Khrushchev, replaced more than a third of the Central Committee. Khrushchev engineered the appointment of five new alternate members to the Presidium, including Leonid Brezhnev and Ekaterina Furtseva, who later became Minister of Culture. Shepilov, editor of *Pravda* and a Khrushchev-appointed Party secretary, succeeded Molotov as Minister of Foreign Affairs; Kaganovich was demoted. By the middle of 1956, Khrushchev seemed to clutch the reins of power firmly in his grasp.

Across the country the dismantling of the Stalinist cult of personality translated into a backlash against regional Party bosses. The debunking of Stalin was reflected in the debunking of hundreds, perhaps thousands, of mini-Stalins. These provincial Party secretaries, factory directors, chairmen of city soviets and the like had consistently suppressed criticism and punished dissenters. They had exercised their power with arbitrary and arrogant disdain for their subordinates, not to mention their constituencies.

Khrushchev's speech at the Twentieth Party Congress and the consequent thaw empowered a passion for truth-telling, expressed in a variety of artistic forms that shared a common concern with the moral compromises endemic to Soviet society. Irina Shilova recalled the euphoria she and her friends, then students at VGIK, felt over Khrushchev's speech, with its promise of the possibility of utopian socialism without the crippling weight of despotism.[22] Those who were slightly older relished the opportunity to revive their idealism, tarnished by decades of Stalinism. They could believe once again.[23] Writers articulated a mixture of anger and guilt over their own acquiescence in falsehood. Evgenii Evtushenko's lengthy dramatic poem 'Zima Station', first published in October 1956, portrays a cynical writer as someone who guards ideas instead of seeking truth; the poet reproaches himself for saying 'what I should not have said' and failing to say 'what I should have said'.[24]

Stories by Aleksandr Iashin, Nikolai Zhdanov and Iurii Nagibin expressed similar anguish. In the autumn of 1956 the monthly magazine *Novyi mir*, under Konstantin Simonov's editorship, published Daniil Granin's startling 'A Personal Opinion' and Semen Kirsanov's controversial poem, 'Seven Days of the Week'. It serialized Vladimir Dudintsev's novel *Not by Bread Alone*, a stodgy text that at the time appeared bold and dramatic. Dudintsev pointedly contrasts the idealism of the ethical inventor Lopatkin with the 'materialism, snobbery, servility to authority, arbitrary use of power, habits of intrigue and ... detachment from the ideals to which, in theory, [he is] dedicated' of the opportunistic bureaucrat Drozdov.[25]

All the arts reverberated with the impact of the Congress, cinema among them. Since cinema appeals so strongly to emotions as well as intellect, and since viewers react viscerally to its edited images and sounds, audiences indifferent or hostile to explicitly political messages responded to such messages

– and their political import – when they were coded in film terms. Whatever the direct impact of Khrushchev's speech on viewers, film-makers heard Khrushchev loud and clear, and absorbed and transmuted the purport of his speech into the images, dialogues and characterizations of their films. The Party had set ambitious target figures for film production, and committed financial resources to implement its goals. It authorized construction of cinemas with a total seating capacity of 500,000, and substantial modernization of equipment.[26] As inducements to would-be film-makers and scriptwriters, it raised authors' fees. Prize-winning films at a newly established annual festival would receive monetary awards instead of purely 'administrative' recognition. (At the first festival, held in June 1958, twenty-six studios submitted over one hundred films.)

The plan called for seventy-five films in 1956, one-third of them from Mosfilm and another dozen from Lenfilm, more than half of which should portray 'contemporary' heroes and 'socialist reality,' including kolkhoz achievements and the life of young people. Films should greet the fortieth anniversary of the Bolshevik Revolution, only eighteen months away, by highlighting both past achievements and future ones, notably the Virgin Lands project, a scheme to develop agriculture by ploughing up huge tracts of land (over 75 million acres) to create new grain regions in Kazakhstan and Siberia.[27] The Party hoped that the Virgin Lands campaign would capture the popular imagination, and to an extent it did so, helped by films that emphasized the 'pioneer' element of the project.

Mosfilm remained the hub of the industry in 1956, adding a department devoted to making films for television, but the republican studios were shaking off their torpor. Georgia and Ukraine dominated the network of satellite studios, eclipsing the Central Asian and Baltic republics. The Marxist–Leninist aesthetic formula of 'national in form, socialist in content' posed problems for all the republican studios, especially those in Central Asia. 'In theory', wrote one Western scholar,

> this phrase means that the values and ideas of the socialist society should be uniform in every culture, though the means by which they are expressed may be – indeed, should be – of a traditional and indigenous nature. The vagueness of this formula, however, has left wide leeway in its application, and … it has become quite meaningless in practice.[28]

In their efforts to translate 'national form' to the screen, republican studios usually resorted to local colour – costumes, rugs, dishes, songs and dances – but local life and national character continued to elude them. Criticism of two movies that 'varnished' reality, for instance, forced Tashkent's studio on to the defensive in 1955. The studio director blamed the failure of *The Rakhmanov Sisters* [Sestry Rakhmanovy] and *The Housewarming* [Novosel'e] on studio administrators who were 'estranged from' Uzbek life, 'ignored' new Uzbek literature, and 'didn't believe' that Uzbek writers could produce good literary scripts.[29] He recommended two solutions: sacking retrograde and isolated bureaucrats and immersing their replacements in Uzbek life. (Writers, Russian no less than Asian, routinely received the same diagnosis – lack of knowledge and understanding of their subject – and the same prescription, a ticket to the appropriate destination to fill in the gaps.)

The republican studios bemoaned the absence of adequate training. Belorussia, which had managed to produce three films in 1955 and planned three for 1956, wanted to emulate Mosfilm by organizing one- and two-year courses for directors, cameramen, editors and sound technicians. Its staff felt professionally isolated. In all of 1955 only one major 'consultant', director Boris Barnet, had visited, despite Belorussia's relative proximity to Moscow: 'Not much', noted the studio director plaintively. He suggested a freer flow of information and greater contact with foreign studios to help his teams learn how to shoot films faster and more profitably; he proposed correspondence courses under the aegis of the State Institute of Cinematography, VGIK.[30]

Apart from the practical benefit of opened Party coffers, the creative space available to artists expanded. The Twentieth Party Congress encouraged a measure of boldness in order to 'accomplish the tasks' it was assigning to art. Disconcerting phrases – 'bold initiatives', 'artistic originality', security and tolerance for the artist's individuality – appeared alongside the more habitual negatives.[31] The language was vague, but its import was clear: 'kolkhoz musicals' and historical hagiographies, portraying the nation as a 'static and unindividuated mass, dressed up in brilliant costumes', had no place in the new order.[32]

What replaced them? Mainly, films about 'everyday life' and films that re-examined the Soviet past, especially the intensely dramatic years of the civil war and the Second World War. The mandated growth in Soviet cinema required a substantial increase in not just the number but also the kinds of films produced, from the familiarly monumental and epic to the unusually restrained. From a later perspective, the early innovations appear relatively minimal. At the time, however, as Lev Anninskii reminds us, 'the goals were more modest, the obstacles more fearsome'.[33]

Film-makers chose a variety of prisms, from the ravaged countryside of the 1920s to the streets of modern Moscow. But whatever the context, their films recognized reality as a primary object of consciousness. After years of imposed aesthetic homogeneity, film-makers were able to explore a spectrum of artistic approaches. Instead of one way to depict objects and individuals on screen, they could choose a variety of ways; instead of a single, predictable and judgemental authorial stance, they could offer multiple perspectives. New physical types made their way on to the screen, and very gradually the preternaturally sharp outlines of character and characterization typical of Stalinist cinema blurred and thickened into something closer to human beings, just as the irreproachably clear diction of actors slurred into something resembling normal speech. After a faltering start in 1954 and 1955, the movies of 1956 offered viewers a new vision of their history, their world and themselves.

2. The Fallen Idol

Throughout 1954 and 1955, as studios began to streamline the production process in an effort to reduce time and money wasted, the Ministry of Culture remained deeply interested in all aspects of cinema. It sought in scripts a combination of potential profit and ideological persuasion that writers and film-makers rarely achieved. Thus it examined with painstaking care Georgii Mdivani's script for what became a pivotal comedy, *Soldier Ivan Brovkin* [Soldat Ivan Brovkin, 1955].

Brovkin's genre invited suspicion. Audiences loved comedies and clamoured for them, but the problematic nature of comedy in a highly ideologized society made the genre a minefield for Soviet directors. As Osip Brik had sardonically commented nearly thirty years before, 'It's difficult to make a Soviet comedy because we don't know what to laugh at.'[1] After Stalin's death, the Party advocated satire as an educational medium, and audiences simply wanted to laugh, but no one could figure out what kind of comedy should supplant the silly smugness of films such as Pyrev's *Cossacks of the Kuban* [Kubanskie kazaki, 1949].

Discussion of *Brovkin* centred on how to create a protagonist who was amusing yet identifiably heroic. Mdivani's eponymous hero, Vania Brovkin, is a hapless fellow [*neputevyi*]. He has the soul of an artist and delights listeners at his collective farm with his accordion playing, but he is a bumbler in all practical matters. In slapstick sequences that provide strong visual humour, he allows the pigs to get into the crops and drives a truck off a bridge into the river. Only his mother weeps as he leaves for his army service.

The army decisively transforms Brovkin. Grigorii Aleksandrov, a recognized master of film comedy, approved. 'It is essential to show such heroes on screen,' Aleksandrov commented during the Ministry of Culture discussion, 'ordinary men who can be reformed under the influence of army training.'[2] Like 'frontier' land-reclamation projects, army service can succeed in turning weakly masculine, asexual or androgynous males into 'men'. (Typically, the arduous pioneering experience makes boys more manly, girls softer and more feminine,

The Fallen Idol

1. *Soldier Ivan Brovkin*

and sexual relations more traditional.) In *Brovkin* the first step away from pretty boy is explicitly gendered, as the hero's gorgeous mop of blond curls falls under the barber's blade. Yet Brovkin continues bumbling, and although his mates and his superior officers like him and enjoy his music, they too despair of him, eventually indicting him for his hopeless incompetence. He accepts their harsh judgement.

Mdivani's script did not slip through easily. Mdivani had too much sympathy for his protagonist, critics complained, given the consequences of Brovkin's ineptitude for his kolkhoz. The kolkhoz itself was sketchy, no more than background for the action, and Mdivani failed to include any lifelike positive heroes. Before filming began, Mdivani added a likeable compensatory character, Brovkin's superior officer, who claims at the trial that Brovkin has given his word (as a Young Communist) to change, and recommends giving Brovkin another chance. Brovkin's mates relent, and the hero – who never promised any such thing – is inspired by the officer's trust in him to make and keep that promise. From that day on he is a new man.

Brovkin follows several patterns characteristic of socialist realist film as well as fiction, including the education of the ignorant, the presence of a politically-irreproachable mentor, and the happy ending.[3] But the choice of Brovkin as hero indicates an expansion of the conventional gallery of heroes. He is not merely a simpleton or ignoramus, he is an individualist, even an oddball. He resembles a folkloric figure (Ivan-the-fool) but with a modern gloss.[4] To the criticism that the comic elements disappeared as the story progressed, Mdivani responded that such a loss was inevitable as Brovkin's character developed and matured. 'Vania Brovkin', said Mdivani, 'is the hero of a comedy, but he is not necessarily a comic hero.'[5]

The criticism of Mdivani's script – for the absence of a positive hero and a clear authorial stance, the superficial and wooden positive characters, and the unacceptable mixture of genres – reflects what the state wanted in 1954 and 1955: an absolute identification of state and society, government and nation. This indivisibility dominates the only major film that actually opened in 1954, Iosif Kheifits's *The Big Family* [Bol'shaia sem'ia]. *The Big Family* packaged a variety of messages, both old and new, in such a way as to please both policy-makers and audiences.

Before the war Kheifits had collaborated with Aleksandr Zarkhi in directing several popular films, including *Baltic Deputy* and *Member of the Government* [Chlen pravitel'stva, 1939]. This, Kheifits's second film as an independent director, depicts the Zhurbins, a multi-generational family of shipworkers ranging from the seventy-eight-year-old Grandpa Matvei, 'grandfather of the whole shipyard', to the newest grandchild, also called Matvei, whose birth is announced in longshoremen's language: 'One more Zhurbin has left the dock/ slipped his moorings!' [*so stapelia soshel*].

The yard workers say there are enough Zhurbins to build a ship all by themselves, and each one of them is devoted to work. Kheifits observed in his production notes that the work-ethic replaced religion for the Zhurbins,[6] though he does not identify the religion in question as the Stalinist cult of personality. With one god dislodged, 'work became the daily prayer to a new god', and the Zhurbins serve Labour and Collective 'like priests serving a divinity'.[7]

Old Matvei hates the very idea of semi-retirement, although the yard manager consoles him that as night watchman he will continue to serve the cause he has fought for all his life. Matvei's son Ilia, who has plenty of practical experience but little formal learning, represents the middle generation, and Ilia's children stand for the younger generation, especially his sons Anton, Viktor and Alesha. Alesha, the youngest, is a worker whose epic achievements are praised over the radio. The state rewards him with a separate apartment, a great prize in those days of acute housing shortage, and he prepares it for his fiancée Katia with eager pride.

A family gathering on the veranda visually epitomizes the achievements of Soviet power. All the generations of Zhurbins relax as the sun sinks; children play in the dirt and adults, slumped comfortably, sing together in sweet harmony. Looking around at her brood, Ilia's wife declares with pride, 'We were workers, and poor. Just look at us now.'

2. *The Big Family*

But human beings, even Zhurbins, can make mistakes, and emotional mis-
judgements create tangles. Son Viktor, while he gazes tenderly at a picture of
his wife Lida, fails to notice the woman herself. Lida's indifference to shipyard
matters that absorb the rest of the family, and her desire for her husband's
attention, swell into such unhappiness that she leaves him. Alesha's plans are

derailed when Katia falls for his antipode, a cynical poseur who impresses Katia by falsely claiming that he once acted with Mayakovsky and who reacts to her pregnancy with horror.

With one foot firmly planted in traditional cinematic soil, *The Big Family* tidily resolves its human dilemmas. Viktor's wife returns for a brief visit, bringing closure (a firm handshake) to their unhappy relationship. After a sadder and wiser Katia rejects her lover and has her baby, Alesha, still in love, marches to her room, grabs her and the baby – blanket, bottle and all – and leads her back where she belongs, into the welcoming folds of the working class. Ilia, who has felt superannuated as technology outpaced his knowledge, turns for help to Zina Pavlovna, the engineer he earlier disdained for her reliance on 'book' knowledge.

The film's final imagery suggests a joyful yet sombre ritual. A new ship slides out of its mooring at the yard as the workers crowd the dock. The ship glides through the water in stately silence while the workers, their shadows visible on the side of the ship, applaud tumultuously. Ilia's wife recalls the names and sailing dates of each ship built in the yard as well as she does the names and birthdays of her children. The new ship symbolically fuses both: it is called the *Matvei Zhurbin*.

Audiences liked *The Big Family*'s portrait of their 'remarkable Soviet life'.[8] Lines that today seem laughably tendentious ('The working class is the basis for all human life,' for example) did not necessarily grate on the ears of contemporary viewers, accustomed as they were to such rhetoric on screen. And officialdom approved: the film was both ideologically sound and aesthetically appealing.

The film's title underscored the reassuring image of Soviet citizens as members of a big clan, 'sons and daughters of a great nation, nurtured by the Communist Party and by Soviet reality'. These offspring of the Soviet state, supremely conscious of their civic responsibility, assess each man's work in terms of the benefit accruing 'to the common effort'.[9] Powerful and productive, the Zhurbins embody labour itself, as the long shot of their shadows against the new boat dramatically implies. The engineers, Zina Pavlovna and her ineffectual male colleague, are outsiders sent by 'the Ministry'; their ignorance is symbolized by the open-toed sandals Zina wears to walk around the debris-littered shipyard. They derive strength from their attachment to the Zhurbins: intellectual and worker unite when Ilia turns to Zina for tutoring.

The film accommodates, even requires, this reading of its title, which harks back to the image of multi-generational close-knit working-class family popular in Soviet cinema of the 1930s (*The Miners* [Shakhtery, 1937], for instance), and again in post-war films like *The Fall of Berlin* [Padenie Berlina, 1949]. But a substantial qualifier pertains. *The Big Family* lacks the middleman traditional in films from the 1930s: the Party commissar who explains and inspires, the Party secretary who mediates between the hero and his faith. And it lacks the Stalin-figure of post-war films, the remarkable individual who defines the course of history for other characters. In *The Big Family* the Zhurbins solve problems by their own efforts. Although the sympathetic yard manager, who urges the aged Matvei to 'decide for himself' what to do next, represents the Party, he has no name, no defined obligations, and no real role in the action. The characters' faith is inwardly sustaining and self-sufficient.

Moreover, this self-sufficiency determines the outcome of the love stories. Alesha must discover for himself the depth of his constancy to Katia, and his ultimate acceptance of her and her illegitimate child. Neither family nor social collective intervenes in an essentially private dilemma. Ilia cannot arrange his children's lives: when he tries to play the heavy-handed patriarch he becomes laughable, as his own father confirms with a mocking box on the ears. (Actor Boris Andreev accentuates the comic aspect of Ilia.)[10] Aleksei Batalov's Alesha projects emotional authenticity, suggesting that what is happening inside him is far more significant than what is happening outside him. He does not even plug in the radio to hear his name broadcast, and shrugs off the public recognition that so gratifies his father.

The failure of Viktor and Lida's marriage most dramatically asserts the primacy of human emotions and needs. After Lida leaves, the Zhurbins offer conventional explanations for her departure. The eldest daughter, a doting mother and bossy wife, attributes the marriage's failure to its childlessness. Mama Zhurbin blames the whole family, for not having taught Lida to share their workers' creed. But despite these nods to custom and ideology, the film itself suggests something at once simpler and much more mysterious: the breakdown of a relationship between two good and decent people, two people with different interests and different agendas. Neither one is 'wrong', they are simply wrong for each other. With the best will in the world, they cannot change that stubborn reality, a reality the film acknowledges without con-demnation.

Kheifits made a concerted effort to avoid what he called 'beauty-shop' charm, to smooth out the wrinkles of real faces with cosmetic artifice, and he took pains to create a truthful *mise-en-scène*. 'Costumes tell more about a person than words,' he noted in his production diary.[11] Yet he still 'varnished' reality. The supposedly cramped room where Katia and her baby live is actually quite spacious; Alesha's boots gleam in a scene when they would more likely be scuffed and dirty. The film's patriarchal model of stable family life, in which fathers succeed grandfathers, and sons succeed fathers, misrepresented the reality of Soviet families profoundly injured by wars and political repressions, where women – grandmothers, mothers and daughters – dominated.

With its avoidance of 'pomposity' and 'schematism', two of the most common shibboleths in the critical literature, *The Big Family* became a yardstick against which other films were measured, and invariably fell short. Soviet viewers recognized and appreciated the familiar theme of harmonious collective labour producing what the nation needed to forge ahead towards the future. They recognized, too, the image of their nation as engendering heroes, a legacy of the 1930s when 'the main product of the country was not wheat, steel or even tanks, but heroes ... "forged" by factories, plants, kolkhozes, schools, newspapers and radio'.[12] After a decade of 'remarkable' heroes, audiences were relieved to see men and women like themselves, who lived in ordinary surroundings and dealt with mundane problems and pleasures.

If they had an appetite for innovation, however, they had to be patient. Throughout 1955 the film industry recovered; the majority of films that came out tendered images of stability in the face of new uncertainties, and official policy manipulated popular demand. When *Iskusstvo kino* published round-ups of readers' views, the first letter routinely reflected the journal's editorial stance; it may well have been written (possibly by a staff member) specifically for that purpose. The August 1955 editorial, for example, urged film-makers to seek 'simple people' as the heroes of films.[13] In a survey of readers' reactions to recent films one month later, the first letter repeated nearly verbatim the August text, requesting 'simpler' heroes, ordinary workers and peasants.[14]

Moreover, it is difficult to ascertain what Soviet audiences actually enjoyed watching, especially since their choice was so limited. In the 1920s, as Denise Youngblood has established, Soviet audiences lapped up entertaining films, imported or domestic, whenever they were available. After the Second World War, confiscated German musicals and Hollywood adventure films and Westerns appealed more than most domestic products, although state propaganda preferred to assert the opposite.[15] Audiences enjoyed *Stagecoach*, *Tarzan* and *The Roaring Twenties* for their acting, music and general style, and handily ignored the distortions imposed by new titles (*Mr Deeds Goes to Town* became *The Dollar Rules*) and ideological prefaces.[16] Western imports disappeared in the early 1950s, supplanted by historical biographies whose heroes led absurdly and totally public lives – as if, commented one critic, historically important figures do not fall in love, get jealous, enjoy their marriages and love their children.[17]

Nevertheless, the dramatically expanded range of reader responses throughout 1955 and 1956 suggests genuine enthusiasm for movies, keen interest in the kind of movies produced and distributed, and a sense of involvement in the decisions made within the industry. The shift from public and collective portraiture to private and individual, from inflated and hyperbolic to life-sized and realistic, seems to have attracted Soviet citizens as much as it satisfied the needs of politicians taking the first tentative steps to dismantle the cult of personality.

Certainly throughout 1955 the leadership, both in the Ministry of Culture and in the Kremlin, persisted in regarding cinema chiefly as a powerful arm of the state, to be wielded in the interests of education and propaganda. Comedy performed 'an important educational function';[18] Soviet cinema's 'chief task' was to provide role-models and to educate workers 'in the spirit of communism';[19] Soviet cinema must not lag behind the major changes occurring in the nation but must lead the way.[20] The phrases recurred with numbing frequency on the pages of *Iskusstvo kino* and in studio discussions.

Occasionally the directives were explicit: following the Party congress that focused on agriculture, *Iskusstvo kino* ran as its lead article 'The Urgent Task of Improving Films about Agriculture'. But, in fact, unless Party directives coincided with what film-makers wanted to do, and even with what viewers wanted to see, those directives bore little fruit. Film-makers were reluctant to tackle farm life, and few such films were made. (Some years later, when the writer Iurii Nagibin tried to find a director for his script about a post-war collective farm, he couldn't interest anyone of prominence. A relative unknown, Aleksei Saltykov, got the assignment, which resulted in a huge hit, *The Chairman* [Predsedatel', 1964].)

Artists had reacted in much the same way between September 1939 and June 1941, during the eighteen months of 'friendship' between the Soviet Union and Nazi Germany. Policy dictated that artists abandon overnight the anti-fascist stance of the 1930s, but most artists were intensely hostile to the pact and many fell silent rather than embrace a pro-German position. The Nazi invasion of June 1941 eliminated the need for hypocrisy; artists responded eagerly to the official demand for 'patriotic' art, which accorded with their own feelings.

Similarly, Party mandates of 1955 and 1956 in large measure corresponded to what film-makers themselves wanted to do. Given the fusion of Party policy, popular demand and artists' desire, the prescriptions and proscriptions articulated in such official organs as *Iskusstvo kino* are more reliable than usual in conveying the mood and preoccupations of the period.

They reveal a mixture of old and new: on the one hand, firm faith in cinema's didactic influence, discomfort with pure entertainment, reliance on the positive hero and other bedrock characteristics of socialist realism; on the other, a desire for realism and complexity, for recognizable individuals who behave in well-motivated and emotionally persuasive ways, for plausible conflicts that do not proceed inexorably towards pat and predictable resolutions. Pedantic, schematic and artificial films, static and pallid depictions of life, were uniformly unacceptable. The head of Gorky Studio advised film-makers to put more trust in their audiences, instead of 'continuously explaining, elucidating, clarifying'.[21]

Critics dismissed the regimental commanders, government leaders, scientific and artistic geniuses who had populated late Stalinist films, but avoided Stalin's name, and did not identify him as the source of and chief reason for the proliferation of such protagonists. Conversely, they valorized 'the individual personality', authenticity and 'the complexity of the era'. The new model of a positive hero existed, in 'the thick of battle with enemies of innovation', and 'the struggle for what is authentic'. The new heroes should be 'simple' people, 'authentic heroes' of Soviet reality, who speak like normal men and women, not like 'bad newspaper editorials'.[22]

Indeed, more than half of the scripts submitted to the Ministry of Culture to fulfil the 1955 thematic plan feature 'foundry workers and wheat farmers, drivers and hydroelectric plant builders, coal miners and metallurgists and policemen, party workers and lab technicians, soldiers, sergeants, salesmen, teachers, pianists and singers, pilots and sailors'.[23] Since the plan appeared only in July, halfway through the year, its pantheon of heroes was destined to be under-occupied.

The line demarcating hero from villain remained clear: positive and negative must be neither confused nor combined with each other. Yet convincing heroes and villains had to be fully developed characters. A promising pair of young men, Aleksandr Alov and Vladimir Naumov, tried to square this circle in their first film, *Restless Youth* [Trevozhnaia molodost', 1954]. Within a conventional story – villain closes local factory-institute, Young Communist hero reports him to the Central Committee secretary, more experienced secretary recognizes villain's fundamental hostility to the Party and takes steps to correct the situation – Alov and Naumov managed to avoid the usual stereotypes. Standard elements of *Bildungsroman* and Party tutelage notwithstanding, *Restless Youth* features attractive and persuasively 'real' young heroes; even the villain is relatively lifelike. As Semen Freilikh, who taught at VGIK and wrote extensively about film, commented appreciatively, Alov and Naumov understood that a cardboard villain makes his opponent (the hero) equally implausible.[24]

Alov and Naumov were among the first of the young film-makers entrusted with their own project. Others included Stanislav Rostotskii, whose first film, *Land and People* [Zemlia i liudi], came out of Gorky Studio in 1955, and Iurii Egorov, whose *Frozen Sea* [More studenoe] appeared slightly earlier. The younger directors who began to replace their teachers consisted of two groups, separated by a significant five to ten years.

The older men – Alov, Rostotskii, Grigorii Chukhrai, Mikhail Shveitser, Marlen Khutsiev – were born in the early 1920s and fought in the Second World War. The cultural freeze of the late Stalin period had forced them to wait ten years in order to portray their experiences with any degree of truthfulness. Shveitser, who had made his first film in 1948, fell victim to the anticosmopolitan campaign, lost his job (at Mosfilm) in 1951, and spent two years in Sverdlovsk making educational films (thanks to Mikhail Romm's help) before Lenfilm hired him in 1953.

The younger men – Georgii Danelia, Rolan Bykov, Mikhail Kalik, Eldar Riazanov, Igor Talankin – were too young to serve at the front. (Kalik was not too young for the Gulag, however: in 1951, Kalik, then twenty-four, and four other students at the State Institute for Cinematography were arrested, convicted of anti-Soviet terrorist activity, and sentenced to twenty-five years. He was released in 1954.) For them, as for the 'youth prose' writers who began publishing in the middle and late 1950s, the thaw occurred at what one critic dubbed the 'appropriate' time.[25]

All of them benefited from the expansion in film production. Many of the younger directors did their first work in the republican studios; Alov and Naumov made *Restless Youth*, for instance, in Kiev. Slowly recuperating from their late-Stalinist paralysis, the studios in Odessa, Riga and Tallinn were functioning if not yet thriving by 1955, Tashkent and Baku a year or two later. Only eight films came out of all the non-Russian studios together in 1953; the figure had nearly tripled two years later.

To encourage young film-makers, the major studios established 'creative workshops' ['*tvorcheskie masterskie*']: teams staffed by film tyros under the supervision of seasoned professionals. At Mosfilm, for instance, Mikhail Romm and Sergei Iutkevich, with more than forty years' experience between them, supervised a team of four directors, two scriptwriters, several cameramen, and so on. The trainees served what amounted to an apprenticeship, and provided the studio with the expanded staff of specialists without whom it could not produce the number of movies demanded by the Party.

Mosfilm was the largest and most prominent studio. Under the leadership of empire-building Ivan Pyrev, its physical plant expanded substantially, acquiring new shooting stages. Pyrev rebuilt Mosfilm's subsidiary branch in Yalta in order to facilitate year-round shooting, and he continually lobbied for money to improve Mosfilm's technical capabilities. He recommended establishing acting schools for teenagers, who would receive both academic and professional training and could then form an acting pool for juvenile roles.

Pyrev also dreamed of creating a union of film-makers comparable to the Union of Writers and Union of Composers, to advance industry interests and protect its members economically and artistically. (It took ten years to realize his dream.) A sense of approaching freedom energized the industry, one critic recalled: 'As before we looked over our shoulders, we tried to guess at the mood "up there, at the top", but we hoped that everything would soon change … that we – not the Ministry, not the Central Committee, not "the boss", as Stalin used to be called – would soon be the masters of our own fates.'[26]

Pyrev's pressure eventually resulted in a two-year training course, with a roster of impressive faculty members, all of them still active film-makers. Eisenstein's cameraman Eduard Tisse taught cinematography; Romm taught direction of actors, shot repetition, and editing while he worked on *Murder on Dante Street* [Ubiistvo na ulitse Dante, 1956]; Iulii Raizman taught ensemble acting as he directed his group of actors in *Lesson of Life* [Urok zhizni, 1955].

The films released in late 1955 and early 1956 were made before the Twentieth Congress, and they often expressed 'old' attitudes. But the terms in which they were discussed, in the spring of 1956, demonstrate the magnitude of change in the post-Congress atmosphere. Three movies received the lion's share of attention. Two of them featured altruistic women as their protagonists, Iulii Raizman's *Lesson of Life* and Fridrikh Ermler's *Unfinished Tale* [Neokonchennaia povest']. In Mikhail Shveitser's *Alien Kin* [Chuzhaia rodnia], set in the countryside, the hero is a newly-married Komsomol member.

Lesson of Life modernizes the nineteenth-century 'unequal marriage' theme, where husband and wife are distinctly mismatched, either because of age or class disparity. In *Lesson of Life*, psychological rather than class differences separate husband and wife. The heroine Natasha is a noble-spirited *intelligentka*, training to be a teacher when she falls in love with and marries Sergei, energetic and talented but insensitive to people – the 'merchant' of older fiction. Sergei's callousness, which intensifies as he becomes more powerful, increasingly dismays Natasha, who takes their son and returns to her hometown. Eventually the authorities discover Sergei's 'errors' and *Pravda* publishes an article 'unmasking' him, at which point Natasha gives up her new and beloved teaching career to go back to him; she hopes they can start a new life together at the far-off construction project to which the Party sends him.

Debate about the film preceded its completion. Critics reacted vehemently to Evgenii Gabrilovich's script. Some of them saw Sergei as an unmitigated monster of egoism, and Natasha's return to him as a craven capitulation; when she says that 'nothing is dearer' to her than her son and her husband, she flips from a positive image of Soviet womanhood to a shockingly negative one.

Others considered Sergei a good man with flaws, who could be redeemed by a combination of Party wisdom and the love of a good woman. For them, Gabrilovich's script demonstrated the power of love, and of faith in man's capacity for change, while avoiding banal, implausible formulas. They argued that wives don't actually leave their husbands over disagreements about construction projects, yet too often

> a soulless and cruel logic rules [on screen]: once a man has made a mistake, a good Soviet woman, true to her principles, is supposed to leave, to condemn him, to break off relations ... That's not how life works. If this is truly a good Soviet woman, if she truly loves her husband, than she won't abandon him for any reason in his time of trouble, won't renounce him.[27]

After the film's release the public joined the fray. 'Perhaps I will be accused of being self-righteous, but I simply want to see justification for a character's behaviour,' wrote one viewer unconvinced by Natasha's devotion. 'Characters shouldn't behave according to the arbitrary will of the director.' A Kharkov viewer disliked the film's title: 'The whole film presents itself as a lesson, and a lesson that is spelled out explicitly and simplistically.' Others criticized superfluous speechifying and 'one-sided and one-dimensional' characters.[28]

However stereotypical its terms, especially its gender components, such a discussion was new and controversial. When *Literaturnaia gazeta* berated *Iskusstvo kino* for publishing articles critical of the film, the journal fought back, eloquently pleading for diversity of voices and opinions. The 'deeply rooted proclivity for clichés and stereotypes' and the sharp division of characters into positive and negative, *Iskusstvo kino* asserted, should be eliminated. 'Only then will art cease to oversimplify; only then will complex and contradictory images appear on screen.'[29]

In many ways *Lesson of Life* is old-fashioned and pleasing. It is visually conventional (Natasha's simple clothing and pulled-back hair mark her as a traditional intellectual), although unpredictable editing occasionally interrupts the tight narrative logic. Thematically, *Lesson of Life* falls back on a stock formula: as Sergei's career prospers, his morals deteriorate. Power, in other words, corrupts. And the film confirms the wisdom of the system, capable of identifying and repairing breaches. Sergei is not a typical representative of a deformed system, but an anomaly.

Natasha's unconventional choice, however, distinguishes *Lesson of Life* as a herald of the thaw. Natasha may be a woman with values solid enough to support her independence, or a woman whose love is strong enough to reform her man. From today's western and feminist perspective, both are stereotypes and almost interchangeable; if anything, the first may seem more radical. Yet in the Soviet context of the mid-1950s the opposite was true. The Soviet state and much of Soviet popular culture had long promoted the virtue of loyalty to the state. Children joining the Young Pioneers pledged to emulate Pavlik Morozov, the teenager who had denounced his father for hoarding grain during collectivization and whose vengeful relatives had then executed him.[30] For decades, state and Party had been 'dearer' than husband and son, at least on the level of public rhetoric.

Within that framework, Natasha's decision amounts to a declaration of the transcendent importance of love. Though she may be a variant of a Decembrist wife – those women who followed their husbands to Siberia after the failed coup of 1825 – she is also intensely modern, perhaps the first 'thaw' individual to be shown on screen in that she ultimately chooses to live by her feelings rather than her reason. Her decision provokes 'the thought that love and goodness may not coincide with justice [*spravedlivost'*]'.[31]

Raizman's innovations become all the more salient when *Lesson of Life* is compared to the other major film of 1955 whose protagonist is female. The heroine of *Unfinished Tale*, Elizaveta Maksimovna, is a dedicated doctor. She eats on the run, standing over the stove; she is invariably the first person out of the house. Her commitment to her work is matched by one of her patients. Despite the fact that Iurii Ershov is confined to his bed, paralysed from the waist down, he inspires his students with his own ardent example, and they respond eagerly. 'Work', he tells them, 'is love, joy, happiness.'[32]

Elizaveta Maksimovna's exemplary devotion to her patients was considered a feminine trait: 'The main quality of a doctor, as of a teacher, is charm and substance of personality,' explained one reviewer.

In all circumstances a doctor should be wise and calm. It's as if this profession requires spiritual superiority [*dukhovnoe prevoskhodstvo nad okruzhaiushchimi*]. If Elizaveta Maksimovna had not received a medical degree, she would none the less have helped people, supported them firmly and without regard for herself ... [She] is entirely contemporary, but also evokes memories of those girls who left their families and went as teachers to the villages, those women lauded by Russian and Soviet poets.[33]

Dr Aganin, an egotist in love with Elizaveta Maksimovna, completes the triangle. His conceit compromises his professional competence. When she spends the night at a child's bedside, he responds with callous incredulity: 'At a patient's bedside one can spend fifteen, maybe twenty minutes, let's say even an hour. But all night?!' He prescribes 'rest, rest, and more rest' for Ershov, precisely the wrong advice for a man with so activist a temperament.

Audiences admired the heroine's selflessness, seeing her as a role-model for young doctors. But they disliked the schematism of 'good' Ershov and 'bad' Aganin: Ershov innovates, while Aganin fears new ideas; Ershov listens with painful intensity to a concert on the radio, while Aganin dozes off in the concert hall.[34]

Everyone dismissed the love triangle as banal and its resolution as absurd. When Ershov overhears Elizaveta Maksimovna weeping, he pounds his thigh in fury at his own impotence – and miraculously feels sensation for the first time since his accident. Skipping (presumably) months of therapy, the camera cuts straight to the happy ending: Ershov staggers onto his feet and stumbles out onto the apartment balcony. A 'whole' man at last, he puts his arms around his beloved and gazes out at the broad boulevards and gleaming canals of Leningrad. The city, spread out below them, signifies the universe he can now master.

Unlike *Lesson of Life*, with its validation of individual human emotion, *Unfinished Tale* takes a more conventional view of the individual's relationship to her society. During a convivial evening with a patient's family, Elizaveta Maksimovna joins them in song; they eat potatoes and herring and toast one another's health with vodka. As she walks home, a large group of singing and celebrating students accost her and absorb her into their happy midst. The sequence implies a social resolution to emotional isolation: the warmth of the larger group can assuage Elizaveta Maksimovna's loneliness and melancholy.

In their attempts to create 'ordinary' heroes and heroines, melodramas like *Lesson of Life* and *Unfinished Tale* responded to changes in the political atmosphere. Yet while both are set in contemporary Soviet society, neither reflects the complexities of Soviet life in 1955, and the 'present' in which they take place is virtually atemporal, lacking the kind of superficial, visible markers – skirt lengths, hairdos, car styles – that identify eras in western films. When Elizaveta Maksimovna finally goes to a beauty salon, the resulting coiffure is so bizarre that she heads straight for a sink to wash it out. The musical score reveals nothing, since the music is either classical (Tchaikovsky at the concert), traditional (folksongs with the patient's family) or generic Soviet anthems (the students).

Predictably, films about the countryside had more explicitly political agendas, if only by virtue of their setting. Like other films of the period, they were seen against the background that preceded them, and derived much of their impact from the contrast with earlier musicals, such as Pyrev's *The Swineherd and the Shepherd* [Svinarka i pastukh, 1941] and *Cossacks of the Kuban*. Pyrev's movies, with their giggling young women and smirking young men, with market stalls that groan under a cornucopia of produce and goods, equated and conflated the individual and the collective. By 1955 one critic could acknowledge their representation of feasting and revelry as synthetic, florid and grotesquely remote from reality.[35]

The two most significant kolkhoz films of 1955, *Alien Kin* and *Land and People*, starkly contradicted that kind of artifice, emulating essayists and prose writers in creating more truthful portrayals of life in the backwaters of provincial Russia. Camerawork favoured medium and long shots, encompassing the entire environment, as if the camera could, simply by avoiding selection, offer images saturated with reality. Cinematographers shot natural landscape so as to make it look boring, not poetic or beautiful. They thought they were moving away from the lyric tradition of film-makers like Aleksandr Dovzhenko, although Dovzhenko's influence is strikingly evident in shots of peasants sitting astride tractors and in close-ups of softly-lit faces angled up towards the bright future.

From the vantage point of ten or even five years later, *Land and People* and *Alien Kin* appear naive and meretricious. Compared to *Cossacks of the Kuban*, however, they broke a taboo and penetrated 'a forbidden zone'.[36] Many viewers knew first-hand the primitive, often impoverished conditions of life in the country, but they did not expect to see them on screen, however ameliorated and prettified.

Stanislav Rostotskii's *Land and People* combined the thematic unmasking of enemies – a commonplace of Soviet movies long after Stalin's death[37] – with the pioneer plot, in which young people leave home and work in a remote and undeveloped area in order to find their happiness. (Hardship was an essential pre-condition to success: in *Land and People*, as in *Unfinished Tale*, only happiness achieved through struggle proves genuine.) The hero of *Land and People*, a young agronomist, is under investigation for an unauthorized experiment. He is eventually vindicated, and the villain is revealed as the kolkhoz chairman, in league with a group of conservative demagogues led by his patron, the 'regional god' [*raionnyi bog*].

The implied dichotomy between 'us' and 'them' characterizes Mikhail Shveitser's *Alien Kin* as well. Like *Lesson of Life*, *Alien Kin* depicts a *mésalliance*, here between private farmstead [*usad'ba*] and collective farm. Stalinist kolkhoz movies, like many Hollywood counterparts, often ended with a wedding, as if to assure viewers that nothing but trivial and easily resolvable misunderstandings could cloud the future of Soviet characters. *Alien Kin*, in contrast, begins with a wedding, a wonderful *mélange* of song and dance, and of understated erotic tension between the hero, Fedor Soloveikov, played by the popular Nikolai Rybnikov, and the radiant heroine, Nonna Mordiukova's Stesha Riashkina. After the wedding Fedor, an industrious and committed member of the kolkhoz, moves out of the dormitory and into the home of Stesha's retrograde parents.

As Shveitser's paradoxical title suggests, Fedor is shocked to encounter obstacles to his happiness not at work or within the bureaucracy, but within his own home, a world alien [*chuzhoi*] to him and his collectivist values. The tension builds as Fedor begins to comprehend his in-laws. Shveitser emphasizes their baseness visually and aurally: angled shots of the low ceiling make their dark house look stifling and oppressive, and when they torment a goat, binding its horns and leaving it helpless, it bleats plaintively for a long time. The farm becomes an 'unpeopled space', where any vile action is possible.[38]

Fedor Soloveikov, whose very name – 'nightingale' – carries a positive connotation, is a generally satisfactory hero. Neither propagandist nor soldier, he is a 'nice guy'. He loves his wife and avoids clashing with her parents until he has no choice. He is an exemplary new Soviet man, revolted by the selfish 'ownership' mentality of the Riashkins. Fedor interprets the Riashkins' desire to live affluently as a sign of spiritual poverty, and so does the film.

With Fedor's departure, a family drama expands into a conflict between exemplars of 'socialist morality' and concern for the group, and greedy, egoistic relics of the past. In the countryside, such people constitute a fundamental obstacle to the healthy growth of the kolkhoz, but 'the Riashkins' disease [*takaia bolezn', kak riashkinshchina*] exists in one guise or another in the city, too – wherever people care only for their private success and prosperity and are indifferent to the interests of the people'.[39]

The Riashkins win a temporary victory when Fedor, despite his love for Stesha and the child she is carrying, walks out, but eventually Stesha herself challenges her parents and joins her husband. The penultimate scene exposes the Riashkins' empty lives, symbolized equally by the neatly stripped bed where Fedor and Stesha used to sleep and by the heavy wooden chest crammed with the material wealth gathered by generations, locked up to moulder.[40] The authoritarian voice of a stern narrator asks the old folks, 'Where is your happiness?', and the camera answers with a shot of Stesha and Fedor behind a curtain in the workers' dormitory. Sitting side by side at their baby's cradle, their faces tilt up towards the future they will create together.

3. Beat the Devil

The hierarchy of power engendered during the Stalin years had begun to teeter before the Twentieth Party Congress. In the film industry, for instance, Lev Kuleshov and Grigorii Aleksandrov were attacked as early as the summer of 1955 for the autocratic way they ran their departments at the State Institute of Cinematography and for considering themelves accountable to no one.[1] But Khrushchev's speech accelerated the process.

Meanwhile, the film industry's growth spurt continued. Gorky Studio hosted a festival of grand proportions. Thousands of viewers in the Rostov, Voronezh and Ivanov provinces met writers, directors, cameramen, editors, actors and actresses in a fortnight of conferences and formal and informal meetings. The studio showed one short film and six feature films, among them *Soldier Ivan Brovkin* and *Land and People*, to collective farmers and factory workers, Red Army officers and soldiers, and students from Rostov University and from medical, pedagogical and railroad institutes.

In the Voronezh area alone, roughly 20,000 people attended screenings and post-screening discussions. Festival organizers distributed questionnaires, asking 'Did you like the film you just saw?', 'What were its flaws?', 'Which of the actors played their roles best?' and 'What themes would you like to see in new films?' Audiences were enthusiastic and responsive, though they tended to echo official appraisals, disparaging 'grey' and 'mediocre' films and 'schematic and banal plots'.[2] Viewers repeatedly requested heroes who worked in their own professions, but director Stanislav Rostotskii thought lack of cinematic realism, not jobs, was the real problem: if films convincingly portrayed essential human conflicts, profession would become irrelevant.[3]

In assessing the significance of such a festival, the 'grassroots' repetition of opinions trumpeted in *Pravda*, *Izvestia* and other state organs must be understood in context. People saw what the Ministry of Culture permitted them to see, since the ministry kept firm control of film distribution for both ideological and financial reasons. When Mosfilm and Gorky Studio organized free showings of feature films in clubs and institutes on their own initiative, they were sharply rebuked by A. Fedorov, head of the Department of Film Production.[4]

Nevertheless, there is no reason to doubt the popularity of such festivals. The inhabitants of Rostov, Taganrog and Novocherkassk were as eager as fans everywhere to meet their screen idols in the flesh, and the memoirs of actors who participated in similar festivals bear out Rostotskii's somewhat gushing account. Moreover, both culture and ideology stressed film's paradigmatic status, on the one hand, and the validity and weight of audience reaction, on the other. Soviet viewers genuinely thought their opinions could make a difference. One Rostov student spoke for many when he asked why there were so few films that profoundly affected viewers, that could 'accompany them throughout their lives'. He articulated what the majority of Soviet movie-goers wanted.

In 1956 the State Institute of Cinematography was prestigious and selective. Its elite student body consisted mainly of Russians, since the Russian republic was always favoured and applicants from other republics were neither numerous nor strong. Entrants encountered an atmosphere of intellectual and creative excitement. VGIK staff and students were able to study western films, to hear the formerly taboo music of Wagner, Webern, Schoenberg and Berg, to see the paintings – still only semi-secretly available – of Russian modernists like Malevich, Kandinsky and Filonov. Unlike most of the reading public, who had no such access, VGIK's privileged few could obtain from the archives the still-unpublished poetry of such early twentieth-century masters as Gumilev and Kharms, the prose of Zamiatin and Pilniak, Proust and Huxley.

Irina Shilova recalled student life as existing on two discrete planes. In the hallways, among themselves and in private conversation with certain faculty members, she and her friends engaged in fierce debate. They confronted one another, demanding independence of thought and judgement. Such polemics were confined to the oral domain, however, and hardly impinged on their lectures or papers.[5] A novelist of the same generation, Vladimir Makanin, describes a similar atmosphere at a Moscow technical institute:

> During the lecture breaks (and in a whisper during the lectures) the students were discussing a biting polemical article that had just come out in *Novyi mir* ... I remember how, after arriving a bit late, I sat at the very top of the lecture auditorium; the view from there was excellent: I could see the volume with the blue cover being passed to Shitov on the left side of the room; a speed-reader, Shitov looked through it in five minutes, if not three, and sent it on to Kozlova; she and Mlynarova read it together, squinting their eyes; in addition, Gavrilets was craning his long neck and reading it over their shoulders. The journal moved down and then up again. Sometimes it was suddenly grabbed right out of people's hands. Outwardly, however, their faces were inscrutable ... The lecturer, meanwhile, was lecturing. Then another lecturer took over; there were

six lecture hours that day, and four of them in the same auditorium, which was considered a great convenience.[6]

Makanin's narrator, despite his avid attention to the revelations published in the leading liberal journal, is more engrossed in a fellow student, Lara; love, he reflects, crowded out everything else. For Shilova and her friends, art intoxicated them far more than revelations about a past that, with all its horrors, was closed off by 'an impenetrable wall' from their normal, daily activities.

Movies mirrored this chasm between public façade and private interests. The metamorphosis of cinema was not necessarily obvious, except when the image on screen sharply diverged from its 'real' counterpart, either lagging behind or leapfrogging over it. Films presenting familiar concepts were comprehensible and comforting. Viewers were accustomed to art that defined love as patience, understanding and fidelity, with self-sacrifice the highest virtue. Movies exploring startling alternatives – love as passionate abandon and intoxication, self-interest as an affirmation of the need for personal happiness – disconcerted them.

In the vernal breezes of 1956, artists in every medium pressed for greater tolerance of diversity. Even the relatively conservative writer Konstantin Simonov, then editor of *Novyi mir*, urged that any literature imbued with 'socialist spirit' be accepted under the rubric of socialist realism. *Iskusstvo kino*'s May issue boldly linked ethics and aesthetics in its lead article. The author, V. Razumnyi, made the requisite obeisance to the 'inseparability' of personal and societal in the life of a Soviet citizen and to the importance of this theme for Soviet art. At the same time, precisely by taking this ideological obligation for granted, Razumnyi shifted the issue from the realm of ideology into the realm of art. How, he asked, can art show this theme? His answer was unequivocal: there is no single way of doing this. Razumnyi argued that an individual's private life need not be juxtaposed with his professional world (a typical construct) in order to demonstrate his 'social' involvement. A character's morality, with all its social implications, could be conveyed quite clearly within the purely personal sphere of activity.[7]

Another critic staked a more radical claim. The contemporary rejection of spuriously embellished portrayals of reality should be accompanied by a return to what he designated the 'specific qualities of art, qualities that had been lost or considered suspect'.[8] No one in the arts could miss this veiled reference to the 'anti-formalist' attacks on aesthetic autonomy that had been common currency for years.

The ramifying of representational possibilities was a slow and uneven process, not a single event. It manifested itself in a variety of ways. Contemporaries noticed new physical types making their way onto the screen. The actress playing the heroine of *Steep Slopes* [Krutye gorki, 1956], for example, lacked the ample proportions and broad features characteristic of kolkhoz milkmaids.

Precisely because she did not conform to type, Galina Vodianitskaia's slim, elegant figure, her thin face and sombre dark eyes made her more believable.[9] Aleksei Batalov followed his acclaimed performance in *The Big Family* with *The Rumiantsev Case* [Delo Rumiantseva, 1955], where he played a long-distance trucker. His lanky, coltish body and his expressive, mobile face, with its shadow of a beard, challenged the more conventional 'powdered and primped' posturing screen heroes. His features combined 'masculinity, strength, even boldness' with something childlike, naive and good.[10]

Well into 1956, screen heroes and heroines were still obliged to present intact images of rectitude, to embody ideological purity. Secondary characters, not required to carry the burden of canonic virtue, allowed directors more freedom to show nuances, but villainy remained unalloyed. Gradually, films acknowledged villains as products of Soviet life, rather than holdovers from the tsarist past such as the Riashkins in *Alien Kin*.

Thus the villain in Pyrev's *Test of Faith* [Ispytanie vernosti, 1954] is a careerist and a cynical egotist, yet 'one of us', as a character states explicitly: born and bred within the Soviet system, educated in Soviet schools, an erstwhile member of the Young Pioneers. The 'Soviet-ness' of negative characters quickly ceased to be remarkable, although the system as such never bore responsibility for them, and easy identification of villainy and pre-revolutionary Russia, like black hats in Westerns, or twirled moustaches in silent melodramas, persisted: in *The Rumiantsev Case*, one of the three villains is a criminal first arrested in 1924.

Impeaching the purity of traditional Soviet role-models (such as security service officers) was more problematic.[11] Their flaws had to result from personal inadequacies, and a colleague, usually of a higher rank, provided balance, observing the subordinate's failings and compensating with his own better understanding. During the investigation of the Rumiantsev case, Lieutenant Afanasev rebukes the obtuse Captain Samokhin, advising him to study the biography of the Cheka's first chief, Feliks Dzerzhinskii, for tips on how to combine ruthlessness against enemies with respect for individuals(!). As late as *Ballad of a Soldier* [Ballada o soldate, 1959], this seemingly 'natural' way of retaining an official hierarchy still obtained: the greedy soldier guarding the troop train is rebuked by his superior officer.

Still, for most of 1956 black remained black, and white stayed white. Koronkov, one of the villains in *Rumiantsev*, not only robs the Soviet state; he also drinks excessively, bullies his wife and turns his Young Pioneer son into an unwitting (though instinctively reluctant) accomplice. The 'good' Lt Afanasev proves clever enough to trick the wily criminal he first arrested in Odessa thirty years earlier; his commitment to his duties is so strong that he works forty-eight hours without sleeping – *and* he loves his wife, whom he affectionately dubs 'my dear Pinkerton' for trying to track him down when he does not come home. After a frustrated and angry Rumiantsev makes a false confession, Afanasev pursues the case, and when Rumiantsev is badly injured from tangling with the chief crook and his thugs, the lieutenant cradles his head, wipes away the blood, and calls him 'son' [*synok*].

Mikhail Kalatozov's 1956 *First Echelon* [Pervyi eshelon] was one of the first films to combine positive and negative qualities *within* one character, rather than parcelling them out discretely. An uneasy mixture of epic and lyric, of 'frontier' adventure and love story, *First Echelon* opens by introducing a trainload of people eastbound to work on the Virgin Lands project. The film suggests that, with rare exceptions, the thousands of young people who responded to Khrushchev's call for volunteers were completely idealistic. One critic strongly objected to this as an obvious exaggeration; plenty of the volunteers had grown up in the difficult circumstances of the post-war years, he noted, and were damaged by them, as well as by the low level of general culture and the poor work done by the Young Communist League. The Virgin Lands project, in other words, reflected society as a whole.[12]

A whole cast of wooden secondary characters in *First Echelon* – Party organizer, agronomist, engineer – do no more than deliver a few lines apiece, but Kalatozov and scriptwriter Nikolai Pogodin resisted the reflexive urge to portray the Komsomol leader as a simple positive hero. Uzorov is relatively complex. Laudably devoted to the project, he is also a trifle foolish, seeming to believe that wish and will alone can make barren land productive. He is over-confident, he tends to magnify the significance of slogans and directives, and he responds mechanically rather than imaginatively to difficult situations. While admirable in many ways, Uzorov is no icon of Soviet heroism. (Indeed, he was faulted for failing to live up to the standards set by Maksim, hero of Kozintsev and Trauberg's popular film trilogy of the 1930s, and Pavel Korchagin, hero of Nikolai Ostrovskii's classic socialist realist novel, *How the Steel was Tempered*, on which a film was first based in 1942.)

Endings consistently posed problems, for a mixture of political, ideological and aesthetic reasons. Since the edifying role of cinema remained a paramount concern of the state, one reiterated regularly by the Ministry of Culture, film-makers frequently relied on the banal conclusion of an edifying speech, addressed by a figure of unimpeachable authority to a rapt audience, 'as if without the affirmation of higher-ups ... a heroic feat would not appear to be a heroic feat'.[13]

Semen Freilikh sardonically described this tradition:

[Such] endings illustrate the victory of the fallen hero: he rises again to raise the banner in battle, or races along in a tank, or, as is often the case in historical/biographical films, stands embronzed on a pedestal while grateful scions (usually Pioneers) lay flowers at the base. If the hero survives to the end, he then assumes a monumental stance, directing his gaze into the future, thus illustrating his communion with the life of the next generation.[14]

Kalatozov and Pogodin followed this formula by completing *First Echelon* with just such a speech, in this case delivered by the Party secretary, Kashtanov. A genuine *deus ex machina*, in the final scene he literally descends from the skies to congratulate the workers for their stellar performance.

Yet although such explicitly prescriptive endings were beginning to grate on audiences and critics alike, the final rhetorical and oratorical flourish of most Soviet films suggested a collection of examples invented to illustrate a thesis, as both viewers and critics were well aware. The heroes, the incidents, even the emotional content all too often merely 'sweetened the sermon'.[15]

Moreover, Italian neo-realist cinema had altered viewers' expectations. Film professionals, film club members and urban residents generally had easy access to Rossellini's *Rome – Open City*, De Sica's *Umberto D.* and *Bicycle Thief*, and to all of De Santis' films; the regime permitted liberal distribution because these movies dealt with social issues and depicted 'simple' working-class characters. The open-ended conclusions of Italian films compared favourably with what one critic called the tidy 'exclamation points' that terminated even such 'fairly good' recent films as *Alien Kin*, *Land and People*, and *First Echelon*. He much preferred inconclusive endings: a panning shot of a city, the glimpse of a pretty girl's smile through a rain-spattered window. Such shots implied that 'life doesn't end here, you've just seen a small piece of life, which is bigger and far more complex'.[16]

The Soviet system categorized movies by subject: 'about workers', 'about the Virgin Lands', 'about the Revolution'. Yet whatever the subject, whatever the style, all the films of 1956 reflected the *desiderata* of less embellishment, greater truthfulness, and more attention to individual human beings.

Historical films dominated the screen, especially those set in the civil war years, a natural and logical choice of context for writers and directors. In rejecting the Stalinist legacy, Khrushchev himself called for a return to Leninist norms, Leninist legality, Leninist ideals. The years of the formation of the Soviet state offered film-makers an inherently dramatic framework for their own hopes and ideals, and they interpreted and represented this period, however naively, as a 'symbol of faith'.[17]

Hence 1956 witnessed a spate of such movies, many of them relying on retrograde ideological clichés or timid deviations from familiar formulas. Iurii Egorov's *They were the First* [Oni byli pervymi], the title referring to the Petrograd Komsomol during the civil war, combined thematic, dramatic and cinematic clichés. Stepa, a working-class youth who yearns to accomplish 'world-class' feats, has a sick mother whom he nurses devotedly. His girlfriend Glasha (like Sholokhov's Bolshevik heroine Anna Pogudko in *And Quiet Flows the Don*) dreams of fighting alongside Stepa for their common revolutionary cause. The Komsomol banner is a sacred object, 'sanctified', says one character, 'by the blood of comrades'. In a montage derived straight from 1920s Soviet cinema, saboteurs plotting against the revolution murder a loyal Young Communist who overhears them; the victim becomes a source of inspiration, much like the martyred Bolshevik sailor Vakulinchuk in Eisenstein's *The Battleship Potemkin*.

Yet new tints – admittedly anaemic in this film – infuse the colourless old stereotypes. The Party organizer, for example, admonishes a journalist for glossing over the ruinous economic situation and the catastrophic lack of food, advising him to 'write honestly'. A young poet, urged to write about the actual situation, replies that 'there's no poetry in broken glass', and learns how wrong he is. A paternal, accessible, forthright Lenin jokes with Komsomol members in a flash forward to the Third Congress of the Komsomol.[18]

Kiev Studio produced Alov and Naumov's *Pavel Korchagin*, based on Ostrovskii's *How the Steel was Tempered*. Alov, four years older than Naumov and a Second World War veteran when he enrolled in the State Institute of Cinematography, had formed an enduring and fruitful partnership with Naumov. At a time when most Soviet films were ponderous, talky and theatrical, Alov and Naumov made movies of unusual lyricism and graphic dynamism. Their debut film, *Restless Youth*, though conventional in most respects, featured distinctively rapid editing and an uncluttered visual texture.[19]

Two years later, in *Pavel Korchagin*, they broke up the sanctified image of the Komsomol, avoiding the platitudes of *They were the First* and the gelid images of Ostrovskii's text. Instead of Ostrovskii's Korchagin – stalwart, politically irreproachable, and an emotional zombie – Alov and Naumov created a Pavel Korchagin whose renunciation of personal happiness, expressed in the phrase 'this isn't the time for love', is shadowed by pain and longing. Rejecting decorative *mise-en-scène*, Alov and Naumov constructed the image of a reality that may have been imbued with revolutionary dedication, but was also squalid, disease-ridden and plagued by hunger.

Mosfilm director Ivan Pyrev reacted with loud indignation: 'Filth, lice, typhus. No brightness,' he objected. 'We knew how to take pleasure in life, we didn't go off [to fight] like people doomed to suffering.'[20] The Komsomol itself was ambivalent: the public's generally favourable response to the film ameliorated the organization's displeasure ('This is *not* how the steel was tempered,' wrote the secretary of a regional branch). The film generated what amounted to good publicity for the organization, so the Komsomol on balance judged it 'useful'.[21]

Cinema professionals applauded Alov and Naumov's work. Apart from Pyrev and a few others, most of the older generation defended the film as a mirror of their own youth ('That's the way it really was'). But regardless of the divide between the *kinoshniki* (cinema enthusiasts) and *komsomoltsy*, the discussion signified an alteration in the nature of intellectual debate: 'No one any longer called "black" "white",' Lev Anninskii wrote. 'No one called asceticism "love of life", nor the absence of difficulties "total happiness".'[22]

Pavel Korchagin's portrait of the 1920s hardly re-creates those years as they 'really were'. Rather, it inscribes the impulse of the mid-1950s to *regard* the 1920s as a relatively noble and passionate period, with its fanaticism and total commitment. Even the miseries attendant on revolutionary dedication became attractive in so far as they embraced a degree of freedom and inspiration unavailable in 'normal' conditions. The heterodox notion of revolution as a kind of ecstasy-producing escape from humdrum reality was certainly not identified as such; the critics spoke, rather, of revolutionary idealism and self-sacrifice.

In venerable Soviet tradition, revolutionaries unwittingly reap rewards for their willingness to sacrifice themselves to their ideal. They do not act out of hope for reward, since socialist endeavour is joyful and optimistic in itself, but reward crowns their efforts. Thus in Aleksei Tolstoi's 1920 novel, *The Road to Calvary* [Khozhdenie po mukam], later made into a film trilogy, the heroes traverse their stations of the cross only to end up at the brilliantly-lit Congress of Soviets, where they hear Lenin give a speech.

Alov and Naumov, in contrast, cast sacrifice in highly ambiguous terms, in part because they exploit cinema's ability to convey the visual drama of illness. The flashback that constitutes most of the film is framed by images of a sightless, paralysed Pavel, and the film opens with Pavel's head on his pillow, his skin pale, his gaze motionless, his face a death-mask.

Pavel overcomes excruciating trials only in order to confront new suffering. Since 'there can be no question of moral fallibility, the only genuine tests [Korchagin] can undergo involve his capacity to stand physical suffering'.[23] Pavel nobly forswears happiness; he becomes, as Troianovskii writes, a 'kind of Christ-figure', offering himself up for the sake of humanity.[24] But the film underscores the cost of his renunciation: emotional happiness, health, ultimately life itself. The film's double ending reinforces that ambiguity: immediately before a reassuring finale in which a healthy Pavel tells the viewer not to believe in his death, the film-makers return to the prologue. The blind Pavel is lying in his bed and wrestling with despair before he makes the decision to start all over again.

The civil war spawned the other major historical film of 1956, *The Forty-first* [Sorok-pervyi], directed for Mosfilm by another recent VGIK alumnus, Grigorii Chukhrai. Chukhrai undertook a remake of a Soviet classic: in 1927 veteran director Iakov Protazanov, back in the Soviet Union after two years (1921–23) in the West, adapted for the screen Boris Lavrenev's story of Mariutka, a Red Army sharpshooter who guards a captured officer of the opposing White Army. After an idyllic interlude on a desert island, when the two fall in love, a boat carrying Whites nears the shore and the officer runs towards them. The Red heroine snatches up her rifle and shoots her lover, thus claiming her forty-first victim.[25] Because of the love between Red and White and because *The Forty-*

The Big Sleep

first had 'already been done', Mosfilm took a risk in approving the film for production, especially with an inexperienced director.

Chukhrai, a twice-wounded and decorated war veteran, had studied direction with Sergei Iutkevich and Mikhail Romm before graduating from VGIK in 1953. He was beginning a successful career in the Kiev Studio when he criticized a script commemorating the 300th anniversary of Ukraine's union with Russia. The studio fired him, and he was fixing radios to support his family when Mikhail Romm, his teacher and mentor, went to Kiev as a studio consultant and ended up rescuing Chukhrai, both by agreeing that the script under discussion was hopeless and by arranging for Pyrev to invite Chukhrai back to Moscow to work.

Romm and Pyrev's importance in launching the careers of younger artists and their influence on the film industry in those years are hard to overestimate. Pyrev assigned serious projects to relatively green young men, and he also enjoyed his role as benefactor and formidable 'boss' [*khoziain*] of Mosfilm. When Chukhrai proposed a remake of *The Forty-first*, Pyrev nominally consulted colleagues but basically made the decision himself, proclaiming, 'We'll do it.' (Pyrev distributed other kinds of largesse just as decisively. Pointing to a building under construction across the road, he told Chukhrai, 'I won't give you an apartment, but I'll give you a room.' For the thirty-five-year-old Chukhrai, living in corners and cubby-holes since the end of the war, the room was as much of a fantasy-come-true as the film assignment.)[26]

Pyrev had a well-developed talent for navigating the bureaucratic quagmire that all too often devoured attractive film projects. He was famous for playacting: on one occasion he fell to his knees before a minister of culture, alternately pleading with him and insulting him as a 'puffed-up turkey' who understood nothing about art. Vladimir Naumov, who knew him well, speculates that Pyrev's theatrics served to neutralize the paralysing force of the system:

> Collaborating as he did with the state, he would perhaps unconsciously, perhaps involuntarily, express his inner protest in this way. He seemed to be trying to destroy the horrible pyramid of subordination that he himself had helped create. With his carnival acts he would destroy, he would roil up the stagnant swamp of conventions that was so closely bound up with toadying [*chinopochitanie*] and with programmed ideas [*instruktivnye myshleniia*].[27]

The Forty-first justified Pyrev's faith. It won a prize at Cannes in 1957 and kudos from the European press; Soviet film-makers ultimately named it best film of the year. But it nearly foundered when Mosfilm's artistic council met to discuss the script. The heroine's love for a class enemy seemed an insurmountable obstacle. Grigorii Koltunov, the experienced scenarist assigned to Chukhrai by Pyrev, had anticipated this objection and included a few scenes in which the film explicitly condemned her love. But Chukhrai was unhappy with that solution and prepared to wage war with his scenarist at the meeting. Iutkevich dissuaded him. Arguing that only a united front would protect the film, he advised Chukhrai to go along with the scenario in public and then shoot it the way he wanted when he was on location.

The meeting was indeed stormy, for *The Forty-first* was considered a barometer of the times, no less in 1956 than thirty years earlier.[28] Grigorii Roshal, whose career was beginning just about the same time that Protazanov's film opened, felt modern audiences would not tolerate a remake. 'If you show Govorukha-Otrok [the White officer] unsympathetically, the viewer will not forgive Mariutka her love for him, and if you show him sympathetically, the viewer will not forgive you for his getting shot.' The characters, especially the heroine, used unpalatably crude language that undermined the 'aesthetic education of the masses', objected one participant. But Pyrev mocked the notion of Mariutka as a refined young lady. He pranced around waving his arms and mincing, 'Ah, pardon! Ah, merci! Ah, bonjour! Ah, guten Morgen!...' Pyrev prevailed.[29]

Chukhrai later commented to an interviewer from the Belgian *Le Soir* (7 June 1957) that he had no ideology in mind when he made *The Forty-first* except the desire to create art. Chukhrai and his brilliant cameraman Sergei Urusevskii shot the timeless idyll enjoyed by Mariutka and her blue-eyed lover on their desert island with such lyricism and beauty that the lovers' passion and tenderness enjoy parity with, if not indeed primacy over, any revolutionary duty. As the film critic Semen Freilikh perceptively noted at the time: 'The theme of love too often seems like an appendage to the main theme. Here love occupies centre stage, it merges with the theme of revolution.'[30]

Nevertheless, the domestic press interpreted *The Forty-first* much as it had *Pavel Korchagin*, as a study in revolutionary courage.[31] Chukhrai himself, notwithstanding his comments abroad, encouraged that reading at home. The film, he said, tried to resurrect for the viewer 'the heroic romanticism of the unforgettable years of the civil war, to bring to Soviet people the idea of indomitable faith in the motherland and in the revolution that is stronger than any personal feeling'.[32]

Revolutionary loyalty dominates the first half of the film, as the remnants of a Red Army unit, 'Evsiukov's regiment', make their way across the Karakum desert to the Sea of Aral. In mostly long and middle shots, twenty-two men plus Mariutka and her prisoner – kept alive because he possesses important information about White strategy – trudge across drifting dunes and endless sandhills. Each receives a mouthful of precious water, and Evsiukov gives bread even to the soldier who, by falling asleep while on sentry duty, cost them the camels crucial to their survival. By the time they reach the Aral Sea and an encampment of Kazakhs, eleven are left. Seven continue overland, but four set sail. Of those, only Mariutka and Govorukha-Otrok survive the storm that wrecks their boat.

The Big Sleep

3. *The Forty-first*

Once the couple comes ashore, the isolation of island existence permits revolutionary loyalty to take a back seat to love. 'Red soldier' and 'White officer', 'escort' and 'prisoner' become, simply, He and She, Adam and Eve. Govorukha-Otrok's arrogance, earlier manifest in a smirk and a raised eyebrow, disappears along with his sodden clothing; he comes to appreciate, without condescension, Mariutka's warmth, her simplicity and spontaneity. She nurses him through fever and delirium, watches him by firelight, catches and cleans and cooks fish for them to eat. She even sacrifices the paper she composes her poems on so he can have a smoke, because she has fallen deeply in love with the man she calls her 'blue-eyed darling'.

In *The Forty-first* love is autonomous and elemental. Chukhrai breaches conventional film presentations of love as constancy (Alesha in *Big Family*) and as friendship (*Unfinished Tale*). However, love can rule unchallenged only in the unpeopled world of nature, where it arrogates to itself such classic symbols of the Revolution as the raging storm. The golden sand and golden skin, the turquoise sea and Govorukha-Otrok's azure eyes form a visual alliance of nature and love. When the human world impinges, it destroys that idyll just as inevitably as Mariutka's rifle kills Govorukha-Otrok.

The title hangs over the picture, its end implicit in its beginning. Mariutka shoots her lover as he splashes through the surf towards the ship carrying 'his' people: 'revolutionary duty' triumphs. But the final close-up is of her anguished face as she weeps over the body clasped in her arms, the rifle forgotten on the sand – a collision of despairing faith and doomed love.

Contemporary Soviet reviews praised *The Forty-first* not only for its 'truthful depiction of revolutionary reality', but also for showing within that reality the human capacity for feelings. They admired Urusevskii's extraordinary gift for portraiture and his ability to endow landscape with emotional content, making nature 'background, atmosphere, place of action, and one of the main heroes'.[33] The desert itself, though nearly fatal to Evsiukov's regiment, is beautiful, its sands sensual and velvety.[34]

Less remarked at the time was the loving, almost caressing homage Urusevskii's camera pays to the human body. In the first half of the film, as the Reds cross the Karakum desert, they are wrapped in their uniforms and boots. Mariutka, her long hair hidden under a fur hat and her body muffled in an overcoat, is deliberately desexed, but so are the men. Even when they reach the Aral Sea their ecstasy is confined to facial expression, as if they have no bodies. The Kazakh natives who feed and help them are nearly as disembodied. For all their ornate and colourful clothing, the only females we see in close-up are pre-sexual: 'She's just a child,' says Mariutka about one of them, 'not a girl.'

By contrast, when Mariutka and Govorukha-Otrok are shipwrecked on their island, Urusevskii shoots their bodies as extensions of nature. Warm firelight flickers on Govorukha-Otrok's lithe muscles; Mariutka's sleeve falls back to reveal the vulnerability of her upper arm. Her thigh and hip are outlined beneath her skirt. When Govorukha-Otrok retells the story of Robinson Crusoe and Friday to his rapt audience of one, Chukhrai and Urusevskii construct out of image and music a wordless montage in which hair, lips and skin have particular beauty.

The dialogue is more troublesome than the images. The words of love exchanged by Mariutka and Govorukha-Otrok are less persuasive and less eloquent than the angry words they hurl at each other when they argue about the Revolution. Their love, grounded in exquisitely-rendered physical reality, is genuine, but politics engage their passions on a different level. *The Forty-first* exemplifies what Troianovskii rightly identifies as a central paradox of the thaw. A profound hunger for personal freedom co-existed and warred with a sincere belief in the 'collectivist divinity', even though the belief would – does – deny the yearned-for freedom.[35] Whether in *The Forty-first* or in *Pavel Korchagin*, the cost of achieving true faith appears frightfully high: one's love, one's very soul.

4. Modern Times

B oth *Pavel Korchagin* and *The Forty-first* satisfied the multiple demands imposed on Soviet cinema by its several constituencies. Both films depict the heroic formation of the Soviet state; both portray revolutionary and paradigmatic heroes. As such, they earned official, if guarded, approbation. The distinctive cinematic gifts of Alov and Naumov in *Pavel Korchagin* and Chukhrai and Urusevskii in *The Forty-first* engaged and gave hope to critics who had despaired over the mediocrity of Soviet cinema. And audiences were moved by the human drama of the two works.

Nevertheless, in 1956 viewers, especially younger ones, hungered for films about contemporary urban life. *A Person is Born* [Chelovek rodilsia], the Georgian film *Our Courtyard* [Nash dvor], *Good Luck!* [V dobryi chas], *Spring on Zarechnaia Street* [Vesna na Zarechnoi ulitse], the slightly later *The House I Live in* [Dom, v kotorom ia zhivu, 1957] – these were movies made for a specific audience of urban students and workers in their late teens and twenties. Like the films' characters, they had been born 'lucky'; they had grown up in 'our courtyard'.

Such modest, unembellished images of everyday life [*bytovaia zhizn'*] satisfied the voracious appetite for 'truthful' art that was one of the most significant, if only partly realized, achievements of the thaw. As so often happened in Soviet cultural politics, classics and foreign material became ammunition in contemporary battles. In spring 1956, for example, the veteran film director Sergei Iutkevich's *Othello* opened in the wake of the Party Congress. Venice and Cyprus took a back seat to Moscow: critics interpreted Iutkevich's version almost exclusively in terms of its immediate significance. They praised its portrayal of 'the pathos of the struggle for truth, for humaneness ... the violent and passionate protest against every sort of lie and hypocrisy, falsification and double-dealing ... the conflict between truth and decency, and base betrayal'.[1] Sergei Bondarchuk's performance as the Moor became a symbol for the decade, as Innokentii Smoktunovskii's Hamlet later became for the 1960s; in Iutkevich's version, Shakespeare's *Othello* became a drama of indestructible faith, shaken but subsequently restored.[2]

This 'passionate protest against every sort of lie' underpinned the hunger for films of contemporary life, and Soviet studios released half a dozen such films between the autumn of 1956 and the spring of 1957. One of them, *A Person is Born*, very nearly failed to make the hazardous leap from script to production, in part because it presents the birth of an illegitimate child quite matter-of factly. Studios most often blocked potentially controversial and risky films at the script stage, before committing substantial financial and human resources, as well as reputation, to a project that might backfire. In the case of *A Person is Born*, as with *The Forty-first*, Ivan Pyrev's patronage once more proved crucial.

The author, Leonid Agranovich, had anticipated problems when he brought his script to the studio's artistic council. Nevertheless, he reeled under the assault: 'Again and again I heard, "slander of reality", "where did the author get this?", "callous society", and so on and so forth ... I stopped listening when the *khudsovet* members started vying with each other to save the nation's youth from me, and tried to teach me the truth about life.' Pyrev, who had read the script overnight and liked it, gave everyone the opportunity to vent their objections. He then summed up: 'Is that it? Well, then we'll write it down: film approved for production.'[3] He appointed Vasilii Ordynskii, a recent VGIK graduate, as director.

A Person is Born opens with a panning shot of infants in a maternity clinic. Unlike the other new mothers, Nadia Smirnova receives not a single visitor, and her only gifts are what the other women, pitying her, provide. A flashback shows Nadia on her way to Moscow to study, instantly identifiable by her braids as a country girl. Her dreams and ambitions falter when she fails her entrance exam ('It's my fault,' she acknowledges, 'I forgot the formula'), and falls in love with Vitalii, a poseur who exploits her innocence and seduces her. (Many movies repeated this cliché, from *The Big Family* through the Oscar-winning melodrama *Moscow Doesn't Believe in Tears* [Moskva slezam ne verit, 1979].)

By the time Nadia and Vitalii split up, she knows how phony he is: 'You have nothing of your own. Your suit belongs to your brother, your apartment belongs to your parents,' she says scornfully. The flashback ends and the film cuts back to the maternity ward, where Vitalii appears on the day Nadia is due to leave with the baby. At first pleased, Nadia kicks him out of the taxi when she realizes that he has surfaced only because the doctor, nurses and other women managed to track him down. She ends up walking the streets with her baby in her arms and nowhere to go.[4]

Prologue concluded, the rest of the film depicts its real subject: how 'a person is born'. The process is patently far more complex, and in ideological terms more meaningful, than physical parturition. Nadia is resting forlornly in a trolley shelter when Gleb, a student, notices her, and finds her a room in a

The Big Sleep

private house on the outskirts of the city. She gets a job as a bus conductor, and juggles the demands of her job with the care of her child. Gleb's attempt to combine similarly conflicting demands of work and school ends with a failing grade in biology that puts his student stipend at risk.

Ordynskii and Agranovich occasionally opt for implausibly simple solutions. Gleb rescues Nadia just when despair threatens to overwhelm her; the gruff landlady proves to have a kind heart. In general, however, the film validates Nadia's friend Sima: 'In books it's all fine,' she says. 'In reality it's not like that.' Both Nadia and Gleb confront serious dilemmas, make difficult choices, and take responsibility for the consequences. One montage, for instance, splices together Nadia's exhausting reality, a treadmill of night-shift work, cleaning, sewing, laundry and baby-minding in a dishevelled, cluttered room.

Individual spokesmen for the system, such as the visiting nurse whom the landlady scornfully dubs 'lady bureaucrat', lack sensitivity. The assistant director at Nadia's job belongs to a large roster of bureaucrats whose decency is compromised as they move up the ladder. Like the Komsomol leader in *Alien Kin*, who condemns Fedor for leaving his wife and child without bothering to find out why Fedor left, the transport official fails to ask why Nadia is requesting a change from night- to day-shift (to take care of the baby). 'Think first of the passengers,' he rebukes her sternly, 'and then of your comfort.' Stripped of the optimism once *de rigueur* for Soviet heroines, Nadia barely avoids cynicism: 'I don't believe in friendship, in happiness, in fairy tales,' she says hopelessly. 'I don't believe in any words.'

Still, the system ultimately supports her. It provides a work schedule that can accommodate child-care ('That's the law. It's your right'). It exempts her from the community work [*obshchestvennaia rabota*] expected of every Soviet citizen, because she is still nursing her baby. And genuine friendships – with Gleb, Sima, the landlady – sustain her. Even the crude bus driver who earlier made a pass at her comes to respect her. 'Nadiusha,' he reminds her, 'without friends you can't make it.' Vitalii's father, a decent man, manages to locate her and offers help. When she refuses, he leaves reluctantly, full of admiration for her courage and regret for his own worthless offspring.

Earlier, Sima had excluded heroism from the realm of everyday life: 'At the front,' she asserted, 'that's the place for heroic exploits. But here?' Nadia proves her wrong. *A Person is Born* takes place 'here', in the world of night-shifts and nappies, and Nadia is clearly a heroine. She is, however, an ungainly heroine, who holds the other characters at arm's length. She succeeds in 'becoming a person' essentially by herself, an achievement that deviates from screen convention. Instead of recognizing the film's originality, however, both viewers and critics considered it a new variant of an old pattern, and they attributed Nadia's recovery to the help of people around her. In fact, she routinely rejects help, and the film does not force her into orthodoxy in the end.[5]

Construing the relationship between heroism and everyday life consistently baffled film-makers. Mandarins in the Ministry of Culture and in their own studios urged them to make movies about the lives of ordinary men and women in typical Soviet milieux. However, they had to contextualize individual concerns, imparting to or extrapolating from them a larger significance. Otherwise they were found guilty of trivializing the social dimension of individual lives.

When the Ministry of Culture met in the spring of 1956 to discuss the following year's thematic plan, it focused on this issue. The plan for 1957 required particular attention, since that year marked the fortieth anniversary of the Bolshevik Revolution. The head of film production criticized 'naturalistic imitations of life', and the ignorance that engendered them. 'They [film-makers] don't know our reality well and they don't study it. They can't always rise above trivial everyday facts to select what is significant.' The Minister of Culture himself concluded the discussion with a resounding *dictum*: 'Soviet cinema will not advance on the basis of minor themes. It can grow and develop only by taking up important issues, matters of principle ... We must direct our attention to themes associated with the simple man who is building the new society.'[6]

In the echo-pattern typical of Soviet cultural politics, the call from on high reverberated like a yodel across Swiss mountains. A short while later, at a meeting between Mosfilm's artistic council and a group of scriptwriters, Pyrev cited Soviet cinema's dwindling concern with 'matters of principle' as its central problem. The writer Mikhail Papava reproached his colleagues for 'equating life and art, as a result of which verisimilitude has replaced the great truths that can be mediated by art. We rightly repudiated our former false concept of scale [*masshtabnost'*]', he continued, 'but we are failing to achieve authentic magnitude, which can best be expressed by creating characters on a grand scale.'[7] The lexical arsenal now added 'narrow' and 'private' to 'schematic' and 'lifeless', as cardinal artistic sins.

This ambiguity explains the reaction to what was arguably the most important film released in 1956, Marlen Khutsiev and Feliks Mironer's *Spring on Zarechnaia Street*. The movie delighted most critics and viewers, but the distinct chill emanating from bureaucratic sources anticipated a major cultural battle of the next few years.

The plot of *Spring on Zarechnaia Street* is a variant of the standard 're-education film', in which labour, or its individual representatives, can reform and improve everything, including human beings – a genre as characteristic for Soviet cinema as the Western was for Hollywood. In Khutsiev and Mironer's film Tania Levchenko, a brand-new graduate in literature, arrives in a provincial city to teach adult worker-students, and ends by learning from them instead. In only slightly less commonplace counterpoint, the hero-worker, in this case stoker Sasha Savchenko, has his eyes opened by his first exposure to a member of the intelligentsia.

Mironer's script, about the relationship between a naive and bookish young teacher and her pupils, had languished for two years. Once production finally began, he and Khutsiev contended with the charge of 'thematic trivialization' [*melkotem'ie*]: supposedly they exaggerated the importance of 'everyday life' [*bytovshchina*], the phrase used by contemporary critics for 'everything that alarmed them'.[8] Pyrev dismissed the finished film as a 'neorealist variation on the theme of *The Young Lady and the Hooligan* [Baryshnia i khuligan]', a 1918 melodrama starring the poet Vladimir Mayakovsky and disdained by him as 'sentimental … rubbish'.[9]

In 1950 Khutsiev and Mironer had collaborated on a film, *The City Builders* [Gradostroiteli], to fulfil graduation requirements at the State Institute of Cinematography. Although a student film, *The City Builders* attracted attention: in a cinematic context of musicals, literary adaptations, concerts, biographies and children's films, when 'even a hint of contemporary life as multi-layered and contradictory was unthinkable',[10] it offered viewers at least some intimations of the density of reality.

Six years later, the significantly altered atmosphere gave Khutsiev and Mironer far more leeway. Khutsiev manipulated the banal elements of the story with the unblinking detachment that came to be the hallmark of his style. Khutsiev traced the subterranean shifts of the era not by digging below the surface, but by fixing his dispassionate eye *on* that surface, on the visible spoor of what was happening below. The *realia* of life pulsing on the streets and in the rooms and courtyards of his southern workers' town formed the texture, style and meaning of the film. The resulting entity is, as Maia Turovskaia observed, far bigger than the plot itself.[11]

The very first moments of the film illustrate Khutsiev's revolutionary approach. A long shot shows people purposefully leaving a train station in an autumn rain; a girl trails behind them, her raincoat and hood glistening and her arms pulled down by two suitcases and a couple of bundles. We see no faces, just the girl's wet coat and bags as she rushes after and misses the bus. A figure flies past her, oblivious to her plight; a trucker pulls up along the muddy road and helps her in. Instead of swelling strings, a pleasant tenor voice sings about 'this street' and 'this crossroads' to the accompaniment of a guitar. (The guitar theme continues throughout the film, a bold choice given the swelling string arrangements and orchestration typical of the time.)

Obviously, we are far from Moscow's spacious central squares and Leningrad's gracious boulevards and embankments. In fact, we are miles away from any conventional *mise-en-scène*, such as the long shots of the shipyard that introduced *The Big Family*. As in *The Big Family*, the horizon of *Spring on Zarechnaia Street* establishes the larger context of the industrial city, with its factory smokestacks and cranes as if seen by Tania from the truck window. But the street is as ordinary as could be, with its rushing cars, its ruts and mud, its impatient lines of people in stiff raincoats. Even the weather is anti-heroic, as it were, not the sparkling, ceremonial rain common to movies then, but a dreary, autumn drizzle.[12]

The camera makes its innovative way through a pre-war workers' settlement. A few years after Khutsiev and Mironer's film came out, Khrushchev initiated a massive housing-construction project: thousands of five-storey residential units were built, intended to be temporary solutions to the acute post-war housing shortage.[13] But the workers in *Spring on Zarechnaia Street* still live in little houses surrounded by crooked fences, and when the roofs peel back the camera shows us equally modest interiors. Tania's mentor lives in a room nearly bare of furniture. She herself rents a room in an apartment whose kitchen is separated from the main room by a curtain.

The film is full of authentic 'signs of the times'. Ficus plants, 'little curtains, picture frames, mirrors, cushions on the piquet spreads on the steel beds' impose some small mark of individuality, just as passers-by, all dressed in the same poorly-fitting clothing, add a scarf or a pin or a cap to express 'their' style.[14] The faces we finally begin to see when Tania pushes her wet hood back and combs her hair are attractive but hardly glamorous. The trucker uses cheerfully crude and slangy language and the young workers gulp down foaming mugs of beer when their shift ends.

Those mugs of beer agitated critics in 1956, who worried about the pernicious influence of screen images, and even the film's partisans felt obliged to couch their praise in terms of the directors' 'courage' in showing such 'negative' characteristics. In turning away from the monumental promenades to the 'alleyways of one-storey houses, where ordinary people live, bear children, drink … beer, which they buy at kiosks for money, cinematography for the first time risked showing the ordinary life of ordinary people of those times'.[15]

Khutsiev and Mironer sought their heroes 'not in the centre, not in the capital, not in offices with nameplates on the doors … but in the very heart of life', and audiences gratefully welcomed such screen images of their world. 'The art of those years', Turovskaia observed, 'felt obliged to tell people the truth about themselves and their lives, even if initially a rather inconsequential and private truth about their personal human relationships … These years witnessed widespread popular enthusiasm for the theme of "family" life, and abounded in stories of unhappy marriages, divorces, abandoned children, young love.'[16]

Khutsiev and Mironer went disconcertingly further, treating Tania quite objectively, and against the grain of convention. The weight of a century-old Russian tradition presumes representatives of the intelligentsia to be not only progressive in political matters but sensitive to human beings. Tania is not. Lacking self-confidence, she stands on her professional dignity in lieu of a more substantial or worthy foundation. She chides a student for falling asleep

The Big Sleep

at his desk without learning why he is so exhausted: in fact, he worked a full day after being up all night while his wife was in labour. When a man tells her his wife must remain seated, Tania insists that the woman stand – only to see that she is eight months pregnant.

In one scene, Tania reads poetry aloud to her class while snow falls outside. Her dry, pedantic reading undercuts the expected contrast between the cold, dark, snowy scene outside and the warmth and light of the classroom. Tania sincerely loves poetry and music, and is genuinely dedicated to her profession, but both her love and her dedication are lifeless, because she has not yet felt the emotions that would give her a profound understanding of either poetry or people.

Sasha, the unpretentious and self-confident representative of the proletariat, is even less conventionally portrayed. Typically, Sasha's attributes would be shown in a flattering light. Instead, Khutsiev and Mironer question their merit. Sasha's swaggering masculinity verges on exploitative arrogance with his girl-friend Zina (though their embraces have a appealing physicality not often seen on Soviet screens then). When he strolls into class late, holding a posy he swiped from a flower-pot en route, he looks foolish.

'Simplicity' is not an *a priori* measure of heroism in *Spring on Zarechnaia Street* nor is it synonymous with worker status. Only one sequence in the film presents labour formulaically. In a montage of static tableaux, to the background of cheerful music, Tania witnesses her students at work in the factory. She – a tiny figure against the gigantic machinery – is transfixed and liberated by the power and beauty she sees.[17]

In a film that customarily shows characters in medium shots, amid a thicket of objects, rooms and streets, camerawork also functions to demonstrate the inner incompatibility between Sasha and Tania. The camera most strikingly contrasts his depth of feeling with her aridity when Tania listens raptly to a Rachmaninov concerto on the radio, completely oblivious to Sasha. In the script the music draws Tania and Sasha together, following the convention of Soviet cinema that associates classical music with emotional depth. (In *Unfinished Tale*, for instance, the Tchaikovsky concerto playing on the radio enthrals the paralysed hero, while the egotistical doctor falls asleep in the actual concert hall.)

Khutsiev retained the scene, but reversed its effect: the music separates them. The camera cuts from Tania's ecstatic face to Sasha's blank gaze. She turns away, unwilling to reveal her rapture; he fiddles with a cigarette and finally leaves softly, his exit as unremarked as his presence. A successful lesson, in other words, is replaced by an unsuccessful one. The predictable alliance between worker and *intelligent* – the pact established, for example, by engineer Zina Pavlovna and shipbuilder Ilia Zhurbin in *The Big Family* – fails to occur.

Sasha is unwilling to be, and to be seen as, a piece of clay to be moulded.

Modern Times

4. *Spring on Zarechnaia Street*

He does change, in the end, but his transformation does not conform to someone else's measure. It springs from his own inner necessity. His impatient attraction to Tania and his superficial enthusiasm for learning become a more profound and more tender attachment to both. 'He grows up,' comments Troianovskii, 'but he is not re-educated.'[18]

Along with Aleksei Batalov, Nikolai Rybnikov as Sasha was one of the first Soviet actors to embody individual empowerment. The thaw permitted men and women to believe that they could define history for themselves, independent of any leader. With his cocky grin and his buoyant stride, Rybnikov seemed wholesome and decisive. He performed no special exploits on screen, yet he was strong enough 'to hold up the planet'.[19]

At a time when the 'concept of totally remaking human beings'[20] dominated every sphere of life, including politics, morality and law, Khutsiev and Mironer refused to create a model hero or a model heroine. Both characters wear blinkers, the result of personal inadequacy. They cannot be slotted into neat categories. Good and bad, 'ours' and 'alien' co-exist within them; neither is right and neither is guilty.

Khutsiev and Mironer do prefer Sasha to Tania, not because he is a worker but because his *naïveté* and ignorance conceal sensitivity and openness to beauty, whereas Tania's 'egoistic erudition' conceals 'spiritual constraint'.[21]

> The image of a harmonious, unified, organic man, such as Soviet man ought to be, turned out to be divided in two halves though no one had ever suspected such bifurcation ... It was not at all easy to accept such an image, since cinematography was after all supposed to set an example, derive from life what was worthy and significant. *Spring on Zarechnaia Street* violated that canon.[22]

Rejecting the typically clear and easily identified authorial positions of Soviet films, Khutsiev and Mironer forced viewers to do some hard thinking for themselves. The ending is unresolved, pregnant with possibility. Sasha and Tania face each other in a classroom; a spring breeze blows through the open window, scattering papers. The breeze, billowing curtains and flurry of pages form a visual image of uncertainty. They do not constitute a happy ending, as they would have in an earlier film; they belong to a love drama that may or may not work out.

The cinematic acknowledgement of human complexity signalled a major shift in both expectation and perception, and film comedy reflected this shift no less than dramas of everyday life. Conventional intellectual snobbery denigrated comedy – Shilova recalled laughing at comedies in private while criticizing them as primitive and vulgar in public – but audiences felt otherwise.

In the summer of 1956, 'passionate, exigent and proprietary' cinema fans (some 40,000), who attended a two-month festival in Kuibyshev and in the Krasnodar and Novosibirsk regions, demanded entertaining films and especially comedies. '"More comedies!" they cried with one voice,' reported Mosfilm. 'And more romance, not necessarily on the basis of political consciousness or industrial relations.'[23] Ivan Pyrev, Mosfilm's director, agreed. Himself a director of lyrical and romantic comedies, he had long urged his colleagues to make enjoyable, engaging comedies.

Comedy, though, could easily lead into the ideological quicksand of 'pure' entertainment, a danger apparent to the Soviet state and its film industry from its earliest days. In 'a society whose appointed and self-appointed spokesmen took themselves exceptionally seriously', the culture of laughter was inherently problematic.[24] These spokesmen suspected irony, 'the faithful companion of unbelief and doubt' that pervaded the high culture of the 1920s,[25] but also low-brow comic manifestations, such as slapstick, farce and the all-too-subversive deviance of carnivals and clowns.[26] The state felt queasy rejecting anything closely allied with 'the people', such as side-shows and fairs; nevertheless, the rebellious and liberating nature of much of folk culture and folk humour disquieted officialdom.

One solution was to freight comedy with tub-thumping, as if comedy could express serious ideas only via explicit homiletics. Another was to concoct recipes for distinctively 'Soviet' comedy: in the 1920s, ideological messages and social significance replaced 'bourgeois' situations and the physical humour beloved of audiences;[27] in the 1930s, a shift away from the farcical antics of Aleksandrov's *Jolly Fellows* [Veselye rebiata, 1934] towards 'solemn joy in the midst of heroic construction', manifest in Aleksandrov's subsequent string of hit musical comedies, *The Circus*, *Volga-Volga* [1938] and *Radiant Path* [Svetlyi put', 1940].[28]

After the war, when 'every new film was to be a masterpiece, capable of instilling communist consciousness into the masses', comedies vanished altogether. Audiences had to make do with repeated showings of the Aleksandrov films and with popular but unpublicized 'trophy' films, the most famous among them the German musical comedy *Girl of My Dreams* [Die Frau meiner Träume/ Devushka moikh mechtei, 1944].[29]

Fifteen years later, Grigorii Aleksandrov tried to explain that the realism dominating mid-1950s cinema militated against comedy, since comedy relies on grotesquerie, satire and eccentricity to exaggerate negative human qualities. When comedy restricts itself to 'real life', he maintained, it becomes merely a 'photograph of the ordinary'. The result is 'boring movies ... [in which] sharp observations are replaced by interminable vaudeville misunderstandings, stunts and dances'. Aleksandrov saw an alternative approach:

> In fact, although we don't have the exploitation of man by man in our country, or class antagonism, remnants of capitalism endure in people's consciousness ... Careerism, callousness, cowardice, sloth, stupidity, subordinating the common good to one's personal satisfaction: all this can be found to one or another degree in various individuals.

These 'remnants of bourgeois mentality', then, provide an appropriate subject for comedy, which can perform 'an important educational function' by exposing them.[30]

Given the onerous double yoke of politics and pedagogy, directors understandably avoided comedy. A few comedies had opened: Mikhail Kalatozov's moderately successful *Faithful Friends* [Vernye druz'ia, 1954], Boris Barnet's *Liana* [1955]. But didactic comedies were, not surprisingly, dull, and funny movies forfeited political relevance. Gorky Studio had complained that *Liana*, for instance, was 'too entertaining': its amusing plot stifled 'the ideological significance' of the work.[31] When the Writers' Union met to evaluate Mosfilm's plan for 1957, orthodox scriptwriter Klimentii Mints spoke for many: the proposed comedies, he feared, would turn out 'thematically trivial and aesthetically weak'.[32]

Amid such widespread suspicions, the creation and distribution of the first thaw comedy, Eldar Riazanov's debut feature film, *Carnival Night*, seems all the more remarkable. *Carnival Night* depicts the comic struggle between a middle-aged, hidebound bureaucrat named Ogurtsov (roughly, Pickle), and his underlings, a group of young and enthusiastic performers, over preparations for a New Year's concert at a House of Culture. Loaded with song and dance routines, the film culminates in the concert itself, ultimately a victory for the innovative young vanguard over the censorship of the old.

The plot sounds innocent enough. Indeed, intense scrutiny of *Carnival Night* today yields virtually no evidence of subversive irony. But in 1955, when Boris Laskin and Vladimir Poliakov first submitted their script proposal, they felt obliged to defend their satiric intent on the basis of its social utility: '[Ogurtsov] belongs to that fortunately rare breed: men who are entirely devoid of a sense of humour. He is a hypocrite who always plays safe and he is prone to analyse any burst of laughter in terms of its expediency and immediate usefulness.'[33]

Everyone understood the pitfalls. Ivan Pyrev, with his usual strategic acumen, took the unusual measure of convening a Mosfilm artistic council to consider the script while it was still being written. Pyrev and the writers wanted to garner support for the project so as to avoid excessive revisions that might destroy the freshness and immediacy of the comedy. At the meeting the script's advocates carefully chose their laudatory adjectives: *Carnival Night*'s brand of comedy was 'healthy' and 'life-loving', the Soviet equivalent of America's 'clean entertainment for the whole family'. 'Youth' and 'conviction' vanquish hypocrisy, sterility and 'false adherence to principle'. Conservatives dismissed the script as stale and derivative.

As was so often the case, Pyrev had the last word. Slyly observing that Ogurtsov-like individuals flourish within many 'of our organizations, including our own artistic council', he relished the thought of a delightful Soviet comedy, 'the likes of which we haven't seen for a very long time'. He even proposed making Ogurtsov the director of the House of Culture instead of the assistant director: 'In our productions the negative character is always the assistant director, never the director; the director goes off on vacation and straightens everything out when he returns.'[34]

Pyrev chose Eldar Riazanov as director. A recent graduate of the State Institute of Cinematography, Riazanov had worked in documentary film-making for several years. He was no different from most Soviet film-makers in his reluctance to direct comedy: when Pyrev proposed *Carnival Night* to him, he tried to wriggle out of it. But Pyrev persuaded him, and although they had many disagreements, Riazanov gives Pyrev a great deal of credit for the success of *Carnival Night*.

Riazanov wanted to sharpen the barbs ridiculing bureaucratic stupidity.

It would be terrific, I thought, if the picture elicited not just laughter but bitterness. Pyrev pushed me towards a more conventional and colourful film spectacle, whose musicality and carnival atmosphere would create a joyful mood, and Ogurtsov would be absurd and funny, but not at all frightening ... At the same time Ivan Aleksandrovich did not reject the film's satiric thrust; he believed its buffoonery and grotesquerie would enhance the satiric impact. I was sure, then and now, that realistic satire is more scathing, more trenchant, more weighty.[35]

The script was controversial, the studio's financial investment substantial and Riazanov inexperienced. Hence Pyrev carefully monitored the progress of the film, watching footage weekly and reporting his reactions to Riazanov. Despite Pyrev's caution, Riazanov nearly lost his job when studio members – most of whom had never directed a comedy – previewed a rough and incomplete version of the film. They disliked the film so much ('boring', 'untalented', 'mediocre') that they were ready to scotch the whole project and forfeit the money already spent. Thanks to Pyrev, Riazanov stayed on as director, and Pyrev's faith was justified when audiences flocked to the film, released in time to celebrate the new year of 1957.

Carnival Night centres its comedy on Ogurtsov. Russian tradition identifies a widespread social phenomenon with the fictional character who embodies its distinctive qualities: *manilovshchina*, from one of Gogol's landowners in *Dead Souls*, suggests dithery inaction and pointless, rambling speech; *oblomovshchina* (from the eponymous hero of Goncharov's *Oblomov*) signifies passivity and sluggish indecision. *Carnival Night*'s contribution is *ogurtsovshchina*, denoting a mixture of stupidity, complacency, hypocrisy and conservatism. 'In our life,' director Abram Room had remarked of the script, '*ogurtsovshchina* exists in art, in literature, in theatre, and in many other areas.'[36]

The humorous lines derive their comic bite from the use of official rhetoric and oratorical demagogy in wholly inappropriate contexts. Ogurtsov is a bureaucrat to the marrow of his bones: he announces the New Year's party with the words, 'Comrades! We have received a directive to celebrate the New Year!' He replies to one of his underlings, 'As Russian fairy tales say, in accordance with the estimate ...' Ogurtsov embodies the bureaucratic Word, and *Carnival Night* wages war on it.[37]

Obsessed with planning festivities to which no one can object, Ogurtsov fears a dance because it is too erotic, a clown act because it is 'unreliable' ('After all,' he scolds the clowns, 'you are adults'), anything that provides pleasure. He is ignorant, ascribing the young hero's love-letter – inadvertently read over the loudspeaker – to Shakespeare, yet he insists on 'educating our audience'. In accordance with the Soviet reverence for 'mass' art, he proposes enlarging a quartet to a chorus, and is eager to replace youthful musicians with pensioners because 'these youngsters aren't sound' [*Eti mal'chishki ne solidny*].

Each of the film's dozen or so musical routines satisfies doubly: besides being tuneful, energetic and well-performed, it is a fount of gall for Ogurtsov. In this sense the film is a 'polemical comedy': with every number the authors

The Big Sleep

5. *Carnival Night*

and director engage in a passionate argument with their opponent – if only because they insist on the 'right of Soviet people' to merriment.[38]

Riazanov cleverly cast the seasoned stage and film actor, Igor Ilinskii, as Ogurtsov. He had won the heart of audiences twenty years earlier with his portrayal of another soulless bureaucrat, Byvalov, in Aleksandrov's *Volga-Volga*. That character, however, was a 'symbolic portrait, a buffoon', while Ogurtsov's mixture of servility towards superiors and arrogance towards subordinates was 'virtually sculpted from life'.[39] Ilinskii's facial expressions and his gestures underscore Ogurtsov's grovelling hypocrisy. 'We must implement our entertainment in such a way that no one can object,' he says, piously waving a hand upwards at the words 'no one'. 'On a high level, comrades!' he warns his team, his finger inscribing a steep downwards trajectory. Mispronouncing unfamiliar words, Ilinskii implicitly parodies the uncultured 'commander on the culture front' who presumed to educate the public. Viewers, echoing Abram Room's *in camera* judgement, appreciated Ogurtsov as a common type within society and they laughed their heads off; they continue to enjoy the annual New Year's Eve broadcast of *Carnival Night* on television.

Apart from *Carnival Night*'s explicit thematic challenge to *ogurtsovshchina*, its authors also launched a specific film polemic. Soviet cinema had its own carnival paradigm, one created in the 1930s by Aleksandrov and his gifted composer Isaak Dunaevskii and by Ivan Pyrev in *The Swineherd and the Shepherd* and, after the war, *Cossacks of the Kuban*. These films suggest that Soviet life is one big holiday, a non-stop festivity that regularly explodes into jubilant song and dance. *Carnival Night*, by contrast, implies that life is *not* a celebration, except on holidays. Its festivity is confined to New Year's Eve, and its comic premise is not life as carnival but life's aberration, a genuine carnival. The New Year's Eve performance makes no pretence of being reality; it is an exceptional masquerade, albeit one with all the liberating deception inherent in masquerade's role-reversals and gender ambiguities.

The young protagonists of *Carnival Night* charmed audiences, just as the young protagonists of *A Person is Born* and *Spring on Zarechnaia Street* and other heroes and heroines of 1956 cinema appealed to them as emotionally and psychologically more complicated than their immediate forebears. While still demonstrably 'positive', they no longer function as unambiguous role-models. Nor are their opponents instantly identifiable as villains. In *The Forty-first*, for instance, where the fat faces and Astrakhan caps of the White soldiers are the equivalent of black hats in Hollywood Westerns, the White captive with whom Mariutka falls in love is by no means an unsympathetic character. The simple and pre-defined cluster of characteristics associated with 'good' and 'bad', the ritualistic opposition between 'us' and 'them', the rigidity of class divisions were losing the stability that had once seemed immutable.

The movies of 1956 looked different, too. Locations shifted from sparkling boulevards and spacious accommodations to the far more commonplace lumpy, bumpy streets and cramped rooms. Lighting generally toned down artificially contrasting black-and-white, preferring more natural shadings and shadows. The camera became much less obtrusive and avoided the self-conscious, acute angles made famous by Soviet masters of the 1920s; uninflected angles and a neutral middle distance proved more effective in revealing characters within their domestic environments, surrounded by the bric-à-brac of their lives.

Aesthetic categories that had seemed equally immutable were losing their stark clarity as well. One critic put it plainly:

> Our art has suffered from the frequent demand imposed on the artist to show this or reflect that. But art does not 'show'; it is not a mirror reflecting everything that falls within the artist's field of vision. It reifies life in a complex system of images created by the artist out of his knowledge and understanding … his talent and taste.[40]

Not everyone welcomed such recognition of artistic autonomy. The old guard singled out *Carnival Night* for opprobrium. Sour Klimentii Mints referred to *Carnival Night* – though without mentioning its title – by denigrating the use of comic surnames as a 'pre-revolutionary gutter press gimmick'. He warned that a negative character who provokes laughter in the audience can also elicit sympathy, and used Ilinskii's very expertise against the film, though without naming him: if 'genuine' actors, griped Mints, play the villains with humour and for comic effect, while novices play the hero and heroine as characters who are bold but who lack humour, 'we will not create comedy worthy of the adjective "national"'.[41]

Mints' comments characterized a newly conservative atmosphere of early 1957. Many people appreciated Khutsiev and Mironer's ability to capture the 'beauty of the everyday' in *Spring on Zarechnaia Street*, but more conventional and unyielding viewers felt that the directors' attention to *byt* compromised the image of heroism. The veteran director Aleksandr Zarkhi, whose career began in the late 1920s and spanned half a century, acknowledged the film's appeal, yet regretted what he considered its shrunken stage: 'It is a very decent and truthful film, but precisely for that reason it prompts one to ask why the young worker Sasha Savchenko is so indifferent to the life around him, so self-absorbed, so concerned with everyday cares?' He wondered why Tania and Sasha's love story seemed so circumscribed.[42] A film whose characters seek and find their happiness within a purely personal existence restricts its canvas to a narrow, bourgeois and philistine world, Zarkhi wrote disapprovingly:

> And can one even call this happiness? Complete happiness can only be found when the life of the couple accommodates the interests of society ... This is all the more natural in our society, where personal and societal are inseparable in human consciousness and the understanding of happiness is exceptionally comprehensive.[43]

Within a year Zarkhi acted on his convictions, directing the film he called *Heights* [Vysota, 1957].

Part II The Rules of the Game, 1957–59

5. The Rules of the Game: Introduction

E ven before the end of 1956, domestic political warfare threatened the hopes kindled by the Twentieth Party Congress. East European upheavals – strikes in Poznan in June 1956, the Hungarian uprising five months later – provided the *casus belli*. Khrushchev's opponents blamed his conciliatory advances towards Tito and his de-Stalinization speech at the congress for lowering Soviet prestige and influence abroad, which in turn permitted the turmoil.

For six months battle raged behind the Kremlin walls. Khrushchev chose to engage his adversaries in the economic arena before moving to a more overtly political struggle. He proposed a decentralizing economic reform that started by creating regional planning organs and ended by abolishing the industrial ministries altogether.[1] By June 1957 Khrushchev had acquired sufficient power to defy efforts to unseat him and to turn the tables on his opponents. He called a special session of the Central Committee and received its virtually unanimous support. The Presidium and the Central Committee expelled Malenkov, Kaganovich and Molotov, Khrushchev's three most powerful rivals, and Khrushchev regained firm control.

Although few details appeared in the media, these intramural tussles reverberated in the arts. Liberals and conservatives duelled on the pages of most periodicals, among them *Iskusstvo kino*. In the first months of 1957 editorials still warned of the detrimental consequences of 'administrative timidity and deference toward the opinions of officials from the Ministry of Culture or the Writers' Union'. Sergei Iutkevich mildly proposed 'not condemning films but discussing them' [*ne osuzhdat', a obsuzhdat'*], as well as discovering 'what our friends and enemies abroad are doing – without a two-year delay'.[2] 'The fear of critical comments anticipated from somewhere "above" ... is a tradition that should stop immediately,' Iutkevich noted elsewhere.[3]

Increasingly, however, such pleas for boldness, innovation and the elimination of bureaucratism and red tape co-existed with intensified Cold War

The Rules of the Game

rhetoric and confrontational responses to foreign criticism. Because of the politically-driven chill, for much of 1957 and indeed most of 1958 as well, lacklustre articles, pedestrian memoirs, archival documents, and verbatim citations from or paraphrases of Party directives dominated all major arts periodicals.

The upcoming fortieth anniversary of the Bolshevik Revolution increased the pressure. The Central Committee instructed the industry to 'prepare films on historical and revolutionary themes and documentaries on the successes of socialist construction in the USSR'.[4] Every studio was expected to turn out at least one or two panegyrics. Alas, the industry fell short, prompting the staff of *Iskusstvo kino* and the editors of *Sovetskii film* to urge mobilizing all departments and dedicating all resources, human and technical, in order to complete such revolutionary epics as *Tales of Lenin* [Rasskazy o Lenine], *The Fiery Miles* [Ognennye versty], the first part of *Road to Calvary* [Khozhdenie po mukam] and *The Communist* [Kommunist] in time for the November anniversary.

A barrage of advance publicity pumped up expectations. When *Iskusstvo kino* announced that shooting on *The Communist* had begun, for example, it appended an editorial note describing *The Communist* as 'one of Mosfilm's most important productions in this anniversary year. The studio must provide the crew with whatever it needs for rapid and fruitful work on the film.' Upper-case letters alerted particularly dim readers: 'IT IS THE DUTY OF THE STUDIO COL-LECTIVES TO CONCENTRATE THEIR ENERGY ON RESOLVING THE MOST CRITICAL CREATIVE TASK: PRODUCING IDEOLOGICALLY AND ARTIST-ICALLY SIGNIFICANT FILMS DEVOTED TO THE 40TH ANNIVERSARY OF GREAT OCTOBER.'[5]

Khrushchev spelled out the new rules when he met with writers and artists in March and again in May 1957. Ominously, he compared the Soviet literary 'opposition' with the Petöfi circle, those Hungarian writers who had played a major role in the events leading to the uprising. All major arts publications reprinted in part or in full Khrushchev's speeches to writers and artists, and editors everywhere recapitulated the main points: artistic obedience to the Party line, conformity to socialist realist patterns, state promotion of ideological orthodoxy.

Anxiety mounted as infractions engendered repercussions. The State Institute for Cinematography imposed disciplinary measures, including expulsion, on students who had been too outspoken in their judgements and who had pub-lished an underground journal.[6] Khrushchev denounced Vladimir Dudintsev, author of the influential thaw novel *Not by Bread Alone*, for 'slandering' Soviet society. He censured the editors of the literary almanac *Literaturnaia Moskva*, Margarita Aliger and Veniamin Kaverin, for failing to admit their ideological errors abjectly enough. He authorized the creation of a Union of Writers of the Russian Federated Republic as a conservative counterweight to the liberal and outspoken Moscow writers' organization. A planned volume of Marina Tsvetaeva's poetry with an introduction by Ilya Ehrenburg was postponed indefinitely.

The state urged or coerced leading figures in the arts into retreating from the candour many of them had warmly welcomed after the Twentieth Party Congress. At writers' meetings held in the spring of 1957, for instance, conservative members of the Writers' Union pressured their colleagues to recant and apologize. Stalin had died only a few years earlier, and the entrenched fear that lingered after twenty-five years of Stalinism outweighed the fragile trust kindled by Khrushchev; most complied.

At the same time, artists resisted surrendering the breathing-space they had craved so desperately. Some balked overtly, like Aliger, a poet who had bluntly denounced the 'moral cowardice' of Soviet society. She, Dudintsev, and a few other stalwarts considered themselves genuinely loyal to the Soviet system and to Leninist ideals. The system disagreed. 'At the very least,' wrote one English observer, 'they were guilty, in the official view, of washing the Soviet Union's dirty linen before gloating foreign eyes; of usurping the Party's prerogatives in diagnosing and prescribing for the ills of Soviet society; of encouraging demagogy and homebred revisionism.'[7]

Others devised more oblique and Aesopian responses, retreating from the fraught present into a seemingly safer past and finding ways to manipulate it to suit their needs. Ehrenburg, for instance, published an essay on Stendhal, whom he invoked as a champion of artistic freedom, a writer who 'hated despotism and despised servility'.[8] Ehrenburg made the argument that art and political commitment can (and in Stendhal's case did) productively co-exist. Readers interpreted the essay primarily as a passionate defence of the artist's autonomy against the encroachments of tyranny and as a challenge to the spineless literary establishment – which upheld its reputation by attacking Ehrenburg for his 'false, mediocre and stupid judgments about Stendhal'.[9]

In Grigorii Kozintsev's version of Cervantes' *Don Quixote* [Don Kikhot, 1957], Nikolai Cherkasov's mad knight confronts rulers who are as arbitrary as they are incomprehensibly cruel. If a few years earlier Iutkevich had made of *Othello* a drama about faith that was tested and shaken, but ultimately survived, Kozintsev now updated Cervantes' novel into a bleak assertion of the human need for faith, however illusory, in those – rulers and populace alike – who don't in the least merit it.

Literature offered 'golden times' ripe for film adaptations. An ever-popular genre expanded explosively as the state attempted to 'extend its mastery of literary classics' by creating film equivalents of books by foreign, pre-revolutionary and Soviet authors.[10] Veteran Sergei Gerasimov made a massive if forgettable screen epic of Sholokhov's *And Quiet Flows the Don* and swept the competition at the All-Union Festival in Moscow in 1958. The film itself took first prize, as did Gerasimov for script and direction, and Petr Glebov for his performance as protagonist Grigor Melekhov. Gerasimov's cinematographer Vladimir Rapoport shared top honours with the cameramen of *Don Quixote*.

Film adaptations of Russian literature contributed a human scale of behaviour, as well as reassurance: 'We are just the same as they were, they are us, only in historical perspective.'[11] Sometimes such an interpretation hardly accorded with the original text: Dostoevsky himself might not have recognized the Prince Myshkin Pyrev put on screen in his adaptation of *The Idiot, Nastasia Filippovna* [1958]. Other authors had more affinity for the values film-makers wanted to endorse, most predictably Chekhov. Beginning with *The Grasshopper* [Poprygun'ia, 1955], half a dozen of his stories were adapted for film in as many years, some poorly (*The Fiancée* [Nevesta, 1957]), some extremely well (*Lady with the Dog* [Dama s sobachkoi, 1960]).

Whatever the genre and subject, the question of heroism preoccupied those who made, those who saw, and those who oversaw Soviet cinema, as indeed it had virtually from its inception. History once again provided a viable framework, although by 1957 the civil war film was losing some of its appeal. Long a staple because it could accommodate audiences' taste for action films while satisfying official ideological requirements, its easy certainties and mythic dichotomy between Whites and Reds as absolute as any outlaw/sheriff conflict in a Hollywood Western, already seemed dated and naive.

In the more than a decade since the end of the Second World War, Soviet film-makers had hardly begun to examine its significance. After the Twentieth Party Congress, however, where Khrushchev asserted that errors made by Stalin during the Second World War had cost millions of Soviet lives, the public and artists alike had access to a more complex and painful history of the war, one that corresponded to their own experiences and that offered greater imaginative potential. Film-makers seized on the theme of the Second World War as a meaningful context within which to elaborate heroic potential and celebrate heroic deeds and to recouch their definitions of heroism.

Politics had accounted for their earlier silence, just as politics accounted for their new voice. During the actual war years artists had supported the national effort, willingly imbuing their art-*cum*-propaganda with heart-felt patriotism.[12] From the fall of Berlin in April 1945 until Stalin's death in March 1953, however, the state rewrote history and forced artists to do the same. Ugly reminders of the war vanished from public display – the police rounded up and deported to the far north crippled and impoverished veterans, for instance – and the Kremlin underwrote a pompous, inflated and unreal artistic version of the conflict. Fedor Bogorodskii's painting of a mother mourning over the body of her son, 'Glory to the Heroes who Died for Their Country', epitomized the official view: 'The artist has aimed at depicting the mother's patriotic readiness to sacrifice her son, rather than her grief,' one art historian commented. 'This Soviet "Pietà" is striking in its indifference to pain and suffering, and reminds one more of an ideological poster than of a piece of art.'[13]

In the visual arts draconian post-war decrees on culture resulted in 'meaningless mass scenes'. Well-fed and well-rested soldiers inhabit a 'dream world' at the front in Peter Krivonogov's 'The Victory' and Ilia Lukomskii's 'The Solemn Oath of the Defenders of Stalingrad'. Happy women work in sunlit fields in Tatiana Iablonskaia's 'Bread', and cheerful, optimistic civilians gather to hear good news in Aleksandr Laktionov's 'Letter from the Front'.[14] Post-war monuments and parade banners featured airbrushed images of Stalin, as did films like *The Fall of Berlin*. Art ignored or falsified the military mistakes and civilian miseries of the war.

The Second World War quickly took a back seat to the intensifying Cold War, however, a struggle requiring the country to 'mobilize its energy for the daunting task of economic reconstruction'.[15] Stalin fired some of his leading military commanders and shipped off others to the Gulag; he abolished Victory Day as a state holiday in 1947 (Brezhnev and Kosygin officially reinstated it in 1965). Stalin's claim that the war was too recent for the necessary 'objectivity' effectively deterred would-be memoirists, although a handful of writers persevered and produced a small body of honest and moving war literature: most notably, Viktor Nekrasov's *In the Trenches of Stalingrad* and Vasilii Grossman's *For a Just Cause*.

The effective prohibition on any honest depiction of the war until Stalin's death paralysed cinema no less than it did the rest of the arts, although Vsevolod Pudovkin defied conventional cinematic presentations of the war and its aftermath in *The Return of Vasilii Bortnikov*, whose unhappy hero returns home to a wife who has given up waiting for him and has found another man. (In Gabrilovich's script the action is set in 1945–46, but Pudovkin advanced the time-frame to 1951–52, thus softening the wife's betrayal; in the film, she has waited quite a few years before committing her 'infidelity'.)[16]

Khrushchev's speech at the Twentieth Party Congress unleashed a wave of memoirs by soldiers, partisans and former prisoners in Nazi camps, and of autobiographical fiction by writers who themselves had fought at the front: Grigorii Baklanov, Iurii Bondarev, Vasil Bykov, Ales Adamovich. New phrases – 'trench truth' [*okopnaia pravda*], 'deheroicizing' – entered common discourse. This revised history of the war, apparent in *The Cranes are Flying* [Letiat zhuravli, 1957] and *The House I Live in*, ascribed the defeat of Nazi Germany not to Kremlin leadership but to the Soviet people, and encompassed *all* the Soviet peoples, not just Russians, civilians in the rear as much as soldiers at the front.

As time went on, however, the excitement faded, and the ready acceptance of each new slogan 'dissipated in the recognition that each new belief was as dubious as its predecessor'. Faith in the 'simple man' became as moot as earlier

The Rules of the Game

faith in the 'leader'.[17] In the domain of cinema the hard evidence of 1957, 1958 and 1959 – reviews, articles and, above all, movies themselves – attests to a pattern of caution and retrenchment. Conservative views drowned out liberal ones; dogma replaced creative energy.

Critics now disparaged psychological complexity and recognizable surroundings, the gratifying 'discoveries' of 1956 cinema, as 'fashionable' and trifling, the latter especially reprehensible in films dealing with historical subjects. Thus one conservative sarcastically rejected the notion that Alov and Naumov's *Pavel Korchagin* 'told the truth' about the civil war:

> What kind of strange joke is this? Magellan perished in discovering the Pacific route. If one wrote only that, would it be the 'truth' about him? A great feat is greater than a man's life, it enters the future of mankind, and a work which fails to affirm that central fact robs the life of its truth ... Let's not play with words. This is the pathos of suffering and sacrifice, more appropriate for early Christianity than the pathos of revolution ... Yesterday film-makers simply asked for the right to portray everyday life and states of mind. Today they are trying to run the show.[18]

The atmosphere of the Soviet political-*cum*-cultural world throughout 1958 and 1959, its cacophony of 'thaw' and 'freeze' signals, contributed to artists' disorientation. In May 1958 the Central Committee revoked one of the bleakest symbols of the Zhdanovshchina, the 1948 denunciation of 'formalism' in music; *Iskusstvo kino* reprinted the resolution on the first page of its July 1958 issue. A few months later, however, the 'Pasternak affair', initiated with mild mutterings when *Doctor Zhivago* was published abroad in November 1957, blew up into a hurricane when the Nobel Committee awarded Pasternak the Prize for Literature on 25 October 1958. Venomous censure of Pasternak in major newspapers forced him to renounce the prize and plead with Khrushchev not to force him into emigration.

The film world felt the chill when Ivan Pyrev was replaced as director of Mosfilm by Leonid Antonov, an undistinguished director and an old Party hack who had held the post from 1946 to 1949, abysmal years for Soviet film-making. Khrushchev's pronouncements on 'catching up with' and 'overtaking' the United States referred primarily to agriculture and industry, but Ministry of Culture bureaucrats and dogmatic film critics were quick to see their relevance to the arts as well. One scriptwriter reminded his colleagues that they were workers not essentially different from stokers or miners. If the Seven-Year Plan called for one thousand films, then scenarists should produce triple that number of scripts, to ensure meeting the quota. Balzac, he thought, had had the right idea: the French colossus went to bed at 6 p.m. in order to wake at midnight and work.[19]

Amid the confusion, that shadowy figure, a 'real Soviet man', was hard to find. The protagonists of undistinguished adventure and detective films in 1959 were both male and 'masculine', but they failed to satisfy either audiences or critics.[20] The hero who did capture the hearts of audiences was barely old enough to shave. Grigorii Chukhrai's *Ballad of a Soldier* [Ballada o soldate], released at the very end of 1959, transformed the concept of the heroic in Soviet cinema. Together with Alov and Naumov's *Wind* [Veter, 1958] and Kalatozov and Urusevskii's *Unsent Letter* [Neotpravlennoe pis'mo, 1959], Chukhrai's film signalled the disappearance of the tragic romantic ethos best exemplified in *Pavel Korchagin*, *Cranes are Flying* and *The Communist*.

6. The Best Years of Our Lives

Two films made in 1957 illustrate the uneasy mood. One, Stanislav Rostotskii's *It Happened in Penkovo* [Delo bylo v Pen'kove], is an ambiguous 'village' film that passed relatively unnoticed when it came out in the first months of 1958. The other, Aleksandr Zarkhi's *Heights*, is an 'industrial' drama from a conformist director.

Rostotskii's film, set in a poor kolkhoz, reveals its central conflict in a flashback that constitutes virtually the entire film. Larisa, the kolkhoz chairman's spoiled daughter, is engaged to and then marries Matvei. She fears Tonia, the Leningrad girl who arrives with a suitcase full of books and a head full of Marxist dreams, because Tonia's vision of the future enchants Matvei: unmanned machines work the fields, directed from afar via video screens, while peasants, freed from drudgery, seek culture in the as-yet-nonexistent kolkhoz club.

Larisa belongs to a well-established Russian fictional tradition of provincial lionesses. So consumed with jealousy that she turns for help to the 'witch' Alevtina, Larisa's basic decency reasserts itself at the last moment and she foils Alevtina's plot to poison Tonia. Nevertheless, an enraged Matvei shuts Alevtina in a cellar, a crime for which he is sentenced to prison. In *Penkovo*'s opening framing scene Matvei returns from prison to the kolkhoz, now full of solid buildings instead of the ramshackle huts he had left several years before, and in the epilogue Matvei greets his wife and the son born during his imprisonment. Tonia, still working at the kolkhoz, appears to pose no threat to the happy, reunited family.

On the very day that the script was first discussed at Gorky Studio, 17 January 1957, *Pravda* published a Central Committee declaration on agriculture. The declaration proclaimed that the Party supplied the countryside with all necessary economic and political sustenance; culture alone was lacking. Participants at the meeting referred both explicitly and indirectly to this directive in evaluating the script.

As was usual, the first speaker supported the film. Liudmila Pogozheva, editor of *Iskusstvo kino*, found the characters well-drawn and interesting. She praised Rostotskii for showing how machinery can improve rural life: 'This image is especially important for the countryside right now ... The technology being sent to the countryside is essential, but just as important is a comparable growth in human consciousness.'[1] (Cinema's pedagogic role was regularly emphasized far more in connection with 'village' than with 'urban' films.)

Pogozheva's colleagues, though, saw a multitude of defects in the script, from structural imbalance and lack of dramatic resolution to a reliance on narration rather than visual means. They faulted the characterization of the Party instructor, Ignatev: his weakness implied that Party leadership itself was passive and unengaged. Ignatev's lines should be rewritten to express the dynamism and commitment 'typical' of Party representatives.[2]

The script faltered, too, in its utopian depiction of life on the neighbouring kolkhoz, New Path: *kolkhoznik*s themselves would reject as spurious such a model collective farm, with its magnificent cowherds and elegant pig-tenders. Sergei Antonov, whose story inspired the script, objected: 'Either we are afraid of being accused of embellishment or else we don't believe that such kolkhozes exist. Such kolkhozes can and do exist.'[3] Perhaps such kolkhozes could hypothetically exist, but – *pace* Antonov, who surely knew better – none did. Indeed, the lustrous example of New Path notwithstanding, *Penkovo* confirms the reality of village life as dreary and boring, a repetitious tedium relieved and adorned by drinking, by the occasional dance or fight, by Matvei's mischief.

And by sex. The love triangle itself is a commonplace, but Rostotskii's visualization of erotic power as the cornerstone of Larisa and Matvei's marriage is startlingly candid for a Soviet film. Larisa is openly seductive, her breasts practically bumping the camera when she reaches to embrace Matvei. Her gaping chemise emphasizes her voluptuous body, and when the two lie in bed, their postures are frankly sensual: Matvei looks up at her above him while Larisa, sexually dominant, gazes down at him.

The flashback structure of *It Happened in Penkovo* potentially guarantees the irreproachable ending, in which collective will supersedes individual wish, and prison rehabilitates the hero. However, the body of the movie undercuts – indeed, substantially contradicts – that ending. Matvei is the odd man out in the kolkhoz, his energy and drive stifled by foot-dragging reality. As the unconventional individual, the one who strays from the herd, he inevitably ends up outside the law.[4] Obedience and lack of initiative finally triumph.

Heights is far more conventional than *Penkovo*, as one would expect from the ideologically orthodox Aleksandr Zarkhi. He had disliked Khutsiev's *Spring on Zarechnaia Street* for failing to show the intersection of private and public; true personal happiness, he asserted, required accommodating the interests of society. Mikhail Papava's script for *Heights* gave Zarkhi the opportunity to fashion his own cinematic response.

The Rules of the Game

6. *Heights*

In *Heights* the heroes and villains neatly line up on either side of the moral faultline. The worker-hero Kolia (played by Nikolai Rybnikov) is a steeplejack who goes from one enormous construction site to another, leaving behind towering structures and dented feminine hearts. He is energetic and idealistic. So is his white-collar counterpart, project-manager Tokmakov, whose traditional virtues include mentoring the young and shouldering responsibility.

These two heroes, one a line worker and the other a manager, are balanced by two matched villains. Khaenko too is a worker, whose rudeness corresponds to his ideological obscurantism. As he huddles in an enormous pipe to get out of the rain – a symbol of Soviet shelter he is quite willing to exploit – he contemptuously shrugs off both socialism and communism as irrelevant to him. Money matters, he says, demonstratively rubbing together the tips of his fingers. When he tosses aside the emblem of faith, the red flag meant to ornament the completed blast furnace, Kolia punches him in the nose for his blasphemy. His white-collar counterpart is chief engineer Deriabin, a cynical careerist who endangers workers by forcing them to work in perilous winds.

Heights offers equally stereotyped women: the worker Katia, outwardly tough and inwardly vulnerable, and the engineer's wife Masha. Katia is the 'good girl' damaged by circumstances. As an individual, she has pluck and verve, lighting her cigarette with a blow torch and dancing on a board suspended high above the ground. Historically, however, she is a casualty. Orphaned by the war, she was obliged to raise herself, hence her ignorance in matters of both politics and etiquette. (Kolia, eyeing the red-and-green outfit she dons for a date, calls her a 'traffic light'). Until she falls in love with Kolia she is on the road to wasting her life.

Katia's educated analogue, Masha, deplores her own inauthentic life as Deriabin's wife. She trained as a doctor, but her husband wants her at home, and she does little except serve tea. When Deriabin teases her for taking an excessive interest in his affairs, she replies, 'That's because I have none of my own.' With her sprigged muslin dress, white shoes, and dainty gloves, she is dismissed by men on the site as a lady [*baryshnia*].

Katia is no prissy patrician. The daughter of a worker, she can appreciate both the beauty and the significance of the blast furnace when Tokmakov shows her around. 'It's a special beauty,' Tokmakov explains, 'created by man.' Both Katia and Masha are symbolic individuals, like many female figures in Soviet culture: love permits them to harness their lives to a larger political cause, in order to find meaning in life, and they need only overcome the press of historical and external circumstances to embrace the right way of life.

Heights was completed early in 1957, to a mixed response from Mosfilm. Grigorii Roshal preferred *Heights* to *Carnival Night*: *Carnival Night* was an 'inadvertent' success, peripheral to the 'proper development' of Soviet cinematography, while *Heights* belonged squarely to the Soviet tradition, 'in the mainstream of cinema'. Mikhail Romm liked the attractive working-class heroes and the film's ability to communicate the 'romance of labour'.[5]

A number of people objected to insipid *mise-en-scène*. Unlike the visually exciting blast furnace shots, the indoor scenes are implausible, marred by furniture, curtains and decorations that reveal nothing about their owners. (Billowing white curtains in Tokmakov's room, for instance, are ludicrously inappropriate.) The camera remains at an uninvolving middle distance from its object for most of the picture, with slight variety provided by standard close-ups of workers' faces and panoramic shots from atop the blast furnace, and repeated dissolves to black break up the action in an annoyingly jerky and lurching rhythm.

Pyrev expressed the general feeling that *Heights* awkwardly glued together two films, one vigorous and fresh (thanks in part to the gifted Nikolai Rybnikov as Kolia) and the other boring and trite. (Pyrev dismissed the 'red flag' as a tired cliché of Soviet cinema for at least forty years.) The particularly banal Deriabin reminded director Iulii Raizman of the scapegoat-villains of the 1930s: 'With this engineer we revert to the era of saboteurs, of engineer-wreckers. He is so objectionable ... that he ceases to be plausible.'[6] Writer Evgenii Gabrilovich agreed: he began to feel sorry for Deriabin, so crude was his characterization and so despicable his personality.

The Rules of the Game

7. *Heights*

In the tense mood of 1957, though, *Heights* was reassuringly safe. Like the members of Mosfilm, reviewers and viewers recognized the banality of the Deriabin–Tokmakov–Masha story line. They chose, however, to concentrate on the worker-heroes Kolia and Katia, on Mikhail Papava's natural dialogue, and on Aleksandr Zarkhi's ability to show the 'beauty of the workers' world'.

Zarkhi himself continued to stress the pedagogic value of the film. Zarkhi admired Papava's skill in revealing the hero's real ambition – 'to break the back of capitalism', no less. 'He labours on the site, he falls in love, he experiences joys and misfortunes, but behind it all and in all of his laconic speech one can sense the goal of his life. From my point of view, that is what makes his image poetic.' For Zarkhi, *Heights* fulfilled Soviet cinema's mission: it inspired young people to live under communism.[7]

The artistic and intellectual climate of 1957 and 1958 nearly guaranteed the mediocrity of most of the films released. Only two of the many films planned to coincide with and celebrate the fortieth anniversary of the Revolution in November were finished on time, *The Sisters* [Sestry], the first part of Roshal's trilogy based on *The Road to Calvary*, and Samsonov's *Fiery Miles*, a civil war adaptation of almost all the thematic and visual conventions of a Hollywood Western.[8] Two others – *The Communist* and *Tales of Lenin* – were not distributed until 1958. A silly if tuneful Tadjik musical, *I Met a Girl* [Ia vstretil devushku], also came out in 1957, as did Mark Donskoi's luridly-coloured Ukrainian historical romance, *At a High Cost* [Dorogoi tsenoi].

Eldar Riazanov followed *Carnival Night* with *The Girl with No Address* [Devushka bez adresa], a mildly amusing version of Boris Barnet's much better silent film, *Girl with a Hatbox* [Devushka s korobkoi, 1927]. Both directors employed the convention of the country-girl-come-to-the-city as an opportunity to portray lovingly the metropolis of Moscow, bursting out in the late 1950s much as it had in the NEP period. Both heroines are idealistic provincial outsiders who sharply contradict the values of the 'new' bourgeoisie.

Amid such undistinguished company, it is all the more shocking to find the first indisputable masterpiece of post-Stalin cinema. Yet Mikhail Kalatozov's *Cranes are Flying* was neither cinematically nor thematically unprecedented; it did not spring full-grown from Mikhail Kalatozov's head and Sergei Urusevskii's camera. Rather, it represents the brilliant confluence of several discrete trends that can be traced in other films, most significantly the choice of the Second World War as a source of hero-images and the preference for private over public. Audiences still sought heroes on screen, yet eyes educated in part by Italian neo-realism, in part by *Spring on Zarechnaia Street* and *A Person is Born*, rebuffed the rhetorical, flamboyant political heroism integral to the set pieces of Soviet history.

Until 1956 the trauma of the Second World War was effectively unexplored by film-makers, except for Pudovkin in *The Return of Vasilii Bortnikov*. *Spring on Zarechnaia Street*, for instance, shows no trace of the war and its pain. Yet it offered a ready-made context for depictions of the kinds of heroism accessible to – moreover, exhibited by – millions of Soviet viewers. After Khrushchev's affirmation of Stalin's responsibility for Soviet casualties, revisionism on screen paralleled its manifestations elsewhere. *Immortal Garrison* [Bessmertnyi garnizon], a 1956 film made by director Zakhar Agranenko with cinematographer Eduard Tisse, transfers to the screen a script by Konstantin Simonov about the defence of Brest, a theme then popular in literature. *Immortal Garrison* was probably the first Soviet film in which Russians, not only Germans, are taken prisoner, and, moreover, die in agony. The film candidly acknowledges the great cost of Soviet victories and the tremendous anguish of its populace.

Brest was lost in the first year of the war. Critic Iurii Khaniutin recalled that year as a time 'of great courage, but also of tragic errors … of firm faith in future victory, but also of the stupid arrogance, the unjustified confidence in our military superiority that characterized the last months before the war'. Khaniutin, exploiting the interval of tolerance between the Twentieth Party Congress and the Hungarian revolution, laid the blame squarely on the cult of personality, its insistence that 'genius could not err', its misrepresentation of early retreats and blunders as 'careful' and 'intentional' strategy. Films made

The Rules of the Game

during the era of the cult had been 'shamefully silent' about failure, he wrote, and had distorted the experience of the vast majority of Soviet citizens by confining their definition of conflict with the enemy to battle scenes.[9]

Beginning with *Immortal Garrison* and climaxing in Andrei Tarkovskii's first feature film, *Ivan's Childhood* [Ivanovo detstvo, 1962], that silence was broken. Cinema expanded the definition of conflict far beyond military engagement, and broadened its designation of war's victims to comprehend virtually all segments of Soviet society.[10]

Immortal Garrison is fairly primitive. Characters lack depth and individuality; the hero never wonders why the army has been left in such disarray. But in its portrayal of war as a nightmarish intrusion into the cosy intimacy of family and friends, *Immortal Garrison* moved cinema significantly closer to the major war films of 1957 and 1958, *Soldiers* [Soldaty], *The Cranes are Flying* and *The House I Live in*.

Mosfilm released *Soldiers* in January 1957. Director Aleksandr Ivanov stayed close to Viktor Nekrasov's script, based on *In the Trenches of Stalingrad*, although Nekrasov's fictional dialogue is more authentic and colourful than the improbably bland curses of the soldiers. *Soldiers* has its share of clichés. Some of them come from Nekrasov's text, like the picture of Jack London tacked up in a Red Army barracks.[11] Others are cinematic: the silent pan of the faces of men who form the 'wall of steel and iron' that the Germans must defeat, the sweet strains of Tchaikovsky's 'Andante Cantabile', which visibly move the soldiers.[12]

Soldiers' presentation of ethnicity is more unusual, because films of that period tended to subordinate ethnic to national (that is, Soviet) identity. In Ivanov's film, however, as in Nekrasov's text, one soldier, a mathematician, 'looks' Jewish; he cannot swim or ride a bike, nor can he fight (though he lies and says he can). Soviet fiction and films (*The Fall of Berlin*, for instance) featured the equivalent of the Hollywood foxhole Italian–Irish–Jewish–Wasp mix, its standard assortment including a Russian (almost always the hero), a Ukrainian, a Jew, one generic Central Asian and one beak-nosed type from the Caucasus. What distinguished *Soldiers* was its candid admission of the existence of stereotypical Jewish characteristics, such as physical ineptitude and intellectual proficiency, and the explosion of the stereotype when the Jew behaves with as much courage as the others.

Soldiers is probably the first Soviet film which blames the Soviet state for the prospect of defeat. 'Ask the lieutenant commander where the Red troops are,' an old man says with a mixture of fear and anger; why, he wonders helplessly, has Leningrad been left defenceless? Egregious military and strategic blunders occur on every level, and corpses lining a muddy field visually spell out the consequences. The captain who sends his men into a daylight attack, in effect a suicide mission, is subsequently reprimanded, stripped of his authority and

The Best Years of Our Lives

8. *The Cranes are Flying*

remanded for trial. 'You will answer for this crime,' the hero tells him, and he actually does.

For all its merits, *Soldiers* quickly forfeited its pre-eminence as an original and daring treatment of the war, supplanted by *The Cranes are Flying*. From the first screening of *Cranes* at Mosfilm in late August 1957, through its general release at the end of the year, to its explosive triumph at Cannes in 1958, where it garnered the Golden Palm award as Best Film, *Cranes* instantly gained recognition as a landmark in Soviet cinema. *Cranes* transformed the way viewers and reviewers considered the war trauma and their expectations of cinematic representations of it.

Cranes was one of the first post-Stalin Soviet films widely distributed in the West as well as in socialist countries. At Cannes, reporters were so entranced by Tatiana Samoilova, for her performance as the heroine Veronika, that when the actress came out of the hall, they applauded her instead of taking her picture.[13] Samoilova, whose stardom *Cranes* guaranteed, received a watch at a festival in East Germany with the telling inscription, 'At long last we see on the Soviet screen not a mask but a face, most important of all in today's world.'[14]

The Rules of the Game

Cranes, based on Viktor Rozov's play *Forever Alive* [Vechno zhivye], recounts a story of love, betrayal and renewal. Veronika, lovely and self-confident in her love for Boris Borozdin when the film opens in June 1941, is devastated by the loss of her parents in a bombing raid and Boris's disappearance at the front. (Presumably for reasons beyond his control, he fails to write to her, his family or his factory.) Boris's cousin Mark, a pianist who deceitfully wangles an exemption from military service, takes advantage of Veronika's misery and Boris's absence to rape her; as he carries her in his arms, the film cuts to the front, where a sniper kills Boris.

Traumatized by Boris's silence, her parents' death and her own failure to prevent the rape, and in a state not far from catatonia, Veronika marries Mark and they are evacuated from Moscow together with Boris's father Dr Borozdin and his sister Irina. They live in barracks and work in a hospital in the rear. Veronika hates herself for betraying Boris, whom she continues to love, and is never happy with Mark, though her suffering is slightly eased when she adopts a young orphan named Borka (the diminutive of Boris). Finally discovering the extent of Mark's baseness, she rejects him once and for all, but she needs to hear Boris's death confirmed by his best friend before she is able to relinquish her unreasoning hope in his survival and confront her own future.

Neia Zorkaia attributed the impact of *Cranes*

> above all to the fact that the screen told, with feeling and pathos, the story not of a glorious exploit but of guilt and atonement. The central character of the film could under no circumstances ... be a 'positive example', yet the authors refused to pass judgement on the girl Veronika who, under tragic circumstances, betrayed the memory of her bridegroom killed at the front.
>
> The technique was also new. The black-and-white picture fascinated by the brilliant 'perpetual motion' of the hand[held] camera, the play of camera angles and of light and shade, and the effects of short-focus optics. The vibrant and inimitable human life returning to the screen seemed to employ and rediscover the entire wealth of the metaphor, composition, and rhythms of cinematic poetry.[15]

Everyone saw *Cranes*: veterans, their wives and widows, young people ready to grapple with the significance of their own early orphanhood. *Cranes* forced viewers first to respond to the film's emotional demands and then to think about the war and their own experiences.

The film's refusal to pass judgement on Veronika also compelled viewers to form their own judgement of her, and by extension of themselves. Veronika hardly resembles traditional Soviet female paradigms. She does not embody civic virtues, like the canonized Zoia Kosmodemianskaia, a high-school girl martyred by the Nazis. She is not the beacon of fidelity enshrined by Konstantin Simonov in his poem 'Wait for Me' [*Zhdi menia*], an 'elegiac if inelegant love poem, that millions recited as if it were a prayer; that women repeated as tears streamed down their faces; that men adopted as their own expression of the mystical power of a woman's love'.[16] She is not simple, loving, and modest like the post-office girl Mashenka, from Iulii Raizman's 1942 eponymous film.

Until the mid-1950s, the 'film hero' unproblematically denoted the main character and his services to society/state. In its conventional meaning, that term could not be applied to Veronika.[17] She is enigmatic, and her decision to marry one man while she never ceases to love another is a paradox at the centre of *Cranes*, resistant to logical analysis. Before *Cranes* such a character would have been typecast as the 'faithless fiancée'. *Cranes* transformed a 'condemned and rejected' type into the subject of 'astonishing sympathy and admiration'.[18] Irina Shilova recalls furious arguments about Veronika. Some people denounced her, others adored her; but, either way, she became a new yardstick, particularly for viewers her own age.

Very young when she was chosen to play Veronika, with an 'asymmetrical and rather strange' face, Samoilova had neither classical beauty nor the charm of the soubrette; she was considered too 'heavy' for comedy, too 'light' for drama.[19] A different, more conventionally attractive actress might have made Veronika banal. In *Cranes*, thanks both to Samoilova herself and to Urusevskii and Kalatozov, 'the unusual type of beauty of her face, the lightness and grace of her full figure' are unexpected and perfect.[20]

Samoilova herself interpreted Veronika as 'a pure person whom it was wrong to hurt or offend ... who was deprived of all her innocence by one catastrophe after another ... who died a little bit every day of the war'.[21] Notwithstanding her betrayal, she became a kind of icon for young women who identified with her. 'In the final analysis,' as Shilova wrote, the film dealt with 'the right to live one's own life – perhaps unhappy, plundered, ravaged, but one's own. It had been an unacceptable idea for entire generations, which had embraced the demands of common, communal, civic obligation.'[22]

Cranes is one of the most closely analysed of post-war Soviet films.[23] At the same time it belonged to an evolving cinematic process and to the more general cultural metamorphoses of the late 1950s, at once an oddity among the films of those years and the 'best representative' of that cinematic era.[24] With a special effort of historical imagination, one can see the film in the context of 1957–58, with approximately the vision of Soviet audiences, before it attained the status of a 'classic' – an effort necessary in order both to understand contemporary criticism of *Cranes* and to assess its place in Soviet cinema.

In that effort it is helpful to compare the released film with a version of the director's script dating from 1956. The completed film substantially replaced what had been explicitly verbalized in that script with gesture, movement, camera and lighting; it eliminated scenes that would have dissipated dramatic

The Rules of the Game

9. *The Cranes are Flying*

effect. In the script, for instance, Boris's father is informed of his son's enlist-
ment in the army by phone, at his hospital; he then goes home. The film omits
the unnecessary phone call. Instead, Dr Borozdin strides into his apartment
and conceals his obvious fear for his son behind a screen of angry sarcasm. In
this sequence, when the family says goodbye to Boris, the camera moves around
to include one or more of the other characters but keeps Dr Borozdin as the
visual focus of almost every shot. Symbol of every parent sending his son off
to war, he is finally alone in his desolation, framed by the doorway of the now-
empty apartment.

In the script, Boris's death scene includes a pointless dialogue between Boris
and Veronika, and a dreadful exchange between Boris and Mark ('You know,
Mark, the main thing is to live honestly, and then even death is not terrible …
Though I want to live').[25] Instead Kalatozov and Urusevskii created a wordless
fantasy of Boris and Veronika's wedding, using triple exposures and a swirling
camera to produce a surreal image.

When Veronika runs from the hospital to the train station in the film, her
purpose is unclear, though her desperation is patent. In the script two interior
voices signal her intention of committing suicide: with one voice she condemns

herself as guilty and contemptible, and desires death as an escape from her anguish; with the other she forgives herself and rejects suicide as weakness.

She instinctively opts for life by darting out to snatch the child rooted to the ground in the path of an oncoming truck. The script contains a lengthy dialogue with the little boy; he says, for instance, that he has lots of brothers (Vanka, Vaska, Fedka). This misguided attempt at lightness was cut; instead, Borka's inverted account of his age ('Three months and three years') adds just a touch of poignant humour. Borka's post-war fate was also changed: in the script, Veronika surrenders him to his mother, who comes back for him. Dr Borozdin 'comforts' her, telling her with uncharacteristic pomposity that her adoption of Borka was good and noble, though in the end she lost him. In the film we are allowed to infer that she keeps him for good.

The film emphasizes the contrast between Veronika and Boris's sister Irina more than the script does. Irina is consistently unwomanly, from her gruff manner to her 'masculine' profession: she is a surgeon, while Veronika helps nurse the wounded, a 'feminine' vocation. Although Irina loves her brother, her farewell is brusque, a mocking salute, and the film deletes Irina's tearful confidence to a neighbour in the shared evacuation lodging that, far from being the 'envious old maid' that Veronika angrily called her, she had been in love with a student at the medical institute. Soft lighting heightens Veronika's delicacy, harsh lighting exaggerates Irina's austerity; Irina's hairstyle is severe, while tendrils of Veronika's bunned hair escape to suggest feminine vulnerability.

The loudly ticking clock, the sole object left intact by the bomb that orphans Veronika, is not in the script. Neither is the contrast signified by the camera's abrupt transition from Mark's feet as he crunches over the glass shards shattered by a bombing raid, Veronika's limp body in his arms, to soldiers' boots slogging through muddy fields at the front.

Other changes, while they may have been dictated in part by aesthetic considerations, appear to reflect political necessity as the thaw of 1956 gave way to the chill of 1957. The script includes dialogue between Dr Borozdin and one of his medical colleagues. Looking up at the night sky, Dr Borozdin says bitterly, 'The newspapers used to write that when the war started, it would be fought on foreign territory. But whose cities are burning, ours or the Germans'? We heard in all the songs, "We're peaceful people, but our armoured train waits in reserve" ... What is it waiting for? Why doesn't it get moving?' His colleague Ivan Afanasevich offers the stock answer: 'The fascists invaded unexpectedly, treacherously.' 'Oh, those slippery fascists!' Dr Borozdin scornfully replies:

'Oh, those nasty men! They didn't even warn us ... What, we didn't know what they were like?'
Ivan Afanasevich looks around anxiously.

The Rules of the Game

'We blundered, we blundered at the beginning of the war ... we missed our chance.'

Ivan Afanasevich, frightened by these words, glances at the chimney to make sure no one is within earshot, but Dr Borozdin continues to yell.

'Now they print shameful reports. You can't make head or tail of them ... On the one hand, we're destroying them root and branch, on the other, we're retreating from one city after another.'[26]

Kalatozov never filmed the scene. Perhaps he feared that it was too blunt for the ideological watchdogs. Or perhaps he eliminated it as a diversion from the core of the film; secondary characters in *Cranes* are nearly always shot together with and in relation to Boris, Veronika or Mark.

He did include another sharp dialogue that fits seamlessly into the main action. When two young girls from Boris's factory come to bid him farewell 'in the name of the factory committee', Dr Borozdin mocks the political rhetoric that debases the genuine human feeling for which it substitutes. 'You mean to say, "Beat the Fascists, Boris,"' he says, angrily beating out the rhythm of the clichés with his clenched fist, 'while in the rear we at the plant will fulfil and overfulfil the plan!' Full of helpless love and fear for his son, and pity for all of them, he continues gently, 'Never mind, girls, better sit down and drink to my son Boria.'

In late August 1957, a couple of months before its general release, *Cranes* was screened at Mosfilm. Grigorii Roshal spoke for the majority of those present: 'We all wept. I, too, wept, and I am not ashamed to admit it.' Mikhail Romm tried to speak calmly, but emotion overwhelmed him.[27] *Cranes* affected these professionals so powerfully that it deprived them of speech (though not for long). Rostislav Iurenev, a conservative critic and longtime bulwark at the State Institute of Cinematography, waxed uncharacteristically lyrical: 'All these unusual aspects are part of a form developed precisely in order to convey the delicate, ineffable spiritual states of the heroes, for which words are inadequate. It is the language of cinema.' He deprecated critics of *Cranes'* artistry as people reluctant 'to speak to artists in their own language, people accustomed to clichés'.[28]

A few viewers resisted the appeal of *Cranes*. Aleksandr Zarkhi, for instance, felt that Veronika lacked 'the special quality to be found in the new individual ... she lacks the spirit of our times'.[29] But not all of *Cranes'* critics had retrograde agendas. Maia Turovskaia felt that 'cinematic effects' occasionally marred *Cranes*, and she rightly singled out the rape scene: 'The entire aesthetic of this scene, with its melodramatic sound and light, with the slaps and with Mark's grotesque obstinacy ... comes from some other, invented war.' (She called the great scene of farewell to the volunteers setting out for the front 'absolutely true', in contrast.) Turovskaia argued that by gradually shrinking *Cranes'* emotional scale, Kalatozov had diminished the power of the film. Fidelity, ordinarily a private matter, takes on broader meaning in wartime, 'when a woman's loyalty expresses the victory of the human spirit over forces of destruction and death'. The more exclusive Veronika's despair, the more trivial it becomes.[30]

Shortly after Mosfilm released *Cranes*, Gorky Studio brought out a rival, *The House I Live in*. Since the theme of *House* – in essence, the war's impact on noncombatants – overlapped with *Cranes*, comparison was inevitable, and by no means consistently to the advantage of *Cranes*. Written by Iosif Olshanskii, who won an All-Union Competition for the best scenario, and directed by Lev Kulidzhanov and Iakov Segel, *House* is far more conventional, both thematically and cinematically. Its very familiarity and realism were reassuring to viewers disconcerted by the iconoclasm of *Cranes*.

House divides its story into pre-war life, portrayed as a generally happy period, and wartime, which abruptly and violently shatters that happiness. The 'house' of the title, a brand-new building when the film opens in 1935, serves as a 'ship of fools', bringing together a cross-section of Soviet society, and functions as a metaphor for that society in general. A worker's family lives across the courtyard from a bourgeois family and next door to an actress and a geologist, representatives of the artistic world and the technical intelligentsia respectively. (The geologist was a favourite heroic figure of the late 1950s, here extrapolated backwards on to the 1930s.)

Neighbours help one another, offering nails and spare furniture to the newcomers; Serezha, the worker's son, teases and plays with Galia, the daughter of the bourgeois family. Time passes normally, marked by the birth of a child, the lines on a doorjamb charting Serezha's growth. As one critic approvingly commented, these pre-war details convey the spirit of an era: 'How good our Soviet life is.'[31]

There are problems, to be sure: the geologist's wife Lida – like the unhappy wife in *Big Family* – loves her husband Dmitrii but is estranged from him and belittles his commitment to his work. Her self-absorption is diametrically opposed to Dmitrii's service-oriented philosophy of life: 'After all,' she says, 'we only live once.' 'Yes,' he responds meaningfully, 'only once. That's the whole point.' She has deferred having children to give them time alone as a couple, and the film decisively condemns both the choice and her reasons.

In her unhappiness, Lida sleeps with Serezha's older brother Kostia, home on leave from the army, while Dmitrii is off on an expedition, and then bitterly regrets it. The neighbours all know what's happened. Kostia and Serezha's mother ostentatiously fails to greet Lida the next morning in the kitchen and remains cool towards her; Serezha angrily dismisses Kostia's justification that he loves Lida. But others hesitate to judge. Their father says compassionately, 'You can't dictate to the heart,' and teen-aged Galia admits that she does not know what she would do in Lida's place. The film condemns Lida less harshly for her infidelity, a consequence of her discontent, than for her childlessness, a result of her egotism.

The Rules of the Game

10. *The House I Live in*

Adultery may be part of usual life, even in the Soviet Union; war is not. The flaming digits '1941' rise up to fill the back of the screen; crowds gather at a bus stop to listen to Molotov's radio announcement of the Nazi invasion, broadcast nationwide over loudspeakers. The intimacy and individuality of the first part of *House* yield to the public canvas as the *mise-en-scène* moves out of the apartment house, and its world of chamber drama, on to the street.[32]

The camera steps back, abandoning close-ups and middle shots for long shots. By placing familiar characters in new, public contexts – Lida and Dmitrii among other silent couples, Serezha in a long line of soldiers on skis – the camera suggests the totality of the war effort. Stirring music enhances the quasi-documentary aspect of these scenes, as does the famous wartime recruiting poster of a woman's face emblazoned with the words, 'The motherland summons!', crossed in one shot by an endless line of shadows of men's heads. Wartime activities – underage kids trying to enlist, civilians practising defensive manoeuvres, people dismantling fences for fuel – are set to the musical accompaniment of the Red Army Chorus.

In the film's wartime, as during the actual war, public and private merge in a rare harmony. When the worker-father goes off to war, a close-up of his wedding picture hanging on the wall motivates his readiness to fight for the sake and future of his family, not to fulfil political and social obligations. The logic is inescapable and emotionally compelling: in order to save his beloved wife, he must leave her. Victory, when it finally comes, is presented not via huge public spectacles, but in 'the simple, intimate homecoming of individual soldiers who are too tired to take their clothes off before falling into bed'.[33]

The war leaves gaps in the house. Serezha's father is killed, his brother Kostia badly wounded. Galia is dead, Dmitrii missing in action. Notwithstanding the depredations of the war, however, the film merges generations to create a sense of continuity, a unitary image of the nation. In its epilogue, set in 1950, Dmitrii's standard of dedication has inspired Serezha to become a geologist. Lida, after ten years of guilt and expiation for one act of betrayal, is finally ready for a new life with the steadfast Kostia, her moral rehabilitation signalled by Kostia's mother's forgiveness. 'He loves you, you know,' the older woman says, giving Lida tacit permission to get on with her life.

At Gorky Studio's discussion of *The House I Live in*, Kulidzhanov, Segel and Olshanskii garnered kudos for depicting the patriotism and integrity of the characters, 'ordinary' people living in 'ordinary' houses. Unlike Veronika, their protagonists fit comfortably within the Soviet framework, a land where every individual is a candidate for heroism. In one of the last pre-war scenes Serezha tells Dmitrii about his literature exam.

> We had three themes: the image of Pechorin, the 'new man' from Chernyshevskii's *What is to be Done*, and one other. Not from books, our own. Your favourite hero. I decided to write about you. Because for me a hero is a person who ... well, let's say who doesn't wait to be called but sets off on his own, and where he goes factories may be built, or a whole city, but he's ahead of everyone else, he goes first, he looks for iron, bauxite, oil. Not for himself, but for other people. I didn't write it, of course. There it's all about Pechorins and Onegins. They'd never understand.[34]

Dmitrii, sitting in the foreground of the frame, hardly hears him; he is reading the note in which Lida informs him that she can no longer live with him. (She returns and tries to blot out the import of the note.) A boy's romantic notions about heroism are contrasted with the excruciatingly emotional complexity of adulthood, but the film uses that complexity to enrich rather than simply reject Serezha's definition.

House is genuinely powerful in its directness. Kostia's return, for instance, laconically conveys the motif of the wounded soldier's return: he stands framed in the doorway, while the camera cuts to a steeply angled shot of his crutch clattering down the stairs. Laktionov's meretricious painting 'Letter from the Front', with its cheerful crowd smilingly gathered to hear the letter read aloud, is implicitly evoked and rebutted by the film's far more truthful image of women meeting the mail girl with tense anticipation; two receive letters, while the third moves away in stoic disappointment.

The Rules of the Game

False romanticism sets off real heroism in a scene when Galia, a budding actress, recites a speech to her elderly mentor, Ksenia Nikolaevna. Galia's voice, gestures and facial expressions are theatrical and overstated. Ksenia Nikolaevna 'corrects' her by responding (with a speech from Chekhov's *The Seagull*) so naturally that Galia mistakes the actress for the character she is playing. Art, the film intimates, should not be artifice, but life. Galia learns the lesson well: when she leaves for the front, she says goodbye to Ksenia Nikolaevna quite simply, ready for 'the ordinary Soviet girl's' heroism without fanfare or histrionics.[35]

At the studio discussion, Stanislav Rostotskii contrasted the accessibility of *House* with the artful flourishes of *Cranes*. In *House*, he commented appreciatively, a 'generalized symbol of great emotional force grows out of extraordinarily simple things that are clear to every ordinary person, who doesn't care about aesthetic questions'. *Cranes* is rather more 'western', he added, by which he intended no compliment. A like-minded colleague praised the 'authentic socialist realist style' of *House*, adding, 'in my opinion, our studio comes out ahead in this competition'. Another expressed a general preference for art that 'lets you forget that it's art', over the distracting self-consciousness of *Cranes*.[36] Olshanskii himself acknowledged *Cranes* as a yardstick, but he mean-spiritedly attacked it in defending his own film: 'Every frame [of *Cranes*] cries out, "What a brilliant cameraman I am! What an inventive director I am!" ... The artfulness, the studied quality of the picture should, I think, have no place in and are alien to our film aesthetic.'[37]

Audiences genuinely liked *House*. With none of the hallmarks of individual genius that are everywhere visible, for good and bad, in *Cranes*, it offered admirable characters, intelligible motivations, affecting relationships. As one appreciative viewer said, *House* is superior to *Cranes* because one cares about the characters. 'In *House*,' he added, 'I noticed neither the director nor the cameraman, but I saw people who remained with me ... The artists were able to create heroes they themselves loved, and they made us love them too.'[38]

No system, whether Hollywood's or the Kremlin's, favours idiosyncratic art over conventional, singular over replicable, unique over formulaic. While popular culture occasionally rewards the unorthodox, it relies wholesale on formula. No one denied *Cranes*' significance, and the lustre of its Cannes award was deeply satisfying, but the system, quite naturally, preferred *House*.

7. Great Expectations

Throughout 1958 and 1959, the Second World War continued to provide a ready-made, familiar and historically-grounded framework within which artists could adumbrate the possibilities of heroism for Soviet men and women. But it was not the only such historical framework. A month-long 'youth' film festival in March and April 1958 celebrated the heroic deeds of the Young Communist League, the Komsomol, on the fortieth anniversary of its founding. Studios submitted more than eighty feature films and documentaries, grouped under rubrics such as 'Youth in the struggle for Soviet power during the years of revolution and civil war', 'Labour prowess of Komsomol members and young people during the First Five-Year Plan' and 'Heroism of Soviet youth during the Great War of the Fatherland'. A simultaneous festival honoured a decade of films for young people (1947–57) and culminated in the World Youth Festival.

Iurii Egorov, one of the younger generation of directors, dedicated *Volunteers* [Dobrovol'tsy, 1958] to the Komsomol members of the 1930s, introducing his five young Komsomol heroes when they come to Moscow to help build the metro system, and following their destinies through the war. Alov and Naumov contributed *Wind* [Veter, 1958], a depiction of three young delegates who make a perilous journey to attend the first Komsomol congress. *On the Far Side* [Po tu storonu, 1958], a Mosfilm potboiler, combined Komsomol daredevilry with civil war melodrama: the young hero must lose a leg in order to save his life and find his true love.

The last significant civil war film to open, though not the last one made,[1] reached theatre screens in 1958 after enormous publicity. Mosfilm's *The Communist*, intended for release in time for the fortieth anniversary of the Revolution, missed that deadline by several months, because the ideological significance signalled by its title demanded exceptional and time-consuming vigilance from both the studio and the Ministry of Culture.

Evgenii Gabrilovich finished his script for *The Communist* in early November 1956, a full year before the anniversary it was meant to celebrate.[2] Its hero, the

The Rules of the Game

Bolshevik Vasilii Gubanov, limps back from the frontlines of the civil war to work on one of the electrification projects so critical to Lenin's national policy. At first reluctant to accept the 'passive' job the Party assigns him, he obeys Party discipline and becomes the supply-master or commissary [*kladovshchik*] of the project, in charge of monitoring and distributing the extremely scanty supplies. When the project nearly founders for lack of nails, he displays true Bolshevik ardour, making his way to the Kremlin and into a meeting room where Lenin is presiding. Lenin hears him out and manages to locate the requisite supplies.

Entwined with the public dimension of Gubanov's life is his growing love for Aniuta, with whom he lodges. Gubanov wins Aniuta's heart and mind away from her husband Fedor, and she leaves Fedor first to work on the site, and then to live with Gubanov. They have a son, whose voice-over narration introduces the film and comments on the action at several crucial points. White Army soldiers ultimately kill Gubanov and burn down the construction site, but Aniuta and the rest of the workers, undeterred, prepare to rebuild what has been destroyed.

Readers all along the political spectrum relished the script. Pyrev read *The Communist* as an implicit rebuttal of the nihilistic cinema he disliked, and a worthy heir to four decades of Soviet film art. Conservatives like Aleksandr Mariamov, who had read with horror of a British magazine competition for the best work to deal with 'no subject more significant than a commode', prized the thematic amplitude of *The Communist*. Its 'artistry, its main idea, its chief image' in every way justified its title.[3] (The studio had debated at length whether the film lived up to so ideologically freighted a name; the original working title had been simply 'The Supply-Master'.)

The studio unanimously recommended the script for its 'high ideological and artistic quality ... This script is important because of its theme, depicting the struggle of our people in building the young Soviet government, and its outstandingly profound and clearly delineated characterizations,' including the image of Lenin.[4] (Mikhail Romm particularly liked the simple, 'ordinary' Lenin depicted in the script.)

Parenthetically, the 'humanization' of Lenin on screen accelerated between 1957 and 1959.[5] In Gabrilovich's script for another film that came out in 1958 as *Tales of Lenin*, politics are decidedly subordinate. The film is told from the point of view of Lenin's nurse, Sasha, who tends him in his final illness. Lenin treats Sasha with warm affection, using fond diminutives of her name ('Sashura', 'Sashentsiia') and smoothing her hair with avuncular tenderness. This Lenin is still boyish; since Sasha is not supposed to 'upset' him, he tries to trick her into giving him news of events transpiring in the country. Mocking himself, he wryly recalls falling in love over the pancakes [*bliny*] Krupskaia prepared for Party cell meetings, and ridicules the 'sighs and flowers' that were so unexpected

11. *The Communist*

and out of place for himself, the earnest young revolutionary who knew Marx and Engels practically by heart.[6]

The Ulianov Family [Sem'ia Ul'ianovykh, 1957], a film directed by Valentin Nevzorov based on a stage play by I. Popov, concentrated on Lenin's mother and the family atmosphere, where Vladimir imbibed the 'classic' values of the intelligentsia: spiritual integrity, refusal to compromise, a stout heart, mutual support. We 'fall in love with' the young Volodia Ulianov, one critic wrote approvingly.[7]

The Lenin who secures nails for Gubanov in *The Communist* is, as Romm said, Lenin on a human scale. He spouts no passionate political rhetoric, he appears in no public venue. He listens to a report on electrification progress as attentively as he listens to Gubanov's problem. After Gubanov ruefully admits that he skipped one possible source of nails, Lenin laughs good-naturedly and immediately places a call to that particular storehouse.

Lenin appears again, at the end of the film, when the local Party worker at the electrification project phones Moscow to inform Lenin of the White attack. At first the local man downplays the damage. Lenin, however, sternly demands the truth. (Mostly; after eliciting information about the extent of the damage, he asks, 'But the people aren't abandoning us, are they?' [*Narod ne ukhodit ot nas?*] A comrade would have to be brave indeed not to supply the vehement 'of course not' that Lenin so obviously expects.) Consistent with his steady concern for the people behind the projects, Lenin asks about casualties. He cannot quite place Gubanov's name until the Party worker reminds him of the nails incident, but he then remembers, sighs deeply and instructs him to look after Gubanov's family.[8]

The first of these two scenes in particular directly responds to the anti-hierarchical, relatively egalitarian spirit of the post-Twentieth Congress reforms. It revises Lenin in a dramatic fashion, permitting the simple citizen to make direct contact with the leader. Gubanov breaches the first line, the sentry on duty at the gate, who bars anyone without a pass. He sneaks past the secretary – a friendly but firm barrier – in Lenin's outer office. Once inside the inner sanctum, he literally brushes aside the Party worker standing between him and Lenin's desk. The conventional but previously essential role of the Party as mediator between believer and deity is here rendered superfluous; 'The spirit of the Revolution and its rank-and-file participant meet and unite.'[9]

A critical establishment hungry for identifiably 'Soviet' heroes and edifying 'Soviet' art greeted *The Communist* with hosannahs, notwithstanding its delay. 'We need this picture nowadays just as much as we need bread,' one writer gushed. *The Communist* reminds us of what is 'so often forgotten in the hustle and bustle of daily life – where we came from'. This 'hymn to the building of a new world' made a 'huge, a grandiose impression' on studio members present at its first screening.[10] They extolled Vasilii Gubanov, a 'simple man of the people' without rank or title, 'neither leader nor superman … [but] a man, one of millions who made the revolution'. They far preferred his muscular, robust type of courage to the 'neurasthenic' weakness of Alov and Naumov's Pavel Korchagin.[11] And at a time when the West avidly construed Khrushchev's criticisms of the cult of personality as a 'crisis of communism', *The Communist* showcased the strength of communism, and the ubiquity of its heroes.[12]

In fact, Vasilii Gubanov is *not* the hero these critics so desperately wanted him to be. He is not a revival of the heroes of the 1920s, nor a new incarnation of the revolutionary communist ideal. He superficially resembles the heroes of the 1920s or 1930s (much as Khrushchev's reforms superficially resembled those of Lenin's New Economic Policy), and his heroism is set within the civil war context, but its nature and performance are redolent of post-Twentieth Congress values. Gubanov never holds a weapon, even amid a barrage of shots. (Some years earlier he might well have been branded a deserter simply for failing to show his mastery of guns.) He does give up his life for his cause, but his self-sacrifice is motivated by what Vitalii Troianovskii calls 'thaw altruism' rather than by revolutionary zeal. Much more a contemporary of his film's audience than of the generation he is meant to represent, Vasilii Gubanov wants to live and be happy.[13]

The Communist sends mixed messages. The voice-over narration and much of its dialogue give priority to canonic values yet, throughout the film, emotion supersedes ideology, whether political or theological. When Aniuta, racked with guilt over her feelings for Gubanov, flees from what would have been their first real tryst, she runs into the church and tries to pray her way back to emotional loyalty. Not surprisingly, it does not work: she continues to love Gubanov, though she remains faithful to her husband Fedor. Marxism is no more effective. Gubanov turns for advice to an older Party member, who counsels him to give up his 'unclean' love for a married woman as unbefitting a communist: 'What would the people say?' he asks sternly. But Gubanov cannot 'give it up', and his anguish bursts out defiantly: 'Love doesn't ask whether she is married or not ... What kind of theory is it, if it doesn't take account of love?'

Fedor, Aniuta's husband, is permitted emotional legitimacy despite his blind resistance to Bolshevik power. In political terms Fedor is a remnant of the past, stuck in a peasant mentality that values individual over common good. He puts profit above friendship, most tellingly when Denis, a Bolshevik, squeezes Fedor on to an overcrowded train car. Fedor is truly grateful, but he forces Denis to trade nearly all the clothes he is wearing for a share of the food Fedor has hoarded in his sack. However, because the scenes are arranged in a progressive sequence, we see Denis gradually stripped of everything but his long underwear, and the impact is comic rather than pedagogic.

Fedor's attitude towards Aniuta is old-fashioned and patriarchal, and he believes the malicious gossips who accuse her of adultery. Yet even at his worst, when he beats Aniuta, we never doubt that he loves her; frustration and pain fuel his violence. *The Communist* presents Fedor as a type that, unable or unwilling to change, will be left behind, but also as a weak man who deserves pity rather than scorn. After Gubanov's death, the still-besotted Fedor offers to adopt Gubanov's son if Aniuta will come back to him. When she refuses – she allies herself with 'the people' ['*Kak narod, tak i ia*'] – he becomes even more pitiable.

One of the most physically imposing of Soviet actors, Evgenii Urbanskii, made his debut performance as Gubanov. His face is strong, his features heavy yet highly expressive, their melancholy lightened by infrequent smiles. His brawny body hints at barely contained power, thus implausible scenes, such as his virtually single-handed demolition of a stand of trees and his near-defeat of the armed White bandits who greatly outnumber him, become less preposterous than they would be with another actor in the role. If Aleksei Batalov's physical elegance and his mobile mouth, twisting in an ironic smile to accompany a sceptically-raised eyebrow, suggested to Russian audiences the *intelligent* (even when he played a worker), perhaps tinged with aristocratic hauteur, Urbanskii's massive presence implied an older Russian national archetype or a folkloric hero.

The voice-over narration parallels and enhances Urbanskii's folkloric qual-ities. Its text consists of political truisms, but the very use of it creates a sense

12. *The Fate of a Man*

of national fable. As the film opens the narrator tells us that he heard this 'story' from his mother. Like an African griot, he preserves the sanctity of orally-transmitted history, punctuating the film with reminders that this story was passed on to him ('My mother often told me how these people lived ...'). When Gubanov picks Aniuta up from the dusty crossroads after she has fled Fedor's house, and carries her off in his arms (like John Wayne hoisting on to his horse a plucky frontier girl who's sprained her ankle), the narrator finally completes his self-identification: 'And these were my parents.'

He treasures his father's 'radiant image' [*svetlyi obraz*], the words connoting a secular icon. The narrator inherits both physical and moral strength and, properly appreciative of his parents' stature, he carries on the traditions bequeathed to him. He represents continuity with those hallowed forebears who lived in what was, with all its hardships, a golden time.

Another folkloric hero, the protagonist of Sholokhov's *The Fate of a Man* [Sud'ba cheloveka], made his way on to the screen early in 1959, in a production starring and directed by Sergei Bondarchuk. Sholokhov's moving story tells of an ordinary Soviet man, Andrei Sokolov, who manages to escape from a Nazi POW camp, bringing back to Soviet lines valuable booty: a German major with a briefcase full of precious information. A German bomb kills Sokolov's wife

13. *The Fate of a Man*

and two daughters; his son perishes at the front, literally on the eve of victory. After the war Sokolov meets up with an orphan, and they form a new 'family'.

Sholokhov wrote his story in 1946, but was unable to publish it until 1956, when the thaw permitted open acknowledgement of recalcitrant facts. For example, Sokolov does not fight for Stalin, the Party, or Soviet power; he fights for his family and for his Russian homeland, a veracious but hitherto unacceptably apolitical motivation. And Sholokhov's story deviated from painful history in Sokolov's hero's welcome when he makes his way back to the Red Army. In reality, many Soviet prisoners of war were greeted with suspicion if not charges of treason. (Solzhenitsyn's fictional hero, Ivan Denisovich, was arrested and sent to the Gulag, a more representative fate.) The censors found the discrepancy between fact and fiction too glaring, until Khrushchev openly alluded to the fate of returning PoWs at the Twentieth Party Congress.

Bondarchuk expands the sections set in the concentration camp but retains the story's modesty: to be anti-fascist, his film implies, it is enough to be Russian. 'Nowhere, neither in the text of the story nor in the film dialogue, is there any explicit mention of the patriotism of the Russian. In Andrei Sokolov's understanding, Motherland takes the concrete form of Family. Family and Motherland were united for him.'[14]

The Rules of the Game

14. *The Fate of a Man*

Critics interpreted *The Fate of a Man*, as they did *The Communist*, as successor to classic Soviet films. Sokolov became the godchild of heroes like Maksim, Chapaev, and – gender difference notwithstanding – Aleksandra Sokolova, the heroine of Kheifits and Zarkhi's 1940 *Member of the Government*. *The Fate of a Man* was compared favourably to Andrzej Munk's 'near-slanderous' film about Polish prisoners of war, *Eroica* (1958). In this reading of the film, Sokolov derives the strength to survive from having the 'character, world view, and morality of a Russian, a Soviet man'.[15] In fact Sokolov resembles Chapaev as little as Gubanov resembles Maksim. His tragedies have damaged him irreparably. He survives, and somehow retains the capacity to love, as demonstrated by the bond he forms with his adopted son, but his heart is literally broken, its beat arrhythmic and tachycardiac.

Furthermore, Bondarchuk repeatedly minimizes the 'heroic' or 'exceptional' dimension of his hero's actions. When Sokolov escapes with his captive major, for instance, Bondarchuk barely shows the hazardous journey, cutting straight to their arrival behind Soviet lines. Earlier, the Russian PoWs are barracked in a ruined church, a setting that allows Bondarchuk to expose the profound hypocrisy of the 'Christian' Nazis: they shoot one Russian, a believer, who desperately attempts to run outside to empty his bowels so that he will not defile the church. Sokolov overhears one Russian matter-of-factly express his intention of denouncing another Russian, who is a Party member. With the Party man's help, Sokolov strangles the would-be informer. The silent execution is necessary, but repugnant, not a heroic feat.

The climax of the film occurs in the concentration camp, whose very air is poisoned by the smoke from the crematoria. The camp commandant summons Sokolov from the barracks: someone has denounced Sokolov, who had incautiously cursed the prisoners' servitude. The Germans are celebrating their army's attack on Stalingrad, and the commandant challenges Sokolov to a drinking duel that resembles the ritualized testing of the hero of folktales. Three times the commandant fills the glass to the brim; three times Sokolov swallows it down in one long gulp. Despite his hunger he retains his dignity, declining the bread proffered by the commandant until, after the third glass, he breaks off just a crumb with painstaking deliberation. (Bondarchuk is compelling as Sokolov, though his solid, fleshy body makes Sokolov's emaciation and ravenous hunger slightly hard to credit.)

The Nazis admire Sokolov's drinking capacity, and the commandant rewards his courage with his life, plus a loaf of bread and a slab of fat. But Sokolov's genuine heroism resides not in his ability to drink; it resides in his ability to maintain rigid control over his fear. Impassive throughout the ordeal, Sokolov gives way to his terror once he is safely outside. He nearly collapses as he clutches the precious food to his chest; then he staggers back to the barracks, to share the booty with his fellow prisoners. Bondarchuk, both as actor and director, chooses to underplay the *podvig*, the exploit. Instead he emphasizes its immense cost to Sokolov, whose wish to live survives even in such a situation.

The Fate of a Man enjoyed critical and commercial success. It made so much money that the authorities allowed Bondarchuk to proceed with filming *War and Peace*, the most expensive production in Soviet film history. But, in the disorienting atmosphere of the late 1950s, it also served as a stalking-horse for officials who wished to ambush more troublesome films.

Amid the customary whining about low production figures and the dearth of worker-heroes and contemporary themes, disquieting new notes sounded. The author of an article entitled 'Against revisionism in aesthetics', for instance, defined revisionism as 'antimarxist views on literature and art' and as 'capitulation to bourgeois ideology that can turn into political treason'. He italicized the ominous final phrase by coupling it with a reference to the Petöfi circle in Hungary.[16]

In 1957, 1958 and 1959, as the Soviet space programme scored major triumphs with its sputnik and satellite launches, the genre of 'popular scientific' films (Khrushchev's favourite, according to his family) expanded dramatically. But national pride in scientific achievement, especially space exploration, was

The Rules of the Game

routinely couched in confrontational terms. 'Two worlds exist', wrote one author, socialist and capitalist. The 'internal contradictions of capitalism' render it incapable of achieving feats of 'human scientific and technical genius for the sake of human happiness'.[17] (One critic belatedly berated *The House I Live in* for ignoring the spirit of its age, when Chkalov flew to Kamchatka and Vancouver, workers built Dneprogas, and 'man considered himself personally responsible for everything on the planet'.)[18]

In this atmosphere, lasting well into 1960, accolades for *The Fate of a Man* became a stick with which to beat Alov and Naumov's tribute to the Komsomol, *Wind*, Tengiz Abuladze's first solo directorial effort, *Someone Else's Children* [Chuzhie deti, 1958], and Marlen Khutsiev's *Two Fedors* [Dva Fedora, 1958].[19] In the official lexicon, all three painted too 'dismal' and too 'pessimistic' a picture of Soviet life.[20]

The heroine of *Someone Else's Children* marries a widower she does not love for the sake of his children, and stays with them when he abandons her for another woman. Though the film, which took first prize for debut films at the 1960 London Film Festival, faithfully recounted an incident reported in *Komsomolskaia pravda*, its forthright depiction of pain and loneliness angered many powerful individuals, including Sergei Gerasimov. Gerasimov condemned Abuladze's film as 'a sham imitation', inspired not by life but by film imitations of life. With its 'spiritual debility and incomprehension of the new socialist world, which opposes with all its might egoistic solitude', *Someone Else's Children* was 'alien' to Soviet values. It was, alas, 'feminine cinema' [*zhenstvennoe kino*].[21]

Party-minded critics found both *Wind* and *Two Fedors* too 'grim'. They disliked the self-conscious camerawork and careful visual composition of *Wind*, and they detested Khutsiev's portrayal of post-war conditions in *Two Fedors*, where food is scarce, and dirty, hungry and homeless children play amid building rubble and a burnt-out landscape.

Khutsiev's film begins with a troop train returning home victorious, a moment when 'festivity reigned' and it seemed there 'was no tomorrow, because war itself had been conquered'.[22] A complex aural montage mixes the Red Army Chorus, accordion music, the train engine and whistle, and children shouting 'hurrah'. Visual pans of waving crowds and smiling girls running towards the train, their faces overexposed in impossibly brilliant sunshine, match the soundtrack. But one soldier is alone, apart and unsmiling: Big Fedor. It was the first role for Vasilii Shukshin, later an exceptionally popular author, actor and director, but in 1958 still a student at the State Institute of Cinematography.

Soviet films about the war commonly invert traditional gender roles: men often 'mother' a child. *Two Fedors* initially adheres to that pattern: when a small boy is caught stealing some food at a station, the soldiers 'rescue' him from the woman he robs, and take him aboard the train as a kind of mascot. That night, at another station, the boy – Little Fedor – goes off on his own, valiantly pretending he has relatives in the area, though earlier he has identified himself as 'nobody's child' ['*Ty malyi chei?*' '*Nichei.*']. Big Fedor sees through the lie, scoops him up and takes him 'home' to a crater and some scraps of walls.

For the best part of the film it is not clear who is mothering whom. The two Fedors look after each other, less adult and child than two peers. Then Big Fedor falls in love with and marries Natasha. Little Fedor tries to banish the interloper by cutting off her hair while she sleeps (thus to break her magic spell over Big Fedor); when that fails, and Big Fedor strikes him in anger, Little Fedor runs away. The film ends with a reunion and reconciliation as stale as the love triangle; Khutsiev resorts to repeating earlier footage to demonstrate Big Fedor's love for the child.

In autumn 1956, when Khutsiev first submitted the script, the studio welcomed it. Then came the Hungarian revolt, and by the time he shot the film 'there were objections to anything "dark"'.[23] As happened frequently, the film itself had not changed so much as the times had. At the Kiev Ministry of Culture, discussion verged on ludicrous: 'The picture does not depict our reality, it is pessimistic and uninspiring. You can't tell what country it's set in. If it's ours, then why don't the school children wear red ties? And what sort of hero is this – sullen, taciturn, unsociable. That's not what our people are like. [*Razve nash chelovek takoi?*]'[24]

Two Fedors was decidedly unorthodox in its near-total avoidance of conventional sentimentality. Unlike *The Fate of a Man*, where Sokolov's emotion-laden flashbacks recall components of pre-war happiness such as his courtship of his wife and the birth and success of his children, *Two Fedors* neither tells nor shows us what either Fedor lost because of the war. With no tugging of heart-strings, it implies: everything.

Moreover, the alliance between the two Fedors resembles 'the ascetic bachelor friendship of two men, two soldiers'[25] more than it does a father–son bond. Little Fedor is not obviously vulnerable like Vania, the urchin Sokolov adopts. He is tough and wary, a pragmatist who knows – much better than the romantic Big Fedor – how to scrounge food or push past a line of people waiting to buy food. Though his head barely tops the counter, his eyes follow unblinkingly every move of the woman weighing out his ration. The man is amazed by the coincidence of their names ('Just think of it!'), the boy matter-of-fact ('Well, it happens').[26] It is the adult who shamefacedly admits losing the precious ration cards, the child who scolds him. When Big Fedor buys ice-cream, the child greedily slurps it down, but knows that the money would have been better spent on potatoes. Big Fedor, not Little, is called by the diminutive Fedia.

The role reversal (which involves its own kind of sentimentality) results from the difference in their war experiences. Khutsiev implies, iconoclastically, that soldiers found post-war life more unsettling than the war. Army life provided food, clothing, structure, an orderly life and a network of support.

The Rules of the Game

Civilian life meant depending on oneself alone, amid chaos and scarcity. Little Fedor has better survival skills because his war taught self-reliance as the first and most important lesson. *He* would never have lost those ration cards.

Viktor Nekrasov, in an eloquent defence of *Two Fedors*, wrote of the generation that left its schoolbenches for the front and returned home to ashes: no house, no family, no friends. Though he carefully, explicitly, denied parallels with the West's 'lost generation' ('We had and have no such lost generation'), he in fact described its Soviet counterpart: boys who learned 'two skills in their 17–18 years – how to kill and how not to be killed. And how are they to live now, when such skills are not needed?'[27] Big Fedor, one such young man, is neither indifferent nor callous, but his grief and loneliness absorb him. The war deprived Big Fedor of his hopes, his faith in himself, his past and, he fears, his future.

Two Fedors had other advocates, among them Iutkevich, but the temper of the times demanded heroism on a large and obvious scale, and *Two Fedors* provided an easy target. Khutsiev's heroes may be 'very dear' people, Iakov Varshavskii rebutted Nekrasov, but they lead 'circumscribed lives', and the film fails to furnish the moral armaments needed to conquer the 'fronts' of life. 'We are sure', Varshavskii wrote,

> that not long before the action of the film, Fedor himself lived, thought, felt on a 'high note', because he felt responsible for the whole country. But the filmmakers chose to present this powerful epic image of the master of the nation from a different point of view. If we can believe them, Fedor in peacetime is not the same man as he was in wartime ... [He] shows no interest in the country, in the world.[28]

Another critic wondered whether the heroes, as they rebuild their house, have in mind the house 'of simple Soviet people, connected to the whole huge nation by a thousand threads', or the bourgeois concept of 'my home as my castle'.[29]

Such bombast characterized the rhetoric of 1959. Even the photos that typically adorned the front and back covers of *Iskusstvo kino* manifest the reversion to grandiloquence and hierarchy: month after month a man, often dressed in uniform, gazes towards distant horizons, his head slightly raised the better to see the alluring future. Sometimes he is alone, often a woman and occasionally a child stand next to and slightly behind him, heads turned to him, eyes fixed on his face in rapt devotion. Their stance reflects the general disappearance from the screen of strong female protagonists in the late 1950s. Many early thaw films featured powerful heroines, whether the doctor in *Unfinished Tale* and the wife in *Lesson of Life* or the more complex Mariutka in *The Forty-first* and Tania in *Spring on Zarechnaia Street*. In 1958–59, with the exceptions of *Someone Else's Children* and Igor Chuliukin's comedy *The Unsubmissive* [Nepoddaiush-chiesia, 1959], such women are hardly to be found on screen.

Certainly the biggest budgets, loudest official applause and top prizes were reserved for resolutely 'masculine' films, such as *And Quiet Flows the Don*, *The Fate of a Man*, and *Poem of the Sea* [Poema o more, 1958]. Women have secondary roles in these films; more, the films themselves consistently denigrate 'womanly' values. In *Poem of the Sea*, directed by Iulia Solntseva from the script by her late husband Aleksandr Dovzhenko, all the main characters are men, though the action involves the flooding of the kind of Ukrainian village in reality populated mostly by women. (In the script the chairman of the kolkhoz says as much, calling himself 'chief commander of women and schoolkids'.)[30] The few women are stock characters: a mother who tries to keep her sole surviving son from leaving the village, a young girl who leaves looking for 'real life', the protagonist's petty bourgeois wife.

The same kind of gender stereotyping characterizes Kheifits's *My Dear Man* [Dorogoi moi chelovek, 1958], a film that traces the life of Vladimir Ustimenko (Aleksei Batalov) from his boyhood in the 1930s through the war and into the post-war years. The heroic, overwhelmingly masculine ethic is patrilineal, transmitted directly from the father, killed as a volunteer in the Spanish Civil War, to the son. The father's revolutionary ardour manifests itself in Vladimir's zeal to work as a doctor deep in the provinces, far from 'civilized' life. Thus *My Dear Man* exemplifies the notion so central to Soviet ideology, that no generation gap such as deforms western societies can separate Soviet fathers from Soviet sons.

Two women, physicians at the front, merit places in this heroic pantheon. They are in their fifties (i.e. post- or de-sexed) and first met during the civil war. The more important of the two, the surgeon nicknamed Baba Iaga (the witch of Russian folklore), is, like Boris's sister Irina in *Cranes*, masculine in appearance and brusque in manner. In a photo of the two as young women twenty-five years earlier, Baba Iaga wears men's clothing. (The lesbian overtones of their relationship are unmistakable, if unintended.) They are physically brave, politically irreproachable, professionally outstanding, and devoted to each other, but, though they cast a long moral shadow, they are hardly women at all.

The two nubile women in the film are both caricatures. Kheifits schematically opposes the selfish materialism of Ustimenko's wife Vera to the dedication of his true love Varia. Varia's brother, self-serving and amoral, is unattractively plump, his buttocks tightly encased in fashionable trousers. He collects tsarist crystal and china – a distasteful passion for a 'real' man, and, with its sacrilegious political connotations, one unworthy of a Soviet citizen.

Only one woman figures (barely) in the most successful film of 1959, Viktor Ivchenko's *Ch.P.: An Extraordinary Event* [ChP: Chrezvychainoe proisshestvie], based on the capture of a Soviet tanker, the *Tuapse*, by the Kuomintang in 1954. The Chinese had imprisoned the Soviet crew, pressuring them for more than a year to renounce their loyalty to the Soviet Union. Actual participants

The Rules of the Game

were involved as scriptwriters and actors, blurring the line between fictional and real heroes.

The line between heroes and villains, however, is crystal clear. The phrase 'Made in USA', stencilled on Chinese equipment and shot in close-up, indicates American support for Chang Kai Shek and complicity in the torture of the Soviets. A magazine advertisement of a toddler at a piano encapsulates western materialist decadence: the caption reads 'Get it NOW or NEVER!' The Chinese bring the Soviet captain to a luxurious dacha, offer him food, wine, a beautiful girl, $300,000 and unlimited credit. When he refuses contemptuously, the Chinese replace the soft sell with physical hardships and psychological torment. They exploit each man's particular vulnerability, locking the sensualist up in a whorehouse, forcing the devoted family man to hear crying children outside his cell, and so on.

Ch.P. asserts that the essence of a human being emerges in the context of an extraordinary occurrence. The crew is an 'ordinary bunch', according to the narrator, but they behave with remarkable consistency once the Chinese overrun the ship. Comradeship sustains them: when tempted to abandon a hunger strike, they link arms and sing. Literature (the Word) is a support: one sailor fondles his copy of Ostrovskii's *How the Steel was Tempered*. So is political solidarity, demonstrated via a montage of sympathetic newspaper headlines from around the world. One man signs a 'confession' concocted by the Chinese when they threaten to rape his beloved (the single female character), but uses a false name. When the crew is finally free and back in Moscow, the grateful and proud country they represented so staunchly hails them as heroes.

Although *Ch.P.* was box-office leader for 1959, attracting 47.5 million viewers in its first year,[31] the film that won prizes all over the world and that became an enduring favourite lacked *Ch.P.*'s melodramatic plot convolutions and political bombast. Moreover, it argued precisely the opposite of *Ch.P.* Grigorii Chukhrai's *Ballad of a Soldier*, released at the very end of 1959, affirmed that a man's essence is disclosed not in the exceptional context, but in the unexceptional. Chukhrai structured *Ballad* as an extended flashback, beginning and ending with a grieving woman standing on a road, fields and forests behind her. The flashback framework emphasizes war as a fatal irruption into ordinary life; the body of the film concentrates on the 'normal', even if that normalcy exists within an alien and abnormal state of war.

In the only 'battle scene' of the film, nineteen-year-old Alesha Skvortsov runs in panic before he shoots at and disables two German tanks. Rewarded with a week's leave, Alesha heads home to help his mother repair the roof, but he uses up almost the entire leave helping others. He barely has time to embrace his mother before he turns back, to the front and to his death. Alesha is a hero precisely in the unexceptional context, and the individuals he encounters are mainly civilians whose heroism reveals itself in prosaic, quotidian reality far from the front.

Not everyone appreciated this aspect of *Ballad*. The script was initially considered 'too ordinary', and Chukhrai was advised to give Shura, the young girl who joins Alesha on the train, an 'exploit' comparable to Alesha's tank manoeuvre.[32] On the eve of *Ballad of a Soldier*'s commercial release, dubious theatre managers in Leningrad's best cinemas substituted *Room at the Top* [UK, 1958], thinking it was more 'reliable'.[33] Even after its release, when it had become the Soviet sensation of 1960, *Ballad of a Soldier* required justification because it dealt with the war instead of contemporary life. Stanislav Rostotskii acquitted the film on the basis of its edifying nature: 'Workers in the arts should think of the souls and hearts of the generation who were children [during the war], to concern themselves with their education ... [Chukhrai] wants the radiant memory of people like Skvortsov to help today's world and to illuminate the future.'[34] A colleague valued Alesha's 'Soviet' character, which 'could not have been forged in the atmosphere of an orangerie or a hothouse', presumably found only in the West. Alesha is 'our contemporary' because 'in the moment before his death [a moment not actually shown in the film] he turned his face towards the future, and his eyes glowed with the reflected light of the morrow'.[35]

Such praise seems grotesquely unsuitable for *Ballad*, and most critics, within and outside the Soviet Union, remarked on the qualities that still affect audiences: the goodness of nearly all the characters, the film's simplicity, its organic, natural flow.[36] At Cannes, *Ballad* presented an attractive anomaly when set alongside Antonioni and Buñuel's surrealism, and Fellini's scandal-provoking *La Dolce Vita*. The British press called it a 'calming note in a discordant symphony'; *Le Monde* acknowledged that 'from time to time it's nice to see normal and healthy people on screen'.[37]

Ballad of a Soldier shares with other deeply satisfying pieces of art the 'journey' motif, that voyage of the soul objectified in physical movement. Figures appear and disappear, but the journey continues, giving the film its unity, its rhythm, the unexpected linking of episodes full of meaning for both the viewer and the hero. 'Alesha Skvortsov's road to his native village becomes his road to himself,' wrote Maia Turovskaia a year after *Ballad* appeared. He truly wishes to get home, so that his reluctance at every turning point testifies that real choice is involved, but each time he chooses the kind, the decent, the noble alternative. Like chronicle, *Ballad* lacks invention; it is driven by the immutability of a fairytale's moral law, where 'beauty equals happiness and ugliness unhappiness, where the hero never fails to help the helpless and never errs, precisely thanks to his naïveté'.[38]

Ballad transformed the concept of the heroic in Soviet cinema. Alesha's flight from the advancing tank, his burrowing into the ground, and his panicky firing at it, constitute 'a plainly ironic attack on the established traditions of front-line heroism'.[39] Chukhrai spurns the simplistic image of the hero who

The Rules of the Game

15. *Ballad of a Soldier*

feels no fear, and he implicitly challenges the more subtle type of heroism exemplified by Andrei Sokolov in *The Fate of a Man*. Sokolov triumphs in the drinking duel in spite of his fear. Alesha performs his feat precisely *because* of his fear.

Moreover, in *Ballad* no single brilliant feat constitutes heroism. Rather, heroism is a mosaic consisting of many separate details, each mini-story a variation on the initial theme. The episodes are linked to one another not by cause and effect, but by thematic unity. The actual 'confrontations' of the film are mild: Alesha defies a greedy sentry on the train, helps a one-legged soldier with his gear, brings soap to a soldier's unfaithful wife and then takes it to a worthier recipient, the soldier's bedridden father. Their meaning and impact occur less on screen than in our minds. But the rhythmic repetition of the theme penetrates our minds with the power of what Eisenstein called 'shamanic incantation'.[40] What would be admirable as a single week's worth of actions becomes something much greater, because we know it is the last week of such actions, and he will have no more of them. Alesha's entire life becomes the exploit.

Cranes are Flying, Quiet Don, The Communist, The Fate of a Man all depict individuals trapped by history. Characters make choices that have decisive consequences, their own survival paramount among them, but they cannot change the inexorable movement of historical circumstances where ultimate meaning resides. Chukhrai shifts the whole domain of meaning so that historical circumstances become, in a sense, irrelevant. What matters is the individual. Alesha Skvortsov does not have to make one fateful choice on which his future depends. He has to make many small choices, none of them decisive, most of them inconsequential. Yet, unlike Veronika, who is for much of *Cranes* the passive object of tragedy, Alesha is consistently hegemon and subject. In the moral logic of Chukhrai's film, as Anninskii observed, good proceeds from within the individual when he acts, and it engenders good; generosity engenders generosity.[41] The wounds cruelly if brilliantly exposed by *Cranes* were healed, three years later, by *Ballad*. But where could film-makers go from there?

Part III The Grand Illusion, 1960–64

8. The Grand Illusion: Introduction

The Soviet Union entered the new decade in a contradictory mood, at once hopeful and wary. Real gains in the economic and social spheres included better old-age pensions and disability pay, shorter work days, more (though still inadequate) new housing and consumer goods and services. The number of visitors – workers and students from 'underdeveloped' countries, as well as students and tourists from capitalist states – shot up in the early 1960s; Soviet citizens embraced their new contacts, however constrained and artificial, with other worlds, and the Soviet intellectual and artistic elite enjoyed exposure to and interchanges with western ideas and colleagues.

Khrushchev made two visits to the United States. The first, in September 1959, took him to midwestern wheat farms. A film documentary celebrated his journey and the hospitable reception accorded Khrushchev by 'ordinary' Americans; the Soviet press (including *Iskusstvo kino*) published dozens of photographs from the trip and overflowed with protestations of international good will. In January 1960 Khrushchev announced cuts in the armed forces, and he repeatedly expressed a desire for more relaxed relations with the United States in order to encourage internal Soviet development, especially of consumer-goods production.

At the same time, however, fissures splintered the socialist bloc, with China adopting Albania as a client state and disputing Moscow on both ideological and policy issues, and strains between the two superpowers persisted. The U-2 incident of May 1960 and Rudolf Nureyev's defection a year later fuelled an aggressive anti-Americanism noticeable in fiction as well as political rhetoric.[1] Khrushchev's second trip, almost exactly a year after his first, brought him to the United Nations for his infamous shoe-banging speech. In August 1961 the Berlin Wall was erected.

Equally mixed signals plagued domestic Soviet cultural politics. The Third Congress of Soviet Writers, held in May 1959, resounded with formulaic speeches. The Central Committee challenged writers to 'show truthfully and vividly the beauty of the people's labour exploits ... to be passionate propagandists of the Seven-Year Plan, and to imbue the hearts of Soviet people with courage and energy'. Great literature requires innovation, the union's head admitted, but innovation must not be confused with 'formalist quirks'. Yet Khrushchev himself implied that the state had more important issues to resolve than questions of literature and art: 'The easiest thing would be to print nothing, then there would be no mistakes ... But that would be stupid. Therefore, Comrades, do not burden the government with the solution of such questions, decide them for yourselves in a comradely fashion.'[2]

The Congress of Writers virtually ignored the controversy surrounding Boris Pasternak's Nobel Prize, and the media barely mentioned Pasternak's death on 30 May 1960. The authorities, following tsarist tradition, hoped silence would discourage attendance at the funeral, and sent no important Party, government or Writers' Union representatives. Notwithstanding the official muzzle, thousands came to pay their respects. Within weeks of Pasternak's death the KGB arrested his mistress, Olga Ivinskaia, and Ivinskaia's daughter. They were convicted of currency speculation and were sentenced to eight and five years, respectively, in a labour camp.

As if to belie such ominous signals, however, that same summer *Novyi mir* published the first part of Ilya Ehrenburg's memoirs, *People, Years, Life*. Konstantin Paustovskii, an editor of the 1956 thaw anthology *Literary Moscow* and a steadfast advocate on Pasternak's behalf, continued to publish his autobiography, *Story of a Life*, as well as articles arguing for artists' need and right to experiment, however foolishly. His and Ehrenburg's immensely popular memoirs exposed Russian readers to their own rich cultural heritage, particularly the modernist movements of the 1920s, so long denied them. Ehrenburg made strenuous efforts to 'introduce' people he had known – and he had known nearly everyone. Thanks to strategies honed by decades of political manoeuvring, he was reasonably successful, though certain subjects, among them Bukharin and anti-Semitism, remained off-limits.[3]

Writers were confused when a controversial literary anthology, *Pages from Tarusa* [Tarusskie stranitsy], appeared in a sizeable print-run (75,000), but was almost immediately withdrawn from sale and remained under ban until 1962. At the same time, Konstantin Simonov published *The Living and the Dead* towards the end of 1960, pushing at the limits of Party tolerance with his probing of war-related issues that were still muffled in secrecy, such as the degree to which the 1937 purge of army officers contributed to Soviet losses when the Germans invaded. A few months later Viktor Nekrasov published *Kira Georgievna*, a novel that refers, cautiously, to the hero's experiences in a labour camp and his readjustment after returning to 'normal' life.

In the months preceding the Twenty-second Party Congress of October 1961, both liberals and conservatives scored victories and defeats, and the congress revealed splits within the Party itself. Khrushchev emphasized the Soviet bloc's military and economic might, and western decline, in order to demonstrate 'that the cause of Communism could be effectively advanced on a world scale without risking the destruction of a thermonuclear war'. Hard-liners, however, among them the Chinese leadership, regarded Khrushchev's position as 'a rationalization for inaction and as a betrayal of the revolutionary cause ... In Chinese eyes, the Khrushchev strategy with its long-drawn-out prospect of competitive coexistence and eventual peaceful capitalist surrender was founded on illusions.'[4] Chou En-lai departed before the end of the congress, leaving the confrontation unresolved and an impression of dramatic disunity between the two most powerful communist nation-states.

If foreign policy issues dominated the first days of the congress, domestic issues dominated its conclusion. As with the Twentieth Party Congress four years earlier, the most sensational speech was reserved for the last day. The head of the KGB, Aleksandr Shelepin, had earlier read out material from KGB archives to support his indictment of Stalin, Molotov and Kaganovich for the Great Purge of 1937. Khrushchev, in his closing address, went further: 'Thousands of absolutely innocent people perished, and each person is a whole story. Many Party leaders, statesmen, and military leaders lost their lives.' He confirmed Ordzhonikidze's suicide and implicated Stalin in Kirov's assassination; he verified that Tukhachevskii, Iakir and other high-ranking military officers had been executed on the basis of Nazi-supplied documents. He demanded the removal of Stalin's body from the mausoleum, and proposed a monument to 'the memory of comrades who fell victim to arbitrary rule'.[5]

'As the congress unfolded,' historian Merle Fainsod wrote soon after,

> both program and rules disappeared into the wings, and a host of absent figures – Stalin and Mao, Hoxha and Shehu, Molotov, Kaganovich, and Malenkov – moved into the center of the stage. The past and the present invaded and displaced the future, and the delegates found themselves being escorted on a journey into Hades instead of concentrating on the vision of the Promised Land.[6]

As for the arts, the lines drawn at the congress followed six weeks of high drama. On 18 September Evgenii Evtushenko had declaimed his poem 'Babi Iar' at the Moscow Polytechnic Institute. Named after the ravine near Kiev where Nazis murdered more than 30,000 Jews, the poem forcefully denounces 'pogrom thugs', and concludes with the poet's ringing assertion: 'There is no Jewish blood in me/ But I am hated by every anti-Semite as a Jew,/ And for this reason I am a true Russian.' The next day, twenty years after the massacre occurred, *Literaturnaia gazeta* published the poem.

Evtushenko received more than 20,000 letters, the overwhelming majority of them positive. The dogmatists, however, who understood the poem as a direct attack on them, responded with abuse. Dmitrii Starikov, editor of *Literatura i zhizn*, led the attack.[7] A month later, on the last day of the Party congress, arch-conservative Vsevolod Kochetov followed up with a venomous speech. As Aleksandr Tvardovskii eloquently pressed the liberal cause by warning against 'residual forms of ... former habits of thought and of literary practice', Kochetov responded with accolades for conservative and conformist writers. He construed Khrushchev's remarks as favourable to socialist realism and to a quasi-Stalinist approach to literature, denounced Evtushenko directly and Ehrenburg indirectly ('morose compilers of memoirs who look to the past ... and drag out into the light of day mouldering literary corpses').[8]

The congress yielded a mixed tally sheet. Kochetov moved up to editor-in-chief of *Oktiabr*, a post he held until his death in 1973. He also received the highly prestigious Order of Lenin on his fiftieth birthday several months later. But, overall, liberals felt encouraged. Tvardovskii, already influential as the editor of *Novyi mir*, gained power as an elected candidate member to the Central Committee of the Party. Evtushenko incurred no official sanctions as a result of 'Babi Iar'. On the contrary, he joined the editorial board of the journal *Iunost* (along with Vasilii Aksenov), while his nemesis Starikov lost his job at *Literatura i zhizn*. Younger and more innovative men replaced older conservatives in the RSFSR Writers' Union.

The general climate of tolerance lasted for a year after the congress, fully blossoming in the autumn of 1962. In October and November, literature appeared that would earlier have been considered impossibly heretical, such as Evtushenko's 'Heirs of Stalin', a passionate and forceful 'assault on the persistence of neo-Stalinism and the possible revival of a full-fledged Stalinism',[9] and two caustic anti-Stalinist poems written by Boris Slutskii years earlier. The November issue of *Novyi mir* contained two bombshells, Aleksandr Solzhenitsyn's *One Day in the Life of Ivan Denisovich*, published in part thanks to Khrushchev's personal intervention,[10] and the first half of Viktor Nekrasov's *Both Sides of the Ocean*. (The remainder followed in December.) In Nekrasov's account of trips to Italy and the United States, he criticized isolationist Soviet cultural policies, recalling his embarrassed admission to an Italian director that he'd never seen a film by Bergman or Antonioni, and similar embarrassment some years earlier at his ignorance of Kafka.[11]

An equally auspicious musical atmosphere reigned. Stravinsky made his first visit to his homeland in fifty years, and met privately with Khrushchev. Yehudi and Hepzibah Menuhin toured the Soviet Union, as did the New York City Ballet under George Balanchine (*his* return after nearly four decades). Robert Shaw's Chorus gave the first Moscow performance of Bach's B-Minor Mass in many years. Shostakovich's Thirteenth Symphony, a musical setting of 'Babi Iar', premièred on 18 December, after a period of 'intense anticipation':

The excitement generated was not purely musical: people were aware of the artistic tensions behind the scene, of the meetings between the arts intelligentsia and the Party. The city was buzzing with rumours of a possible last-minute cancellation of the performance ...

The first movement, *Babyi Yar*, was greeted with a burst of spontaneous applause. At the end of the hour-long work, there was an ovation rarely witnessed. On the stage was Shostakovich, shy and awkward, bowing stiffly. He was joined by Yevtushenko, moving with the ease of a born actor ... Seeing the pair together, the audience went wild.

Shostakovich's *Katerina Izmailova*, a revised version of *Lady Macbeth of Mtsensk*, opened 'almost surreptitiously' eight days later, a 'last-minute' – but, within Moscow artistic circles, expected – substitute for Rossini's *Barber of Seville*.[12]

The rigidly conservative art world had been opening up as well. *Izvestia* carried a defence of abstract art; Vladimir Turbin's *Comrade Time and Comrade Art* proclaimed the twentieth century 'an age of triumphant abstractions'.[13] Canvases by Benois, Bakst, Larionov and other modernist masters graced gallery walls after languishing for decades in museum basements (though Chagall's work had to wait a further twenty-five years for a full exhibition).

In the last days of November 1962 conservatives and liberals confronted one another at an officially-sponsored three-day conference on socialist realism. Conservatives such as Vladimir Serov, president of the Soviet Academy of Arts, found themselves heckled and hissed off stage. Mikhail Romm spoke openly of Jewish members of the film community who had been victimized during the anti-cosmopolitan campaign (Iutkevich, Trauberg) and denounced the failure to hold the victimizers accountable. He condemned the Soviet habit of claiming authorship of major inventions, and advocated greater contact with western intellectual life. Two exhibits, one of students' paintings, many of them non-realistic, and one of Ernst Neizvestnyi's work, were timed to open during or just after the conference.

On 1 December the tide turned. Flanked by conservative artists (Serov and Aleksandr Gerasimov, among others), Khrushchev and an entourage of Presidium and Party members visited the Manège. They examined modernist paintings and sculptures, predictably reacting with loud and crude dislike.[14] Within days, three conservative artist-bureaucrats regained the leadership of leading art institutions, and the Neizvestnyi show was cancelled.

The Manège visit initiated a period of struggle between liberals battling to retain their hard-won breathing space and conservatives equally intent on regaining the prerogatives they felt slipping away. Three meetings between Party leaders and artists and intellectuals punctuated the next six months. In each case the major speeches delivered by Khrushchev and Leonid Ilichev, chairman of the Ideological Commission created in November 1962, were published within days in *Pravda*, *Literaturnaia gazeta* and *Izvestia*, and while their content and tone varied, they shared three central themes: insistence on

The Grand Illusion

Party control of the arts, rejection of western (and/or modernist) influence on Soviet art, and shrill denial of anything resembling a generation gap in Soviet society.

The first meeting, held on 17 December at the Pioneer Palace in the Lenin Hills, was still a dialogue: conservatives struck, liberals parried. Ehrenburg defended modernist art, Evtushenko challenged Khrushchev's crude hints at renewed repression ('The grave straightens out the hunchbacked,' Khrushchev warned).

By the third meeting, three months later, the atmosphere had deteriorated decisively. Six hundred artists and writers gathered at the Kremlin on 7 March. Romm recalled the chilling presence of 'unknown young men in modest dark suits and tidy collars', and Khrushchev's bizarre 'invitation' to 'willing informants of foreign agencies' [*dobrovol'nye osvedomiteli inostrannykh agentstv*] to leave the room. (The foreign media had accurately reported the first meeting, and Khrushchev blamed the presence of 'lackeys of the bourgeois press'.)[15] This time conservatives clearly had the upper hand, and frequently interrupted those liberals who attempted to speak. Ehrenburg left the hall after Ilichev's particularly venomous tirade.[16]

By late spring conservatives in all cultural spheres had retrieved much of their eroded authority. The dogmatic Aleksandr Chakovskii replaced *Literaturnaia gazeta*'s moderate editor, Viktor Kosolapov. Articles and speeches targeted individual artists, with censure ranging from relatively temperate (Voznesenskii, Okudzhava, the artist Pavel Nikonov, the composer Andrei Volkonskii) to vicious (Ehrenburg, Nekrasov). After its triumphant première, Shostakovich's Thirteenth Symphony was not performed for months, until 'adjustments' had been made in the first ('Babi Iar') movement.[17]

Cinema, unlike literature, had barely figured in speeches at the Twenty-second Party Congress. Still, the films produced in its wake map the contours of the shifting cultural terrain with striking fidelity. A remarkable number of significant movies came out in 1963, 1964 and 1965, films made within and reflecting both turmoil and tolerance. Whether critical success or failure, box-office triumph or dud, released or – in one notorious instance – not released, these films dealt with the critical themes of the period: generational friction, class tension, gender conflict. The adjectives added a startling new dimension to age-old themes, signifying struggle between individuals previously presumed to co-exist harmoniously, and within a society previously presented as a human symphony with few discordant notes.

The surge of energy unleashed in 1956 by liberation from the dead weight of Stalinism involved recovering a dormant revolutionary romanticism disencumbered of its Stalinist deformations, and rediscovering the ordinary heroes of everyday life. Innocence, excitement that occasionally spilled over into self-congratulation, belief that honesty sufficed to repair what had gone awry,

Introduction

unalloyed faith in emotional sincerity – these had buoyed artists throughout the mid-1950s. By 1961 they were no longer feasible, particularly after the concluding speeches of the Twenty-second Congress, with their implication – however unintended by the Kremlin – that a craven political apparatus had abetted in and enabled the excesses of Stalinism.

Hence the Kremlin's extraordinary sensitivity to the broad question of 'fathers and sons', one fraught with both political meaning and emotional resonance. It denoted two sets of generations: the Leninist 'fathers' who made the revolution and the Stalinist 'sons' who subverted and deformed it; and the Stalin-era (if not necessarily Stalinist) generation of fathers and their children, the thaw generation reaching maturity in the late 1950s. The 'fathers', mostly of the older generation, insisted on evidence of a clear legacy, an intact inheritance that admitted no fissures; the 'sons', not all of them younger, repudiated the lies and inauthenticity of their predecessors.

In the politics of cinema, where polemical declarations repeatedly affirmed the values and the aesthetics of the 'new' generation, the reality was complex. Older directors, such as Romm and Raizman, felt as uncomfortable with the pomposity and duplicity of the high Stalinist style as did their students; members of both generations spurned films like *The Fall of Berlin* and *The Battle of Stalingrad*.

Most of the 'elders', whatever their own aesthetic inclinations, cared passionately about their young colleagues' work. Uneasy with their own earlier conformism, they exorcized their chagrin by dedicated teaching and by electing to work with younger colleagues. The startling number of such collaborations suggests that youth itself was considered a prerequisite for starting out 'clean' and getting things right. The older men, who lived in a kind of privileged isolation, may also have envied those more directly involved in the metamorphoses of their society.[18]

The imbroglios of the winter of 1962 and spring of 1963 initially exempted film from special attention, but by the March meeting, where Khrushchev pointedly and stridently attacked Marlen Khutsiev's film, *Ilich's Gate* [Zastava Il'icha, 1961; rel. 1965 as *I am Twenty* (Mne dvadtsat' let)], cinema's relative immunity vanished. Although Khrushchev seemed to support film-makers' autonomy when, at the same session, he abruptly reversed the Party's planned dissolution of the Cinematographers' Union, the industry panicked. Uncertain of the future, powerful individuals took refuge in tried-and-true self-protective tactics: self-flagellation and remorse, copious citations from Kremlin speeches, repeated references to Lenin's handful of cinematic dicta.

For the rest of 1963 and well into the following year, issue after issue of *Iskusstvo kino* harked back to the March meeting: its 'affirmation of Leninist principles' and 'profound analysis and principled articulation of the tasks facing artists';[19] its unmasking of artistic pretension and egoism; its mixture of

The Grand Illusion

Bolshevik rigour and generous regard for the welfare of artists (because 'no one was considered incurably ill').[20]

Critics, actors, actresses, set designers and writers were enlisted to provide their own versions of the Party line. In June, for example, an actress echoed the Party's disappointment with cinema's failure to 'speak about the life of the Soviet people candidly and courageously', and a painter thanked the Party leadership for its repudiation of formalism and abstractionism: 'Successful development of decorative art is unthinkable without principled, profoundly Party-minded criticism.'[21]

Most of these contributors had little renown, so it is startling to find among them the exceptionally gifted actor Rolan Bykov. Bykov wondered whether the heroes of Vasilii Aksenov's fiction concealed a 'natural fear of falsity or the cynicism of the philistine' behind their 'fear of fine words'. He came close to a categorical indictment: 'A certain kind of finicky hero, who avoids "loud phrases", in fact sells them off to all sorts of rascals instead of fighting with all his passion for the great truth of fine words about communism, the Party, the people!'[22]

The Party's authoritative voice, *Kommunist*, devoted two articles to cinema's sins, especially those committed by film critics. *Iskusstvo kino* had failed in its mission 'to orient readers in properly understanding films'. Its writers neglected the 'social thought and significance' of films in favour of formal analysis; they denigrated, as outmoded and old-fashioned, films 'that continue the fighting tradition', instead saluting 'ambiguous and ideologically weak films inaccessible to mass audiences'.[23] (The journal quickly ran a compensatory essay on 're-actionary concepts in contemporary bourgeois cinema aesthetics'.)[24]

An interesting discussion of elitism and mass culture, initiated by an article in *Iskusstvo kino*'s November 1962 issue,[25] ceased, and by the time the Cinematographers' Union plenary session occurred, in November 1963, the official stance admitted no gap between elite and mass films. 'We have always rejected the modish western notion that cinema is for the elite,' Ivan Pyrev said in his opening remarks. 'From its inception our cinema has grown and developed as an art for the broad masses.'[26]

Luckily for embattled liberals, the extreme hard-line softened in late spring and summer of 1963, partly thanks to pressure from western communists, whose support the Kremlin wanted in disputes with China. *Pravda* ran an editorial on 19 May disclaiming the Party's need to 'watch over every step' taken by intellectuals, 'to explain in detail how to write a book, stage a play, make a film, compose music. Setting forth the main aim of creative work, the Party urges the masters of literature and art to creative boldness and independence.'[27]

A conservative-sponsored plan to amalgamate all creative unions into one was dropped, and jamming of Voice of America radio broadcasts ceased on

19 June. Two days later, when Khrushchev reaffirmed the Party's absolute control of the arts at the Central Committee plenum on art and literature, he mentioned only one film-maker, Mikhail Romm, as having 'incorrect views' about cinema, and added that Soviet artists who had succumbed to 'bourgeois ideas of nonpartisan ideology' constituted a small minority. Ilichev avoided ideology and concentrated on the material losses sustained by the state because of poor management of production schedules.[28]

Khrushchev may have intervened personally to avert a major scandal at the Third International Film Festival, held in Moscow in July. Six jurors from non-communist countries (France, India, Japan, the US, Italy and the United Arab Republic) voted to award first prize to Federico Fellini's *8½*, while nine jurors from Soviet bloc countries voted against. The 'nays' reversed their vote, but the film was not released within the Soviet Union and the press ignored it; *Iskusstvo kino* printed a bare statement of competition results.

Watchful and guarded, the film industry reverted to routinely political evaluations of new films, paying scant attention to individual artistic vision. A review of Aleksei Sakharov's *Colleagues* [Kollegi, 1962], for example, praised dramatically weak scenes that, however, carry the most explicit messages.[29] Words that had receded from the active vocabulary of film criticism years before, such as 'revolutionary pathos' and 'scope' [*masshtabnost'*], re-emerged in an essay on *Optimistic Tragedy* [Optimisticheskaia tragediia, 1964], a political struggle set on board a ship in 1917.[30]

Larisa Kriachko, a relatively sophisticated exponent of Party orthodoxy, disparaged the tendency to evade rather than resolve problems. Sympathy for passive characters, for failures and eccentrics, gives them false significance, she argued.[31] Authors in search of safe cinematic examples and references felt obliged to reach back, past *Cranes are Flying*, to the icons of the past, *Chapaev* and the *Maksim* trilogy.

Artists, film-makers among them, must have greeted the end of 1963 with relief. It had been a nerve-wracking year, and although the Party-led conservative assaults had subsided by the autumn, anxiety lingered.

9. Children of Paradise

B *allad of a Soldier* had no direct epigones. It was at once too simple and too abstract. Its self-contained narrative frame and its nearly unbroken lyric intonation created a completely achieved portrayal of goodness. Alesha Skvortsov's personality, perfect in its own way, belonged to the realm of folklore rather than realistic fiction. Film-makers who wanted to create a contemporary Alesha Skvortsov would almost inevitably sacrifice the 'main quality of a ballad – its grace and structural harmony'.[1] They had to look elsewhere for their heroes.

The hypertrophic and wholly public celebration of Iurii Gagarin's flight into space on 12 April 1961 suggested one possibility. Gagarin's flight appeared to offer an updated version of the heroic paradigm enshrined in the 1930s, when polar ice-breakers, Arctic explorers and aviators such as Chkalov (flying the 'Stalin route') were celebrated in fiction, poetry, in song and on screen.

Upon his return, Gagarin announced, 'I am an ordinary Russian man. There are lots of us in the Soviet Union, dozens and hundreds of young Soviet men and women.'[2] The subtext of his scripted line was plain: the real miracle is not my astounding trip to outer space, but the fact that I am a Soviet, like all of you. As a popular ditty of the time ran, 'How good it is that our Gagarin/ Is no Armenian or Tatarin,/ No Jew, no Lett or Moldovan,/ But just a simple Soviet man.'[3]

An official biography modified and shaped the distinctive facts of Gagarin's life, emphasizing his participation in the common Soviet experience. In this version of his life he witnessed partisan exploits in the Smolensk region and grew up remembering the stench of smoke and fire in his village. His brother and sister, forced into slave labour by the Nazis, managed to escape and served in the Red Army. His favourite book was supposedly Boris Polevoi's *Story of a Real Man*, the harrowing saga of a legless pilot. The destruction of the war left him thirsty for peace.

Gagarin seemed a genuine hero, one ready-made for cinema: 'Let the

Children of Paradise

contemporary hero on our screen be a modest man, full of good-will, practical and hard-working, a man of generous heart and spacious intellect, to whom nothing human is alien,' wrote one critic.

> To be an accurate and enduring image, the [cosmonaut] hero must be shown in struggle. We must witness his difficult victory, we must see that victory demanded … a total effort of mind and heart, we must share the hero's suffering, follow his thoughts, feelings, the forging of his character. Together with the hero we must wonder, doubt, stray from the path to victory, falter and pick ourselves up again … Victory must not await the hero like winning a lottery that has no losers, like an inappropriate gift bestowed by the scriptwriter and director.[4]

Yet despite the barrage of media attention to the flight of the *Vostok* and to Gagarin himself, this living example of a new positive hero, whose feats were performed in the most public sphere conceivable, apparently failed to inspire film-makers or indeed other artists.

Instead, the films of the period reflected a static mood, at least on the surface. Escapist adventures, often set in exotic locations, were popular. Modernized industries continued to overfulfil their plans, misguided characters regularly learned to subordinate wayward impulses to the interests of the collective, kolkhoz chairmen and women presided over remarkable harvests. The protagonist of *A Simple Story* [Prostaia istoriia, 1960], for example, the widow Sasha Potapova (Nonna Mordiukova), manages through persistence and sheer grit to transform three villages, 126 households, and eighty-five disgruntled if able-bodied workers into a model kolkhoz. Films required happy endings, no matter how implausible or inappropriate.

Film-makers sought a cinematic form that could accommodate a less meretricious portrait of reality yet plausibly justify a happy ending, and a hero who could live within the real world yet legitimately retain the innocence of an Alesha Skvortsov. They found one answer in a new kind of hero: the child. In 1960 and 1961 at least half a dozen films featured children or adolescents as their protagonists, including Georgia Danelia and Igor Talankin's *Serezha* and Mikhail Kalik's *Man Follows the Sun* [Chelovek idet za solntsem, 1961].

Of these child-images, the first and purest is the five-year-old protagonist of *Serezha*, played by the entrancing Boria Barkhatov. His first words, addressed to the bigger kids he runs after, proclaim the theme of the film and introduce a larger generational concern: 'You know,' he says with pride and amazement, 'I have a heart!' The feelings prompted by that heart are powerful and unmediated. Happy or sad, Serezha's emotions illuminate the screen. When the other children usurp his brand-new bicycle, the screen fills not with his tearful face but with the leaf on to which his tears drop, one by one.

Danelia and Talankin – the ink barely dry on their diplomas – co-directed *Serezha*; Vera Panova adapted the script from her 1956 novella. Danelia and

The Grand Illusion

16. *Serezha*

Talankin created a cinematic equivalent of the child's fresh point of view, conveying Serezha's wonder at the universe he discovers around him by keeping Anatolii Nitochkin's camera at Serezha's eye-level for much of the film. Even when the camera shoots 'objectively', a small child somewhere in the frame serves to remind us of that perspective, and of the relativity of size. 'We never for a moment forget', one critic aptly observed, 'that this is about a Lilliputian in a land of Gullivers.'[5]

Serezha's small world expands throughout the film, most significantly when his widowed mother remarries. Her sovkhoz-chairman husband Korostelev (Sergei Bondarchuk) brings into Serezha's life both unalloyed delights (the bicycle, a bus ride, a stuffed monkey) and ambiguous ones, chief among the latter a baby brother. When Korostelev is given a new assignment, far away, the adults decide to leave Serezha behind until he fully recovers from a fever. Korostelev carefully explains the concept of duty to Serezha, giving him lessons in 'how to be a man' ('There is a word, *must* ... '). But Serezha has given Korostelev lessons too, in how to be a caring human being, and Korostelev shows himself an apt pupil. In a last-minute *volte-face*, his feelings overrule logic. He scoops Serezha up in his arms and they ride off. The heart triumphs.

Korostelev is sensitive, principled and loving, but he is an adult. This film belongs to the children, especially to Serezha. The youngest and smallest of the village children, he is often overlooked, even by the kindly older boy Vasia who lets him tag along. But Serezha always watches and listens and tries to understand. Neither Panova's script nor Danelia and Talankin's direction is condescending towards Serezha; his apprehension of what he sees around him is given as much weight as any adult's 'mature' understanding.[6] His convictions emerge from observing those around him, and he judges accordingly. When a visitor ceremoniously presents Serezha with a candy that turns out to be an empty wrapper, and then laughs uproariously at his own trick, Serezha matter-of-factly calls him a fool.

Danelia and Talankin validate such truth-telling in their own approach to film-making. At one point Serezha and Korostelev watch the 'News of the Day' newsreel projected onto a screen at the sovkhoz. The sovkhoz *is* the news of the day, having overfulfilled the planned targets for milk and meat deliveries. On screen, Korostelev wears a hat and suit, the only time we see him dressed so formally, and he speaks stiffly. Korostelev's discomfort in front of the camera contrasts with his usual warmth and energy, manifest in the very next scene when he strides around the sovkhoz itself.

The viewers watching themselves on screen like what they see. They find the clichés and lack of spontaneity appropriate, and ask the projectionist to run the newsreel again and again. But Danelia and Talankin challenge that attitude. They show that life begins outside the auditorium, on the roads and fields of the sovkhoz, and that the life of the actual sovkhoz is far more complex and absorbing than the artifice of the so-called 'actuality' caught (or invented) in the newsreel.

Danelia and Talankin tried in *Serezha* to fashion a new Soviet man from scratch, without the deformations of Soviet history. Subsequent heroes (Alesha in Tumanov and Shchukin's *Aleshka's Love* [Aleshkina liubov', 1960], Sandu in Kalik's *Man Follows the Sun*) are adolescent Serezhas, a few years older but retaining his integrity and appealing purity. None of these films problematizes sentiment or sentimentality; on the contrary, sentimentality is simply 'one more argument in behalf of ennobling, liberating, redemptive feelings and experiences'.[7] It was a persuasive argument, and one that audiences welcomed. Practised critics found ways to reconcile the apolitical virtues of these films with the requisite ideological baggage. One otherwise sensitive analysis of *Serezha*, for instance, attributes the child's fresh perceptions to his luck in living in a land of discovery that is 'outstripping other [nations] along unknown roads ... [A]udiences discover for themselves the spiritual wealth and sunny world-view of a new society.'[8]

Certainly all these films about children and adolescents are optimistic and affirmative, strikingly so in comparison with contemporary West European films about children, such as Truffaut's 1959 *Four Hundred Blows* [Les Quatre cents coups]. Even Andrei Tarkovskii, in *The Steamroller and the Violin* [Katok i skripka, 1960] – the forty-five-minute 'diploma' film he made to fulfil graduation requirements at the Institute of Cinematography – does not explicitly reject such optimism.[9] Its heroes, seven-year-old Sasha the violinist and Sergei, the steamroller operator working on his street, become genuinely attached to each other. Forming a traditional worker–*intelligent* alliance, they learn from each other: Sergei teaches Sasha about manhood and protecting the weak, Sasha reciprocates with the power of art.

In *Steamroller*, as in *Serezha* and other films, the 'good mother' is a male figure who displaces the biological mother; he demonstrates more love and understanding towards the child than the 'natural' parent. When Serezha calls the visitor who tricked him a fool, his mother punishes him for his impertinence, while Korostelev simply endorses the obvious: the man *is* a fool. In *Steamroller*, Sasha's mother is cold and forbidding, abbreviated with Gogolian terseness to a fashionable skirt and hat, stockinged legs and high heels. She personifies a rulebook mentality and the stifling power of convention, preventing Sasha from keeping a date with Sergei (to see *Chapaev*!) because the worker is a stranger to her.

If Tarkovskii shared Danelia and Talankin's preference for a young hero, he sharply disputed their predilection for reality over art. They included the newsreel scene in *Serezha* in order to reject art's 'illusory' potential; they embrace its devices, such as contrived camera angles, only as a means of depicting reality from a particular point of view. In *The Steamroller and the Violin*, by contrast, reality assumes menacing forms: Sasha's sinister mother; a pecking order dramatically symbolized by a small boy hitting a smaller boy for no reason whatever; the ambush plotted by Sasha's neighbours, children who scorn him as 'the musician'. Art, however, can blot out ugliness and beautify reality. Sasha's violin-playing enthrals and transports Sergei. The bevelled mirror Sasha spots in a shop window multiplies a ray of sunlight into a brilliant explosion of light.

In Kalik's *Man Follows the Sun*, art's magic accompanies the hero on his journey of (self-)discovery. Sandu's exploration combines elements of Alesha Skvortsov's moral education in *Ballad* with Serezha's exploration of the larger world. In the course of a day, Sandu encounters life's tragedies and life's joys, from a soccer-mad shoeshine man, who lost his legs in the war, to a baby's birth. He witnesses the beauty of a glorious garden, with sunflowers in one corner planted by the girl gardener to remind her of her village, and the malice of a bureaucrat who lops the heads off the sunflowers.

Sandu discovers a world full of natural light, towards which people gravitate as naturally as sunflowers turn their heads to follow the sun. But art enhances its beauty: a pair of magical eyeglasses can turn the world red, blue, green … In his final dream, Sandu himself becomes a kind of artist or perhaps a sorcerer's apprentice. He restores the bootblack's legs and the flowers' heads, and he transforms the bureaucrat into what he really is, a mannequin.

Films about adults were not permitted the freedom and fancy of child-oriented movies. In 1960 Semen Lungin and Ilia Nusinov fashioned an action-packed script out of the memoir of an old Party member who had returned from the Gulag. Before the 1917 Revolution, he mentioned in passing, he had been involved in smuggling political prisoners abroad. As directed by Mikhail Shveitser, *Midshipman Panin* [Michman Panin] manipulates the standard material of revolutionary commitment into a semi-realistic, semi-fantastic adventure movie culminating in a courtroom drama.

When Panin takes the stand during his trial, he describes his sojourn in France, actually spent in revolutionary activity, as a relentless round of gambling and whoring. He borrows corroborative details from the lurid fiction he read while under house-arrest, lent him by a friendly tsarist captain. His 'testimony' is cleverly shot as a flashback, without words but with a silent-movie melodrama score; its images of dissipation are so delicious that the men in the courtroom – including one envious judge – deem such a month worth any punishment.

Predictably, orthodox voices disparaged the liberties *Midshipman Panin* takes with doctrinal truth as falsifications of historical reality. The film makes the tsarist officer who helps Panin entirely too sympathetic, they said, and Panin himself was a poor excuse for a communist. In the original version of the film Lenin appears in several scenes, but the actor playing Lenin displeased the ideologues. Shveitser refused to reshoot the scenes with another actor, and the film was shelved until Shveitser agreed to cut those scenes entirely and substitute a letter sent by Lenin to Panin.[10] The patronage of an old Bolshevik who had known Lenin helped to win the film's release. 'After all,' she commented, 'this is an artistic work. There has to be some invention in it.'[11]

As always, cinema reflected – however obliquely – the moods of the period, and the movies of 1960 and 1961 teem with contradictions. Truthful moments and ambiguous images co-exist with and occasionally confute the obvious messages. The women of Sasha's kolkhoz in *A Simple Story*, for instance, who sleep alone in their cold and empty beds, are far more convincing in their bitter anger than when the camera pans their smiling, hopeful faces at the end.

Similar inconsistencies characterize two films that seemed to lend support to Khrushchev's flourishing anti-religious campaign. The campaign itself had been launched several years earlier with the forcible closing of churches. Moscow's immense outdoor swimming pool, built on the site of the Cathedral of Christ the Saviour razed by Stalin in 1931, opened in 1958, and the monthly journal *Science and Religion* [Nauka i religiia] began publication in 1959. In the early 1960s Party militancy intensified to combat clandestine religious sects and the yearning, apparent even among non-believers, for answers to moral and ethical questions that politics and ideology could not adequately address.[12]

The Grand Illusion

In 1960 Vladimir Skuibin directed *The Miracle Worker* [Chudotvornaia], Vladimir Tendriakov's adaptation of his own 1958 novella. In the remote northern landscapes of Russia, twelve-year-old Rodia clashes with his traditional mother and grandmother when he finds a 'miracle-working' icon. (In the novella Rodia is taught that science can disprove superstition: his physics teacher explains a mysterious noise in the local church as an acoustic echo of passing trains.)[13] Ancient village tradition designates as a saint whoever finds the icon, and the women force Rodia, a Young Pioneer, to 'become Christian', to pray and wear a cross. They beat him when he tries to destroy the icon. A desperate Rodia throws himself in the river; his teacher rescues him.

It was possible to interpret *The Miracle Worker* as a broadside against religious faith, 'initiating for the first time in many years a cinematic discussion of the most ancient and one of the most dangerous deceptions in human history', as one reviewer wrote.[14] Yet *The Miracle Worker* is ambiguous about such faith, affirming at the very least the vitality of religion in Russia; it seems as if every village woman in *The Miracle Worker* is a believer.

Similar ambiguity qualified Vasilii Ordynskii's *Clouds over Borsk* [Tuchi nad Borskom, 1960], a film originally blessed by the KGB. When writers Lungin and Nusinov had turned to the KGB for information on religious sects, the KGB identified a group that believed in speaking in tongues and sent the pair off to a prayer meeting. But the film proved 'overly sympathetic' to the heroine's religious experience; Lungin and Nusinov suggest complex and often compelling reasons for choosing religious over secular creeds. As a result *Borsk* was initially shelved as 'politically harmful', a ban reversed thanks to a KGB officer who, after watching the first scene and enjoying the first song, authorized the film's distribution.[15]

Anticipating by several months the second stage of de-Stalinization of the Twenty-second Party Congress, in May 1961 Grigorii Chukhrai released a film that tackled with unusual candour the Party's ostracism of Soviet prisoners of war after their return home. *Clear Skies* [Chistoe nebo] meshes – via awkward flashbacks – two stories, the first a romance set during the war, the second a post-war drama, both featuring Evgenii Urbanskii as Aleksei Astakhov and the diminutive Nina Drobysheva as Sasha.

Chukhrai relies on conventional if well-drawn portraits and striking *mise-en-scène* in the otherwise banal first half of *Clear Skies*, where Astakhov, a famous pilot, performs exploits that are celebrated in newscasts, is wooed and won by Sasha, and receives posthumous decorations after being reported killed in action. Indeed, Chukhrai stakes out his place in the classical Russian realist tradition by including cinematic quotations from the greatest literary practitioner of that tradition, Lev Tolstoi: Sasha's first meeting with Astakhov, when he comes to her older sister's party, deliberately evokes Natasha Rostov's entrance in *War and Peace*, and her teenage flirtation with a boyfriend in the school

17. *Clear Skies*

library, conducted soundlessly via Pushkin quotations from the text in front of them, evokes Levin and Kitty's communication at the billiard table in *Anna Karenina*.

One wordless scene is particularly effective. A troop train passes through the local station where a throng of lonely women wait in the hopes of catching a glimpse of their men. They hand around a small mirror, squinting to smooth back their hair and pinch colour into their drawn cheeks. But they primp in vain; the train races past the platform in a blur of noise and motion. Not one visage can be discerned.

When Astakhov comes home after the war, having survived a German PoW camp, his ugly physical scars are trivial compared to the psychic wounds inflicted on him by his own society. He has no place in this post-war world. He is not allowed to resume flying because, as a former PoW, he is automatically suspect. A Party member articulates the distrust that so often hounded returning PoWs: 'It would be interesting to know what he did while he was a prisoner. Why didn't he escape?'

Astakhov remains an idealist who believes that the 'great goal' justifies any means and outweighs the fates of individuals. 'When a forest is chopped down, chips fly,' he quotes Stalin. But his bitterness erupts when Sasha guilelessly wonders why the Party blames him: 'I'm guilty because my plane was shot down. I'm guilty because when I was half-dead they took me prisoner! I'm guilty because I ran, and got caught ... I'm guilty because I wasn't shot, because I didn't go up in smoke.'

The war between idealism and scepticism blazes up in a row between Astakhov and Sasha's younger brother Sergei. 'Words, words!' Sergei spits out in disgust. 'I've had it up to here with all those pretty words!' He fiercely spurns Astakhov's tired formula, 'when I was your age ... ': 'Next you'll say that I didn't storm the Winter Palace, that I didn't fight in the Great Fatherland. Well, I didn't storm it, and I didn't fight. So what?' And when Astakhov charges him with cynicism, Sergei cruelly retorts:

> 'Where is it, your justice? I was still sitting on a potty when you were already flying planes. You fought the Germans, you sat in a camp. I was proud of you ... And what happened? You're a trainee and I'm a trainee. We get the same salary! So where's your famous justice? ... I know you're a real communist. Okay, you're a communist! Then why aren't you in the Party?'

Wounded almost beyond speech, Astakhov replies, 'Apparently that's how it needs to be' [*Znachit, tak nuzhno*]. 'Why?' Sergei hurls back. 'Who needs it? I'm asking you, who? Her [Sasha]? Me? ... The Party? Or maybe the powers you fought for?' Astakhov has no answer.

Anninskii remembered the impact of this scene: 'In 1961,' he wrote, 'when similar arguments were spreading like wildfire from poetry readings to the pages of prose, from prose to theatre stages, such a dialogue between the representatives of two generations hit a nerve and looked like a real argument between real people.'[16] Casting heightened the tension: Oleg Tabakov, one of the most talented younger actors, played Sergei, while Urbanskii had the weight of the one-legged soldier from *Ballad* and Vasilii Gubanov (*The Communist*) behind him; indeed, his Astakhov extends Gubanov's earthbound, indomitable, stubborn power.

In *Clear Skies* the situation radically alters almost the moment that Stalin dies. Chukhrai abandons Tolstoi for Pudovkin and Eisenstein, quoting film images of revolutionary idealism to depict the impact and meaning of the thaw. Ice blocks break up and melting water rushes downstream; a montage that could come from any Eisenstein film unites workers and machines. When the Party summons Astakhov, he reassures a worried Sasha that 'times have changed', and emerges from Party HQ unsmiling but vindicated, his Party membership restored and a medal in his hand.

Both the montages and the dialogue may seem hopelessly trite today, but as the first such references on screen, they were explosive: 'A person with a clean dossier has the future open to him with no obstacles, while one unclear item clouds a man's whole life. Alas, this absurd approach to people took root at one time and became an unwritten law,' one contemporary critic wrote.[17] Sasha herself, though symbolizing the force of love, embodies the double-think of the period. She believes in Astakhov's innocence, yet accepts the need to prove innocence, not guilt. Trusting Astakhov, she trusts equally in the principle that is destroying him. Nothing in her life enables her to conceive that the ideas expressed by the Party committee might be false.

The energies and tensions expressed in *Clear Skies* were accumulating below the relatively placid surface of Soviet society. Sergei resembled the young men who populated Vasilii Aksenov's popular fiction. In Aksenov's 1959 novel *Colleagues*, for instance, one of the heroes shares Sergei's disgust with hollow rhetoric:

> 'Ugh, I'm fed up with all of this! With all these high-flown words! ... A great many idealists pronounce them, but so do thousands of scoundrels ... They've become tinsel. Let's do without the babble. I love my country, I'd give up an arm, a leg, my life for it without thinking, but I answer only to my own conscience, not to some verbal fetishes. They only get in the way of seeing real life.'[18]

Words were at once crucial and impotent, debased by overuse yet the *sine qua non* for an authentic life. In Shilova's recollection, the thaw *meant* words: 'People started to talk and could not talk themselves out. In and of itself that was a great joy.' Words had immense psychological power, they could overcome fear and censorship. She continued: 'In the general context, however, the newly empowered word already began to sense its limited opportunities. It existed as if separately, in the domain of discussion, and could extend its power neither to intimate relations between people ... nor to the sphere of practicality.'[19]

No film expressed this duality better than Alov and Naumov's *Peace to Him Who Enters* [Mir vkhodiashchemu], released in September 1961. Set in and near Berlin on the last day of the war, *Peace* traces the journey of three Russian soldiers, assigned to transport an official dispatch and a heavily pregnant German woman. Words serve as nearly impermeable barriers, isolating even the three Russians, who supposedly share a common language. One of the three soldiers, Iamshchikov, is concussed, deafened and mute. The second, the driver Rukavitsyn, jabbers incessantly, to his own face in the truck mirror when no other listener is available. The third, Junior Lieutenant Ivlev, fresh out of military training school and hungry for action, spouts textbook maxims that everyone with actual war experience knows to be nonsense.

The Russians cannot understand the German woman, nor she them. They can converse with a group of former concentration camp inmates only thanks to one man who knows a little Russian. A lanky American GI, whose Studebaker Ivlev commandeers, shouts and trades punches in lieu of talking.

The Grand Illusion

18. *Peace to Him Who Enters*

The film's final image is hopeful: urine from the newborn baby splashes on to a pile of weapons. Yet *Peace to Him Who Enters* is a bleak movie. Virtually every attempt at contact fails. The German woman is so terrified of the Russians that she slaps Iamshchikov, the closest to a heroic figure in the film, and jumps off the truck. With nowhere to go, she huddles on the road in a blinding downpour until Iamshchikov brings her an umbrella and walks her back to the truck. She pleads for forgiveness; he cannot hear her.

At one point the Russians exchange first names (Pasha, Shura) with the German woman, domesticating her Teutonic Barbara to the Slavic Varia. Individual human identities seem to supersede national differences. But soon thereafter she, perhaps artlessly but none the less treacherously, points them in the wrong direction at a crossroads. In the ensuing ambush Rukavitsyn (Pasha) perishes, a death that calls into question any affirmation of shared humanity.

Unlike *Ballad of a Soldier*, in which Alesha's decency is reciprocated, *Peace* offers goodness without recompense. Kindness fails to unite people, as language fails to achieve clarity or communication. In *Ballad* war was unpeopled, an empty field where clumsy tanks inexorably pursue a solitary human figure. The camera flipped over, capturing an absurd and unnatural reality. Alov and

Naumov's war is chaotic and full of people; the camera remains right-side-up, since reality itself is upside-down.

The cultural bureaucrats at the Ministry of Culture who saw *Peace to Him Who Enters* in November 1960 exploded in anger. 'Slander of the Soviet Army!' vied with 'Get rid of the film together with the directors!' 'How could they film such rubbish?' led to 'The film must not be released, and its authors must answer for it!'[20] The portrayal of Soviet people as 'crude and vulgar', 'ugly, at times even repellent', unsettled and offended Anatolii Golovnia, who had worked with Pudovkin on *Mother* and *End of St Petersburg*. 'Even in wartime our people were beautiful,' he asserted, 'when they were moved by patriotism and selflessness in the name of the Motherland.'[21]

Given such outrage, Alov and Naumov were lucky to have the friendship of Minister of Culture Ekaterina Furtseva. Like her cordially detested predecessor as Minister of Culture, N. Mikhailov, Furtseva had tried to dissuade Alov and Naumov from making the film, and she voiced her displeasure at their work during the Ministry of Culture discussion. ('Did you think about the Soviet veteran? ... The characters are servile, nearly bestial ... As Chernyshevskii said, "Man must be beautiful in body and soul".')[22] However, because she liked the two directors personally, she took *Peace to Him Who Enters* with her to the 1961 Venice Film Festival, where it won a special gold medal for 'originality and innovation', as well as an award from Italian film critics. Foreign acclaim helped win authorization for (restricted) distribution of the film within the Soviet Union.[23] Critics objected to Alov and Naumov's unconventional version of war, as they had to Iakov Segel's *First Day of Peace* [Pervyi den' mira] (1959), and as they would to Bulat Okudzhava's autobiographical novella *Lots of Luck, Schoolboy!* [Bud' zdorov, shkoliar!], included in the 1961 literary anthology *Pages from Tarussa*. Films ought to celebrate, with unambiguous joy, the victorious conclusion of four years of war, and the defeat of Nazism; they ought not intimate the fragility of peace. 'That's not how we recall the first day of peace,' one reviewer had written of the Segel film. 'Not with mournful melodies, but with the greatness of the nation's soul.'[24]

Their failure to distinguish between 'just' and 'unjust' wars and their focus on the irrationality, chaos and victims of war branded Alov and Naumov (like Okudzhava) as 'pacifists'. *Peace to Him Who Enters* betrayed symptoms of 'Remarquism', a diagnosis repeated when Grigorii Baklanov and Vasilii Bykov published war novels a few years later: that is, 'painting war in such dark colours [as to imply] that war itself was wrong'.[25]

In the conservative monthly magazine *October*, Lenina Ivanova indicted Alov and Naumov for sentimentality and 'false humanism':

Now, years after [the war's end], it is obvious that what awaited 'him who entered' was not peace but an ongoing struggle. And difficult circumstances, and

The Grand Illusion

doubts, and mistakes, and hostile influences, and – most important – the need to choose sides in this continuing battle in the world ... It is not for our [Soviet] art to soften the contradictions, to replace stern, courageous truth with sweet, false words![26]

Her belligerence typified the increasing polarization that, in the autumn of 1961, preceded the Twenty-second Party Congress.

10. Lost Horizon

L enfilm released one of the first films that responded (indirectly) to the father–son tension implicit in the revelations of the Twenty-second Congress. *The Amphibious Man* [Chelovek-amfibiia], based on a popular story by Vladimir Beliaev, became the top box-office success of 1962, though critics deplored its 'vulgarity'.[1] Co-directors Gennadii Kazanskii and Vladimir Chebotarev made no other films of distinction, but they scored a hit with *The Amphibious Man*, an engaging mixture of science fiction, romantic adventure and exotic underwater photography. Its script features a brilliant scientist, Dr Salvator, who dreams of establishing an underwater society where equality and justice will reign. The first and sole citizen of this Utopia is his amphibious son Ikhtiandr, into whom Salvator transplanted shark's gills during a childhood illness. Ikhtiandr has thrived in his oceanic eden of undulating flora and translucent, beneficent sea creatures. He has known no human except his father; he is emotionally virgin.

And then he rescues a drowning maiden, the good and beautiful Guttiera. Smitten, he loses his contentment and goes out into the world to locate her. Guttiera meanwhile marries the wicked Don Pedro in order to save her father from debtors' prison. Eventually Don Pedro is thwarted and the young lovers find each other, but despite their mutual attachment they must part, she to remain on land and he to return to the sea he needs to survive.

The Amphibious Man borrowed many elements familiar from dystopian fiction, such as Huxley's *Brave New World* and Zamiatin's *We* (at that time still unpublished in the Soviet Union), and film, such as Fritz Lang's *Metropolis*. It shared themes with Eldar Riazanov's allegorical comedy, *The Man from Nowhere* [Chelovek niotkuda], released for a very brief run less than a year earlier, in which an anthropologist discovers and brings back to Moscow a stone-age man, Chudak (Eccentric).[2] Both Chudak and Ikhtiandr have kind hearts, but because they deviate from the norm they are feared. Both fall in love at first sight ('Is there any other way?' Ikhtiandr asks gravely), and, untrammelled by society's conventions and hypocrisy, declare their love forthrightly. (Chudak literally shouts it from the rooftop of Moscow's Luzhniki stadium.) Neither can grasp the meaning of ownership or of money, as Ikhtiandr confirms when, Christ-like, he distributes a basketful of fish to hungry children. Puzzled by the fisherman's anger, he gives him a wad of currency, and is just as bewildered by the fisherman's delight.

As is typical for this genre, love spurs enlightenment: the hero, seeking his beloved, travels through realms of reality hitherto unknown to him. In *Metropolis*, Fritz Lang's Freder sets out to find his Maria; before he can, he must first encounter both the gruelling world of the workers and the fleshpots of the gilded youth. Similarly, Ikhtiandr wanders the noisy, colourful streets of a vast port, dismayed by cramped courtyards and dazzled by its man-made wonders.

When Ikhtiandr's father Salvator unfolds his vision to a journalist, Olsen, he meets a sceptical response: given human nature, Olsen cautions, people will long for *this* world, however imperfect, no matter how beautiful *that* world. Ikhtiandr proves Olsen's point. 'I no longer want to live among the fish,' Ikhtiandr tells his father. 'I'm dying of anguish ... If I'm a man, I have the right to love.' Love humanizes even Don Pedro, whose demonic qualities are signalled by a Mephistophelean moustache and backlighting. He genuinely loves Guttiera, and does not force himself on her, despite the scorn of a grotesque hag who derides him as a 'dishrag" and taunts him to 'be a man' or 'sleep like a dog on [Guttiera's] threshold'.

Beyond its common themes with dystopian art generally, *The Amphibious Man* reflects the particular Soviet preoccupation with the broad issue of fathers and sons, and the film industry's pattern of collaboration between members of the older and younger generation. *The Amphibious Man*, co-directed by the fifty-one-year-old Genadii Kazanskii (whose career began in the early 1930s) and the thirty-year-old Vladimir Chebotarev (a 1952 graduate of the State Institute of Cinematography), comes down squarely on the side of the children, who are paying for the dreams and desires of their fathers. Both fathers love their children, yet both exploit them, Guttiera's father out of selfish motives and Dr Salvator out of idealistic ones. Once cognizant of the harm they have done their children, they try to make reparation. Guttiera's father helps her escape from her marital prison and Dr Salvator trades places with Ikhtiandr, who is dying from lack of water in prison. 'I wanted to make you the happiest of men,' he apologizes. 'And instead I made you unhappy. Forgive me.'

The obsessed scientist frequently figures in works of political fantasy-*cum*-science-fiction (Rotwang in *Metropolis*, Kubrick's Dr Strangelove, Dr Persikov in Bulgakov's *Fatal Eggs*). Dr Salvator deludes himself with the thought that he does not 'interfere in politics', yet his ambition to use science to create a paradise where the poor and unfortunate will dwell in harmony and egalitarian happiness is patently political. Like Dr Persikov's Red Ray, Salvator's 'experiment' in *The Amphibious Man* is an obvious analogue to the utopian experiment of the Bolsheviks.

Salvator's profession also had specific relevance to the intense debate waged by Soviets on the social role and responsibility of science. By 1961 and 1962, scientists had edged out geologists as the most modern of heroes, a cross between magicians – modern alchemists – and cult-idols, 'tenors' of the twentieth century.[3] Boris Slutskii provided the name for the polemic in his 1960 poem 'Physicists and Lyricists' [*'Fiziki i liriki'*]. In the age of atomic energy, cybernetics and space travel, he wrote, science had surpassed the popularity of poetry and eclipsed literature in imagination; its language 'resonated like contemporary music'. Indeed, arts journals abounded with words like 'quantum' and 'light years' and references to Nils Bohr; readers snapped up Fermi's memoirs.[4]

The controversy involved genuine ambivalence towards scientific progress, with its exciting galactic exploration, on the one hand, and the dangers of thermonuclear weapons and nuclear radiation, on the other. Scientists understood the perils of nuclear policy, and those in the 'liberal' wing advocated increased dialogue with foreign scientists. Andrei Sakharov tried and failed to halt the series of nuclear tests planned for 1961–62, convinced that it was 'no longer necessary on scientific grounds, but was being undertaken for purely political reasons'.[5] Fiction often scrutinized the issue, sometimes within an anti-American context. And the debate provided a framework for *Nine Days of a Year* [Deviat' dnei odnogo goda], Mikhail Romm's first film in nearly six years and one of the screen sensations of 1962.

The sixty-year-old Romm wrote the script for *Nine Days* together with Daniil Khrabrovitskii, a much younger colleague. (Romm's cameraman, German Lavrov, was thirty-one and had shot one feature film.) The two men first became acquainted a few years earlier, when Romm ran an experimental mini-studio within Mosfilm meant to encourage new work and younger film-makers. The mini-studio's remarkable autonomy, with weekly discussions of ongoing work held behind closed doors to stimulate candour, attracted the most innovative and original of the younger generation, including Alov and Naumov, Chukhrai, Shveitser and Vladimir Ordynskii. Ordynskii had directed Khrabrovitskii's first screenplay, *Four of Them* [Chetvero, 1958], and brought him along.

By 1960, Romm's studio had been shut down and he had lost his position at the Institute of Cinematography.[6] He was available, and as part of his creative credo – a tacit repudiation of his own earlier compromises – he was actively seeking contemporary subjects. Romm vowed to make films only about people he knew, only about contemporary material, only about subjects that genuinely engaged him, and with whatever aesthetic approach he considered appropriate.[7]

The studio urged Khrabrovitskii to write a script about physicists, while Romm had read an article in *Ogonek* about an intriguing case of irradiation. In reality the physicists recovered, but Romm rejected this 'fairytale' ending in

The Grand Illusion

favour of a far more likely tragic resolution. Khrabrovitskii feared official disapprobation: 'In our country they don't like deaths' [*U nas smertei ne liubiat*], he knew. Indeed, objections were raised on this point with the first very sketchy version of the script, dated 19 April 1960: two of the four handwritten comments on the cover sheet question the doom-laden ending.[8] But Romm insisted and, as the film ends, the hero is dying.

The script took shape mainly in the summer of 1960. In the early 1960s, perhaps because of the successful flights of cosmonauts Gagarin and Titov, Khrushchev felt sufficiently self-confident to moderate the secrecy that had shrouded scientific establishments. He established Akademgorodok near Novosibirsk and opened up Dubna, a centre for theoretical research in atomic physics on the Volga. Nevertheless, when Romm and Khrabrovitskii first applied for permission to meet nuclear physicists at a closed institute, the authorities pretended total ignorance of any such place. Thanks to the help of leading physicists Igor Tamm and Lev Landau, Romm and Khrabrovitskii were eventually able to visit Bolshevo, a secret research institution, and observe scientists at work.

Romm and Khrabrovitskii developed a script driven not by plot but by ideas. The two main characters incarnate ideas: brilliant, obsessed and doomed Gusev (Aleksei Batalov), and Innokentii Smoktunovskii's Kulikov, equally brilliant and with the self-assurance of a spoiled only child for whom everything comes easy. Aleksei Batalov recalled his excitement when he read the script:

> In those days physics, physicists, their discoveries and problems – all that was perhaps the most animated point of discussion among young people. Disputes and arguments raged, as much about physicists and poets as about the new morality, about Picasso's paintings, and so on. It was just then that the fog finally cleared, revealing what just the day before had been shrouded in deep mystery. The action took place in a world no one had known about before. It's hard to imagine today, but before Romm no one (except the narrowest of specialists) – not just in the Soviet Union but all over the world – had seen these installations and labs ... For us then it was like making a picture about Martians. No one knew how they lived, how they worked, what they talked about.[9]

When Romm, Khrabrovitskii and two actors read the script aloud at VGIK, the primarily student audience shared Batalov's excitement.[10] So did Mosfilm, which approved the fourth version of the script on 6 December 1960. Finally, a hero – better, *two* heroes, both young, intelligent and serious, both committed to their work. Romm and Khrabrovitskii had deliberately spurned the 'absent-minded professor' cliché, and their colleagues applauded: 'Why does a scientist have to be an Einstein, either a fool or some kind of god?' one queried.[11]

The lightweight and two-dimensional heroine, Lelia, however, dissatisfied nearly everyone. Gusev's lover for six years, she has grown tired of his obsessive devotion to his work, and decides to marry Kulikov. She abruptly reverses her decision and marries Gusev after learning that he has been irradiated in a lab accident. Her decision made no sense, except to those who shrugged it off as typical feminine waywardness. ('Women are complicated,' one man observed sagely, 'you never know what to expect from them.') Chukhrai put his finger on the problem: 'Right now this woman acts the way the scriptwriters want, and not the way real flesh-and-blood people … actually behave.'[12]

Nine Days deals with sensitive political issues: splitting the atom, its potential as a destructive tool, the short- and long-term goals of scientific research. A high official in the atomic energy division of the Council of Ministries, to whom the script had been sent for vetting, admitted that it contained no secret information, but felt it distorted work conditions: 'The authors of the scenario turn this one case of irradiation into a law, suggesting that the danger of radiation is inevitable.'[13]

Such hopelessness dismayed Mosfilm, as well. When large chunks of the nearly finished film were screened a year later, several people feared that the film might not be approved because it was too gloomy, and also too non-committal – always a sticking point for the 'organizations on whom acceptance or rejection of the picture depends … In each of our pictures the author's idea and point of view must be expressed with perfect clarity,' one man warned.[14]

Romm understood the pitfalls. He chose to confront them head on. When he rose to speak, he recalled Oppenheimer's opposition to the building of the hydrogen bomb as inevitably spurring a destructive and unwinnable arms race between the USA and the USSR. He cited Oppenheimer's testimony before the United States Senate in 1954, adding delphically, 'Oppenheimer's extremely interesting argument would have been unthinkable here. None of our physicists simply could have thought that way or come to such a conclusion. Over there, as you see, physicists have their own thoughts' [*U nikh, kak vy vidite, odinokovye mysli u uchenykh*]. He concluded incontrovertibly, 'The difference between those atomic physicists and our own is that they work for capitalism while ours work for socialism.'[15]

When the film was finished, Romm used his considerable skill and experience to steer it through official channels. Since he knew that some scientists from atomic energy research labs were opposed to its release, he arranged a screening at the Academy of Sciences. The distinguished audience included Mstislav Keldysh, president of the Academy, as well as academicians Skobeltsin, Prokhorov, Tamm and Basov. As the lights went up, there was silence, and Romm asked Keldysh whether he liked the film. When Keldysh nodded, Romm asked him to tell Furtseva. Keldysh agreed, and his approval was decisive in getting the film released.[16]

Actor-director Rolan Bykov recalled that when a director knew his movie might provoke opposition, he would 'confide' in one or two people that an important personage – a Politburo member, perhaps, identified solely by his first name and patronymic – had seen the picture and raved about it. The gossip would percolate up to the bosses. And 'though everyone knew that the director could have made the whole thing up, the slight possibility ("And what if? ... ") was enough to clear the path of hurdles'. In the case of *Nine Days*, Romm borrowed this manoeuvre to manipulate Leningrad Party members gathered expectantly for a screening. Before the lights were dimmed, in the taut silence, Romm walked to the front of the auditorium and announced, 'I showed the picture to the Politburo. They liked it very much ... And now let us begin!'[17]

Tension permeates *Nine Days*. The film begins with an accidental irradiation and ends with Gusev's almost certain death. The human triangle itself is unstable, at times dominated by the sexual alliances, at other times by the intimacy between the two intellectual equals, Gusev and Kulikov. And camera and *mise-en-scène* significantly contribute to the tension. The film is shot in black and white, in a style reminiscent of German films of the 1920s. Foreshortened angles and compositional contrast convey a sense of anxiety, like the disorienting painted sets of *The Cabinet of Dr Caligari*.

News of the first accident travels visually: the camera slowly dollies down a dark corridor towards a steep flight of stairs deep in the background, while white-coated figures run inexplicably in both directions. The set design is geometric and austere, and people are often shot from a low angle against a bare wall, with no curves, pictures or decorations to soften the starkness. In the institute, heavy doors, elaborate banks of controls, an oversized desk and a network of massive interlocking pipes add to the aura of dread.[18] So does the absence of music: Romm decided at the last minute to discard the score that had been composed for the film, so as not to distract attention from its ideas.[19] Against the background hush, the ongoing arguments of the intelligentsia, spoken aloud or inwardly voiced thoughts, are all the more audible.

Nine Days is above all a movie of words. After the first accident the fatally stricken older scientist, Dr Svintsov, feverishly pours out a torrent of words, aware he has little time left to express his thoughts. Kulikov chatters incessantly, peppering his stream of words with his trademark phrase 'so to speak' [*tak skazat'*]. Lelia thinks aloud, the scientists in the hallways of the institute quarrel, the guests at Gusev and Lelia's wedding party cannot shut up.[20]

Talk does not merely replace action in *Nine Days*, talk *becomes* action: the film documents the 'destruction of silence' signified by the thaw and celebrates the polyphony that triumphed over unitary, unindividualized speech.[21] As Wiktor Woroszylski commented at the time, Romm broke all the rules about dialogue, yet produced 'the best dialogue I've heard in film ... [Dialogue] constitutes the film'.[22]

Gusev alone is taciturn. He listens silently to Svintsov's linguistic deluge, he is mute when Lelia presses him for explanations. But his silence and Kulikov's logorrhoea are two sides of the same coin, a distaste for inflated rhetoric.

Kulikov plays with the rhetoric via ironic inversion and parody; Gusev avoids it altogether. The result is that neither one is left with a language in which to express feelings, whence derives much of Lelia's frustration. The love of these two exceptional men for her is barely convincing; they reserve their passion for ideas.

Gusev abandons his reticence only once, during an argument with Kulikov about their work and its long-term benefits for mankind. For Gusev, scientific research is a means to an end, providing sources of energy. Kulikov sardonically notes the human preference for destruction: 'Scientists perfected chemistry – and the Germans created poison gas. The principle of internal combustion was discovered – and the English built tanks. Atomic reactors – and the Americans dropped a bomb on Hiroshima.'

Gusev embodies the dedicated personality, the self-sacrificing scientist, whose pedigree stretches from Pasteur to Chekhov's Dr Dymov in 'The Grasshopper' and Pasternak's Zhivago. The fear of radiation, however, is new. Soviet literature in the early 1960s offered a number of such scientists, including the hero of Aksenov's *Ticket to the Stars* and the two physicists in Granin's *Into the Storm*, who are based on Tamm and Landau. Writers had also devised plots involving scientific accidents: I. Grekova's *Beyond the Checkpoint*, Chakovskii's *Light of a Distant Star*.[23] In Gusev's case, obsession is humanized by Batalov's intellectual charm and the humour the script allows him. But he remains predictable, a slightly dated figure, right down to his peasant roots. (Batalov's appearance and demeanour contradict Gusev's background: he and his peasant father share nothing except a distaste for fine words.)[24]

Lelia, the woman who garners little emotional reward for sacrificing herself for her beloved, remains as flat as she was in the script. Her accomplishments as a physicist are purely titular, and her behaviour towards Gusev conveys obligation and respect but no passion whatever. The film itself seems uncertain about Lelia. Is she, as she calls herself, a 'bad housewife' and a 'bad wife', because she wants a husband who notices her, and because she finds no fulfilment in preparing his breakfast? Is she selfish because she ponders love as she watches Kulikov and Gusev animatedly discuss scientific matters? One hardly thinks so: Gusev's absorption in his work leaves little room for Lelia. Yet because *Nine Days* insists on Gusev's valour, it appears to underwrite Lelia's self-criticism. Halfway to creating a new kind of heroine, one who is sexually and intellectually independent, *Nine Days* stops short, and Lelia remains little more than an irritating distraction.

Smoktunovskii's Kulikov, on the other hand, is absolutely engrossing. Kulikov operates on a different level from Gusev. No less gifted, he is more skilful in debate, a magician of words. He deploys them to amuse and confound others, and occasionally to screen a kind of moral cowardice. (His verbal dexterity and some of his arguments recall Dostoevskii's Underground Man, although Kulikov

The Grand Illusion

19. *Nine Days of a Year*

has a self-confident charm entirely absent from Dostoevskii's character.) Kulikov is unshackled, his own man, 'free', in Romm's words, 'of dramatic twists and turns. In essence, he does nothing. Perhaps that's why his character is more successful than the others.'[25]

Certainly Kulikov was controversial. He could not be tagged either 'positive' or 'negative' according to some textbook list of qualities. When he glances around a restaurant and dismisses his fellow diners as neanderthals, mocking the idea that human beings have become more clever in the past 30,000 years, he directly challenges Marxist teleology and affirms the 'illusory nature of ideals of social development'.[26] Gusev risks his life, becomes irradiated, and submits to a dangerous operation. Kulikov, in contrast, wants to dance, drink and enjoy life. Before *Nine Days*, such an 'intellectual, almost a cynic, always elegant, tidy and well-pressed', would have been shown as 'a successful young careerist, well-entrenched in the capital not far from ministries, a snobbish and indifferent egoist'.[27] Instead, Kulikov rather than Gusev 'spoke' to sophisticated young audiences, his taste for paradox and irony similar to their own.

Delighted with a movie about intellectuals,[28] but more cautious than young viewers, liberal critics hoped to forestall conservative backlash by focusing on Gusev. The March editorial of *Iskusstvo kino*, for instance, spoke of 'the hero' of *Nine Days,* referring solely to Gusev; Gusev understands the connection 'between what is happening in our country and what goes on far beyond its borders ... [and] clearly acknowledges the international significance of his research, and this is characteristic for Soviet man'.[29] Its reviewer described the film as the 'story of a scientific exploit' and stressed the continuity of the heroic line, with Dr Svintsov passing on the baton of scientific discovery to Gusev.[30]

They failed. In two separate articles, the monthly *Oktiabr,* one of the fiercest conservative journals under Kochetov's editorship, assaulted *Nine Days.* The film's malignancy, according to one article, derived from Kalatozov and Urusevskii's earlier partnership: from *The Cranes are Flying,* with its 'fall of a hopeless philistine unable to remain faithful' and its abandonment of genuine heroism, and from *Unsent Letter,* where man's doomed struggle with nature is 'completely alien to socialist humanism'.[31]

In *Nine Days* the cancer had metastasized. Romm's 'socially myopic' characters lack perspective and demonstrate a 'strange' apoliticism. Gusev is 'courageous in science alone. In everything else he embodies amorphousness and inertia, some kind of odd passivity. Gusev is uncompromising in achieving his goals, but quite tolerant as far as ideological views are concerned.' The authors wondered why Gusev didn't 'oppose to Kulikov's snobbish nihilism his own harmonious, integrated, optimistic programme'.[32]

A second broadside repeated these charges as part of a more general onslaught on Soviet mimicry of western film trends. Its author, Pavel Strokov, could not deny the success of *Nine Days,* but he ascribed it solely to Batalov's and Smoktunovskii's acting. On behalf of 'every viewer' he reacted with horror to Kulikov's comment about neanderthals and to his observation that war advances science:

> Are there really such troglodytes among Soviet scientists, who are famous for their humanism and their struggle for peace? ... If art is true to life, this collective of scientists should be shown as true citizens of their Motherland, with a broad intellectual sweep, politically mature and far-sighted. But the heroes of the film seem to live on some kind of little island, cut off from the whole country.[33]

Language like Strokov's and indictments such as the articles in *Oktiabr* found targets besides *Nine Days,* which drew fire partly because of Romm's stature within the film community. The search for acceptable heroes continued to worry the authorities, particularly in films made for young audiences. Iulii Raizman's *And What If It's Love?* [A esli èto liubov'?], which opened at the same time as Romm's movie, had little in common with it, but critics found they shared 'pessimism' and 'objectivity', qualities the cultural mandarins had disliked throughout Soviet history.

For months before Raizman's film was released, even the relatively liberal

The Grand Illusion

Iskusstvo kino lambasted the 'profound pessimism' of western art and its pernicious influence on certain Soviet film-makers. One such director, Iurii Pobedonostsev, presented adolescents as crude egoists, their parents as idiots, and other adults as fools and drunks in *Mishka, Serega and I* [Mishka, Serega i ia, 1961]. If reality were this egregious, *Iskusstvo kino* wondered, why didn't Pobedonostsev 'take up arms' instead of withdrawing?[34] 'Discontented and angry' protagonists, devoid of moral courage, failed to represent 'our young people', and hardly qualified as 'heroes of our time'.[35]

Iulii Raizman intended *And What If It's Love?* to join this discourse, and it did. He based the film on press reports of an innocent high school romance that ended tragically: after teachers, parents and peers crudely intervened, the young couple committed suicide. Raizman softened reality: only his heroine Ksenia attempts suicide and she survives. Nevertheless, the film unblinkingly examines a code of values and a milieu that violate and destroy love's potential. In the bleak world depicted by the film, the two teenagers never have a chance.

A painstakingly realistic *mise-en-scène* captures that world. Raizman filmed *And What If It's Love?* in a new district of Kiev, where concrete apartment blocks surround an enormous open square still bare of trees and playgrounds, and children and adults dart across a wide road full of incessant truck traffic. Cinematographer Aleksandr Kharitonov's repeated panoramic shots, the harsh daylight and the wide screen visually confirm Raizman's thematic approach: the social overshadows the individual, the general dominates the particular. Kharitonov avoids unusual angles, relying on neutral front shots; the single exception is when the teenagers escape to the woods for a few hours. Their nascent feelings awaken in an elemental environment full of natural shapes and sounds.

The alleyways and arches of old Kiev or Moscow would have been a more conventional setting, with the terrain and architecture convenient symbols of 'old' ways of thinking. But Ksenia and Boris live in the unadorned geometry of vast outdoor squares where people hang out their washing, play dominoes and stand around gossiping. The teenagers inhabit domestic environments scrupulously constructed by Raizman to explain their personalities. (When Raizman shot a living-room corner, he furnished the entire room.)[36] Ksenia is surrounded by the 'appurtenances of village *byt* transplanted into the modern, light apartment'[37] – bazaar rugs, clay cats, a hand-operated sewing machine. In Boris's home, the apartment of *intelligenty*, matching polished furniture rests on highly waxed floors.

Raizman generalizes the human milieu as much as he does the social. When the camera follows the crowd of students leaving school in the opening sequences, it isolates none of them. We have no idea which of this group of teasing, lively teenagers are the film's protagonists. (The single hint is the familiar face of Zhanna Prokhorenko, recognizable as Shura from *Ballad of a*

20. *And What If It's Love?*

Soldier.) When a love-letter is discovered, we are as ignorant of the writer's identity as any of the characters in the film.

Once revealed as hero and heroine, Boris and Ksenia hardly resemble Romeo and Juliet. Boris is bright and willing to explore his feelings, Ksenia is sweet, not especially clever, rather conventional. Their very 'ordinariness' helps Raizman shift attention from them to those who interfere with them, in order to understand the mechanism that destroys the 'fragile embryo' of their love.[38]

That 'mechanism' includes everyone in Boris and Ksenia's two worlds of school and courtyard. The teacher who discovers the tell-tale note and inveigles a student into identifying the author is ruthless and self-righteous. (Teachers protested the implication that they were training informers and conformists.)[39] Those with better intentions nevertheless do almost as much damage simply by interfering. Ksenia's careworn, provincial, loving mother is all too quick to believe the worst that her neighbours can imagine as they stand in the courtyard gossiping. (The scene recalls the scene in Murnau's 1925 film, *The Last Laugh* [Der letzte Mann], where neighbours stand on their balconies, gleefully shouting gossip across the courtyard of their tenement.) 'Bad people trample around one's soul in galoshes – but then "good" people march in without asking permission! ... Benevolent or hostile, it's all a bazaar, all torture.'[40]

And What If It's Love? broke major taboos. It has no positive hero. It regards the 'collective, that eternally reliable buttress of the typical', as neither irreproachable nor wise. It not only insisted that audiences judge for themselves but that they judge *themselves*. Shilova remembered her shock of recognition:

> Each one of us in the audience had spent a lifetime bumping up against people like that: in school, where private affairs could be condemned [in public meetings] and where the only way of saving yourself was repentance and self-criticism; in the communal apartments ... in squabbles on the street and in the bus, in scandals about the *stiliagi* [young people favouring modish western clothes], in a general intolerance towards young people.[41]

Raizman's comprehensive sweep infuriated conservatives: 'Yes, such things occur in our life. Yes, we still have bribetakers and embezzlers, hypocrites and phonies, malingerers and speculators ... But can one conceive of the Soviet collective consisting primarily of philistines, hypocrites and phonies?!' Why does Raizman's film depict school as bad, home as worse, and Boris and Ksenia as passive victims of circumstances, instead of warriors who would fight for their happiness?[42]

Viewers reluctant to accept the image of Soviet society constructed in *And What If It's Love?* could take comfort from Lev Kulidzhanov's *When the Trees were Big* [Kogda derev'ia byli bol'shimi], released like Raizman's film in March 1962. *Trees* assured its viewers that they lived in a generally tolerant and forgiving society. If two neighbours in the kitchen of the protagonist's communal apartment disdain him as a disreputable scrounger, a third regards Kuzma Kuzmych as a decent, unhappy man deserving of pity. When Kuzma Kuzmych falls down a flight of stairs, the kind old lady who had employed him comes to visit, having shrewdly tagged him as alone in the world.

After she mentions a girl in her village whose parents disappeared during the war, the old drunk is inspired to pretend to be Natasha's long-lost father. With that, *Trees* moves to the country, where village life idyllically balances community and solitude, labour and leisure. Natasha, surrounded by loving adults and friends, wins her lover away from the local siren without compromising her standards. When the 'father' she has never forgotten, and in whose death she never believed, turns up, she redeems him with her steady, unquestioning and unconditional love. Kuzma Kuzmych regains his sense of self-worth and his respect for work. (Thanks to Iurii Nikulin and Inna Gulaia's exceptionally fine performances, the film is less treacly than it sounds.)

Where Raizman asserts the tyranny of social values and the frailty of love, Kulidzhanov's film affirms the fundamental decency of Soviet society and the redemptive potential of human love. *When the Trees were Big* is as consoling as

And What If It's Love? is distressing. The rural milieu of *Trees* offers satisfying hard work and beautiful surroundings: we first see Natasha swimming in the river and then gazing into the sunset. Authority is benevolent (a young, clean-cut major in the militia does his best to help the obdurate Kuzma Kuzmych, a warmly paternal registrar marries Natasha and Lenia) and the city, though less friendly than the village, contains cosy spaces, not Raizman's asphalt deserts.

If Boris and Ksenia are battered by their social environment, Kulidzhanov's characters consistently derive strength from theirs. There is no discrepancy between their individual desires and the collective's. Work is a source of pride and pleasure, neither the drudgery that has worn out Ksenia's mother nor the tension between individual and system audible in the school principal's voice when she argues with her superior on the phone. Innocence is presumed. After their marriage Natasha and her Lenia fall asleep in a hayloft, yet no one thinks about sex; when Boris and Ksenia play truant, nearly everyone assumes that they are 'up to no good'.

Kulidzhanov rewards goodness. Natasha and Lenia face a happy future; Kuzma Kuzmych can anticipate years of productive work and a loving family. Raizman, in contrast, ends *And What If It's Love?* with a deeply sad meeting between Boris and Ksenia months after the main events of the film. Boris's parents shipped him off to a distant work project after Ksenia's suicide attempt. Now he is back, full of boyish enthusiasm and the hope that they can resume their relationship. Ksenia, wearily trudging across rubble with a string-bag full of empty bottles, has 'grown up'. Stripped of her sunny joy and disillusioned with the very idea of love, she seems years older than Boris.

All three films – *Nine Days*, *When the Trees were Big* and *And What If It's Love?* – opened nearly simultaneously, attracted the same number of viewers (about twenty million each), and presented decidedly different images of Soviet society. Kulidzhanov's film harks back to the optimistic mood of the early thaw years, pregnant with possibility, accepting traditional values and willing to believe in the perfectibility of individuals. Romm's film beguiled audiences with its irony, humour and intellectual engagement; its heroes belonged to their age, but they remained heroes. Raizman, in contrast, portrays a society untouched by the thaw. Boris and Ksenia are not bold and self-confident, like Romm's young men. They are average, hardly different from legions of their peers, and their aborted romance speaks volumes about pressures to conform and the price of non-compliance. Raizman's film, whether or not the authorities approved, catches the anxiety and questioning mood characteristic of the early 1960s, after the Twenty-second Party Congress. Taken together, the three films suggest the spectrum of Russia's mood at the time.

11. Kameradschaft

In September 1962 Maia Turovskaia discussed contrasting styles of contemporary Soviet cinema. She dubbed them 'prosaic' and 'poetic'. She chose *And What If It's Love?* to exemplify the former. To illustrate the latter she chose another film in which innocence is destroyed, albeit for very different reasons: Andrei Tarkovskii's *Ivan's Childhood*.

Ivan's Childhood, Andrei Tarkovskii's first feature film, launched a body of work widely celebrated for its individuality and imagination. As the Soviet film-maker closest to the European definition of an *auteur*, Tarkovskii was for many years the post-war Soviet director most highly regarded by western critics. A powerful influence on both Soviet and western film-makers, his work has received detailed and careful analysis.[1]

Certain thematic elements of what has been called 'the Tarkovskian agenda' already exist in embryonic form in *The Steamroller and the Violin*, most notably the image of the artist as outsider in a cold and comfortless world.[2] But in *Ivan's Childhood* Tarkovskii's principal preoccupation, 'the collision of two forces, two substances: man and history, man and his time',[3] emerges far more forcefully, and in an eloquent artistic language. *Ivan's Childhood* introduces themes and images developed and deepened in later works made within the Soviet Union (*Andrei Rublev* [1966, rel. 1971], *Solaris* [1972], *Mirror* [Zerkalo, 1975], and *Stalker* [1979]) and in his last works, *Nostalgia* [1983] and *The Sacrifice* [Sweden, Offret, 1986], completed in emigration.

Ivan is one of Tarkovskii's child-protagonists, 'burdened by knowledge and experience beyond their years. Their childhood is blissful only in the rare flash of memory, for in the present they are emotionally orphaned, often literally so. Their fathers are absent, or dead in war, and thus replaced by surrogates (who fail them).'[4] Much more than the young violinist Sasha, Ivan foreshadows subsequent Tarkovskian heroes in his traversal of psychological as well as physical space; his journey, like theirs, takes him into forbidden zones.

Tarkovskii's aesthetic agenda is also set in *Ivan's Childhood*. The mysterious, brooding landscape through which Ivan picks his silent path, dead water (separating this world from the other world) and purifying water (in his dreams), the bell he rings – these images recur in *Andrei Rublev, Stalker* and *Mirror*. The use of sound and light introduced in *Ivan's Childhood* became Tarkovskian 'signatures'; so did his preference for tracking shots over montage to create or shape time.

In view of Tarkovskii's subsequent career it requires some effort to see *Ivan's Childhood* in its own right and not merely as a precursor to a remarkable *oeuvre*. With all its astonishing individuality, however, it is a film made within the Soviet studio system, by a young man educated in traditions of Soviet cinema as well as the innovations and discoveries of the French New Wave. Like *Cranes are Flying, Ivan's Childhood* opened in the midst of intellectual, artistic and political ferment, and it was welcomed and spurned in that turbulent atmosphere. Examining it within its temporal and artistic context is useful both in order to understand the film better, and in order to assess its relationship to other films of its time and place.

The choice of child-hero exemplifies how Tarkovskii at once accepted and subverted Soviet tradition, radically revising a convention of Soviet cinema to alter its accepted meaning. Literary and film re-creations of the civil war frequently featured the youngster who 'hid the wounded commissar in the loft and dreamed of serving in Budenny's regiment'. He metamorphosed into the bright orphan who, twenty years later, acted as liaison for a partisan unit, or the schoolboy, 'son of the regiment, in a fine soldier's shirt and boots',[5] moving audiences with his brave but sad smile. In *The Fate of a Man*, for instance, Vania's guileless questions and limpet-like attachment to Andrei Sokolov had viewers brushing away tears in ready sympathy. Khutsiev's Little Fedor, toughened by his war experiences, is cockier and less innocent than Vania, but the veneer hides an emotional hunger apparent in a close-up of him clinging to Big Fedor in his sleep, and the suppressed grief that emerges as he watches the excavation of a buried Soviet tank, a coffin for Soviet soldiers like his own father.

Ivan, at twelve several years older than Vania and Fedor, has seen his childhood blasted into smithereens by the Nazis. He is hardly a child at all, except in his dreams. During the first extended sequence in the dugout Ivan demonstrates a wholly adult poise as he insists that Lt Galtsev contact HQ, writes up his report on German troop strength, wearily sips his tea and warily sleeps an uneasy sleep. All the more shocking, then, when he exhibits childlike behaviour for the first time, with his flying leap into the arms of Captain Kholin.

In the film's 'waking' reality Ivan combines physical immaturity (pre-puberty bodily contours and child's soft skin) and frailty (ribs that are clearly visible when he strips) with a most unchildlike ferocity and self-assurance. The result is not far from frightening. Thanks principally to the dream sequences, we

The Grand Illusion

21. *Ivan's Childhood*

watch him with hearts pinched with pity, but horror accompanies the pity, not just because of what this child has lost but because he has become the embodiment of his hatred.

Hatred is the meaning of his life; it alone makes survival desirable. Ivan is the first Soviet film hero since Veronika in *Cranes* who does not wish to survive, or, more accurately, who is indifferent to survival, and such indifference is all the more appalling because of his youth. Bondarchuk's Sokolov, despite the inhumanity of the concentration camp, does whatever he must in order to endure, sustained by thoughts of his family. Even the exhausted and concussed Iamshchikov, in *Peace to Him Who Enters*, is able to smile at the sight of a newborn infant, herald of peace. Ivan, however, wants to live solely in order to take vengeance. When the Red Army enters Berlin and Galtsev discovers Ivan's dossier in the underground torture chambers of the Gestapo, the record of Ivan's execution conveys the awful sense of a destiny fulfilled.

The hatred-driven Ivan skews one commonplace of thaw art, the innocent child-hero. Another, the orphan's adoption by an adult male, is similarly disrupted. Conventionally the relationship is necessary to both child and adult as emotional compensation and healing for the traumatic losses inflicted by the war. They save each other. (Even a film set years after the end of the war, such as Kulidzhanov's *When the Trees were Big*, relies on this formula.)

Ivan's Childhood, however, is the story of an unsuccessful adoption. Ivan cannot be saved. None of the adults, from solidly paternal Katasonych to charming but feckless Kholin, can protect Ivan. Moreover, though they love him, they are reluctantly forced to exploit the advantages of his age and size for their own military purposes. Before the final fantasy sequence, interpolated documentary footage – including a row of small corpses, Goebbels' poisoned children – marks the 'suicide' of fascism and suggests the twin motifs of vengeance and of ravaged childhood. Not only our Ivan (and his Russian peers) have lost their childhoods to war: all children have.[6]

Ivan's Childhood depicts the war without battle scenes, by 1962 hardly an innovation in Soviet films. The entire action occurs in the interstice between two scouting missions, neither at the front nor in the rear; it takes place in the no-man's-land between and beneath them. Here Tarkovskii's originality lies in the depiction of that space, its limbo-status emphasized by the stagnant icy water Ivan must traverse to reach the dugout at the start and again towards the end of the film, when Kholin and Galtsev row him out for another mission.

Urusevskii had given visual form to the paradox of 'unnatural' nature in *Cranes are Flying*, as Boris trudges through dead swampland and barren trees before dying amid the circling image of living birch trees, and again in the 'evil' sun of *Unsent Letter*. But nature in *Ivan* is not simply deformed by war. It provides the building blocks for war. The trees of Ivan's dreams become the stumps of waking reality. The 'preternaturally mature and ... eerily intense'[7] boy-soldier is torn from the world of nature of which he is organically part, the world of sunlight and apples, goats and horses, where he follows a butterfly through the air and listens entranced to the cuckoo. He must use his knowledge of that world, now rendered a stagnant world of lifeless nature, to help the war effort. The landscape is less external than internal, Ivan's blasted interior world.[8] The emotional devastation is complete. Chaliapin's song on the gramophone, itself about incomplete love ('Masha isn't led across the river' – in other words, cannot marry), breaks off. *Peace to Him Who Enters*, notwithstanding its desolation, acknowledges the possibility of new life: the film is framed by two symbols of renewal, a green shoot growing out of a newly-cut cross and the new-born baby. Just such an affirmation ended the original script for *Ivan's Childhood*: Ivan survives and Galtsev utters the last words of the film, 'Blessed be peace.'[9] In Tarkovskii's *Ivan's Childhood*, however, potential vanishes. Love, whether erotic or paternal, is blighted in this context, reduced to the nurse Masha's anaesthetized passivity or impotent in the face of its inversion, Ivan's hatred.

Tarkovskii achieved an unprecedented aesthetic effect in *Ivan's Childhood*. In the original novella, an outsider – young Lieutenant Galtsev – tells Ivan's 'story'. By shifting the point of view and by adding the dream sequences, Tarkovskii avoided the narrativity of the original story, brought us inside Ivan and created a new way of linking and organizing his material.[10] Uniting emotion and reason via the 'logic of associative links', he offered a vision equally removed from 'poetic' films such as *Man Follows the Sun* and from 'prosaic' films such as *And What If It's Love?*

Yet just as Tarkovskii combined and revised multiple thematic elements characteristic of the thaw in *Ivan's Childhood* – the child at its centre, the surrogate parenting, the primacy of emotions – so, too, he 'borrowed' many of the component devices of *Ivan's Childhood*. Romm used interior monologue in *Nine Days*. Kalatozov deployed fantasy in *Cranes*. Kalik and Chukhrai turned their cameras upside-down, and several film-makers incorporated documentary footage. In that sense, Tarkovskii's aesthetic choices emerged from his context and era no less than did his thematic preoccupations. Marlen Khutsiev made many of the same aesthetic choices and used many of the same devices for entirely different purposes in his film *Ilich's Gate*. *Ilich's Gate* (the title designates a Moscow neighbourhood) is the cinematic equivalent of Sherlock Holmes' dog that didn't bark; one of the most significant films of 1961, it was not released until 1965, and then in a severely truncated form under the title *I am Twenty*. Because of its belated release, its impact was substantially diluted, both by the cuts forced on Khutsiev and by the release of other films made under its influence. Overtaken and overshadowed by politics, the film had shifted from precursor to source.

Ilich's Gate follows the maturation of three friends, neighbours in a Moscow courtyard, after one of them, Sergei, returns from two years' army service. Slava has undergone the biggest visible changes: married with a small child, he is burdened by and resentful of adult obligations. Peter Pan-like Kolia is deliberately carefree, eager to play jazz and chase girls. Sergei hovers between adolescence and adulthood, proud to turn his first pay cheque over to his mother but thoughtless enough to stay out all night without phoning home.

The Moscow in which these three live and work is far more than mere 'setting': the city is all-inclusive, a cosmos. Background details move 'decisively into the foreground, becoming a generative source of ideas, not merely auxiliary but essential'.[11] Public spaces dominate the first half of the film, where much of life is social and public: an impromptu soccer game, thronged streets on May Day, dancing on a street corner to early rock-and-roll. Sergei and Kolia whistle greetings to each other across the courtyard, and meet in the street, where Slava joins them. A doorway and a park bench provide better venues for passionate conversation and argument, lighthearted teasing and flirtations, than the kitchen of a crowded communal flat. Sergei first spots Ania, the girl he falls in love with, on a crowded bus, and jumps off to follow her.

The first half of the film climaxes in the May Day parade. With its music, myriad faces, balloons, and banners of Gagarin as well as of Lenin, the parade sequence whirls and pulses with movement. Film scholar Evgenii Margolit observes that crowds in Soviet cinema tend to be either chaotic and vulnerable (Eisenstein's fleeing civilians in *Potemkin*, for instance) or organized instruments for reform, visually shaped in geometric forms like the wedge or pyramid, with an orator or flag-carrier at its apex. Khutsiev's crowd, however, is neither a mass of randomly swarming Browning particles nor an obedient regiment; it is a host of distinct individuals.[12]

The camera shows us a variety of people, both those we know as characters and those we don't, as part of that streaming life. Slava strides alongside his smiling wife, his son on his shoulders; Sergei catches sight of Ania and tracks her through the laughing, snaking line of paraders. One critic called it: 'the first and perhaps the last image on screen of an unforced, joyful procession of free people, the holiday as a natural manifestation of the national soul and not an official, organized demonstration squeezed by cordons of police cars, barriers, instructions and warnings'.[13]

Whatever 'national soul' may mean, Khutsiev's May Day parade does portray an unforced celebration of the Soviet Utopia and the union of individuals and society. Yet much of *Ilich's Gate* details precisely the opposite: the departure from that Utopia and from its ideals. Indeed, the very next morning Slava is on the street, brooding over a fight with his wife. He, Kolia and Sergei sit and muse about love, while the unofficial Soviet anthem, 'My Homeland is Broad', plays in the background. 'A nation must know its heroes,' one of them intones with mock gravity when Kolia's face, caught on camera during the parade, appears on TV later that day.

All three heroes are painfully maturing, troubled by the discrepancy between their everyday lives and their dreams. And if Slava just wants to watch hockey on TV, Sergei and Kolia worry too about the distance between the proclaimed ideals of their society and its reality of hypocrisy and lies. Kolia's crisis of conscience occurs when he is first told to stop writing 'disorienting' poetry, and then asked to report on a colleague at work. Despite his irate refusal, he remains confused and depressed. Sergei oscillates between 'wanting to question and think for himself and wanting to distance himself from that kind of struggle and to accept on faith such sacred cows as the Revolution, war, love'.[14] Ania's father impatiently advises his daughter and Sergei to grow up and accept responsibilities, but his own life exemplifies compromise, the surrender of ideals for material rewards. Ania angrily rejects his advice: 'All your life you say one thing and do another'; Sergei more politely spurns the older man's justification that he has sought and achieved success for the benefit of Ania, of younger people, 'of the future'.

Age is not a prerequisite for cynicism, however. Ania's friends, privileged offspring of the elite, attend art exhibits and knowingly comment on abstract painting. Although Sergei admires their cleverness, his own, sounder values protect him from their brand of irony. His love for Ania grounds him in adulthood, but by the end of the film even love and friendship – succour when all else disappoints – are tottering. The three heroes sit on a bench in a metro

The Grand Illusion

station until the train comes, loath to accept that their different choices will, ultimately, take them their separate ways.

Khutsiev co-authored the script for *Ilich's Gate* with Gennadii Shpalikov, who was roughly the same age as the heroes of the film and was still studying at the Institute of Cinematography. The mood of the early 1960s, its mixture of 'elevated and awkward, radical and ritualized, naive and cynical', suffuses the script.[15] Exhilarated members of Gorky Studio loved it: 'First class!' exclaimed the co-author of Bondarchuk's *War and Peace*. 'It is the only scenario that comes to grips with our times, with what most concerns everyone today ... Without ready-made formulas and clichés, it forces each one of us to think about these issues.' Valentin Ezhov, co-author of *Ballad of a Soldier*, agreed that the script was refreshingly free of banality, unlike so many in which 'the author sets up a series of questions at the beginning and then, in a highly demagogic manner, provides a full set of answers to his very own questions at the end ... This is the first profound and major examination of our contemporary life.' 'We need this picture right now,' someone from the floor interrupted with heartfelt yearning. 'Boy, do we need it!' [*okh, kak nuzhna*].[16]

Yet in the months of filming and editing that followed, excitement warred with jitters. The assistant head of the studio's production section sent a warning to the studio director:

> The dispassionate tone of the script is a serious fault, as is its social passivity [*sozertsatel'naia, a ne aktivnaia grazhdanstvennaia pozitsiia*]. The authors consider their heroes typical representatives of today's youth, yet their spiritual and civic interests are exceedingly narrow, and their conception of Soviet life is primitive.
>
> The film-makers ... artificially isolate these young people from everything connected with their work and social existence. It goes without saying that such a life can impart nothing good, meaningful, or optimistic to either the heroes of the picture or its future viewers.[17]

To support the project, the script was published in *Iskusstvo kino* in July 1961, and Iurii Khaniutin provided an afterword, as if to forestall and refute the inevitable criticism. He defended the young heroes' lack of certainty about their future. 'Of course,' he wrote,

> the general historical goals of our society are clear and indisputable, of course there are many young people who immediately recognize their path in life. But not everyone finds his way, his particular place, so easily. Such are the heroes ... And the authors treat their search and their spiritual dramas with respect. They understand that truths won by suffering are always more precious and firmer than those adopted mechanically.[18]

Filming began on 1 May 1961, with the May Day parade, and was more or less complete a year later. Khutsiev deliberately enhanced the topicality of the film at every turn. He chose to work with a man a dozen years his junior, whose language would be authentically up-to-date, and he used students from VGIK – future stars of Soviet cinema – for many roles. (Among Ania's party guests, for instance, are Andrei Tarkovskii and Andrei Konchalovskii.) Sergei escorts two Ghanaians around his factory, and two African faces stand out among the passengers on the metro, emblems of the first large wave of Africans to work and study in Moscow in the early 1960s. Arabs in *kefiyas* march in the May Day celebration, and a girl twirls a hula-hoop. With an uncommon insistence on actuality, Khutsiev sought out real construction and demolition projects for his characters' work-sites, to ensure that the film both looked and felt wholly contemporary.[19]

The Minister of Culture, Ekaterina Furtseva, was instrumental in the film's completion. Furtseva, who occupied that post from 1960 to 1974, became increasingly dogmatic, but in the years before Khrushchev's ouster she was relatively sympathetic to younger film-makers.[20] When she saw the rushes towards the end of the summer of 1962, she suggested creating a climax for the second half of the film parallel to the May Day parade. Khutsiev requested permission to film a poetry reading. The reading at the Moscow Polytechnic Museum was specifically organized for the film crew, but differed in no way from the many readings that occurred in 1961 and 1962. It forms a lengthy sequence in the film, almost a separate set piece, with poet after poet approaching the microphone and reading (or, in Bulat Okudzhava's case, singing) to a packed house. Margarita Pilikhina's camera brilliantly captured the almost exalted mood of the reading; Khutsiev himself later said that her camera 'dived and swooped' as if echoing the movement and rhythm of the poetic lines.[21]

The camera pans rapt faces, singles out Sergei as he squeezes through the mob to join Ania, follows the request notes passed from the auditorium to the floor. The sequence looks spontaneous as well as authentic, as 'real' as the documentary footage of the May Day parade. Indeed, life and art blurred: the actors had to elbow their way into the auditorium through the throng outside the door, and members of the audience protested that the cameras obstructed their view of Evtushenko, Slutskii, Rozhdestvenskii, Akhmadulina, Okudzhava and the others.[22]

By the autumn of 1962 *Ilich's Gate* was ready for review by the Ministry of Culture. Despite rumblings and portents, Khutsiev had reason to hope for the Ministry's approval. Art was blooming in a climate of unprecedented tolerance. October and November were banner months, with the publication of Evtushenko's 'Heirs of Stalin', Slutskii's anti-Stalinist poems, Solzhenitsyn's *One Day in the Life of Ivan Denisovich*, Nekrasov's *Both Sides of the Ocean*, and comparable excitement in the world of art and music.

Then came Khrushchev's visit to the Manège, and the subsequent meetings between Party leaders and artists and intellectuals. Film initially attracted no special attention. At the 17 December session, where Ilichev concentrated on painting and sculpture, he lumped together cinema, music and literature as contaminated by 'formalist' tendencies, but spoke rather mildly of 'ideologically immature' films and 'films that suffer from a studied cleverness and complexity of form'. Nikolai Gribachev, a writer whose notoriety spread after he published a nasty poetic parody of Evtushenko, assailed Mikhail Romm, but not for his film-making: Romm had sharply criticized Gribachev (along with two other conservatives, Kochetov and Sofronov) a month earlier, and Gribachev reciprocated by calling Romm politically deficient, a 'provocateur' and 'slanderer', all the while 'assuring his Jewish friends that he was no antisemite'.[23]

But cinema was not to be spared. Innovative films in general and Khutsiev's *Ilich's Gate* in particular came under critical scrutiny. After the December meeting Polikarpov, head of the Central Committee's cultural department, demanded a screening of the film. Furtseva tried to protect Khutsiev by saying the film was not yet ready, but she was forced to acquiesce, and after the screening Ilichev summoned Khutsiev to discuss the film. The very first image of the film, preceding the titles, depicts three Red Guardists marching away from the camera down a cobblestone street; after the titles, the figures who turn and approach the camera are again three soldiers, this time in Second World War uniforms.[24] The loud footsteps of the Red Guard patrol particularly disturbed Ilichev. Khutsiev, puzzled, tried to explain that footsteps always sound louder at night than during the day. 'At night people should be asleep,' his interlocutor replied. 'Footsteps are that loud only in prison.'[25]

By the March meeting in the Kremlin, Khrushchev had seen *Ilich's Gate* as well. He interrupted Romm's praise of the film to object to the dialogue between Sergei and his ghost-father, killed eighteen years earlier in the war, when Sergei seeks guidance in how to live his life. When Khrushchev took the floor for his major peroration, his tone lacked the slightly absurd paternal good humour still audible in December's performance. After repeating his earlier condemnation of abstract art, he turned to cinema, a medium so influential that it required, he noted, the exacting attention of the Party, and to *Ilich's Gate*:

> The real meaning of the film is to assert ideas and norms of public and private life that are entirely unacceptable and alien to Soviet people. That is why we categorically reject this interpretation of a great and important theme.
>
> The film's title, *Ilich's Gate*, is allegorical ... We are meant to accept the main characters as representing the vanguard of Soviet youth, who staunchly guard the achievements of the socialist revolution and Lenin's legacy.
>
> But whoever watches the film will say this is not true. Even the best of the characters – the three young workers – do not personify our wonderful youth. They are shown as not knowing how to live or what to live for. And this at a time of all-round building of communism, a time illuminated by the ideas of the Communist Party Program! ... These are not the sort of people society can

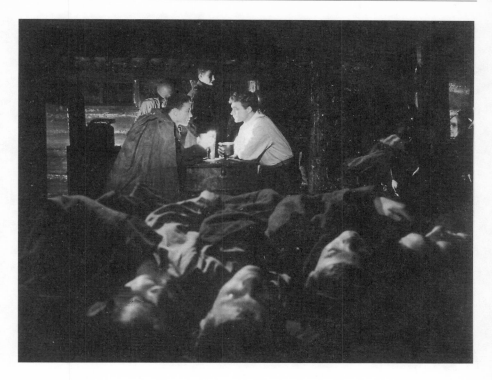

22. *Ilich's Gate*

rely upon. They are not fighters, not remakers of the world. They are morally sick people, who have grown old while still young, who have no high aims or vocation in life ...

The meeting between the hero of the film and the ghost of his father killed in the war raises serious ideological objections. When the son asks how he should live, the ghost in turn asks his son how old he is. And when the son answers, 'Twenty-three,' the father says, 'And I'm twenty-one,' and disappears.

You really want us to believe that this could be true? No one would believe it! Everyone knows that even animals don't abandon their young. If you take a puppy from its mother and throw it into the water, she will immediately jump in to save it, at the risk of her own life.[26]

Can anyone believe that a father wouldn't answer his son's question and wouldn't help him by advising him how to find the right path in life?

There's more to this than meets the eye. It has a particular meaning. The idea is to impress upon the children that their fathers cannot be their teachers in life, and that there is no point in turning to them for advice. The film-makers think that young people ought to decide for themselves how to live, without asking their elders for counsel and help.[27]

Ilich's Gate became a scapegoat for two reasons. The first involved its treatment of the 'fathers and sons' issue, the extreme sensitivity of which may be inferred from Khrushchev's passionate condemnation. In Romm's words, 'all the old men ... were putting the younger men through the meat grinder', while insisting that there was no tension between generations and that 'anyone who suggested otherwise was a scoundrel'.[28]

The second reason pertained less to the film *per se* than to Viktor Nekrasov's remarks about it in *Both Sides of the Ocean*. Nekrasov especially liked the absence of standard answers to the searching questions posed by the heroes. 'I am endlessly grateful to Khutsiev and Shpalikov', he had written, 'for not dragging in the old worker by his greying moustache, the one who understands everything and always has exactly the right answer for anything you ask him. If he had come by with his instructive sayings, it would have ruined the picture.'[29]

Khrushchev was irate: 'That was written by a Soviet author in a Soviet magazine!' he sputtered. 'You can't read something like that, written about an old worker in a haughty and contemptuous tone, without becoming indignant. I believe it is absolutely impermissible for a Soviet writer to adopt such a tone.'[30]

Nekrasov had offended on several counts in *Both Sides of the Ocean*. He explicitly repudiated didactic art and implicitly repudiated Party control. He was open to and curious about western art. Worst of all, he described 'home-grown Soviet follies: the arrest of a well-meaning Italian publisher for taking snapshots of the Kiev marketplace; the walling off of Soviet intellectuals from the writings of Kafka and avant-garde foreign films; above all, the inclusion of secret police watchdogs in Soviet tourist groups traveling abroad'.[31]

Izvestia had already published a broadside against *Both Sides of the Ocean*, accusing Nekrasov of 'bourgeois objectivism' and blindness to American class contradictions and to 'the war psychosis fanned by imperialist circles'. Between March and mid-June, when Khrushchev clamoured for Nekrasov's expulsion from the Party, Nekrasov joined Ehrenburg and Evtushenko as the most prominent victims of the conservative campaign. Like them, he came under increasing Party pressure to recant his views. He steadily resisted, compromising only to the extent of writing a letter that was considered an unsatisfactory admission of his political errors. His praise of *Ilich's Gate* could not have been worse timed.

The film's future hung by a thread. Khrushchev's speech prompted a carefully orchestrated round of negative letters and reviews, beginning with a letter from indignant steelworkers at the Hammer and Sickle Factory. Without seeing the film, they wholeheartedly endorsed every word of Khrushchev's: 'He expressed our thoughts, our workers' attitude towards such works of art'.[32] At Gorky Studio, where Sergei Gerasimov supervised the unit within which Khutsiev worked, Gerasimov strove to minimize reprisals against Khutsiev and to keep the film in the director's hands.

Khutsiev and Shpalikov, though they expressed no contrition, wanted to retain a measure of control over their work. They protested the sincerity of their intentions and their readiness to continue working, and they had supporters at the studio, among them Iakov Segel and Lev Kulidzhanov. Their antagonists ranged from Party hacks to fellow directors. 'I must speak!' the actress Maria Barabanova huffed at the 12 March meeting. (She was also a member of the studio's Party control commission.) 'If comrade Khrushchev had not held this assembly, the picture would have been released!'[33]

The animosity of fellow directors must have been more painful, if occasionally ludicrous. Mark Donskoi splutteringly dismissed the film's heroes as 'some kind of Hamlets and bums' [*shalopai*] who even 'smoked like bums' [*dazhe kuriat shalopaiski*]. Sergei's bad manners – spending a night with a girl and slipping off the next morning – appalled him ('I would have brought the girl flowers, would have said thank you and only then good-bye'), but were to be expected from a 'neo-nihilist' film with a 'dilettantish' [*intelligentstvuiushchii*] script.[34]

Directors Stanislav Rostotskii and Tatiana Lioznova consistently masked hostility with 'friendly' concern. Rostotskii considered the Party's reaction too mild ['*partiia ... imela pravo i mogla by dazhe bol'she rasserdit'sia, chem rasserdilas''*']. He warned that Khutsiev and Shpalikov's film could prevent Soviet art from developing in the proper 'Party orientation', reproached the film-makers for creating an artificial and unsoviet division between work and life, and demanded proof that they were 'Party-minded' artists. Lioznova was blunt: 'Why are you embarrassed to acknowledge openly your love for Soviet power?' she asked. She advised Khutsiev to 'have guts' [*Bud' do kontsa muzhestvennym*] and candidly declare for or against his heroes. ('You don't admire strength,' she added contemptuously.)[35]

Proposed amendments included rewriting Ania's father as a positive character, with his virtues to be inferred from the pictures in a family album Sergei leafs through, and adding a meeting on the Cuban missile crisis, where Sergei would either openly condemn the United States, or, since public oratory does not fit Sergei's style, would paraphrase the speaker's condemnation for a woman standing nearby.

Khutsiev made changes, but they were deemed inadequate.

We have already said that you are talented, but your talent was not directed towards Party ideology. Our Marxist–Leninist ideology does not need it ... Everyone knows that when *Ivan Brovkin* came out, 25,000 tractor and combine drivers set out for the Virgin Lands territories. That's what the Party wants. And we wanted young people to grow up as a result of your picture. But does your picture encourage anything of the sort? No![36]

Gerasimov angrily refused to take over from Khutsiev: 'Appropriating someone else's work does not accord with my notions of honor, morality and decency.' The film's fate was uncertain.

In late July 1963 Aleksei Romanov, chairman of the cinema committee of the Council of Ministers, received a letter from the studio. Aleksandr Dymshits, chief editor of the script division, and a colleague, A. Skripitsyn, recommended an array of revisions: eliminating the poetry reading, shortening Sergei and Ania's visit to the art exhibit because the film-makers do not 'clearly express' their attitude towards 'formalistic tendencies'; rewriting dialogue to avoid 'notes of scepticism'; cutting Sergei's one-night stand ('amoral') and Sergei and Ania's candle-lit dance ('people will copy it and start fires').[37]

Khutsiev acceded to some suggestions, declined others, and continued to rewrite and re-edit. More than a year later, on 18 January 1965, the revised and abridged *Ilich's Gate* finally opened under the title *I am Twenty*. But inevitably, the Soviet Union that watched *I am Twenty* was not the same society as the one in which Khutsiev had made his film.

12. Meet John Doe

Until the December 1962 meeting in the Lenin Hills, the film industry enjoyed and exploited the prevailing atmosphere of relative cultural tolerance. A large number of the films released in 1962 were individually distinctive; as a group, they spanned a remarkable breadth of styles and approaches and demonstrated a high level of professional competence. Members of the Soviet film community had much more access to western films, and often met with European film-makers both at home and abroad. In France in the early spring of 1962, Grigorii Chukhrai felt secure enough to comment that Soviet film-makers encountered just as many difficulties as western film-makers, though 'they are of a different nature'. He described his own directorial approach: 'I never consider a film in terms of whether I will show something positively or negatively, whether I will defend or condemn.'[1]

Sprightly discussions and thoughtful reviews were the norm rather than the exception in the cinema press during this period. Mikhail Romm eloquently defended himself and *Nine Days of One Year* against the poisonous piece that had appeared in *Oktiabr* the previous May; he accused its authors of a tendentious and disingenuous interpretation of his film, as well as of *Cranes are Flying*, *Unsent Letter* and other scapegoated movies.[2]

In one of *Iskusstvo kino*'s most provocative articles, 'Nine Films of One Year', critic Vera Shitova explored the distinction between two outstanding films of 1962, *Nine Days of One Year* and *Ivan's Childhood*, and seven mediocre films. The first years of renewed, post-Stalin film-making had spawned equally undistinguished movies, she notes, but those uneasy [*nespokoinye*], questing films were part of a process of rebirth. Despite their mediocrity, they were in some sense 'experimental', simply because they reflected the experimentation and searching going on within the society.

> Now it's as if two different cinematographies exist. In one, schools of thought and opinions collide, aesthetic concepts conflict. This one is always interesting.

It tends to be difficult for both the artist and the viewer. It produces great triumphs and terrible frustration. In the other, a constant, calm temperature prevails. Some films are better than others, but between the best and the worst there is a sort of harmonious mutual understanding. The second-rate is not disdained, sometimes it is openly preferred. Film feeds on film in this kind of cinema. Apprentices do not choose a mentor because he is a great artist; rather, they engage in a strange and superficial apprenticeship of clichés.

For Shitova, *Twelve Companions* [Dvenadtsat' sputnikov], *The Confession* [Ispoved'], and five equally forgettable movies are not simply run-of-the-mill but meretricious: 'There is the black bread of art, and always will be and it is not merely unavoidable but necessary. And then there is grey bread. It is a surrogate. It offers neither nourishment nor taste.'[3]

She was not alone in discussing the gap between 'serious' and popular films, a split that had widened as the Soviet film industry expanded throughout the late 1950s and early 1960s. When relatively few feature films were made in the Soviet Union, each one had at least to attempt to fulfil the competing demands of ideology, art and market (or, though the equation is at best inconsistent and reductionist, state, film-maker and audience). By the early 1960s, the studios produced so many movies that such multiple roles received no more than token acknowledgement, yet the concept of 'B grade' movies remained unacceptable. The authorities welcomed the revenues generated by box-office hits, whatever their genre, but disparaged 'frivolous' films for failing in cinema's educational mission. Critics, scorning such movies even when they were professionally adroit, disregarded their directors and writers.

Despite the portents of the December 1962 meeting, the first few issues of *Iskusstvo kino* in 1963 remained hospitable to an assortment of opinions and approaches. Pyrev could continue to deplore the 'gloomy atmosphere' of many Soviet films, as he had done for years. Never a fan of what he considered overly aestheticized film-making, he scoffed at the 'contrived camera movements, equally contrived camera angles [and] occasional quotations from modernist styles borrowed from the bourgeois West'. He branded as snobbery Soviet film criticism that focused on such stylistic issues at the expense of content.[4] Undaunted, *Iskusstvo kino* published an entirely apolitical and sophisticated analysis of Vadim Iusov's dramatic use of lighting in *Ivan's Childhood*.[5]

Comparable diversity characterized a round-table discussion on cinema. Vladimir Baskakov, assistant director of Goskino, clearly articulated the official line, but Iakov Segel and Gennadii Shpalikov, among others, expressed very different views. Segel began by castigating films that failed to support the Party, a seemingly irreproachable stance. His explanation of their failure, however, was hardly orthodox: such films undermined the Party, he argued, because they are like

Meet John Doe

schoolbook arithmetic problems for early grades, where examples are offered and solutions given. The viewer waits for something more complicated, where x and y stand for unknown factors and where the direction of a solution may be indicated but must be reached independently and without the author's prompting. We live in a complex era, and must show viewers life in all its complexity, not simply that two times two equals four. We must be equal to our era. Then we will help our country in its struggle to build communism.

Shpalikov stridently identified a chasm between life and contemporary cinema. Life is less logical, more intricate and more interesting than what the screen shows us, Shpalikov asserted, citing René Clair's comment – deeply subversive of Soviet pieties – that 'cinema is what cannot be told in words'.[6] The cold wind of the March meeting, particularly the blasts at *Ilich's Gate*, put an end to such open expression of heterodoxy in the press and on screen. Of the dozens of feature films that opened between the autumn of 1962 and the autumn of 1964, virtually none made a mark. Most ran briefly to little critical or popular acclaim. A select few secured official approbation, reified in massive press coverage and in print quantities and theatre distribution patterns that ensured large audiences.

Goskino was responsible for the preliminary classification of new movies, assigning them to one of five categories. Subsequent rating of each film determined the number of authorized copies, from a very rare maximum of 2,000 to an equally rare minimum of perhaps a dozen, with the norm for average Soviet films a few hundred. The Moscow-based Office for Film Reproduction and Distribution also decided whether the copies should be black-and-white or colour: some low-rated pictures filmed in colour were distributed in black-and-white to save money. Regional and urban officials could choose to order a film or not, and in how many copies, although Goskino tended to promote its own favourites.[7]

In 1963 and 1964 the box-office blockbusters leavened ideological orthodoxy with a judicious measure of action, adventure and pathos. *Optimistic Tragedy*, about a ship's crew caught between the arguments and authority of an anarchist on the one hand and a female Red Commissar on the other, attracted 46 million viewers in 1963; the following year Aleksandr Stolper's adaptation of Konstantin Simonov's war novel, *The Living and the Dead* [Zhivye i mertvye], and *Stillness* [Tishina], Iurii Bondarev's post-war saga transferred to screen by Vladimir Basov, had similar success.[8] All three were reviewed extensively, with *Stillness* and *The Living and the Dead* receiving more than one hundred newspaper notices, most identical in wording to those published in *Pravda* and *Izvestia*.

All three films, despite some good acting, are tedious and formulaic. *Stillness*, set during the cult of personality, is typical. The cowardly villain, Uvarov, had been responsible for the destruction of his battery during the war; he thrives in the miasma of the post-war years. The honourable heroes, dedicated communists, manage to preserve their ideals and serve the nation despite personal and political blows, among them exclusion from the Party, until the Twentieth Party Congress vindicates them and re-establishes their authority.

What had been politically bold in Chukhrai's 1961 *Clear Skies* had by 1964 been co-opted into nothing more than a sanctioned cliché. *Stillness* affirms the sagacity of the Khrushchev-led Communist Party in exposing the wrongs of late Stalinism, and it implicitly reiterates Khrushchev's contention that he, and those like him, had sincerely trusted Stalin and had believed in the guilt of those arrested.

Stillness confirms as well the hallowed postulate of father–son continuity: an old professor at the institute gives comfort and advice to Sergei, the beleaguered hero. Film-makers certainly took to heart Khrushchev's criticism of Khutsiev on this issue: an extraordinary proportion of the movies released in this period, whatever their genre, proclaim that no generational division of any sort existed in the Soviet Union. On the contrary, the older generation continued to teach, nurture, mentor and protect the younger generation, men and (a scattering of) women worthy of inheriting the legacy bequeathed by those who stormed the Winter Palace, those who fought in Budenny's regiments and defeated the Nazis.

Even an oddity such as *Hussar Ballad* [Gussarskaia ballada], Eldar Riazanov's musical, with a script in verse about the Napoleonic invasion, substantiated this generational continuity. (It opened on 7 September 1962, the 150th anniversary of the Battle of Borodino.) The great symbol of Russia, aged General Kutuzov, shares common values with the young heroine-in-hussar's-uniform, seventeen-year-old Shura Azarova.

Khrushchev's explosion at the March 1963 meeting precluded the kind of balance that characterized Villen Azarov's comedy *Grown-Up Children* [Vzroslye deti], released a year earlier. In *Grown-Up Children*, the differences between parents and children are matters of taste and style rather than fundamental values, but neither generation has a moral advantage over the other.

Lusia, an idealistic fledgling architect, and her new husband Igor live with Lusia's parents, disrupting what Lusia's parents had fantasized as a serene retirement. Lusia and Igor reject the somewhat philistine tastes of their parents. The young people hang abstract paintings in place of old-fashioned portraits; they play jazz instead of sentimental music; they prefer a sleek aluminium alarm clock to the dignified grandfather clock. They lack consideration: their friends swarm over the apartment, dancing till all hours, and destroying Lusia's mother's prize orchid. Eventually, however, the two generations learn to value each other without imposing their own tastes or standards.

Grown-Up Children resolves differences with a placatory and explicit moral: 'We're building new cities, but we can't be happy till we learn to live together,' Igor pontificates. Reconciliation, it appears, can be achieved with a modicum of tact and tolerance on both sides. Nevertheless, *Grown-Up Children* quietly implies that children will not grow up as long as they remain in the parental home, a mildly heretical notion that is nowhere to be found in the preponderance of films completed in 1963 and 1964. Most of them demonstrate, explicitly or tacitly, that continuity rather than conflict distinguishes relations between generations, and that discerning sons will learn from their sagacious fathers. At the same time, the older generation must learn to look beyond the offensive music, narrow trousers and slang, so as to identify the core of idealism that binds their children to them. These patterns characterize at least half a dozen films, including two made from Vasili Aksenov's popular novels, *Colleagues* and *My Younger Brother* [Moi mladshii brat, 1962].

Both films feature the typical quartet of three boys and a girl. In *Colleagues* they are doctors just finishing their medical training, in *My Younger Brother* they are high school graduates who want a summer adventure before continuing their educations. Each trio of boys consists of one idealist, one 'cynic' and a cypher as the third, barely fleshed-out character. Better movies, such as *Ilich's Gate* and *I Walk Around Moscow* [Ia shagaiu po Moskve, 1963], suffer from the same asymmetry: three characters, whether all men or two men and a woman, create a dramatically viable triangle, while a fourth seems superfluous and ends up little more than a sketch.

In *Colleagues* Sasha sets off for a rural community that has been without a doctor for two years, not because it is his obligation [*ob"iazannost'*], a matter of civic contract, but because it is his duty [*dolg*], a matter of personal commitment. Alesha disdains such 'big words', and signs on as a ship's doctor, a position that promises excitement, exoticism and romance. Instead, he finds tedium and corruption. Their analogues in *My Younger Brother* are two brothers, Vitia, a scientist who refuses to defend his dissertation – the expedient choice, and recommended by his supervisor – because subsequent work invalidated its conclusions, and Dimka, the young scoffer, who rebels against the rigidity of conventions and doubts all sacred cows.

Tension between older and younger generations proves to be more apparent than real. In the opening scenes of *Colleagues* two aggressively drunk middle-aged men accost the three buddies: 'You young people,' asks one belligerently, 'what do you live for? At your age we knew what to do.' However, he lives in Sasha's medical catchment area, and later, when he sees Sasha's dedication to his work, realizes he was unjust. For his part, Sasha learns to supplement his book-knowledge with sensitivity towards people very different from himself.

My Younger Brother, the film version of *Ticket to the Stars* [Zvezdnyi bilet], blunts much of the iconoclasm of Aksenov's novel: 'I'm a law-abiding man. When I see a red light, I stop,' says Vitia in the novel's first sentences. 'But my younger brother is another story. Dimka always crosses the street against the light.'[9] Aksenov and director Zarkhi were told that if the film resembled the book too closely, it would not be approved, and although Zarkhi retained some of the novel's mischievous humour, students at a screening in Moscow State University felt the movie betrayed what they considered 'their' novel.[10]

The film does retain Aksenov's subversive reversal of direction. The compass of desire points west, to Tallinn, instead of east, towards Siberia. Tallinn is lovely and exotic, with cobblestoned narrow streets and Gothic church spires. Aksenov's characters are entranced by its combination of semi-familiar and semi-alien: the heavily-accented Russian spoken by the Estonians, the work-clothes and folk costumes worn by Estonian women.

In Aksenov's fiction, choice of language, clothing and music often external-izes profoundly-held beliefs, and suggests resistance to state-imposed values. In these early novels, however, such resistance is relatively superficial, and in the film versions it degenerates into little more than adolescent rebelliousness: stylistic differences signal generational conflicts that can and will be reconciled. In *My Younger Brother*, for instance, the three male protagonists (Alik, Dima and Iurka) and Galia, the girl who makes up the quartet, live in a Leningrad courtyard that throbs to the heavy bass beat of loud rock-and-roll. The older generation impotently fumes. One man tries to drown it out with a folksong, 'one of *our* songs', while crabby matrons gripe about the din and the disgrace. But music also testifies to the fundamentally sound values that lurk beneath youth's pseudo-sophistication: Estonian folk music delights them, and tears roll down the face of the bespectacled aspiring writer Alik, a jazz fan, as he slumps on the sidewalk outside a church listening to Bach.

Both explicitly and symbolically, individual members of the older generation serve as role-models and mentors to the younger protagonists. In the end, all the characters in *My Younger Brother* grow up, which the movie defines as learning to appreciate the best values and the ideals represented by their seniors, and to see the value of absorbing those 'old' values and ideals into the new society they will create. Alik will learn his craft by studying Shakespeare and Aristophanes, the classics he earlier disdained. Galia is ready for real pro-fessional commitment to the theatre, no longer blinded by its glitter. Iurka, the shadowy third boy, will return to the girl and the job he found in Estonia. And Dima, the main hero, is ready to emulate his brother. Once he modishly affected to believe that love was a myth; now he trusts his feelings for Galia. Once he raised a toast to painted stars, because 'what's painted is preferable to what's natural'. Now he sits where his brother sat (though he doesn't know it), looking out the same window at the same scrap of sky and admiring the real stars just as Vitia did.

My Younger Brother takes a mediatory approach to the generational issue, as do most other films of 1963 and 1964. Two of them, *Come Back Tomorrow* [Prikhodite zavtra] and *Everything Remains for People* [Vse ostaetsia liudiam], are formulaic if well-acted depictions of mentoring seniors and responsive juniors, distinguished in the first by the acting of Ekaterina Savinova as the Siberian would-be singer Frosia, and in the second by Nikolai Cherkasov as Academician Dronov, a dying physicist.

In Evgenii Tashkov's *Come Back Tomorrow*, Ekaterina Savinova plays the Siberian Frosia, newly arrived in Moscow to study voice. She is dowdy in her mother's 'best dress', a foot longer than the current fashion, and ignorant: two students at the conservatory introduce themselves to her as Stanislavskii and Nemirovich-Danchenko, certain she will not recognize the names – nor does she. The skyscrapers, shot at acute angles for emphasis, stun her, as do restaurant prices; the indifferent crowds repel her ('It's awful,' she writes home. 'So many people, and nobody says hello'). Frosia conforms to tradition by being honest and uncorrupted, sincere in her dealings with other people and spontaneous in her interpretation of and responses to art. And she has a splendid voice.

Typically, culture and education centre in Moscow, but authenticity resides in the periphery, where Frosia's widowed mother is raising six children alone. Before moving into a dormitory Frosia stays with a sculptor, Kolia.[11] Kolia and his lady friend, the librarian Natasha, admire the simplicity of Frosia's life: like Abe Lincoln, she walked miles to school every day. But whereas Kolia qualifies his admiration ('All the same, she's so far away from everything'), Natasha is less deluded: 'Maybe we're the ones who are far away from her,' she muses.

Frosia has missed the deadline for registering at the conservatory, but she haunts the building, pestering an older professor, Aleksandr Aleksandrovich, for an appointment. After impatiently telling her repeatedly to 'come back tomorrow', he finally consents to listen to her. Her provincialism amuses him. 'A Russian folk song, "Along the banks of the Piterskaia",' she bellows, looking straight ahead from a fixed stance behind the piano. 'Performed by Burlakova, Frosia.' Perform it she does, with great gusto, *fortissima*, and in nearly a baritone register. She follows it with a beautiful rendition of Rosina's aria from *The Barber of Seville* ('Composer, G. Rossini; performer, Burlakova, Frosia'). The purity of her voice, her range, and, most of all, her transparent love for the music more than compensate for her clumsy stage presence. Aleksandr Aleksandrovich negotiates the bureaucratic obstacles barring her late admission and gives her special tutorials. No generation gap mars the relationship: fifty years his junior, Frosia is Aleksandr Aleksandrovich's artistic peer and his heir, eagerly matching his rigour and his devotion. 'If you please,' says Aleksandr Aleksandrovich to Frosia years later, 'let us start from the beginning.'

Everything Remains for People, a screen adaptation of a popular play directed by Georgii Natanson, repeats the doomed scientist motif of *Nine Days*. If Romm chose to focus steadily on the younger scientists, however, Georgii Natanson's gaze remains fixed on elderly Academician Dronov (Nikolai Cherkasov). The narrative frame of Dronov's dying moments encloses the body of the film, told in flashback. When doctors sternly warned Dronov to abandon the work that gave meaning to his life, he yielded the directorship of his institute to an unworthy successor, the careerist Morozov, husband of Dronov's devoted physician. Dronov bequeathed his intellectual rigour and scientific curiosity, symbolized by his notebooks, to a young woman scientist.

Everything Remains for People specifically denied the relevance of a generational conflict within the scientific and artistic intelligentsia.[12] The divisions in the film are not between age and youth, but between honesty and corruption, idealism and egoism. Dronov's doctor remembers that her husband, Morozov, failed to support her ten years earlier, 'during the unpleasantness about the doctors', and spoke up on their behalf only after their release (in other words, after Stalin's death). He hasn't changed.

Dronov, in contrast, belongs to a group of fictional scientists, modelled on older physicists like Tamm and Kapitsa, whose unquestionable devotion to their calling rivals their sensitivity to the morality of human relationships. He withheld his notebooks from the young woman, for instance, until he deemed her worthy. Like Solzhenitsyn's hero Nerzhin in *The First Circle*, Dronov's gods are scientists of profound ethical commitment: Einstein's picture hangs on his wall.

Dronov argues with his wife's cousin, a priest, on behalf of humanist–scientific values. The priest, echoing Dostoevskii's Grand Inquisitor, asserts that such values are adequate for strong personalities like Dronov, but that most people are weak and need faith in an afterlife and a divinity in order to lead good lives. The film endorses Dronov's point of view by portraying those characters who exemplify and act on his philosophy – Dronov, his wife, his disciple, his doctor – as unambiguously meritorious. Nevertheless, *Everything Remains for People* in no way derogates the priest's spiritual values.[13] He is a thoughtful man, nearly Dronov's intellectual equal (they play chess together regularly), and while he may underestimate the potential of human beings, he is motivated entirely by compassion, untainted by the slightest shadow of contempt for others or self-aggrandizement.[14]

A popular film of 1964, Georgii Danelia's *I Walk Around Moscow*, exemplifies the circumspection of the period. Released in April 1964, *I Walk Around Moscow* was one of the last in a long line of 'male buddy' Soviet movies. It starred the boyish and engaging Nikita Mikhalkov as Kolia, a construction worker on the metro. He is flanked by Volodia, a Siberian visiting Moscow en route for home, and Sasha, a childhood friend on the brink of marriage. The female member of this quartet is Alena, a pretty salesgirl with whom Kolia is slightly smitten, but who herself falls for the more serious Siberian visitor. Kolia is the moving force of the film: it follows him around for one day as he shows Volodia around Moscow, escorts Volodia to visit a writer, pursues Alena, helps Sasha arrange a deferral of Sasha's army service so he can marry, and so on.

Gennadii Shpalikov turned to the script of *I Walk Around Moscow* during the lengthy process of revising *Ilich's Gate*. He replicated a number of attractive

23. *I Walk Around Moscow*

features from *Ilich's Gate*, including its slangy, wise-cracking dialogue and a loving attention to Moscow. As in *Ilich's Gate*, the Moscow of *I Walk Around Moscow* is increasingly international, as we see from an encounter with a Japanese tourist and from a concert of Latin American music. The city is constantly expanding, and its crowded but clean streets, streams of pedestrians, river lights, statues and squares become part of the film's action, a visual means of conveying youth's mastery over their own future and the future of the nation.

However, nothing controversial, let alone subversive, shadows *I Walk Around Moscow*. Because the three protagonists are roughly five years younger than the trio in *Ilich's Gate*, their enjoyable high jinks simply illustrate the ebullience of youth. They are immature because they are eighteen, like the boys in *My Younger Brother*, not because they are irresponsible young adults reluctant to grow up, like Khutsiev's twenty-three-year-olds. The prevarications and neglect of Slava, husband and father in *Ilich's Gate*, are consequential, for himself, his wife and his child; the inconsistency of Sasha, who in a childish fit of pique with his fiancée calls off the wedding and heads back to his draft board to enlist, is amusing.

Furthermore, *I Walk Around Moscow* ignores or treats conventionally what are ambiguous or complicated issues in *Ilich's Gate*. Rock-and-roll is not heard; instead, an ordinary working stiff requests Tchaikovsky's First Piano Concerto at Alena's music counter in Moscow's emporium GUM, which is filmed so as to showcase its ornate balustrades and walkways. The film closes with Kolia vaulting the metro escalator steps two at a time and singing about how fine life is; the theme song, 'I Walk Around Moscow', has a catchy tune that fits in with the film's pleasant but stylistically neutral score.

Fanaticism is gently mocked when a Young Pioneer, his kerchief round his neck, indignantly refuses to compromise his principles by entering a church to find the owner of a dog tied up on the street. At the same time, when Kolia does go in, the camera keeps a respectful distance, tracking the liturgy and the congregation (a few elderly women) as if eavesdropping on an entirely alien and quaint ritual.

Similarly, the references to the war are standard. Kolia's grandmother identifies her sons in a family picture hanging on the wall, and adds, 'They were all killed in the war.' The draft board official tells Kolia and Sasha that 'at their age' he was fighting outside of Kursk. When Sasha berates himself for treating his fiancée so badly, he is seated in front of a photograph of his late father in Second World War uniform: unlike Serezha's father in *Ilich's Gate*, Sasha's father symbolically guides his confused son.

Indeed, in *I Walk Around Moscow* the generation of fathers, alive or dead, provides a clear-cut moral example for the generation of sons. Old and young are allies. The older writer who read and liked Volodia's first story in *Iunost* invites his help in compiling an anthology of young Siberian authors. When the obstreperous Kolia grimaces at his reflection in a subway door, two older passengers look at each other and smile benignly. From an official point of view, *I Walk Around Moscow* was obviously preferable to *Ilich's Gate*. It portrayed Soviet life, and especially Soviet youth, as energetic and idealistic, joyful and helpful. Nevertheless, that was only half the right answer: 'While showing *that* everything is good,' Rostislav Iurenev chided, 'it never explains *why* everything is good.' He wondered why such talented young artists as Danelia and Shpalikov avoided complexity and depth.[15]

Iurenev had a point, but, by failing to mention *Ilich's Gate* and its controversies, he was also disingenuous. Khutsiev and Shpalikov had created a film of complexity and depth, and the authorities tried to eviscerate it. Warily responding to the realities of 1963 and 1964, Danelia and Shpalikov made an anodyne, diluted replacement in *I Walk Around Moscow*. With its affection for youth and its sense of life as a package of pleasant surprises, *I Walk Around Moscow* may well be considered the last film of 'thaw illusions'.[16]

Part IV Strange Interlude, 1964–65

13. Strange Interlude: Introduction

T hroughout the autumn of 1963 and the winter and spring of 1964, tension permeated the artistic community. Aleksandr Solzhenitsyn was in the running for the Lenin Prize for literature, a prestigious and lucrative honour to be awarded the following spring, and rumours preceded the formal announcement of the roster of candidates. Liberals favoured Solzhenitsyn, and *Novyi mir* staunchly defended the writer and itself for publishing him, but the stories Solzhenitsyn had published after *One Day in the Life of Ivan Denisovich*, 'For the Good of the Cause' and 'Matryona's Home' in particular, infuriated conservatives.[1]

The cautious prize committee threaded its way between the Scylla of Solzhenitsyn and Daniil Granin, on the one hand, and the Charybdis of conservative choices Aleksandr Chakovskii and Galina Serebriakova, on the other, to award the prize to the Ukrainian novelist Oles Gonchar in late April 1964. In choosing an undistinguished writer whose work stressed 'the theme of harmony between the older and younger generations',[2] the committee probably satisfied no one except the Party.

Anxiety abated slightly during the new year, as *Novyi mir* continued to publish prison camp memoirs and *Literaturnaia gazeta* celebrated Anna Akhmatova's seventy-fifth birthday. At the same time, the authorities curtailed poetry readings and concerts by the popular guitar poets Bulat Okudzhava, Aleksandr Galich and Vladimir Vysotskii, and in February 1964 arrested Joseph Brodsky on charges of parasitism. A transcript of the trial, circulated in *samizdat*, revealed the judge's patent hostility towards Brodsky and the complicity of witnesses from the literary community on behalf of the prosecution. Although Brodsky was relatively little known at that time, except to a small circle of poetry-lovers, his conviction and sentence of five years' internal exile shocked the intellectual community.

Throughout 1964 the arts community kept a low profile, wondering and watching. *Iskusstvo kino* circumspectly filled its pages with 'safe' subjects –

chemistry, film design, popular actors and actresses – along with Party doctrine and many references to the restorative if not regenerative results of the Party's wisdom as articulated at the various forums of 1963. In their New Year's greetings, for instance, the editors echoed Khrushchev, rejecting 'on behalf of' the Soviet public films that 'evoke apathy and pessimism, films under the influence of an alien scepticism, films that imitate the formalistic quests of the bourgeois West'.[3] In several issues 'ordinary' Soviet citizens described what they sought in cinema; a television programme provided a similar outlet for *vox populi*.

Every context served as an opportunity to emphasize the vital role of the *narod*, the people, in Russia's history and culture. When *Iskusstvo kino* published the script of *Andrei Rublev*, for example, an afterword clarified that essential point. Its author, a historian, defined the 'simple people' as craftsmen inspired by ideals of national liberation and social protest, who directed their anger against all exploiters, whether Russian or Tatar, secular or clerical. Rublev's art reflected 'their faith in self-preservation on earth, their will to exist in the hell of contemporary evil and violence'.[4]

When Lenfilm released Grigorii Kozintsev's stunning black-and-white *Hamlet* [Gamlet], starring Innokentii Smoktunovskii, in 1964, the national press interpreted the play to fit the exigencies of the period.[5] One reviewer, for instance, pitied Ophelia as a symbol of all victims of absolute despotism, and praised Hamlet as a genuine freedom-loving 'warrior', neither indecisive nor threatened by madness. In this reading of the film, Hamlet is courageous and strong, motivated by righteous anger at the prison Claudius has made of Denmark; his life-or-death struggle with Claudius acts as a crucible in which to forge and mature his intellect.[6]

For cinema, the summer and autumn of 1964 were curiously schizophrenic. On the one hand, after nearly a year's worth of mediocrity, September and October witnessed two significant directorial debuts, Vasilii Shukshin's *A Boy Like That* [Zhivet takoi paren'] and Elem Klimov's *Welcome, or No Trespassing* [Dobro pozhalovat', ili postoronnim vkhod vospreshchen], and the year closed with the release of a third major film, Aleksei Saltykov's *The Chairman*.

On the other hand, official fiats multiplied. *Kommunist* devoted a lengthy article to 'art in a heroic epoch', sections of which were reprinted as a supplement to *Iskusstvo kino*.[7] The Central Committee advised Mosfilm to improve fiscal discipline, avoid uncritical borrowing from the West, demonstrate the 'Soviet way of thought and action' while 'unmasking' the bourgeois way of life, refrain from making 'weak' pictures, and plan appropriately triumphal movies for the fiftieth anniversary of the revolution and hundredth anniversary of Lenin's birth.[8]

Mosfilm's director concurred, citing chapter and verse of the studio's delinquency. The studio failed to provide exemplary films on subjects like the

Komsomol and 'youth's leading role in industry', he said. Mosfilm too often hired (and paid in advance) inexperienced writers who furnished inadequate scripts; it spent too much money on lighting and production; it permitted overcommitted directors to undertake new projects, which they then neglected in order to fulfil prior obligations.[9]

In April 1964 Khrushchev had celebrated his seventieth birthday with great public pomp. But behind the façade of Party unity, 'the Great Decade' of his rule was 'drawing to a close amid economic failure and political intrigue'.[10] Many people within the power apparatus disliked Khrushchev's efforts at destalinization, perceiving them as destabilizing to Party authority. And Khrushchev's growing intolerance of even the mildest criticism frustrated his subordinates.

The General Secretary had made many enemies. He had antagonized heavy industry by diverting funds towards consumer-goods production. His agricultural policies – cultivating the Virgin Lands, planting corn and reducing the size of private plots and the number of privately-owned cattle – had proved disastrous, forcing the Soviet Union to spend precious foreign currency to import grain in 1964.[11] The Cuban missile crisis had compromised Soviet prestige and credibility abroad, the European satellite nations seemed determined to go their own ways, and foreign communist parties were increasingly disinclined to come to heel at Moscow's command.

Throughout the summer and early autumn of 1964, Khrushchev's colleagues engaged in intricate and secret preparations, anticipating a counter-attack by the wily Party boss. However, Khrushchev, perhaps from age and fatigue, perhaps from fear that his enemies possessed and would use documentation of his complicity in Stalinist repressions, chose to resign quickly and quietly. On 16 October 1964, Khrushchev announced his resignation from the post of General Secretary, and a day later Leonid Brezhnev and Aleksei Kosygin deplored and distanced themselves from his 'hare-brained schemes' and 'half-baked ideas'.[12] Without fanfare, Khrushchev vanished from the public domain. After ten years in which probably not a single *Pravda* or *Izvestia* had omitted a reference to him, Khrushchev's name appeared in the central press only once before his death in 1971: when he denounced as bogus his (authentic) memoirs published in the West.

New starts usually generate a sense of possibility, and Khrushchev's 'retirement' was no exception. In the first half of 1965, the collective leadership of Brezhnev and Kosygin appeared to redress some of Khrushchev's more egregious policies. The expansion of private agricultural plots pleased peasants. The reappearance of flour, a scarce commodity for months, delighted consumers. Scientists were heartened by the demotion of the influential geneticist Trofim Lysenko, whose wrong-headed Lamarckian theories had damaged agricultural science for years. Although Lysenko had begun to lose Khrushchev's support,

Strange Interlude

in part thanks to the opposition of scientists led by biologist Zhores Medvedev, he was not fired as director of the Institute of Genetics at the Academy of Sciences until Khrushchev resigned.

Liberal intellectuals and artists continued to scrutinize events for favourable portents. They welcomed such reversals of Khrushchev's policies as the resumed publication of Ehrenburg's memoirs: a Central Committee ban that had interrupted their appearance was revoked shortly after Khrushchev's departure. Prose by Nekrasov and Pasternak, authors previously in disgrace, also appeared in *Novyi mir* in January 1965.

Other encouraging reversals occurred in January and February. The Writers' Union ousted the most doctrinaire members of the secretariat – Kochetov, Sofronov and Markov – and replaced them with younger liberals. The Leningrad branch quickly followed suit, electing Daniil Granin deputy secretary. A few months later Ilichev, who had chaired the ideological commission since its establishment in November 1962, and who was detested for his onslaughts on the arts, was transferred to the Ministry of Foreign Affairs; the commission itself was dissolved.

In late February *Pravda*'s recently-appointed editor, Aleksei Rumiantsev, ran a signed editorial entitled 'The Party and the Intelligentsia'. Rumiantsev cited the Party resolution of 1925, which rejected Party interference in literary affairs, calling it 'the most important Party principle in matters of artistic creation'. Progress demanded 'different schools and trends, styles and genres competing with one another', he wrote, and no one should 'impose subjective evaluations and personal tastes as the yardstick of artistic creation, particularly when they are expressed in the name of the Party'.[13] A month later, consistent with this modestly liberal line, *Pravda* published a sharp attack on the dogmatic journal *Oktiabr*.

In an invigorated artistic community, musicians exploited what one composer called 'the freest period of Soviet culture ... since the days of Stalin' to perform new symphonies by Shchedrin and Karaev as well as Shostakovich's long-unheard Third Symphony and some of his most daring and experimental pieces.[14] The film world experienced a burst of creative vigour, the fruits of which emerged towards the end of 1965 and in 1966, and a few controversial films reached Soviet screens, most prominently Marlen Khutsiev's *I am Twenty*.

Hindsight can discern in the vicissitudes of 1965 the formation of the Brezhnevite patterns that dominated the next twenty years. Though the year began with a surge of energy and in an atmosphere of relative tolerance, the latter, at least, dissipated quickly. By late summer the beacons of liberal journalism, *Novyi mir* and *Iunost*, were under attack for publishing 'negative' work. After six months of Aleksei Rumiantsev's relatively liberal editorship, *Pravda* gave space to an article by Sergei Pavlov, head of the Komsomol, in which he indicted literature and movies that 'glorified suffering' and 'preached hopelessness'. The Party must be concerned, he wrote, when art fails to stimulate revolutionary energy, instead promoting scepticism, especially among young people. And Pavlov spelled out the mission of contemporary art: to help the Party combat 'nihilism' and 'rejection of authority', and to educate those ignorant of or scornful towards 'the historical experience' of the older generation.[15]

Early in September a dispute broke out between *Pravda* and *Izvestia*. *Izvestia* excoriated literary depictions of the seamier side of life as nihilistic. *Pravda* retorted that by exposing such defects, authors were trying to correct them. 'It is unrealistic', Rumiantsev wrote, 'to expect absolute balance from every writer.' He argued on behalf of trusting artists who were devoted to communist ideas, yet felt no need for Party control of the arts. The Party should 'defend the artist's freedom to choose theme and subject, style and manner of execution'.[16]

Ten days later Rumiantsev lost his job. Rumiantsev's firing followed hard on the heels of the arrest of Andrei Siniavskii and Iulii Daniel. The two men, both prominent writers and critics, had smuggled their fiction out of the country in order to publish in the West; they were accused under Article 70 of the Criminal Code of anti-Soviet activity, and tried five months later.

Rumiantsev's dismissal and the Siniavskii/Daniel arrest in September punctuated an on-going chronicle of increasing repression. In the middle of 1965, serious harassment of Ukrainian activists began, and continued for the best part of a year. Of the hundred-odd artists, scholars and scientists arrested, about a score were tried and sentenced to hard labour. In August one of the Party's chief ideological bosses had advocated much tighter ideological controls. The campaign against Solzhenitsyn had been steadily intensifying since the previous winter; in April 1965 *Ivan Denisovich* was accused of 'disorienting youth about the Soviet past', a grave charge, especially because it appeared in the party's theoretical organ, *Kommunist*. In September the KGB confiscated three of the four copies of *The First Circle* that Solzhenitsyn had hidden with friends.[17]

On the surface the film world seemed relatively untroubled. The Cinematographers' Union, Ivan Pyrev's long-time dream, finally became a reality, convening formally in November 1965, in the Kremlin. The presidium included many younger film-makers, among them Riazanov, Tarkovskii and Danelia. The union represented an institutional voice for the industry, giving its members a status formally equivalent to that of writers, artists and musicians. Despite declining attendance and television's disquieting ascendancy, cinema still represented a leading leisure activity for Soviet citizens, and the industry promoted itself via organized festivals, retrospectives dedicated to stars, and lectures and exhibits on Soviet film history. Taking to heart the Central Committee's earlier complaints about fiscal irresponsibility, the studios were turning out movies more quickly, hence more cheaply, and production figures kept rising.[18]

Strange Interlude

Back in June 1965, when Lev Kulidzhanov addressed the organizing committee of the union, he felt confident (or brash) enough to chastize his colleagues for their spurious unanimity. 'Our film critics', he said, 'must have the opportunity to express their opinions candidly. So what if their views are controversial, so what if they polemicize with one another – we need an atmosphere of free debate and unprejudiced discussion about our films and our industry the way we need oxygen.'[19]

At exactly the same time, however, oxygen was disappearing, for cinema as for society generally. Over the next few years, individual acts of repression – searches, harassment, interrogations, arrests – became more frequent. Official sanctions blocked the expanding national self-awareness of Jews, Ukrainians, Crimean Tatars and other groups. Memoirs and historical investigations written in the hopeful heyday of the Khrushchev thaw vanished into locked drawers or slipped across borders to be published abroad. Psychiatry became an instrument of state policy to be used against dissenters, whether poets like Esenin-Vol'pin or military heroes like General Piotr Grigorenko.

As for cinema, 1965 was a fateful year: 'Bureaucrats, perched in wait for artists on the border of the Brezhnevite stagnation, put their scissors to work: they would cut, they would ban, they would shelve. There would be an enormous number of casualties.'[20]

14. Odd Man Out

Taken together, the three major films that opened in the last months of 1964 mark a crossroads in Soviet cinema. While obviously indebted to their cinematic predecessors and continuing the evolution of several trends already discussed, they also nudged Soviet cinema on to new paths. Of the three, Vasilii Shukshin's *A Boy Like That* departed most radically from the prevailing thematic emphasis on the autonomous, self-defining individual.

Gorky Studio released *A Boy Like That* on 1 September 1964, a date calculated to draw attention to the film, since cultural life resumed with the commencement of the new school year; few movies of importance opened during the summer. The public already liked Shukshin as an actor (in *Two Fedors*). His first collection of short stories, *Village People* [Sel'skie zhiteli], had appeared to critical acclaim the previous year. (A man of prodigious energy as well as abundant gifts, in the decade before his death at age forty-five Shukshin managed to direct four more movies, to act in another dozen, and to publish a play, two historical novels and four collections of stories.)

Shukshin based the script for *A Boy Like That* on two of his own stories, 'First Class Driver' and 'Grinka Maliugin'.[1] The opening frames of *A Boy Like That* – a map of vast, sparsely populated space traversed by a highway – introduce Shukshin's territory. The camera pans the road, 'inviting one to take a good look at the surrounding world. Like a newcomer who has happened upon a town, it scans the distant mountains ... the steppes at their base, the unceasing flow of the Katun [River]'.[2] It comes to rest on a solitary wooden-frame building with steps in front and a fenced yard: a *chainaia*, where long-distance truckers on the Chuiskii highway take a break, drink tea and chat.

The hero, Pashka Kolokolnikov, gets back into his cab and sets out, and the rest of what is essentially a 'road movie' follows his encounters with riders and drivers, and his visits to villages where he flirts, meddles, strikes poses, lies, entertains others and himself, indulges in fantasies of his ideal. Eventually he lands in hospital after driving a burning truck into a river before it explodes.

Strange Interlude

Tightly constructed plots had been fading out of Soviet films for some time. Films of 'discovery' – whether child-centred, such as Kalik's *Man Goes Beyond the Sun*, or coming-of-age, as, for example, *Ilich's Gate* – relied on an episodic structure to expose their heroes to a variety of enriching experiences. But Shukshin entirely abandoned cause–effect linkage in favour of mini-stories spliced together only by their protagonist. As Shukshin himself later wrote: 'Plotless narration is more flexible, bolder, it is devoid of preconception and ready-made definitions.'[3] A year later, he even discarded the single protagonist as unifying element, structuring *Your Son and Brother* [Vash syn i brat] as three discrete stories about three brothers.

Pashka belongs to Shukshin's fictional brotherhood of village boys who yearn for something different, an ideal they cannot define, let alone realize. Torn between the vital kinship ties of home and its stultifying boredom, lured by the opportunities of town, but repelled by its atomization, his heroes cannot settle down in either milieu, and their frustration often leads to self-destructive behaviour and scenes of scandal worthy of Dostoevskii.

Shukshin's vivid, rich language invigorated a familiar dilemma, and his mixture of humour and pathos strongly appealed to audiences. They laughed at Pasha's antics, but valued his 'good heart'; he was at once a 'folkloric hero in a folkloric reality' and a living contemporary.[4] A colleague of Shukshin's recalled how 'at countless evenings dedicated to Shukshin's memory and work, especially those that took place in workers' clubs and palaces of culture, viewers spoke of how Pashka Kolokolnikov had become part of their family'.[5]

Critics, while appreciative, had problems 'placing' Shukshin's art. Both pre-revolutionary and Soviet aesthetic traditions tended to define 'serious' literature as art that treated life's problems in an appropriately serious tone; they dismissed as frivolous and insubstantial what seemed to be mere 'entertainment'. Shukshin's work, on paper and on screen, hardly fitted either category.

Despite his Siberian peasant background, his limited formal education and his blue-collar jobs, Shukshin seemed to belong squarely among the intellectuals and artists most directly affected by and committed to the political revelations and psychological liberation of the thaw (the *shestidesiatniki*, people of the 1960s). Upon enrolling in the State Institute of Cinematography in 1954, Shukshin joined Moscow's liberal circles. He studied with Mikhail Romm, and he began his acting career in *Two Fedors*, directed by a director deeply engaged in 'thaw' themes, Marlen Khutsiev. Both Shukshin's fiction and his films accentuated the individual's search for identity and freedom, a central thaw concern. When *A Boy Like That* opened, then, it was initially interpreted as a variant of many works created by like-minded artists in the late 1950s and early 1960s.

Yet careful consideration of *A Boy Like That*, especially in conjunction with Shukshin's other films, reveals Shukshin's perception of the world as fundamentally illogical, irrational and deeply sad. Neither the perception, nor the world, has much in common with those of Khutsiev or Romm. Indeed, for all Shukshin's admiration for his teacher Romm, his own deliberate avoidance of intellectual heroes signalled a tacit polemic with the cult of science and scholarship symbolized by Romm's *Nine Days of a Year*.[6] Shukshin's trans-Siberian truckers and mechanics, carpenters and construction workers, convicts and muscle-men, are not even distant cousins to Romm's clever physicists and Khutsiev's quick-witted Muscovites. Moreoever, Shukshin's heroes require the very familial and domestic chains that they repudiate. Pashka and his successors define themselves on their native Siberian soil, within a domestic context, whatever its constraints and however urgently they try to escape it.

In *A Boy Like That*, and again in *Your Son and Brother*, the Siberian ambience in which the characters work and live is filmed with sensitivity and without sentimentality. It is beautiful, but it is not romanticized. (Shukshin met his cameraman, Valerii Ginzburg, when the latter was shooting *When the Trees were Big* for Lev Kulidzhanov, and recognized Ginzburg's gift for landscape.) Long pans and dollied shots convey the omnipresence of nature. Never mere illustration, the environment is the essential pre-condition for the film's action, the bedrock from which its characters emerge. 'A fence, bushes on a bank, the Katun river in spring flood ... Before each film, before any action, before the hero appears, Shukshin gives this kind of prelude. One knows nothing, but one already senses where the heroes come from.'[7] When Pashka and his friend Uncle Kondrat sprawl on the riverbank to smoke their cigarettes, the natural world is as much part of them as they are of it: Kondrat's fantasies lodge there, as he imagines lying outside at night, looking up at the stars.

The camera moves indoors with equal care. The wood-burning stoves, cloth-covered table, framed photographs on the log walls, cupboard for the good glasses and decanter with vodka are not quaint, ethnographic objects to be observed with cold detachment. Nor are they fetishes or icons to be venerated. The *realia* of people's lives, they merit respect.

Shukshin often hired villagers to play bit parts, thus enhancing the verisimilitude of his films, and he inspired his professional actors with his own flair for natural, appropriate language. Nina Sazonova recalled the scene when Pashka brings together tongue-tied Uncle Kondrat with her character, lonely Aunty Anisia:[8]

> The shoot went well, it seemed genuinely inspired. But then came the point when Boris Balakin [Kondrat] and I, desperately embarrassed by Pashka's impudence in pushing us together ... had used up all the dialogue written in the script, everything we'd rehearsed. The camera was still running, Vasilii Makarovich [Shukshin] was silent, watching us with mischievous expectation. Boris Balakin, to have something to do, uncertainly reached a hand towards the decanter. Out of my mouth came the question, 'And do you esteem our vodka, Kondrat

Strange Interlude

24. *A Boy Like That*

Stepanovich?' [*Vodochku-to uvazhaete*]. (The casual question masked Anisia's
anxiety.)

'Uh-huh,' Balakin replied without thinking, but immediately caught himself,
withdrew his hand and corrected his mistake: 'No, just on holidays.'

'Well, holidays are another matter. Let us have a drink,' I said, calming down
and cheering up the timid suitor.

Vasilii Makarovich was very pleased, simply delighted. He laughed and said,
'You've come up with such good dialogue [*Tekst-to vy kakoi lovkii smasterili*].
Thank you. I would never have thought of it.'[9]

In his fantasies Pashka wears tails and a top hat, while his 'ideal' woman
lounges in a room full of ornaments or, sheathed in white, beckons to him
from a stand of birch trees. He snaps back into a reality of sheep blocking the
highway and a man (supposedly 'cultured') who assumes he is ignorant and
probably dishonest simply because he is a trucker.

His world consists of small towns and collective farms, where a travelling
'fashion show' models outfits designed for 'Natasha, Shock Worker of Communist Labour' and 'Masha the Poultry-Girl', who studies for her correspondence
course while she feeds the hens. The audience – guffawing men and work-worn
women in muddy boots – have as much use for a two-piece swimsuit with
matching sundress as they would for stiletto-heeled fur-trimmed pink mules.

Pashka seeks attachment in innocent flirtations. His deceptions are transparent: soon after he pretends to the librarian Nastia that he is a Muscovite, his ignorance of Moscow's geography betrays him and he cheerfully acknowledges the lie. He is at worst a scamp, at best good-hearted and – as played by Leonid Kuravlev – enormously attractive, his charm enhanced by the slight stammer that belies his apparent self-confidence.

Nevertheless, Pashka's lack of education and his compromising fantasies concerned the Moscow branch of the Union of Journalists. Before organizing a screening in Voronezh, they debated at length the pedagogic potential of *A Boy Like That* and Pashka's 'positive' or 'negative' status. 'In an age when everyone studies', Larisa Kriachko wrote disparagingly, why praise ignorance? 'In an age of great socialist revolutions', why advocate 'some kind of homespun truth', and seek the meaning of life in 'mindless pleasures'? (A kindergarten teacher concurred: Pashka's 'uncultured' speech and behaviour would corrupt her charges, not to mention the bottle of vodka ('Horror!') that appears at one of his stops.)[10] For Kriachko, the film's 'ideological muddle' [*ideinaia neraz-berikha*] doomed Pashka to a bad end unless he found himself a 'great goal' to pursue.[11]

Kriachko notwithstanding, the summer before its official release *A Boy Like That* won a prize 'for its life-affirming joy, lyricism and original resolution' at the All-Union Film Festival in Leningrad. Shukshin had not planned the film as a comedy:

> I never thought about making a comedy … As I understand comedy, someone must be funny. Usually the hero … The hero of our film is not funny. He is a good-natured, responsive fellow, smart, thoughtful, though with a slightly arti-ficial idea about life. He doesn't always think before he acts, but whatever he has, whatever he knows and has managed to learn in his life he is ready to give to other people.[12]

The comic rubric accommodated more comfortably Elem Klimov's first feature film, *Welcome, or No Trespassing*, with its depiction of a Young Pioneer summer camp and its hide-bound director. Klimov's 'villain', camp director Dynin, is a familiar type, obsequious towards authority and resistant to innova-tion, although in Evgenii Evstigneev's performance he becomes a rather hapless tyrant. But Klimov's fresh and witty comedy satirizes a great many Soviet pieties, shuns conventional cinematography, and relies on highly unorthodox fantasy. Klimov's revisions of Soviet comic tradition shaped subsequent comedies, his own (*Adventures of a Dentist* [Pokhozhdeniia zubnogo vracha]) and those of other directors, including Riazanov and Danelia.

The plot of *Welcome, or No Trespassing* is simple. Camper Kostia Inochkin breaks the rules once too often by swimming across the river to an island where the local kids congregate, and Dynin expels him from the camp. Un-willing to face his grandmother's reproaches, Inochkin sneaks back into the

Strange Interlude

25. *Welcome, or No Trespassing*

camp. The other children successfully hide him, with help from the town children, their pig, and staff accomplices. The ritual and requisite 'unmasking' occurs on Parents' Day.

Since the film portrayed a Pioneer Camp, the Komsomol had to vet the script, and its Central Committee gave wary approval to early drafts. Mosfilm remained none the less apprehensive. 'This is a very dangerous road,' worried Aleksandr Khmelik, a scriptwriter whose own *My Friend, Kolka* had run into some difficulties a few years before. 'Our Young Pioneers do good work, under the supervision of representatives of the Central Committee of the Komsomol'; Dynin shouldn't be too young, because camp directors cannot be immature, but he shouldn't be too old, because then he becomes just another Ogurtsov, 'a Young Pioneer Ogurtsov [from *Carnival Night*] in a different genre'.[13]

They allowed Klimov to proceed, but he knew he was on notice. 'Every morning, I would ask the accountant in charge of our money how much we had spent, and would then try to spend more, because the more we had spent, the less likely they were to close us down.'[14] On location at the Black Sea, Klimov received a telegram from the authorities instructing the team to stop all work and return to Moscow. Luckily, by then most of the footage was already in the can. Klimov hastily shot the rest while Semen Lungin, who wrote the script together with his collaborator Ilia Nusinov, flew back to Moscow and provided a smokescreen by 'rewriting' the script.[15]

Lungin and Nusinov's script (the real one) explicitly mocks the truisms and bombast of official Sovietese. As Inochkin slinks past a line of statues to hide under the raised dais, for instance, a voice-over intones pompously, 'Thus Kostia Inochkin placed himself outside the law' [*Tak Kostia Inochkin pereshel na nelegal'noe polozhenoe*]. During the rehearsal for Parents' Day, director Dynin reads from worn-out, barely legible instructions: 'Spectators applaud. Applause ends,' and when a pretty young counsellor objects, he retorts that the instructions may be old but no one has rescinded them. The highlight of Parents' Day is the crowning of 'Queen Corn', empress of the fields, a burlesque of Khrushchev's catastrophic agricultural policy. The husk falls away to reveal not the little girl Dynin chose because of her family connections – her uncle is a Party official – but our hero, Kostia Inochkin. To Dynin's dismay, 'spectators applaud'.

The children's conspiracy itself signifies an intrinsic subversion of authority. A banner proclaims that the children run the camp ['*Deti – vy khoziaeva lageria*'], but Dynin does not believe it for a moment. In the end, however, they *do* run the camp, with a little help from sympathetic adults. While they are preferable to the adults, however, they are by no means 'positive heroes'. They ostracize the misfit among them, in this case a dim-witted, oversized youngster with a loopy smile, who wanders around with a butterfly net and continually asks the others what they are doing. ('Scram,' they usually reply.) In order to abort the Parents' Day festivities, when Inochkin's grandmother is bound to turn up in search of her grandson, one of Inochkin's pals conceives of 'creating' a mysterious epidemic; the symptoms are achieved by a brave leap into a thicket of nettles. Later, however, the same boy breaks under pressure. He draws a picture of Inochkin for the camp newspaper, on whose 'editorial board' he serves, to be used as an Awful Warning: 'My colleagues chose me,' he explains to Inochkin apologetically. Another camper, whom we see from the knees down, routinely reports on the other kids to Dynin.

Inochkin's fantasies punctuate the film. Sent off to make his ignominious way home, Inochkin imagines arriving at his grandmother's door with news of his expulsion. An expert on adult admonitions – having, doubtless, heard more than one – Inochkin can anticipate with precision. 'You're driving me into my grave,' she will say in despair, and into her grave she will go, via an elaborate funeral procession shaped as a gigantic question mark, while bearded eulogists point aged but unwavering fingers at the culprit, Inochkin. (Her round face adorns a huge banner carried by mourners, and one censor, who saw a resemblance to Khrushchev, accused Klimov of implying it was Khrushchev's funeral.)[16]

Strange Interlude

Hidden beneath the dais, Inochkin overhears Dynin rehearsing his Parents' Day address. He fantasizes that Dynin, stricken with a fatal malady, desperately requires a blood transfusion. Naturally, Inochkin alone has the matching blood type. His heroic donation to his enemy is greeted by 'stormy applause', a truism of Party meetings. Despite his gratitude to his 'blood brother', Dynin stubbornly refuses to readmit Inochkin to the camp.

Filmed in black-and-white, with the lush landscape sharply contrasted to the simple camp structures,[17] and with whimsical fantasy contrasted to precisely observed reality, *Welcome* achieves a visual balance between metaphoric and literal. Klimov explained his approach: 'We shot everything head-on, like posters or portraits ... If the picture has any originality, it lies in the eclectic style, the mixture of theater-poster and documentary.'[18] The final fantasy is particularly vivid: Inochkin, his grandmother, and the hopelessly dull boy take flight, soaring over the river to the island beyond, and the dull boy flies back to announce that the film is over. Their exhilarating flight triumphantly transcends limitations of age, ability and 'real' space. It is, as well, illusory. In the Soviet context such fantasies may be more admissible in a child than in the adult Pashka Kolokolnikov, but they still constitute an unacceptable evasion of reality.

When studio members convened to watch sections of the film in late November 1963, their discussion suggests people tiptoeing through a minefield. One writer repeated 'we have nothing to fear' so many times that he must have been scared to death. The word 'complicated' [*slozhnyi*], a tocsin to well-tuned Soviet ears, recurs many times. 'Under no circumstances should the film be completed hastily,' warned one participant. 'The film has friends,' admitted another, 'but it is provoking a large number of hostile responses.' One man tripped over his own circumspection. 'We need balance,' he began. 'I'm not afraid of the word. For me there are not enough appealing, upstanding adults. I would like to see them alongside the fine boys and girls. Not in order to balance the scales,' he continued confusingly, 'but because that would really give a picture of our actual, living world in all its particularity.' Aleksandr Zarkhi closed the discussion with a reference to the 'anxiety' *Welcome* had evoked both within the studio and from 'a whole variety of organizations'.[19]

After months of nervous handwringing, the studio released *Welcome* in early October. According to Klimov, Khrushchev personally intervened: he saw the film, liked it, and asked why it was not being shown in cinemas.[20] If so, it was one of the General Secretary's last forays into the arts before he 'resigned for reasons of ill health' on 16 October, twelve days after the film's release.

In the press, praise for the film's freshness and originality competed with often absurd attacks. 'There's no discipline in this camp,' Lungin recalled one critic writing. 'A person is sitting under the platform and no one notices!'[21] Distribution was limited, but compared with a number of controversial films released just after Khrushchev's fall from power, *Welcome* had a relatively happy fate. In its first year of release it was seen by 13.4 million viewers, a small number by Soviet standards, but sizeable compared to the handful who somehow managed to see Klimov's second film, *Adventures of a Dentist*. Another comedy, Leonid Gaidai's *Operation 'Y' and Shurik's Other Adventures* [Operatsiia 'Y' i drugie prikliucheniia Shurika], was the box-office blockbuster of 1965, with 70 million viewers.[22]

The film that ushered out 1964 in a gust of glory was hardly humorous. *The Chairman*, released on 28 December 1964, had been trumpeted for months in the press. The December issue of *Iskusstvo kino* (which made no mention of Khrushchev's resignation) formally announced the completion of *The Chairman*, 'a work affirming and raising to new levels the best traditions of Soviet film art'.[23] In spite of such a benediction, the film nearly foundered; according to its author, Iurii Nagibin, permission to release the film was in dispute until the very last moment.[24]

Based on Nagibin's script and directed by Aleksei Saltykov, *The Chairman* is a saga of post-war village life. In the first part, 'Brothers', war veteran Egor Trubnikov (played by Mikhail Ulianov) returns to his family home, intending to become chairman of the collective farm, Konkovo. The kolkhoz is a shambles, the cows so enfeebled by hunger they can barely stand on their feet, the peasants disgusted and disheartened. Egor's brother Semen, who remained in the village during the war, bitterly remarks: 'Your Soviet power didn't do much to defend us. Just leave us alone.' And he thinks Egor's plan is mad: 'Stay the night, rest, and in the morning go to the station. Don't slide into our mud. The people have turned into beasts, drunks, womanizers. That's how it is.'

Instead, Egor sets about putting things right. Despite the loss of his right arm in the war, and an artificial limb that pains him as if it were flesh, he wields a whip with his left hand to get the cows up off their haunches. The women, though they mock his clumsiness, help the cows stagger to the barn door, shouting to encourage one another while Egor enlists an old drunk to play on his flute.

At the pre-election meeting neither Egor's Party credentials nor his pie-in-the-sky promises (a cow for every family within a year) impress the roomful of peasants, mostly women munching sunflower seeds; what, after all, does he know about farming? But they do appreciate his candour. He admits that their suffering may in fact increase, especially at first, if he is elected. He admits that Semen did not come to the meeting because 'maybe it would have been awkward for him to vote against his own brother'. He admits, too, that his marriage has failed, and turns the question back on the women: 'How is it for you without your men? Where are they?' With very little to lose, they vote for Egor.

As kolkhoz chairman, Egor is authoritarian, ruthless and unrelenting. He drives everyone hard, himself hardest of all, making no exception for his recalcitrant brother, envious sister-in-law and reluctant nephew. Although Egor resembles Stalinist heroes of the 1930s in his passion and his will, his mission is significantly different from theirs. Heroes like Pavel Korchagin were surrounded by self-motivated masses, people driven by their own energy; the hero had to direct and channel that energy. Egor, in contrast, must become a source of energy for everyone else, mired as they are in apathy and fatigue.[25]

Moreover, he must galvanize the kolkhoz with no help from an obstructive and dogmatic bureaucracy. He relies on a combination of coercion, concern and pragmatism. He curses vociferously and threatens physical violence and legal sanctions to get the peasants out into the fields. But he pays them a cash advance out of his own pocket when government funds are not forthcoming, and – without 'higher authority', at the risk of expulsion from the Party – he returns some of the harvest to the peasants instead of giving the state the entire yield. (When asked who gave him the order to start harvesting, he replies, 'The grain. The highest authority.')

The women are fiercely derisive for a long time, at one point mooing at him till he turns away in anger, and they remain sceptical of his 'fairytales' (a club, a sanatorium). But they come to trust Egor, to tease him affectionately and playfully. After he offers to mind his sister-in-law's baby so that she can work in the fields, even that savage opponent yields, amazed by the tenderness he reveals. Egor cannot, however, win over his brother. When Egor sees Semen scything grass to feed his cow ('A cow isn't a *kolkhoznik*,' Semen says defiantly. 'It needs to eat'), their antagonism explodes in a near-fatal confrontation. Semen remains obdurate, but by the end of the first part of *The Chairman*, when Egor runs for a new term as chairman, Semen is forced to attend the meeting and to accede to the will of the majority. Egor is elected unanimously.

The weaker second part of *The Chairman*, subtitled 'To Be a Man' [*Byt' chelovekom*], continues the saga, with conflicts of every sort increasing until the magic moment of Stalin's death. En route to Moscow when he hears the news of Stalin's death, Egor leaps off the train and hurries to the fields. Immediately thereafter the kolkhoz sprouts new homes and new trees, telephone wires, farm machinery, a hospital. Egor makes one final attempt to redeem Semen, offering him a job at a good salary, but Semen, his family in tow, leaves Konkovo, obstinately unwilling to adjust to the new reality.

On its release *The Chairman* prompted an exceptional response. (Nagibin wrote in his diary, 'literally every adult saw the film',[26] and indeed, some 33 million people saw *The Chairman*, an unusually large number for a two-part film.) Professional reviews, rural conferences and discussions proliferated. 'We argued about *The Chairman*', one critic wrote a few years later, 'both in print and aloud, in a way in which we argued about no other recent film.'[27] The argument continued for years, driven less by considerations of art than of agriculture and farm life.

The controversy pre-dated the film. Nagibin first submitted his concept for a film about post-war kolkhoz life to Mosfilm in the winter of 1960–61. The studio embraced Nagibin's proposal, hoping the result would satisfy the official clamour for pictures about rural life. Mosfilm's directors were more ambivalent, either because the script was obviously controversial or because they felt uncomfortable with the kolkhoz milieu. The job was given to Aleksei Saltykov, a young director with one co-directed film (*My Friend, Kolka*, with Aleksandr Mitta) and one solo project (*Bang, Drum!* [Bei, baraban!, 1962]) under his belt.

In January 1963 Mosfilm appraised the script, entitled 'My Russia'. (The title was changed several times before industry chief Aleksei Romanov himself proposed *The Chairman*.) Saltykov defended Nagibin's script with circular logic:

> I believe that the Stalinist cult of personality was not able to destroy the norms of Soviet power and Soviet society because Soviet power and society were stronger than the cult of personality ... Everyone speaks and knows about the mistakes and the cult of personality, but no one speaks about the thousands and thousands of heroic acts. This script is ... wholesome, and demonstrates love for one's people, for one's country. Cult or not, the country grew, developed, people lived and worked, children were born.

As for Trubnikov's authoritarian leadership, Saltykov offered a quasi-Stalinist rationalization: 'Kindliness to the detriment of productivity is impermissible; the people themselves would not forgive that' [*Nel'zia byt' dobren'kim v ushcherb proizvodstvu, sam narod ne prostil by ètogo*].[28]

Of those who disagreed with Saltykov, none spoke more forcefully than Maia Turovskaia. She criticized the script's reliance on verbiage rather than visualization, and its lack of chronological clarity, but her most serious objections involved Trubnikov's appalling methods:

> He revives the kolkhoz all by himself, not together with the *kolkhozniki*. He strides about giving orders and instructions which the *kolkhozniki* fulfil. He never makes a mistake, and people follow him in a crowd, like a herd of cattle ... He deals harshly and arbitrarily with the peasants, yet they cherish and embrace him ... Literature first deified and then repeatedly exposed this type of commander, who hacks away left and right, but here he exists without the slightest reconceptualization.[29]

A realignment of 'conservatives' and 'liberals' formed about *The Chairman*. Liberals disparaged its implicit endorsement of quasi-Stalinist tactics, while conservatives honoured the script for showing how socialism continued to be built by the 'millions of Trubnikovs' in the countryside, despite the oppressive effect of the cult. Industry bureaucrat Aleksandr Macheret applauded Trubnikov's heroic stature, squarely in the socialist realist mould: Egor 'achieved his successes not because he was well-versed in agricultural technology, and not because he created particular opportunities for agricultural enterprises ... but because with his whole soul and with the immense force of inspiration and love for his people, he genuinely and selflessly wanted to help them.'[30]

But liberals and conservatives alike pleaded for greater complexity, and rejected flatly the spurious 'happy ending'. Pyrev commented that happy endings suited comedies, such as his own *Cossacks of the Kuban*, but not *The Chairman*, and Valentin Tolstykh, a film theorist, contrasted the false resolution with what actually happened: 'The Party's service and the service of its leadership in criticizing the cult of personality did not consist of solving all problems, but of clearing a path towards solving them, towards speaking about them honestly. The problems themselves for the most part remained in place.' A colleague went considerably further: 'I think', he said, 'that in ten years, when some film script is being discussed, someone will ask: and where were you, and why were you silent? Because the very same kinds of things go on today as occurred then, in spite of the speeches made at both the Twentieth and the Twenty-Second Party Congresses.'[31]

Two months later Mosfilm considered a revised script, now called 'Black Bread'. ('Black Bread' was the studio's favourite title, but it could not be used because Odessa Studio released Aleksandr and Kira Muratov's *Our Honest Bread* [Nash chestnyi khleb], a drama about a kolkhoz chairman, at about the same time.) Difficulties remained, such as Trubnikov's response to the news of Stalin's death. In reality, director Lev Arnshtam recalled, no one had been unmoved, neither Stalin's acolytes nor his detractors. 'I too had tears in my eyes, and for one whole day I went around stricken, like someone ill, though I understood everything that had been happening.' ('Not everyone wept,' Pyrev retorted, 'not everyone was devastated.') The script was still too verbose, its psychological conflict too rudimentary. Pyrev wondered how Trubnikov was able to win over his peasants: 'The collective farmer is practical [*khoziaistvennyi*], he must be shown that something works before he gets excited.'[32]

Everyone recognized the politically sensitive nature of the script. Turovskaia recommended checking the script with farm experts: 'Why, when we attach such major political importance to the picture, should we set ourselves up for ridicule afterwards? We'll have to deal with Nikita Sergeevich Khrushchev, who, whatever he knows about other things, knows plenty about agriculture.'[33] (Saltykov asked peasants in the village of Myshkino, outside of Moscow, to verify its accuracy. They confirmed that they had indeed been hungry after the war, and that they had been forced to plough with cows, but they couldn't quite believe the film would faithfully reflect the misery of their post-war lives.)[34] One conservative protested that the film showed the undernourished, poorly dressed and poorly shod peasants in too negative a light, but Turovskaia and others continued to press for more realism and plausibility.

By mid-summer of 1963, operating under 'unprecedented' time constraints, the studio unenthusiastically chose Mikhail Ulianov for the lead, and debated how to make the kolkhoz look authentic, not like a dacha colony. Cameraman Vladimir Nikolaev had found locations where the landscape would provide an effective and lyrical contrast with the small dark interiors, but Saltykov wanted a less opulent landscape, and their relationship degenerated to the point that Nikolaev wanted to quit, as did the unit director.

Amid a contentious atmosphere on the set, insults ('traitor', 'scab') flowed freely. Mosfilm held Saltykov primarily responsible. 'In the West a producer says, Do this, do that,' Saltykov was told. 'Whereas we give you everything – lots of money, the best scriptwriter, the most experienced unit director.' 'You need to shape up [*polomat' svoi kharakter*], Alesha,' Pyrev began avuncularly, 'and stop thinking you're the centre of the universe.' Soon enough, however, the famous Pyrev temper began to boil. 'You probably behaved offensively on the set. Don't you remember what people who worked with you earlier said about you? The same thing. When you made *Bang, Drum!*, [production manager Nikolai] Vladimirov was able to exert some influence and you had to control yourself [*vy ne smogli tam proiavit' svoi nevazhnyi kharakter*] … You think you're the most important person, you're god-the-director, everyone has to bow down to you.' Finally Pyrev exploded: 'Don't think', he shouted, 'that Soviet power will give you whatever you want. That you are a young genius and we will fall on our knees before you: Go ahead, do whatever you like. No, that will never happen! We will never agree to that!'[35]

Replacing Saltykov so late in the shooting would have meant unacceptable delays, so the studio allowed him to finish the film, and he screened a rough cut in October 1963. Pyrev chaired the meeting and complimented the film's veracity, excepting only the 'Asiatic wildness' of the drinking scenes and the jarring speed with which life improves after Stalin's death. He and others wanted the film to end with the announcement of Stalin's death, but, as Saltykov said, clearly alluding to higher Party intervention, 'it's not up to us to decide. [Pyrev] will recall Baskakov [Assistant Director of Goskino] saying that they would let this picture through in order to show that times have changed.'[36]

Times had indeed changed – up to a point. To the extent that *The Chairman* 'tells the truth about the countryside', it does so because it portrays not the kolkhoz of 1964, but the post-war kolkhoz, the poverty and misery of which result from the war. Nevertheless, inferences were drawn. The critic Lev Anninskii, admittedly more perceptive than most, recalled watching *The Chairman* and consciously registering that this impoverished village 'of 1947' had been filmed nearly twenty years later, yet the situation had not materially altered: the farmers still ploughed with cows.[37]

Shilova remembered that she and her friends, privileged Moscow students and professionals, knew from their own experience the kind of arbitrary and authoritarian methods Trubnikov employed on the kolkhoz. 'At that time,' she wrote, 'knowing little history and less political economy, we doubted that the post-war village could have been saved from its lethal hunger and deprivation ... without shouting, coercion, orders and violence. Skewed logic suggested that there had been no alternative, and the Kosygin reforms just then beginning left me (and most of us) in the dark.' Nor did Semen represent a viable alternative to his brother: three and a half decades of Soviet rhetoric militated against honouring Semen's simple desire to take care of the family's cow, whose milk fed his children. 'We still lived in a world ruled by old stereotypes,' she continued. 'We smothered the anguished sympathy evoked by his departure from the village.'[38]

Yet polemics continued. Conservatives justified Trubnikov's despotism: whatever the rights of those who wished to leave the kolkhoz, they did not have the right to destroy the kolkhoz. Trubnikov's passion 'to make people happy' vindicated his cruelty; 'there was and could be no other means of attaining the desired ends at that time'.[39]

Opponents responded. The liberal critic V. Kardin echoed Turovskaia's earlier objection: 'Fifteen or twenty years ago such people were hailed: master [khoziain]. Egor Trubnikov is just such a master: vehement, hard, despotic. His attitude towards people is that of a suzerain towards his subjects, who are deprived of rights, voices, faces.'[40] Trubnikov's integrity and his unselfish dreams for the kolkhoz do not excuse his arrogance, his treating the peasants 'like a herd of sheep', his disdain for women. Why should Egor Trubnikov be entitled to make his own choices, while other characters are denied that same right?

Kardin articulated a version of 'Leninist' ideology that was characteristic of like-minded liberals, though it was hardly the orthodox Party line:

> The future will be created by free, considered, inspired work, and not from under the shepherd's crook, the weight of curses, the whistling knout. Egor Trubnikov's earthly kingdom, were it to be realized, would be no more than the kind of society referred to in Marxist literature as 'barracks communism'...
>
> Trubnikov's despotic behaviour oppresses others, places them in absolutely subordinate positions. As for equality, there isn't a whiff of it.[41]

Audiences did not care. In a detailed survey conducted in the region of Sverdlovsk in early February 1966, *The Chairman* placed third in urban attendance, first in rural attendance, and first in terms of quality among city and country viewers alike.[42] (A reader survey conducted by *Sovetskii ekran* for 'best films of 1965' yielded the same result.) Egor Trubnikov was the single most popular film hero mentioned, receiving three times the number of votes given to the second choice, the eponymous hero of the Georgian film *A Soldier's Father* [Otets soldata, 1964]. Viewers preferred 'simple heroes, such as those you often encounter in real life', and they admired determination in the face of difficulties, fidelity to goals, openness [*dushevnaia otkrytost'*], sincerity.[43] Trubnikov fitted the bill. 'We found no trace whatsoever', the Sverdlovsk researchers reported, 'of criticism or condemnation of the "dark" side of Trubnikov's character, about which the professionals argued so bitterly ... Viewers accepted Trubnikov *in toto*, they accepted him as an organically whole personality, a fighter selflessly dedicated to people. For them, this is what made him a *contemporary* hero.'[44]

In the welter of political and ethical issues that dominated discussions of *The Chairman*, aesthetic issues took a back seat. The acting was lauded. So was the authenticity of the kolkhoz; despite their altercations, Saltykov and his camera crew successfully conveyed village destitution against the backdrop of natural beauty, and real collective farmers appearing in mass scenes alongside the actors enhanced the film's veracity.

In the heat of passionate polemics, no one understood that the hyper-realism of *The Chairman* transcended simple verisimilitude and denoted a distinctive cinematic approach. Other films, whatever their particular style, presented film as a quintessential 'other' reality. *The Chairman* turned away from alternative realities; its documentary truth – fictional gloss notwithstanding – is more compelling than invented truth. In this film about the obsessed chairman, 'reality resembles itself'.[45] *The Chairman* challenges the freedom, however illusory, intimated by Kostia Inochkin's flight over the river and by Pasha Kolokolnikov's fantasies. Trubnikov is mired in village mud, and there is no escape.

15. The Last Laugh

In the early months of Brezhnev and Kosygin's reign, a few controversial films reached Soviet screens. Marlen Khutsiev's *I am Twenty* was the most prominent of them, but the film's long-delayed release had deprived it of its original freshness and immediacy, casualties as much of time's passage as of the cuts Khutsiev and Shpalikov had made. Audiences reacted with indifference, and the press was generally hostile, though sympathetic colleagues and critics tried to shield the film from its detractors. *Sovetskaia kultura* published a harsh assault on the film's 'philosophical confusion', but also printed Anatolii Grebnev's rebuttal, in which the scriptwriter for Khutsiev's next film, *July Rain* [Iiul'skii dozhd', 1967], examined Khutsiev's innovative narrative strategy.[1]

Iskusstvo kino ran a critical round-up of responses to *I am Twenty*. Typically, the journal reserved such surveys for movies of political significance, such as *The Chairman*, and for the work of especially respected or illustrious directors. One was devoted to Mikhail Kalatozov's *I am Cuba* [Ia – Kuba, 1964], for instance, a wildly melodramatic exaltation of Castro's Cuba (with a script by Evtushenko and cinematography by Sergei Urusevskii) that viewers ranked among the worst dozen films of the year.[2] The editors acknowledged the failure of *I am Cuba*, but stressed the importance of its artistic experimentation. In the case of *I am Twenty*, too, the editors explained that although the film 'was not a great success with viewers', it merited attention as a 'talented work of contemporary cinema and an artistic experiment'.[3]

None of Khutsiev's advocates in the survey mentioned Khrushchev's attacks on the director, the long delay in the film's release or the cuts Khutsiev had made in order to win permission for the release of *I am Twenty*, so their defensive allusions to Khutsiev's 'profound patriotism' must have puzzled readers without insiders' status and knowledge. Iosif Kheifits, for example, observed that although he was 'warned of pessimism, undramatic structure and other bogeys', he didn't notice any of that: 'Sadness is not the same thing as pessimism,' he observed. Vasilii Shukshin, echoing Viktor Nekrasov, thanked

Khutsiev for eschewing 'formulaic prescriptions on how to live', nostrums that 'we wouldn't believe anyway'.[4]

Larisa Kriachko was nearly alone among *Iskusstvo kino*'s contributors in her antagonism towards *I am Twenty*. She had already disparaged it once, in *Oktiabr*; now she repeated her objections to the film's 'naturalistic' depiction of everyday life. With brusque confidence she asserted that Slava's problems could be solved 'with a good crèche or the presence of a grandmother who could look after the child'. As for Sergei, whom she considered neurotically passive, he needed to stop brooding and take an interest in the larger world. Kriachko dismissed Sergei's conversation with the ghost of his father as old-fashioned and 'something of a cliché'.[5]

In a sense it hardly mattered to viewers what film critics and film-makers said about *I am Twenty*, since distribution was so restricted. Lev Kulidzhanov, reporting on the state of the industry to the Cinematographers' Union a few months later, professed himself puzzled: 'I have no idea why the suspicious atmosphere around the film hasn't dissipated to this day. *Kinoprokat* [the official rental bureau] released it with hardly any advertising. Why? The words "modest" and "advertising" scarcely belong together.'[6]

Another seminal film, Sergei Paradzhanov's *Shadows of Forgotten Ancestors* [Teni zabytykh predkov, 1964], received equally poor advertising and equally limited distribution. Paradzhanov's remarkably beautiful film is based on a folk legend fictionalized by the turn-of-the-century Ukrainian writer and revolutionary democrat Mikhail Kotsiubinskii. Set in a community of Huzuls, Ukrainians living deep in the Carpathian mountains, *Shadows* combines extravagantly lush landscape and *mise-en-scène* with the sparest of plots. A family feud separates Ivanko and Marichka, in love since childhood, and poverty forces Ivanko to hire himself out as a herder far from the village. Marichka drowns while trying to save a lost lamb, leaving Ivanko disconsolate and half-mad. Eventually Ivanko marries Palagna, but the marriage is unhappy and he is killed in a fight with Palagna's shaman-lover.

Paradzhanov's visual passion characterized all of his films. He saw the cinematic frame as an autonomous canvas, and himself as a painter. He revered the work of Bruegel, Abram Arkhipov (one of the nineteenth-century group of painters known as the *peredvizhniki*), and the primitivist artists for whom colour was 'not just mood, emotional supplement', but part of the content of their work.[7] Paradzhanov's use of colour is extraordinary: the death of Ivanko's father, for instance, is announced by a shocking wash of crimson spilled across the screen. *Shadows*, where colour serves not merely to render reality plausibly, is a genuinely 'colour' film, not simply a film made in colour.

Shadows makes equally striking if less exceptional use of folklore. Physical ornament, dress, household art, music and religious rituals dominate the film. Paradzhanov painstakingly avoided treating the material as exotic archaisms, and the Huzuls who participated in the film abetted his efforts. 'They demanded absolute truth,' he recalled.

> Any trace of falsehood, any inaccuracy stung them. They dressed themselves, knowing ahead of time what we would be filming. They were offended when they saw an actress's manicured nails or an alien detail in a costume. When we invited them to the studio to tape them playing their *trembity* [long wooden horns], they would not play until they had put on the appropriate clothing and brought fresh flowers to the instruments.[8]

As a result, *Shadows* lacks the 'masquerade effect' of a costume drama, picturesque routines played out on sweetly sentimentalized farms. Despite its patently historical setting, it looks and feels timeless.[9]

Shadows powerfully influenced film-makers outside Moscow. Its mixture of lyricism, highly individual directorial vision and scrupulous attention to the physical particularity of a milieu and a community became prototypical for 'national' cinema, especially Ukrainian cinema, in 1966 and 1967. But charges of formalism and abstractionism dogged *Shadows*.[10] Regional cinema administrators, who routinely decided ahead of time which films people would and would not like, shelved movies they considered 'too difficult'.[11] *Shadows* barely ran in commercial theatres.

Still, Soviet cinephiles did have a fairly extensive choice of movies in 1965. In the Sverdlovsk region, where researchers surveyed both urban and rural audiences, some two hundred films were available during 1965, mostly domestic productions. While audience response had been studied sporadically in Soviet history,[12] the Sverdlovsk project represented the first carefully and rigorously designed scholarly attempt to assess systematically who went to which movies and how often, as well as why they went and what they thought. Both the industry and the state hoped that the resulting data and analysis would enable them to identify target audiences more precisely and to stimulate ticket sales.[13]

About one-third of the respondents went to the cinema hoping for 'relaxation and entertainment', and liked adventure movies with a light ideological overlay, such as *Government Criminal* [Gosudarstvennyi prestupnik, 1964], third at the box-office for 1965, about the KGB's discovery and apprehension of a man responsible for hundreds of deaths during the Second World War, and *What Are You Called Now?* [Kak vas teper' nazyvat'?, 1965], a thriller about a Soviet intelligence officer who uncovers a Nazi plot.

Another third wanted 'to learn something new, to reflect on life'.[14] They favoured psychodramas, among them *Here, Mukhtar!* [Ko mne, Mukhtar!, 1964], an appealing adventure story about a supersleuth police dog and his trainer. *Believe Me, People!* [Ver'te mne, liudi!, 1964], second at the box-office with 40 million viewers,[15] featured as its hero a labour camp inmate, Aleksei Lapin, who under duress escapes shortly before the end of his term in 1956. When he eventually turns himself in, Lapin learns that his father, a Red Army commander repressed during the Terror, has been rehabilitated thanks to the revelations of the Twentieth Congress – a dash of historical piquancy to spice up an otherwise pedestrian picture.

General audience preferences clearly emerge from the surveys. Viewers wrote comments on their questionnaires as well as ranking films numerically, and consistently responded to heroes with whom they could empathize emotionally. 'I remember Kostia [from *Stillness*] because we're the same age,' wrote one. 'I can understand a lot of his behaviour.' A twenty-year-old was moved by 'films about young people whose relatives perished during the war'. Although younger adults enjoyed movies with romantic and swashbuckling heroes (and exotic foreign films, such as *Scaramouche* and Vittorio de Sica's *Marriage Italian-Style*) more than their parents did, both generations admired film heroes who persevered in the face of obstacles and who remained faithful to their goals. 'Aleksei Lapin ... attracts attention because of his will-power,' one nineteen-year-old worker wrote. 'He helped me become stronger when things went wrong, helped me achieve my goals.' A girl of the same age liked Shukshin's Pashka Kolokolnikov (from *A Boy Like That*) for his joy: 'I'd like to find people like him among my peers.'[16]

Beginning in the mid-1950s, the thaw had validated the attributes viewers identified so approvingly: simplicity, emotional authenticity, sincerity, perseverance, warmth, sentimentality. Audiences loved the ageing peasant in *A Soldier's Father,* Revaz Chkheidze's account of a man who sets out from his Georgian village in search of his wounded son, and follows him all the way to Berlin. (In *Sovetskii ekran*'s 1965 survey, *A Soldier's Father* was placed third, after *The Chairman* and *Marriage Italian-Style*.) The hero's 'typically Georgian' behaviour is lovingly caricatured: a wine-grower like many Georgians, he cherishes the vines with near-mystical devotion, to the point of jumping in front of a Soviet tank that is trampling a German vineyard, shaking his fist and shouting 'Fascist!' at the bemused driver. But Sergo Zakariadze's restrained and poignant performance as Georgii Makharashvili, for which he won a Lenin Prize in 1966, exemplified all the qualities esteemed by viewers. 'I like his simplicity, his spirit [*dushevnost'*],' one eighteen-year-old student wrote; another cited his 'purity and warm heart'. The same qualities were adduced for other appealing protagonists: the old man in Chukhrai's *There Lived an Old Man and an Old Woman* [Zhili-byli starik so starukhoi, 1964], the heroine of *Blood Kin* [Rodnaia krov', 1963].[17]

Viewers claimed to dislike 'tasteless' and 'vulgar' films that 'can have a baneful influence on young people' (the 1964 Czech film *Lemonade Joe*, Hollywood's *Magnificent Seven*). One worker in her late twenties prudishly dismissed 'all pictures that show the heroes' intimate life'. Heroes who behaved

Strange Interlude

in a morally ambiguous manner – Andrzej Wajda's young hero in *Ashes and Diamonds* [Poland, 1958], for instance, a member of the anti-communist underground who is assigned to kill the newly-arrived communist official – discomfited them.[18]

Above all, audiences wanted to laugh. Respondents of all ages and social and educational categories ranked comedy the genre most poorly represented on screen, and they embraced the comedies at long last provided by the film industry. Between April and October 1965, four comedies opened and played to substantial audiences. Two, each seen by upwards of 25 million people, were appreciated as good-natured comedies featuring appropriately committed heroes: *Zaichik*, whose hero resolves to use what he mistakenly believes to be his last few days on earth to help people, and *Green Light* [Zelenyi ogonek], a cheerful saga of a cab-driver who meddles in his passengers' lives.

Eldar Riazanov's *Give Me the Complaint Book* [Daite zhalobnuiu knigu] and Leonid Gaidai's *Operation 'Y' and Shurik's Other Adventures* were even more popular. The latter, a comic triptych linked by a single protagonist, opened in July, and by the end of its first year's run had broken box-office records. Two slapstick sketches, skirmishes between the student Shurik (played by Aleksandr Demianenko) and hapless petty crooks, frame a romantic vignette in which Shurik and a pretty student study together for exams, so absorbed in their textbooks that neither notices the presence of the other. Shurik's dark-framed eyeglasses act as a comic prop and sired a clutch of bespectacled comic heroes, *ochkariki*.

Gaidai, who began his career assisting Boris Barnet on *Liana*, a 1955 comedy, had already demonstrated a gift for visual humour and for comic timing. An earlier short film, *The Dog Barbos and the Unusual Race* [Pes Barbos i neobychnyi kross], included in a portmanteau film entitled *Absolutely Serious* [Sovershenno serezno, 1961], is a witty silent comedy involving three hapless pyromaniacs and a dog. A year later Gaidai directed a trilogy of short comic films based on stories by O. Henry, *Businessmen* [Delovye liudi, 1962].

In *Operation 'Y'* Gaidai kept tone and characterization consistent. He offered 'grotesque without excuses, clowning without psychological burden ... The more comic the situation, the more serious the characters.'[19] Much of the film's humour derives from a trio of actors Gaidai used regularly: Iurii Nikulin, Georgii Vitsin and Evgenii Morgunov (the three pyromaniacs in *The Dog Barbos*). They made a wonderful team: Vitsin, looking like a slightly seedy, permanently half-sloshed *déclassé* aristocrat; big, brawny Morgunov as the cunning but dumb strong-man; Nikulin, with a mournful expression on his long face, as the crook whose brilliant schemes never quite come off.

So beloved were the three actors that Eldar Riazanov deliberately included them 'as a quotation' when he came to make *Complaint Book*, early in 1964.[20] He also wanted to enliven Aleksandr Galich and Boris Laskin's script. Riazanov initially resisted the project: he found the scenario artificial and old-fashioned, and he was eager to make *Watch the Car* [Beregis' avtomobilia, 1966], from a novella he had co-authored with Emil Braginskii. But he agreed: once *Complaint Book* was done, the studio promised, he could go ahead with *Watch the Car*.

This version of Riazanov's favourite satiric topic, bureaucratic intransigence, involves a typical Soviet restaurant. The manager of The Dandelion [*Oduvanchik*] is usually drunk; so is the troika of customers played by Nikulin, Morgunov and Vitsin. 'Service' runs a short gamut from grudging and aggressively rude ('Coffee should be drunk at home,' the waitress sternly lectures, 'not in a restaurant!') to non-existent: waitresses lean over the bar, chatting to one another, or serenely knit, oblivious to a roomful of increasingly desperate customers. When one of them chides a journalist who has been waiting to be served for an hour and a half, calling him 'Young man' [*molodoi chelovek*], he replies plaintively, 'We were young when we came in.'

In revenge, he publishes a sardonic *feuilleton* about The Dandelion, provoking its young director, Tatiana, to propose a major overhaul. Her boss Postnikov objects. 'I went to restaurants when I was abroad,' he sniffs. 'Everyone smiles, but what do those smiles mean? They're just smiles for money.' The journalist rejoins that he would like Soviet waitresses to smile, though 'not for money, of course'. 'For what, then?' Postnikov queries uncomprehendingly. Tatiana cleverly chooses to enlist the support of Postnikov's superior, a paragon of benevolent authority: open to innovation, unspoiled by power (at the market he cheerfully agrees to try on a coat for an elderly peasant unsure of her son's size), and retaining a sense of humour.

In the end, *Complaint Book*'s satire remains conventional, well within the limits of officially mandated social criticism. But while it breaks no new ground thematically, *Complaint Book* represents an aesthetic departure from traditional comedy. Critics and audiences alike complained that comedies were unrealistic, full of incessant action and noise, with interchangeable sets and characters. Riazanov remembered the typical comedies of those years:

> A certain specifically cinematic world was created, peopled by unnatural comic figures who strained to get laughs from the viewer. The action of such comedies took place in a polished and manicured reality, and the pretty blue-eyed heroes recalled pomaded and coiffed cherubim. The viewer would watch the screen and could not recognize the world he knew; in the primped heroes he saw neither himself nor his friends.[21]

Riazanov began to move away from that kind of 'unnatural' comedy with *Give Me the Complaint Book*. He rejected the full colour called for by the script, making the film in black-and-white (his first black-and-white feature). He dressed the heroes and heroine in ordinary clothes instead of fancy costumes. He abandoned the musical formula he himself had used in his earlier films, of

Strange Interlude

set-piece song-and-dances, and restricted music to scenes that accommodated it naturally. 'I began to shift the characters and situations towards the most natural shots and towards natural acting without comic turns,' he wrote.

By and large I chose 'dramatic' rather than 'comic' actors. I was trying to create a truthful comedy on the basis of an artificially constructed script. We would not use studio-made props and sets. Together with the young cameramen Anatolii Mukasei and Vladimir Nakhabtsev and the designer Vladimir Kaplunovskii I shot the picture only in real interiors and on location. Beyond the windows genuine, disorganized life bubbled. During the shooting of street scenes we used a hidden camera, so that the actors played out their scenes amid totally unsuspecting crowds, and the camera caught all that.[22]

The mixture of realistic episodes and traditional comic turns is not entirely successful, but *Complaint Book* joined Klimov's *Welcome, or No Trespassing* in introducing to Soviet screens new varieties of film comedy and new forms in which to express humour. Over the next few years, as comedy enjoyed a renaissance, a number of directors followed Riazanov's and Klimov's lead.

Riazanov was able to complete and release *Watch the Car*, the film he had wanted to make all along, in May 1966. Klimov had less luck. His barbed *Adventures of a Dentist* officially opened in October 1965, but hardly anyone saw the film; the same thing happened to Georgii Danelia's iconoclastic *Thirty-three* [Tridtsat' tri]. Both directors challenged the consecrated values of Soviet tradition, at least in the uncomplicated form that contented many viewers, deflating such sacred cows as the wisdom of the collective.

In Klimov's film, for example, a novice dentist, Chesnokov ('garlic'), begins work in a provincial clinic and discovers to his own astonishment that he has a magic touch: he is able to extract teeth painlessly and instantaneously, with a flick of his drill and a soft 'ding!' Chesnokov's colleagues admire his skill, but their initial approbation quickly curdles when their patients desert them for the miracle-working newcomer. The patients themselves first honour him as a wizard but turn on him as soon as he falters. A community with little tolerance for difference ostracizes the exceptional individual, whether dentist or, by implication, artist.

Klimov and writer Aleksandr Volodin submitted the script to the editorial committee at the end of 1964. 'The story of a man who reveals an extraordinary talent, and whom everyone tramples in the most friendly Soviet way, could hardly inspire any special joy' in official circles, Klimov recalled, the more so since 'the pencil-pushers [chinovniki] were doubly scared' in the months of uncertainty following Khrushchev's departure. Chief editor Aleksandr Dymshits wanted to pass as a liberal and someone who valued art, but his fear dominated: 'You disparage and oversimplify ordinary Soviet people,' he warned; Chesnokov was weak and neurotic.[23]

Nevertheless, Klimov was permitted to proceed. He tried to sharpen the parodic elements of Volodin's script both visually and verbally. When Chesnokov's parents visit their depressed son in order to cheer him up, for instance, Klimov shoots them frontally, like Soviet equivalents of Grant Wood's American Gothics. They stare straight ahead and preach earnest pieties about 'manliness' and courage, each recommending the other as a model of determination and fortitude. In one scene a supervisory commission comes to observe Chesnokov, who is so paralysed by fear that he cannot extract the offending tooth. The parallel to ideological controls on film-makers is obvious.[24]

In the conclusion of the film, one of Chesnokov's students manifests the magical talent he himself has lost. But far from providing a happy ending, Klimov implies that history will repeat itself, and that society will ostracize the student just as it did her mentor. Aghast editors told Klimov to alter the ending 'to avoid the impression that difficulties inevitably await every talented person'. Klimov refused. In consequence, *Adventures of a Dentist* received a 'category three' classification (the next to last group) and virtually disappeared: released two years after its completion, in only twenty-five prints, it was seen by perhaps half a million viewers.[25]

Danelia's *Thirty-three*, in which the anatomical anomaly of an extra tooth appears in the mouth of the hero, Ivan Sergeevich Travkin, suffered a similar fate, and for similar reasons. Like *Adventures of a Dentist*, *Thirty-three* satirizes the 'wisdom' of the collective – when, for instance, the community elects a commission of worthy citizens to verify the presence of the extra tooth. They ascend the podium, stare into Travkin's mouth and loudly count out his teeth in choral unanimity. Instead of displaying sagacity, the masses are foolish and gullible: supposedly sophisticated Muscovites believe any rumour, including one that brands Travkin a Martian, and they are so star-struck that total strangers besiege the hapless Travkin, eager to wine and dine him. (With tremendous comic panache, Inna Churikova plays an adoring proto-groupie.) Misha, an astute provincial with whom Travkin shares a Moscow hotel room, sardonically observes, 'Your tooth is not your tooth, but national property' [*narodnoe dostoianie*].

Danelia deflates the prestige of high culture in the figures of a pompous writer interviewed on television, and an eager curator from the regional museum, who pesters Travkin's wife to promise Travkin's skull (or at least his jaw) to their collection. (He apologetically offers sixty rubles as the paltry compensation their limited budget permits.) Danelia parodies film itself when the male chorus to which Travkin belongs sings the theme song from *I Walk Around Moscow*, and he reduces the cult of heroism to the level of media publicity: national television terms Travkin's tooth an 'epic exploit' [*podvig*]. Finally, Travkin – as played by the moon-faced Evgenii Leonov – is hardly a conventional (or even unconventional) positive hero, despite his sweet smile, his attachment to his family, and his dedication to improving the non-alcoholic drinks produced by his factory.

Danelia attempted to dilute the mordancy of *Thirty-three* with a final dream sequence that shifts from satire to farce, but he could not save the film from virtual prohibition. Although technically released, the film played in one theatre in Moscow, and received not a single review.[26] Danelia had not yet mastered the hybrid cinematic genre – a delicate balance between social satire and moral affirmation – that he himself, in a subtitle to his 1980 *Autumn Marathon* [Osenii marafon], called 'sad comedy'.

Such conspicuous oxymorons and disintegrating generic boundaries characterized a growing resistance to tidy categories, manifest in the intertwining of two trends that dominated Soviet film-making in the mid-1960s. On the face of it, documentary art and 'poetic' or lyric art contradict each other. The first suggests objectivity, evidence, dispassion and fact; the second subjectivity, emotion, individual voice. But although critics in the mid-1960s forced the two into a binary opposition, hindsight discerns in the movies of these years an overlapping of document and lyric, warp and woof of a complex tapestry. A documentary trend was certainly apparent in Soviet cinema (as it was in France's *cinéma verité*, Britain's 'free film' movement and the 'New York School'), and it took shape via a range of aesthetic choices. But it found a distinctive counterpoint in a lyric intonation provided at times by narrative, at times by camera, at times by soundtrack.

Even the apogee of documentary film-making of the mid-1960s, Mikhail Romm's *Ordinary Fascism* [Obyknovennyi fashizm, 1965], united documentary and lyric. All of its images are documentational, but Romm's voice-over narration and the unifying image of children's drawings added a lyric dimension, 'virtually destroying the wall between feature and documentary film, and enriching the latter with artistic passion, bold intellectual flight, emotional colour'.[27]

Maia Turovskaia and Iurii Khaniutin had proposed the project in October 1963, after watching thousands of yards of Nazi footage and becoming fascinated not so much by the politics of what they saw as by the mentality it revealed. They hoped to probe 'those psychological and moral features of the German petty bourgeoisie which Hitler took into account and which, in particular historical circumstances, permitted him to take power in Germany'. As a political fig leaf to their proposal, they planned to include material illustrating 'those features of a bourgeois *Weltanschauung* which today still serve as the petri dish for a rebirth of fascism'.[28]

For Turovskaia and Khaniutin, the documentation – texts and music, as well as footage – did not record incident so much as testify to emotion and frame of mind, usually the domain of 'lyric'. They wanted to avoid a slavish dependence on fact, to escape the limitations of the impersonal narrator and the camera of conventional documentary. For these reasons, they brought their idea not to the documentary film studio, but to Mosfilm, where the script was approved, and to Mikhail Romm.[29]

The project intrigued Romm. He had often incorporated documentary footage into his Stalin-era feature films: columns of German PoWs march through Moscow in *Person 217* [Chelovek No. 217, 1945]; a rapid montage of America opens *The Russian Question* [Russkii vopros, 1948]; American troops appear in *Secret Mission* [Sekretnaia missiia, 1950]. And he liked the idea of scrutinizing Nazism's psychological roots, the instincts and motives of individuals. He agreed to work with Turovskaia and Khaniutin.

Soviet interpretation had traditionally regarded fascism as morally threatening and horrifying, occasionally as absurd, but never as 'ordinary'.[30] Hoping to create a visual, as well as thematic, contrast to the imperial façade, Turovskaia and Khaniutin sought footage documenting everyday life in Nazi Germany, but they found very little. 'Ordinary' life had not interested Nazi-era filmmakers, who preferred to film the 'little man' goose-stepping in uniform and helmet in a military column, or 'squashed … by the borders of the frame' in crowd scenes.[31] Turovskaia and Khaniutin succeeded in locating one image of a worker eating bread, and Romm used it repeatedly as the symbol for 'the other' Germany that endured, however marginally, within the Nazi environment.[32]

Turovskaia and Khaniutin compressed over one hundred themes into fifteen 'chapters' plus epilogue. A content-heading ('Culture of the Third Reich', 'The Great National Idea in Action', etc.) introduces each chapter. Although the chapters are arranged in loose chronological order, the film is idea- rather than chronology-driven.

Romm made two crucial additions to Turovskaia and Khaniutin's concept. He appropriated the fundamental thaw image of the child as prism of moral judgement and as symbol of innocence – developed in such films as Danelia and Talankin's *Serezha*, Kalik's *Man Follows the Sun* and Tarkovskii's *Ivan's Childhood* – but added an explicitly political dimension by contrasting the child's purity of gaze and innocence of spirit with the perversions of morality integral to Nazism. Childhood represents a system of ethics opposed to fascism.

Ordinary Fascism opens with a sequence of children's drawings of cats and ends with a small girl reciting a poem. In between, images of children abound, most painfully in the tenth chapter ('We Belong to You'), where children are transformed into citizens of the Reich. The drawings of the opening sequence are reprised, except that these children of Nazi Germany draw the letter H: they are making birthday cards for Hitler.

Romm also contributed his voice. Turovskaia and Khaniutin wrote their narrative text to include sarcasm, irony, even humour, as well as anger and pain, and Romm's voice – in turn reflective, bemused, stern, sardonic –

powerfully expresses all of those emotions as he considers aloud the images presented on screen. His point of view is normal and healthy, like the implied viewer's, to whom he often discloses the provenance of a shot, simultaneously introducing the search for material and documenting that material. 'He doesn't read,' one critic commented. 'He converses with viewers, and his vocabulary and intonation are directed to each viewer individually.'[33] The dialogic motif so essential to *Nine Days of a Year* here becomes a dialogue between the 'author' and the viewer.

Both the factual veracity and emotional sincerity of *Ordinary Fascism* resonated among audiences. In his speech at the long-awaited First Congress of the Union of Cinematographers in 1965, Lev Kulidzhanov claimed that viewers loathed 'not just explicit falsification but any kind of half-truth', and wanted to see things 'as they are'.[34] Kulidzhanov's confidence that the elite knew every thought and wish of the *narod* may have been a myth cherished by both the pre-revolutionary intelligentsia and Soviet leadership, but surveys and questionnaires bore out his assessment of what audiences wanted. Sincerity and authenticity consistently ranked at the top of the scale of thaw-era values; audiences preferred artless, 'natural' acting, which seemed proof of those qualities, and gave their affection to those actors who best exemplified that style: Innokentii Smoktun-ovskii,[35] Donatas Banionis in *No One Wanted to Die* [Nikto ne khotel umirat', 1966], Rolan Bykov in *Someone's Ringing, Open the Door* [Zvoniat, otkroite dver', 1965]. Banionis, Bykov and Smoktunovskii (for his performance in *Watch the Car*) were close rivals for critics' choice as Best Actor for 1966; Bykov won.[36]

Film-makers strove to satisfy the popular thirst for *verismo*, which corres-ponded to needs of their own. A variety of cinematographic means enhanced authenticity and attestation. Long shots, for instance, underscored the observer's perspective, while shots of longer duration gave audiences time to examine the shot-content. The *mise-en-scène* moved deeper within the frame, forcing the viewer's gaze further into the screen environment to see the action. Narrative linearity receded, and cause–effect logic yielded to the vagaries of the hero's emotions or the unpredictability of the author's thoughts. Interior monologue revealed the individual psychology and consciousness of the characters.

Preferring roughness to refinement, what one critic called 'ms. rather than calligraphy',[37] directors commenced their films *in medias res* and ended in the equivalent of mid-phrase, catching the 'capricious movement of life'.[38] Often films were ordered as a series of autonomous episodes. Segments simply begin, like those of *Your Son and Brother*, or are formally divided by headings indicating chronology (Day One, Day Two of *Nine Days of a Year*, the year designations of *Andrei Rublev*), content (the titles of *Ordinary Fascism*) or point of view ('I remember ...', begins the narrator of Kalik's elegaic *So Long, Boys*).

In *Your Son and Brother* and *Shadows of Forgotten Ancestors* non-professionals appear alongside trained actors and actresses, as they do in Andrei Mikhalkov-

Konchalovskii's first feature, *The First Teacher* [Pervyi uchitel', 1965]. In his second, heavily censored *The Story of Asia Kliachina, Who Loved but Didn't Marry* [Istoriia Asi Kliachinoi, kotoraia liubila da ne vyshla zamuzh], Mikhalkov-Konchalovskii employed only three professionals, and encouraged the villagers to repeat dialogue in their own words. He incorporated their improvisations into the rewritten script.[39]

Otar Ioseliani's *Leaffall* [Listopad, 1966] opens with a lengthy sequence of a feast celebrating the grape harvest. Shot from a distance, with the celebrants milling about and drinking, the episode looks like documentary footage. In fact, such harvesting rituals no longer existed in Georgia, and the revellers are actors, but Ioseliani deliberately enhanced the naturalness of the sequence by shooting them without their knowledge: he called 'Action!' after he had already finished filming.[40]

Curiously, in the mid-1960s black-and-white more often served to express the lyric impulse than the documentary. In the early thaw years the choice of black-and-white had signified a rejection of the garish colour films that 'occupied the highest rung on the planning and production hierarchy' in the late Stalin years. Like simple musical scores (the guitar theme of *Spring on Zarechnaia Street*, for instance) and unadorned *mise-en-scène*, black-and-white refuted the earlier ostentation characteristic of every genre of film. Paradoxically, although black-and-white film deprives the viewer of a central characteristic of objective reality, it affirms the veracity of what is on screen. Film-makers who were attempting to catch life 'unawares' perceived black-and-white photography as a signifier of reliability and truthfulness.[41]

By the mid-1960s, colour had become a neutral cinematic norm, though only a small number of privileged film-makers had access to high-quality Kodak colour stock; the rest managed with inferior Soviet stock. Directors who chose black-and-white were making an aesthetic statement, 'deliberately avoiding the naturalism endowed by colour', the risk of 'picturesque decorative art'.[42] Andrei Tarkovskii, for example, wanting to bypass the museum-replica quality associated with traditional historical films, chose black-and-white for *Andrei Rublev*, reserving colour for the final frames of Rublev's icons. Directors now embraced black-and-white not in order to represent reality truthfully, as their predecessors had done ten years earlier, but to generate their own singular vision and version of it.

Certainly this explains Andrei Mikhalkov-Konchalovskii's choice of black-and-white for his 1965 adaptation of Chingiz Aitmatov's novella, *The First Teacher*. Mikhalkov-Konchalovskii and his cameraman Georgii Rerberg worked together very closely, as they did a year later on *Asia Kliachina*, to create a film that, in Mikhalkov-Konchalovskii's own estimation, 'looks as if it has been edited from documentary footage' which the director didn't shoot himself.[43]

Wanting 'every shot to be seen as a piece of living reality', Mikhalkov-

Strange Interlude

26. *The First Teacher*

Konchalovskii and Rerberg filmed the desolate steppe in very long takes and often in absolute silence, except for the rush of a river or the wind. Extreme long shots alternate with extreme close-ups. At the same time Rerberg broke with the unobtrusive use of 'even, expository' light typical of late 1950s and early 1960s cinema, where it served primarily to create a visual context for actors and objects. Harking back to the work of Sergei Urusevskii, Rerberg used 'natural light ... with a mass of expressive variations'. Sometimes he overexposed the image, setting people and objects on fire in the rays of the sun; sometimes he preferred near-total darkness, with the object filmed barely discernible.[44]

In Mikhalkov-Konchalovskii's film, Diuishen, the young Bolshevik dispatched by the Komsomol to teach youngsters in the Central Asian steppe, is rigid and humourless, himself uneducated beyond basic political and alphabetical literacy. He tries to establish his authority ('I spoke on the telephone. Has your mullah seen a telephone?') but his dogmatism and impatience hinder his ability to engage with the villagers, children as well as adults. When one child guilelessly asks whether Lenin, like all other creatures, will die, Diuishen hurls the expletive '*Contra!*' (counter-revolutionary) at him like a brick. Though he later weeps at his own helplessness, he does not change.

The villagers live amid drudgery and ignorance, interrupted by sporadic fights, violent carousing, rape. In one shot the heroine Altynai, a young orphan, bangs a wooden post downwards. Probably she is pounding grain, but because the camera cuts off the foreground, so that we see neither bucket nor bowl, it seems no more than repeated, pointless banging. In another scene we hear the children chanting the word 'So-cial-ism' while the camera pans a vast barren desert, its emptiness underscored by one lone animal grazing on a hillside. Involuntarily one thinks, 'What earthly relevance does socialism have here?'

Despite Diuishen's protests, Altynai is given to a wealthy *bai* [landowner], who carries her off on the back of his horse. Her wedding night is conveyed entirely in sound: cloth ripping, her voice saying 'No,' his panting breath. The next morning she covers her head as if to make herself invisible to the curious, unsympathetic gaze of those gathered at the campsite. Diuishen returns with the police and leads Altynai away, but despite his pity for her he treats her brutally, as if – one critic aptly observed – 'to avenge his own inability to defend her'.[45]

The community ostracizes her and penalizes Diuishen for his interference, refusing to send the children back to school. When Diuishen returns from taking Altynai to the train station (to study in the city), he finds the school burned down; Lenin's picture flaps forlornly in the breeze. Indomitable, Diuishen takes an axe to the landscape's solitary tree, a poplar, in order to begin rebuilding the school, and one old man joins him, but the reconciliation characteristic of Soviet tradition, the 'merging of hero and mass', never occurs. In the pitiless environment of the steppe, deprived of any exoticism that colour might provide, force is conquered by force. The old defends itself savagely, the new shows no mercy.

'Documentary-like' became an all-purpose commendation, one the authorities felt more comfortable with than 'poetic', with its connotation of individual voice. But attestative consistently overlapped with lyric, whether via explicit text, such as Romm's voice-over narration in *Ordinary Fascism*, or via the expressive image, especially in films from the republican studios. Documentarism thus became 'the basis of poetry in the cinematography of the 1960s'.[46]

Part V Forbidden Games, 1965–67

16. Forbidden Games: Introduction

The last chapters of this book outline the central cinematic shifts of 1965, 1966 and 1967, the last of the thaw years for Soviet cinema, as they were for Soviet society writ large. In subsequent years Brezhnevite 'stagnation' took firm hold. The invasion of Czechoslovakia in August 1968 proclaimed the limits of Soviet tolerance for autonomy in its satellite states, while at home, where repression intensified on all fronts, victims of legal and professional sanctions often belonged to the artistic and scientific intelligentsia. Ivan Svetlichnyi and Ivan Dziuba, for example, arrested in 1966 and charged with smuggling 'nationalist and anti-Soviet' literature to the West, were prominent Ukrainian literary and film critics. The prosecutor at Andrei Siniavskii and Iulii Daniel's trial cited lines from their fiction as evidence of the authors' intent to 'subvert or weaken the Soviet regime'.

The film world suffered depredations during the Brezhnev era that were largely invisible to the public. Political, ideological and moral evaluations continually hobbled the studios, and the checklist of 'permissible' and 'impermissible' hypertrophied, scuttling projects on a range of subjects and styles. Certain films were 'needed', while others – 'inaccurate', 'unheroic' – were not. A larger than usual number of mediocre films flooded movie houses, stimulated, and summoned, by Lenin's birth-centenary and the fiftieth anniversary of the Bolshevik Revolution. 'Leniniana' included six (of a planned series of fourteen) documentaries that would 'reveal the basic stages of the life and activities' of Vladimir Ilich, among them Sergei Iutkevich's *Lenin in Poland* and Mark Donskoi's diptych, *A Mother's Heart* [Serdtse materi, 1966] and *A Mother's Loyalty* [Vernost' materi, 1967], in which Lenin, who 'always showed tenderness and affection for his mummy' [*mamochka*], provided a sterling example to young people.[1]

The state expected a flourish of cinematic fanfare to herald the sixth decade of Soviet rule, films that would, like their glorious predecessors, take a 'dialectical and historical approach to the reality they depict'[2] and continue to

Forbidden Games

educate people morally and ideologically.³ Party proclamations and many *Iskusstvo kino* editorials repeated the truisms of years past, demanding 'broad scale' and the 'creation of a new man' and reprehending equally banal transgressions, among them 'dogmatism' [*nachetnichestvo*], opportunism, and parasitic reliance on foreign sources [*izhdivenchestvo*]. Vladimir Baskakov, Goskino's chairman, particularly disliked 'slavish imitation' of stylistic fads: too many Soviet film-makers, he remarked, 'cut their hair the way Antonioni does, instead of covering up their bald spots'.⁴

Most of the acceptable films produced to celebrate Soviet power either disappointed at the box-office or failed with the critics, occasionally both. A mere handful of viewers – fewer than six million – saw Mikhail Shveitser's costly two-part blockbuster, *Time, Forward!* [Vremia, vpered!, 1966], based on Valentin Kataev's novel of the same name;⁵ not many more saw Valeriu Gazhiu and Vadim Lysenko's *Bitter Seeds* [Gor'kie zerna, 1966], about the establishment of Soviet power in Moldava after the Second World War. The screen version of Aleksandr Serafimovich's revolutionary classic *The Iron Flood* [Zheleznyi potok, 1967], directed by veteran Efim Dzigan, attracted substantial audiences but sank into critical oblivion. *The Republic of Shkid* [Respublika Shkid, 1966] and *The Boss of Chukotka* [Nachalnik Chukotki, 1966], two films about the 1920s, garnered both profits and critical respect, but as films with a primary target audience of children and adolescents, they ranked as secondary in significance.

The anniversary inspired genuinely interesting films, but audiences rarely saw them in the form their creators had intended, if they saw them at all. Aleksandr Ivanov's *The First Russians* [Pervorossiiane, 1967], from a script by Olga Berggolts about Petrograd workers who start a commune in the Altai region in 1918, was released in thirty-two copies. Aleksandr Askoldov's *The Commissar*, with Nonna Mordiukova as a Red Army commissar who boards with a Jewish family during her pregnancy and rejoins the fray after her child is born, mouldered on a shelf for twenty years.

Mosfilm's Experimental Studio, which permitted film-makers unusual freedom, planned a portmanteau film, *The Beginning of an Unknown Age* [Nachalo nevedomogo veka], and produced three of five segments, all based on revolutionary stories. One – Genrikh Gabai's *Motria* – was shown on television, two years later. The other two, Larisa Shepitko's *Homeland of Electricity* [Rodina elektrichestva] and Andrei Smirnov's *Angel*, disappeared for decades, and Baskakov crudely told Smirnov to get out of the business. ('You son of a bitch, we'll help you change professions!' [*My tebe, bl..., pomozhem smenit' professiiu.*]) In fact, since the system attempted to retain, if not co-opt, gifted, wayward individuals, Smirnov was accepted into the Union of Cinematographers shortly after the movie was shelved. The Experimental Studio, on the other hand, was closed down.⁶

Introduction

The cult of personality proved a theme particularly sensitive to political vicissitudes. Apart from Chukhrai's *Pure Skies*, the cult and its collateral issues had been confined to marginal plot lines, individual scenes and glancing references. In the months before Khrushchev's resignation, films were on the verge of atoning for what Valerii Fomin called their 'crooning hymns to a bloody regime',[7] but with Khrushchev gone and Brezhnev and Kosygin in power, neither film-makers nor censors knew what the new Party line would be.

In early 1965 the censors, facing several scripts that dealt with the cult, were still cautious and tentative. The first plenum of the Central Committee under the new leadership had not dealt explicitly with ideological questions. Without clear guidelines, and without what one editor called 'cooperation' with Central Committee members, the editors were altogether too likely to make worrisome mistakes. Not knowing 'exactly how the anti-cult theme was now regarded', Fomin notes, 'but definitely sensing a change of direction, they openly nudged their immediate superiors to go up the ladder' for specific instructions.[8]

The head of the script and editorial committee (GSRK) of Goskino relied on a few useful formulas with which to discuss the subject. The cult had assuredly violated legality, Aleksandr Dymshits admitted, but 'the question is one of measure, of how one treats this subject in films':

> One must know when it belongs and when it doesn't. One must understand one's responsibility to educate the people ... Some pictures show nothing but outrages and breaches of the law. As if there had been nothing else ... Certainly there were difficulties. No one is trying to keep it in the dark. It was our Party that revealed the secret to mankind. And the Party made necessary judgements. But the Party is not interested in people – irresponsible, undemocratic people – exploiting this subject.

Even allusions to this subject could dangerously blemish the image of the Soviet citizen. 'I am not in the least opposed to this theme,' he asserted in late January, 1965. 'But I am opposed to frivolous treatment of it in film after film.'[9]

The theme actually appeared in no more than a dozen scripts under consideration in the spring of 1965. In most cases GSRK chose safety, killing the scripts with the vaguest of justifications or no justification at all. Alov and Naumov had hoped to direct *The Law* [Zakon], from a script by Leonid Zorin. Mosfilm submitted the script to GSRK for the first time in November 1964, and again in January and February 1965. In May the answer came back: 'At the present time,' the commission explained, 'a script dealing with the theme of the cult of personality is unacceptable [*predstavliaetsia k spisaniiu*] for thematic reasons.'[10]

Lenfilm wanted to produce a film based on *The Diary of Nina Kosterina* [Dnevnik Niny Kosterinoi], the wartime diary of a young girl whose father, arrested in 1937, spent seventeen years in the Gulag. (He became a human rights activist in the mid-1960s, defending the rights of Crimean Tatars.) Dymshits and his colleagues disliked the script's 'incomplete and one-sided' treatment of the subject. Instead of showing 'how the steel was tempered', the scriptwriters demonstrated a 'false and dangerous' leaning towards 'Dostoevskian purification through suffering'. More than two years later, despite Lenfilm's many efforts to salvage the project, Baskakov's successor Aleksei Romanov finally buried it.[11]

By the end of June, 1965, bellicose self-confidence had supplanted uncertainty. When GSRK debated Armenfilm's proposal to produce Mikhail Papava's 'Mountains on the Path' [Gory v puti], Dymshits spoke bluntly:

> This film should not be about the era of the cult of personality, for there was no such era. Rather there was an era of transition to communism burdened by specific manifestations of the cult of personality ... 1949–53 were difficult years, but ... you focus exclusively on the wounds in people's souls, with constant importunate reminders and no sense of proportion. An epoch of construction looks like an epoch of repression. We need films about the history of our society, after all, about the epoch of heroism.[12]

Between January and June, a policy reversal occurred that set the tone for the next twenty years. 'It took many years for the anti-cult theme to ripen, however timidly,' Fomin observes. 'It took just half a year to crush it.'[13]

Other themes were only marginally less delicate than the cult, and scripts advancing alternative interpretations or constructed along aesthetically 'inappropriate' lines fell victim to the new standards. The intensified censorship severely affected projects about the Second World War, for example. With the restoration of Victory Day in 1965 and the grandiose celebration of the twentieth anniversary of victory, Brezhnev and his cohorts enlisted the memory of the war in the service of their political exigencies and reinforced the official myth of the war as a 'well-rehearsed romantic–heroic spectacle, with the positive outcome known ahead of time, and a rousing finale'.[14]

A large number of films complied, portraying Soviet soldiers as brave defenders of their fellow citizens (*Moscow is Behind Us* [Za nami Moskva, 1967]); as martyrs (*Alpine Ballad* [Al'piiskaia ballada, 1965]); as liberators of Eastern Europe (*The Tunnel* [Tonnel', 1966], a Soviet-Rumanian co-production). Iurii Nagibin and Aleksei Saltykov, who had collaborated on *The Chairman*, scored another major success with *A Woman's Kingdom* [Bab'e tsarstvo, 1967], about the women of an occupied Soviet village: nearly 50 million viewers saw it during its first year of distribution.[15]

Thus Mosfilm's Experimental Studio knew the hazards of accepting a script about Soviet and Finnish pilots who, adversaries in the air, found themselves dependent on each other for survival in the inhospitable tundra. 'In spite of its clear anti-war sentiments,' ran the cautious wording of the proposal, 'the script is far from pacifist.' Discretion proved futile. GSRK assessed the script as 'abstractly anti-war, almost pacifist', and the culture division of the Central Committee concurred. The authors, according to the official refusal, 'take not so much an anti-war as a pacifist position'. They are 'untruthful' in their treatment of issues of war and peace.[16]

At Lenfilm, venture after venture foundered. GSRK rejected one script for 'failing to show the nature of [wartime] heroism', and another, based on Vera Inber's diary of the blockade years, for minimizing Nazi barbarity and Leningraders' heroism. When Lenfilm proposed Anatolii Kuznetsov's *Babii iar*, which had the requisite 'scale', the authorities decreed that the film should be produced in Kiev, contrary to the express wishes of the author himself. Vasil Bykov's script 'Sotnikov' (the hero's name) was deemed gloomy and hopeless. (Ten years later Larisa Shepitko filmed it as *The Ascent* [Voskhozhdenie, 1976].)

GSRK often tried to pre-determine the fate of a script by assigning it for evaluation to editors known to favour or dislike certain kinds of work. Mikhail Bleiman, for instance, generally favoured traditional psychological narration. So GSRK gave him *King Mateusz and the Old Doctor*, a Lenfilm script that blended fact and fable in depicting the Jewish pedagogue Janusz Korczak, who perished in Treblinka together with the children of his Warsaw orphanage. On this occasion the choice backfired: Bleiman liked the script and recommended that Mikhail Kalik (one of its authors) direct it because of his lyrical style of film-making.[17] Nevertheless, without any explicit official refusal, GSRK quietly buried the Korczak script. Igor Chekin, a GSRK functionary, wrote to his boss that the script didn't really fit into the 'industry plan'. And that ended it.[18]

The authorities equally mistrusted Sergei Paradzhanov's script for a 'war film', *Kiev Frescoes*. In 1965 Kiev studio members, despite concern that Paradzhanov's kaleidoscope of images might bewilder viewers, trusted him enough to approve his unusual script; they respected its fluidity, poetry and internal integrity. Even old-timer Evgenii Pomeshchikov, a scriptwriter whose career had begun in the early 1930s, championed the project, albeit warily: 'It has the right to life,' he said; 'We have an obligation to support this [artistic] quest.'[19]

The studio's backing emboldened Paradzhanov. Why shouldn't Kiev, like Moscow, have an experimental studio for unusual projects? he wondered, and he defended the primacy of the image as the language of cinema. Some directors 'cannot say everything with precision in a literary form ... God grant that our studio should be accused of formalism, God grant us symbols, Dovzhenko['s films] rely on symbols.'[20]

Beware what you wish for ... Paradzhanov's 'self-indulgence' elicited accusations of formalism. Precisely what others admired – Paradzhanov's unique stamp, his patent 'authorship' – infuriated the authorities. They blocked *Kiev Frescoes* because of its 'erroneous, subjective and mystical representation of the

Great Fatherland War', confiscated Paradzhanov's footage and destroyed all but some twenty minutes of fragments.[21]

Unlike Paradzhanov, Tarkovskii did manage to complete *Andrei Rublev*, but he had similar problems with it, since Soviet interpretations – unlike those of Western critics – always focused on the film's historical content rather than its aesthetic achievement. The studio and the editors approved Tarkovskii and Konchalovskii's script in April 1964, but by the time Tarkovskii began shooting a year later, substantial budgetary cuts had forced him to drop such planned scenes as the first major Russian victory over the Tartars, the 1380 Battle of Kulikovo.

In late August 1966, Tarkovskii showed the first cut of his film, then entitled *The Passion According to Andrei*, to studio members. They criticized its length (three hours and twenty minutes) and violence, but provisionally approved the film. Tarkovskii edited out about fifteen minutes, including a few of the most graphic images of physical brutality, but complained to Aleksei Romanov, Goskino's chairman, that 'further cuts would seriously damage the film's artistic integrity'.[22] (He did cut a bit more in the hope of achieving the film's release.) Despite *Andrei Rublev*'s generally favourable reception when it premièred at the film industry's headquarters early in 1967, and despite a request for a print from the 1967 Cannes festival organizers, the film 'existed in a kind of administrative limbo for five years, discussed at the highest levels of Mosfilm and Goskino, and even at a large gathering of the Central Committee of the Communist Party'.[23]

In *Andrei Rublev* powerful images of brutality and physical cruelty – slitting a man's neck, a horse falling to its death, blinding – contribute to Tarkovskii's subversion of Soviet cinema's conventional glorification of the Russian past, as does the absence of 'heroic' images of the Russian people. Without a positive national leader and with a 'detached and passive' hero rather than the activist of the original script,[24] *Rublev* could hardly expect official approbation. Furthermore, Tarkovskii dwelled on 'naturalistic' (that is, negative) aspects of medieval Russian life; he eschewed teleology, presenting history as a panorama of enduring violence; he foregrounded the role of the artist within a community dominated by powerful figures and institutions (the Grand Duke, the church).

In an increasingly nervous and rigid cultural environment, *Rublev* transgressed in the same ways and for many of the same reasons as other films, such as Alov and Naumov's adaptation of a Dostoevskii story, *A Nasty Tale* [Skvernyi anekdot]. Dostoevskii satirized the complacent 'new liberalism' of the early 1860s: after an evening of drinking, a civil servant of good breeding and great vanity decides to try out his half-baked theories about democracy and the common touch by dropping in on the wedding of one of his underlings. 'The consequences of [his] *beau geste*', observed Joseph Frank, 'are exactly what might have been expected': the revellers freeze in their tracks, while young

Introduction

General Pralinskii's 'efforts at conversation, so successful in various *salons*, here fall completely flat'. Eventually, however, the tension abates, so much so that a young radical contemptuously denounces Pralinskii as a hypocrite, and the once-deferential guests mock and deride him. Completely soused and incoherently maudlin, Pralinskii spends a miserable night in the bed intended for the newly-weds (who are forced to sleep on a row of chairs) and makes his escape at dawn. '"Severity, severity, nothing but severity" – these are his final words as he renounces once and for all the treacherous pitfalls of "humanity".'[25]

Back in 1965, when costly projects overloaded Mosfilm's studio plan, Alov and Naumov had pledged to film the Dostoevskii story quickly and cheaply, with few characters and sets, and as a comedy, always in short supply. So the studio had agreed. From the start, however, editors at GSRK fretted, because the 'progressive' characters verged on caricature, while the *narod* consisted of knaves and fools. 'Who needs a film like this now?' one editor asked in February 1965. Another dismissed the idea as 'reactionary', 'anti-social', 'anti-democratic', and alien to the ideas of Dobroliubov, Belinskii, Herzen, Chernyshevskii – the roster of nineteenth-century progressive critics.[26]

Still, GSRK acquiesced, in part as a sop to Alov and Naumov, whose project about Stalinist repression (*The Law*) had been squashed flat in the wake of Khrushchev's removal. The directors worked fast, as promised, showing the edited film to the studio on 1 December 1965. They retained much of Dostoevskii's dialogue verbatim, and employed a claustrophobic visual style to emphasize the grotesque and repulsive aspects of the story. Cameraman Anatolii Kuznetsov used a fish-eye lens for distorted close-ups of leering and grimacing mask-like visages, while silent, staring, dark faces and oblivious merrymakers fill the background.

Revising not so much Dostoevskii as their own earlier myth-making in *Pavel Korchagin*, Alov and Naumov created a world stripped of all beauty and reason. Instead of hatred sanctified in the name of love, hatred alone endures.[27] Their lampoon destroyed the myth – beloved of nineteenth-century intellectuals and Soviet ideologues alike – of the people as the 'moral source' of Russia, as the 'god-carrier' and foundation on which everything rests. In *A Nasty Tale* the *narod* is vile and bestial. At the studio discussion, mild reservations about style quickly degenerated into ominous references to Kafka's 'Metamorphosis' (human beings 'should not be confused' with bugs) and to Buñuel's *Viridiana*, whose heroine seeks redemption among the disfigured and crippled. Lev Arnshtam blamed Dostoevskii for writing a story 'devoid of a moral ideal', but more orthodox voices charged Alov and Naumov with caricaturing the 'ever critical, ever socially-responsible Dostoevskii'. The 'filth', 'human foulness', and 'primitive, barely human existence' portrayed on screen outraged Pyrev. 'These are cattle,' he fumed, 'not people.' Alov and Naumov were pandering to the West, eager to embrace an ugly image of Russia; the film would deeply offend 'people of

Forbidden Games

our nation, of our homeland'.[28] Bad enough to exclude democracy 'from above', in the film's wretched examples of the educated elite; intolerable to exclude it 'from below'.

Even individuals who disliked *A Nasty Tale*, such as Igor Talankin, pleaded the case for its release, on behalf of a more catholic Soviet cinema.[29] Mikhail Shveitser cited Chernyshevskii's dictum that cruel truth must be spoken aloud in order for healing to begin; 'not everywhere in the world have such generals disappeared', said one advocate, 'and plenty of titular councillors still creep around licking their boots'.[30]

Although the authorities permitted a screening in January to a group of literary historians, philosophers and writers, and another at the Union of Cinematographers (where Pyrev repeated his objections), the film's adversaries proved more powerful than its patrons. No document of a formal ban survives, if one ever existed, so no official 'reason' for the film's disappearance exists. But by late September 1966 all discussion of releasing *A Nasty Tale* ended, and the film vanished for more than two decades. Its fate signified the onset of 'the era of administrative persecution of cinema'.[31]

17. To Have and Have Not

alcification did not occur overnight; it was a process, not an event, and it took time for directors, film teams and studios to internalize the constraints imposed from outside. In 1966 and 1967 both the central Russian studios and the expanded and thriving republican studios produced films, not all of them approved for release, of great power and strength. Many of them suggest a growing disquiet about the individual's place within society, distrust if not outright rejection of the core myths of Soviet history and society, and dissatisfaction with the cherished values of the generation that came of age during the thaw's heyday. Together, this suspicion of traditional Soviet interpretations of the past, apprehension about the present and discontent with values venerated only a decade earlier effected a radical transformation of screen heroes and heroism.

In the early 1960s, film heroes still embodied wholeness and stability. Mikhail Ulianov's Egor Trubnikov (*The Chairman*), Nikolai Cherkasov's Academician Dronov (*Everything Remains for People*), Evgenii Urbanskii's pilot Astakhov (*Pure Skies*), Zakariadze's Georgian peasant-soldier (*A Soldier's Father*), Umurzakova's soldier-mother in the Kazakh *Tale of a Mother* [Skaz o materi, 1963] all suggest 'the unwavering moral foundation of national life'; not coincidentally, they are often the heads of families and personify the family hearth.[1]

Within a few years, however, the old-fashioned rock-solid screen *pater familias* had lost the ability to keep his family together. By the mid-1960s, children were leaving home not in order to fulfil a social ideal celebrated explicitly or tacitly by the film-maker, such as constructing vast hydroelectric plants or tilling barren soil, nor to honour their obligations to the state, like Aksenov's young doctors a few years before. Whether they sought advancement, education, jobs, indoor plumbing, or simply amusement and excitement, their goals were personal, not social; individual, not shared. The films of 1966 and 1967, rejecting Stalinist centripetal values, depict an attenuated bond between the small family and the Big Family, and question what both family and Family mean and achieve.

The wide screen mirrored the mobility of Soviet life. Audiences saw for themselves how space was physically opening up, as film characters traversed city streets and took to the road. But whether pedestrians or chauffeurs, they were far less light-hearted than their eager and hopeful older brothers and sisters. The trio in *I Walk Around Moscow* roamed Moscow self-confidently; the heroes of *Ilich's Gate* demonstrated cheerful if ultimately eroding solidarity. By 1967, the heroine of Khutsiev's *July Rain* hurries through Moscow's crowds, glancing uneasily over her shoulder. Only a sudden rainstorm forces temporary contact between strangers as they huddle under a cornice for protection.

Film-makers had earlier welcomed their heroes' travels as evidence of commitment to a collective goal. Now they shared their characters' anxiety. Whether Shukshin's Siberian village in *Your Son and Brother* or Kozintsev's Elsinore in *Hamlet*, the places where the heroes grew up became reminders and symbols of lost values and a disappearing way of life, of past stability and present apprehension. A sense of loss is particularly acute in films made in republican studios, where the family home often symbolizes national culture. Children forsake it for educational and professional opportunities, but in doing so they abandon their roots and an essential part of their identity.

Iurii Ilenko's highly stylized *Spring for the Thirsty* [Rodnik dlia zhazhdu-shchikh, 1965] so forcefully exemplifies this theme that the authorities held it back for more than twenty years. Its experimental style disturbed them: it is visually stunning, as might be expected from the man who shot Paradzhanov's *Shadows of Forgotten Ancestors*, but has no plot and very little dialogue. Its political implications disturbed them too. (The Party expelled its author, Ukrainian activist Ivan Drach, in 1966.) The 'spring' of the title, a well that once gave pure water to family, friends and strangers, suggests national past and traditional culture. Now the protagonist, a white-bearded old recluse whose children live elsewhere and who is haunted by ghosts from the past, has allowed it to become muddy and impure.

Similar images – a dried-up well, absent children, a tottering old father – express abandonment in Vadim Derbenev's *Last Month of Autumn* [Poslednii mesiats oseni, 1966]. The four sons in Vitautas Zalakavicius' *No One Wanted to Die*, a stylistically startling drama about the post-war conflict between kolkhoz workers and Lithuanian opponents of Soviet power, have also made their lives far from the village where their ageing, beautiful and fierce mother remains. They return to avenge the murder of their kolkhoz-chairman father, but they won't stay. Sometimes parents send their children to town for schooling and lose them for good. All the offspring of an older couple in the lovely Kirgiz film *Sky of Our Childhood* [Nebo nashego detstva, 1967] have settled in the city, far from the vast and unpopulated mountainous expanses where their nomad parents pasture horses. Only the youngest son still comes home for the summer, travelling by helicopter and then on horseback; his brothers and sisters send a photograph. Although his parents want to keep him at home, to help them in

27. *The Sky of Our Childhood*

their old age and to carry on their traditional life, they reluctantly accede to the inevitable and send him back to the city for the new school year.

The script of *Sky*, by director Tolomush Okeev and Kadyrkul Omurkulov, genuflects to enshrined values of education and progress. At the same time, Okeev, with the help of cinematographer Kadyrzhan Kydyraliev, records the collision between traditional nomadic life and Soviet modernity in highly ambiguous terms. Our elders, Okeev commented in an echo of the Russian Village Prose writers (*derevenshchiki*), 'don't drink, don't smoke, they are not mercantile, they never lie ... They themselves are a part of that pure nature within which they live.'[2] The Russian engineers who are blasting a highway through the Kirgiz steppes understand very little about the indigenous culture, no matter how much they enjoy drinking the local *kumis* (fermented mare's milk). Their explosions kill the fish and frighten the horses, despoiling the natural landscape and its ecological balance.

For decades Moscow had been the hub of national life; Soviets dreamed of going 'to Moscow! to Moscow!' no less than did Chekhov's three sisters. But as the sense of national commonality disintegrated in the mid-1960s, so did Moscow-centrism and the mental map it engendered.[3] Films with historical contexts, such as Bondarchuk's *War and Peace* and screen adaptations of Turgenev and Ostrovskii, portrayed nineteenth-century Russian provincial life as cosy and attractive, while contemporary characters often found economic opportunity and personal contentment in provincial cities that no longer seemed merely inadequate substitutes for the 'real' metropolis. Georgii Danelia's *Thirty-three*, for example, begins as if to parody sleepy provincial life: to the accompaniment of groans and moans from an unidentified source, the camera pans gleaming onion-domed churches and dusty, empty streets before zooming in on a goat absorbed in steady munching. As the film progresses, however, it becomes clear that the hero's small town permits a far more authentic life than Moscow's rat-race.

When peasants leave the countryside, as they do in Pavel Liubimov's *Women* [Zhenshchiny, 1965] and Kira Muratova's *Brief Encounters* [Korotkie vstrechi, 1967], they go no further than nearby cities. In *Women*, three generations of women from the same village follow one another to town, where the cleanliness and collegiality of the factory they work in represent a clear improvement over the isolation and physical hardship of farming.

In Muratova's *Brief Encounters*, a country girl, Nadia, turns up at the door of the urban heroine Valia. The film concentrates on the relationship between the two women, and between them and the man they both love, not on the depopulation of the countryside; nevertheless, at every stage of making *Brief Encounters* – literary script, director's script, post-production editing – Muratova was pressured to expunge negative references to the rural life her characters are desperate to escape. She had to cut a scene in which Nadia's girlfriend speaks about her hatred for kolkhozniki, and Nadia's statement that people were leaving the kolkhoz as fast as they could.[4] Nadia herself, though she wrinkles her nose at the foetid city water, ran from the pure well-water of her village 'like the devil from incense'.[5]

Shukshin recognized the reality of rural flight as well. Three of the four sons in *Your Son and Brother* have left the Siberian village where their parents and two siblings still reside. Recalling *A Boy Like That*, *Your Son and Brother* opens with the essential prelude of the physical environment that tells us where the heroes come from – long shots of the glistening river and distant hills, middle shots of the social and human reality: a man getting his hair cut in a fenced yard, unhurried morning routines, girls in muddy boots.

The first episode involves Stepan, the son whose homesickness impels him to escape from prison three months before the end of his sentence. Stepan remains emotionally close to the clan life of his village. When the neighbours come over to welcome him, they ask questions about prison without the least embarrassment and with no trace of moral judgement, and Stepan answers the same way. Prison is not a cause for shame; it is simply a world unknown to them, and therefore of interest. He is one of them; they sing without flourishes and without self-consciousness, and he responds by singing an underworld song the same way. (Shukshin was criticized for the impropriety of Stepan's thieves' song.) The camera dollies around the house, respectfully filming furniture and faces.

The second episode involves another son, Maksim.[6] Having trailed his elder brother, Ignat, to Moscow, he dislikes the city's impersonality and the crowds. He searches exhaustively for snake venom liniment for his mother's lumbago, only to be told the medicine is sold out wherever he goes. He has none of the connections necessary to obtain such products, and his frustration and fury explode at the last in a long line of brusquely indifferent pharmacists.

His brother Ignat, a champion wrestler and circus trainer, has 'mastered' city life. He locates and obtains the liniment. He advises Maksim to marry a town girl with a residence permit, as he has done. Ignat's wife teases her hair into a towering beehive and paints her nails. She wears trendy capri pants in their kitsch-laden apartment and ludicrously inappropriate high heels and a slinky dress when she meets her in-laws for the first time.

Genuine attachment to and love of one's homeland have little to do with Ignat's rhetoric. 'We Russians are a tough little nation [*My, russkie, krepkii narodishka*],' he boasts, puffing out his chest. 'Greetings, mother Katun!' he loudly hails the river that nourishes and sustains the village. In fact, he has cut himself off from his roots, has no real affinity with home and its values. He doesn't even speak the same language as his family: 'Why are you pessimistic?' he asks his father, as if sadness and pessimism were synonyms. His father is silent, his reply a look of bewildered disgust.

Vasilii, the youngest son, and Vera, the deaf-mute sister, remain physically within the communal life of the village that supports them emotionally. Vera's handicap does not prevent her from participating in village life, where she is matter-of-factly accepted. She parades her gift from Ignat, a 'town' dress, throughout the village for all to admire, her animated face and eloquent gestures expressing her pleasure at the compliments she receives.

Impulse and inchoate longing drive Shukshin's unpredictable, temperamental heroes, who often appear foolish, if only because they make choices that are illogical and, by conventionally sensible standards, counter-productive. But he cherished them precisely for their emotional spontaneity. 'I love [Stepan],' he wrote in a draft of a letter to his harsh critic Larisa Kriachko. 'Of course he's a fool for not waiting out his last three months and for escaping. But he didn't escape in order to steal. He came openly to his village to breathe the scent of his native soil, to see his mother and father. I love a fool like that.'[7]

Stepan is wiser than his 'successful' brother Ignat; he knows he cannot manage alone, while Ignat erroneously believes he is self-sufficient. Shukshin's heroes, like so many wandering movie heroes of the mid-1960s, need support, yet they do not know where to find it. Traditional sources – religion, family, native soil – have lost much of their meaning and power, undercut by decades of Soviet insistence on their ideological unsuitability. Yet archetypal Soviet buttresses, such as the dream of progress, the sanctity of labour, the wisdom of the people, and the strength of collective will, appear to be equally inadequate.

The Party, concerned as ever with the nature of screen heroism, demanded modern Pierre Bezukhovs, Dr Dymovs (from Chekhov's 'Grasshopper') and – naturally – Chapaevs. It had to be contented with Aleksandr Mitta's *Someone's Ringing, Open the Door* and Eldar Riazanov's *Watch the Car*, films that cleverly subverted conventional Soviet heroic paradigms without rejecting the possibility of heroism *per se*, and that leavened social critique with sensitive psychological portraiture in one and humour in the other.

Open the Door depicts a society where adult guidance is minimal and children raise themselves. Supposedly a neighbour minds twelve-year-old Tania, whose mother has joined her geologist husband in the field, but really the child looks after herself, eating her solitary meal on a corner of the table or, alone in the tidy apartment, perching on the sofa to listen to music. Her friend Gena has a mother too weary to greet or smile at her son, let alone embrace him. When Tania sets out to find members of the first generation of Young Pioneers, cranky men and women slam the door in her face.

The two putative heroes – Petia, Tania's beloved Pioneer leader, and a former Pioneer, now a famous violinist – have clay feet. Petia 'betrays' Tania by ice-skating with a girl his own age, and he traduces his vaunted ideals by missing fencing training and performing poorly at school. The violinist is completely self-absorbed, a narcissist whose memories focus exclusively on himself.

Tania, however, is genuinely heroic. She trusts her own feelings, however absurd and hopeless they may look to an outsider. Tania ignores the mockery of the other children and relinquishes her love for Petia only when she herself is disappointed in him. Unlike Ksenia, Raizman's heroine in *And What If It's Love?*, who lacks the emotional confidence to withstand the scrutiny of outsiders, Tania can firmly tell a woman who tries to comfort her, 'It's none of your business.'

Tania finds an ally in the meek trumpeter Pavel Vasilevich, Gena's stepfather. Though not himself one of the early Pioneers, he can explain to the children the historical context in which the Pioneer organization was formed, and its fierce battles against illiteracy, tuberculosis and 'bourgeois influence'. (He laughingly adds, 'If we'd decided that soccer showed bourgeois influence, we would have battled against soccer.') When the violinist fails to attend the children's ceremony as promised, Pavel Vasilevich steps in, hesitantly mounting the podium to describe a Pioneer from his courtyard who later became a war hero, to whom he blows a musical tribute on his horn. Like Tania, Pavel Vasilevich is unconventionally but authentically heroic: responsible, kind, sensitive. As played by Rolan Bykov, whose very eyebrows manage to convey pathos, Pavel Vasilevich reveals inner nobility and strength, the dignity of a weak and slightly comical man.[8]

To Have and Have Not

28. *Watch the Car*

The hero of Eldar Riazanov's *Watch the Car*, Iurii Detochkin (Innokentii Smoktunovskii), is a good man who steals cars for the sake of justice. He robs members of Moscow's new bourgeoisie who have acquired valuable possessions by exploiting their positions unethically if not outright illegally. Detochkin sells the stolen cars and donates the proceeds to an orphanage. In his spare time, Detochkin is an amateur actor, and he meets ace police detective Maksim Podberezikov (Oleg Efremov) when he plays Hamlet to Podberezikov's Laertes in an amateur production. (Audiences, who loved Smoktunovskii's Hamlet in Kozintsev's film a year before, knowingly relished the spoof.)

Riazanov's casting of Smoktunovskii as Detochkin nearly foundered in official shoals. Smoktunovskii had just played Lenin in two films, *On One Planet* [Na odnoi planete, 1965] and *First Visitor* [Pervyi posetitel', 1965]. Aleksei Romanov, chairman of the cinema commission of the Council of Ministers, so disliked the idea that the same actor would appear on screen as a crook that he vetoed the choice. Riazanov argued that Detochkin was a noble and honest fellow, if a thief, and Romanov eventually capitulated.[9]

Riazanov and Emil Braginskii had published the novella *Watch the Car* in *Molodaia gvardiia* a few years before, partly to facilitate making the film; studios preferred literary adaptations to original screenplays because the former had already been vetted and accepted by a publishing house.[10] According to one source, the screenplay passed muster only after statistics demonstrated that the book's success had not inspired an increase in the incidence of car theft.[11] The film darkens its fictional source: 'We wanted to make a good-natured but astringent comedy whose meaning would not be confined to the plot,' Riazanov wrote. 'We wanted it to be ambiguous, to elicit sadness as well as laughter, to make people think about what they had seen.'[12]

They succeeded. Melancholy shadows the humour of a film that depicts 'the impossibility of achieving justice within the boundaries of reality, about the attempt to achieve it outside the law'.[13] Detochkin goes to jail, despite Detective Podberezikov's testimony as a character witness on Detochkin's behalf. The real criminals, those who steal for their own gain, from the state and the society, accuse Detochkin of violating 'sacred values': the individual's right to private property, to have a car, a dacha, money. In a bitter mockery of the foundation of Marxist philosophy, one of them piously intones, 'From each according to his ability, to each according to his need.'

Watch the Car uses an ironic voice-over narration to unite components of various genres. The opening sequence, for instance, parodies the detective genre: phantoms lurk in the darkness, *Pink Panther*-type music plays, and the narrator at once acknowledges and lampoons the iron rules of the genre: 'The spectator likes detective films,' he says. 'It's pleasant to know how it will all come out. This story occurred ... somewhere ... perhaps ... ' Later the narrator portentously comments on the inevitable confrontation between thief and detective as they 'approached each other from opposite ends of the big city', and introduces a farcical car chase sequence with the mocking preface, 'A detective story without a chase is like life without love'.

Riazanov took pains to cast as his two protagonists strong actors who would appeal to audiences equally, if in different ways, so that viewers would not sympathize exclusively with either the noble detective (*à la* Sherlock Holmes) or the noble criminal (*à la* Robin Hood):

> Although one wears a uniform and the other does not, although they would seem to be on opposite sides, both heroes are profoundly decent and honourable and full of good will towards those around them ... . One had to be odd, a bit of a kook [*chudakovat*], the other had to be full of common sense. One was the principled avenger who would not compromise, the other an inflexible but just guardian of the law.

Riazanov, cameramen Vladimir Nakhabtsev and Anatolii Mukasei, and designer Boris Nemechek tried to compensate for the fantastic plot with realistic presentation, 'an authentic, unembellished environment'. They shot on location, using a hidden camera to enhance realism. The car chase, although entirely staged, seemed 'real' thanks to the sustained sobriety of the actors. Smok-tunovskii as the fleeing culprit and Georgii Zhzhenov as the pursuing policeman were so persuasive that after the film's release, one viewer asked Riazanov if Zhzhenov actually was a policeman.[14]

Both *Open the Door* and *Watch the Car* pleased audiences who, as always, wanted to enjoy themselves; *Sovetskii ekran* readers chose Smoktunovskii as their favourite actor for 1966. In early 1967, in a survey of Moscow's Arbat film club (with over 1,300 members, many in their twenties), comedies, psycho-logical dramas and adventure films topped the list. Although, as Muscovites, members may have been more sophisticated than viewers nation-wide, their preferences ('aesthetic pleasure', 'better knowledge of life', 'favourite actors') reflected general taste.[15]

Thus, the box-office front-runner for that year, Gaidai's romantic comedy *The Prisoner of the Caucasus, or the Further Adventures of Shurik* [Kavkazskaia plennitsa, ili novye prikliucheniia Shurika], drew 76 million viewers. Two melodramas, Pavel Liubimov's *Women* and Georgii Natanson's *Older Sister* [Starshaia sestra, 1966], did well at the box-office, the latter thanks to a stellar performance by Tatiana Doronina, *Sovetskii ekran* readers' choice as best actress of 1967. Tatiana Lioznova, one of the few women who began a successful directing career in the 1950s, earned fame with a series of dramas made in the 1960s: *Evdokiia* (1961), *Early in the Morning* [Rano utrom, 1965], and *'Three Poplars' in Pliushchikh* [Tri topolia na Pliushchikhe, 1967]. (*Sovetskii ekran* readers again chose Doronina as 1968's best actress for her role in *Poplars*.)

Like the extremely successful middle-brow fiction of Vera Panova (with whom Lioznova worked) and I. Grekova, especially Grekova's 1963 novella 'Ladies' Hairdresser' ['Damskii master'] and 'Summer in the City' ['Letom v gorode', 1965], Lioznova's movies appealed because of their recognition and apparent resolution of the 'collisions of daily life'. Characters manoeuvre through the same worlds in which their viewers live, enjoying accustomed satisfactions, particularly maternal pleasures. They bump up against frus-trations and constraints, but the films usually end on an upbeat if often sweetly melancholic note. In Lioznova's pictures 'the screen became a mirror of daily life. Its commandments were satisfying, its recognition was pleasing, it con-formed to the concepts of ordinary members of society about goodness, about mutual help, about the dangers of nonconformity, about how those who live and work, simply and honestly, merit the respect of their brigadiers, friends, and relations.'[16]

Audiences found little such reassurance in three cinematic interpretations of modern life, Larisa Shepitko's *Wings* [Kryl'ia, 1966], Kira Muratova's *Brief Encounters* and Marlen Khutsiev's *July Rain*. All three feature complicated, not particularly happy heroines with strained personal lives and stressful professions. In the world of these films, people who 'live and work simply and honestly', whatever they may deserve, incur at best indifference, at worst anger and resentment.

Shepitko's heroine, Nadezhda Stepanovna Petrukhina, flew bombers during the war; twenty years later, she has become the principal of a vocational training institute and the estranged adoptive mother of a newly-married daughter. Petrukhina is 'a museum exhibit in both a literal and a metaphorical sense':[17] literal because the local museum honours her wartime career, and metaphoric because her capacity for spontaneity and joy froze when her lover, a fellow pilot, perished.

As written by Natalia Riazantseva and Valentin Ezhov and as played with wonderful subtlety by Maia Bulgakova,[18] Petrukhina explodes the Soviet clichés of the conventionally 'tough but fair' heroine, who wins reluctant respect and admiration despite her sternness. This woman is disliked. Her amalgam of competence and awkwardness alienates rather than endears, and although she means well, she is unable to shed her officious manner.

Petrukhina lacks insight into her own behaviour. She seeks out a student whom she expelled (without hearing his side of a dispute), but cannot understand his angry rebuff of her friendly overture. When Petrukhina calls on her daughter and son-in-law, a man Petrukhina has not even met, the air crackles with mutual incomprehension. Shepitko scrutinizes her heroine 'with unprecedented delicacy and implacability', rendering a 'profound analysis of the causes of a rupture between generations that is not only ideological but human as well'.[19] The cliché of mother–daughter intimacy disintegrates before our eyes.

So does friendship. It provides no emotional buttress, as it did for many heroines of this era, in films like *Women* and in the fiction of Maia Ganina, and Irina Velembovskaia (on whose novel *Women* was based). Petrukhina has no friends. The nearest she comes is an unlikely chat with a waitress; they dance a waltz together while dumbfounded men stand outside and stare at them through the café window. She sees her 'real' friends, fellow pilots, once a year, on Victory Day.

Professional gratification, maternity, friendship – *Wings* undercut one truism after another. But Shepitko reserved her most radical reinterpretation for Petrukhina's war experience. The heroine of *Wings* did not sacrifice herself for the security of later generations. She did not survive the trauma of war in order to enjoy contentment. Rather, war exhilarated Petrukhina. It demanded intense skill and effort, but offered satisfactions unparalleled in peace-time. In the film's last scene Petrukhina settles into the cockpit of a plane as a nostalgic exercise, only to roar off down the runway. She points her plane towards the sky, the element where she is genuinely at home, and although we do not see anything more, she will probably dive down in a suicidal crash.

With its revisionist treatment of the war, the complexity of its heroine, and the discomfiting ambiguity of its ending, *Wings* received relatively limited

29. *Wings*

distribution: only about eight million viewers saw *Wings* in 1966, though film critics nearly unanimously chose Bulgakova as best actress of 1966.[20] Muratova's *Brief Encounters* fared even worse. Muratova portrays Soviet society as deeply fissured, with apathetic bureaucrats and a rural population hell-bent on fleeing to the city. Moreover, the film's principal characters embody inappropriate values: eros matters too much to them, family too little.

Muratova's heroine, Valentina Ivanovna, is a water and sewage inspector in a southern city. Valia's probity is patent as she tries to draft a speech to persuade young people to go to work in the countryside. Her hunched posture and repetition of the salutation (she cannot get beyond 'Dear, dear comrades', the first words of the film) suggest deep fatigue and aversion; her phone call to a city official, whose rote blandishments she properly understands to be sugar-coated commands, reveals her extreme reluctance to spout rhetoric that she knows is hollow. She has none of the toughness typically associated with the 'Party broad' [*parttetia*]. The books and old photos that crowd her dim, dark apartment suggest her priorities, as does the sink piled with mismatched dishes, testimony to her indifference towards housewifery and its attendant pride in maintaining appearances.

Forbidden Games

30. *Brief Encounters*

Yet no one values Valia's integrity. When she refuses to certify for residency a new housing block that lacks running water, the would-be tenants, desperate to escape their overcrowded communal apartments, are enraged. She has logic on her side: if they move in before the water is connected, it will never be connected. But they have experience on theirs: if they wait until the water is connected, the new flats may never be ready for occupancy. Besides, as one man tells her to jolt her out of her obstinacy, they already carry water up stairs.

An 'abyss of social misunderstanding'[21] looms beneath the thin ice of Soviet egalitarianism. The hairdresser who rattles on about her son as she combs and sets Valia's hair seems to speak openly, one woman to another. No sooner is Valia out the door, however, than the beautician and manicurist trade barbed gossip about her, dismissing her as 'just an ordinary broad' [*baba*], as if Valia thinks she is better than they are.

Similar tension thickens Valia's relationship with Nadia, who remains wary and secretive despite Valia's friendly warmth. Sexual rivalry compounds class and educational differences: although Valia never knows of it, we discover from a series of flashbacks that she and Nadia both love Valia's peripatetic lover Maksim, with whom Nadia had had a brief romance while working at a roadside bar. (Goskino found particularly objectionable the conjunction of 'important government official' and 'love triangle'.)[22]

Brief Encounters ends on a note of irresolution. Nadia accepts that Valia is the emotional centre of Maksim's life, and decides to leave before he comes home. She sets the table in Valia's apartment for two, carefully constructing a beautiful still-life out of tablecloth, crystal, cutlery, fruit. But though Valia and Maksim may enjoy the beauty and bounty, nothing in the film suggests that this reunion will have different results from all their earlier meetings.

From the authorities' point of view, the ambiguous ending of *Brief Encounters* merely capped its many defects. Nadia's romance with Maksim amounted to a series of fleeting encounters, at the bar and at his campsite. (Scenes of physical intimacy between Maksim and Nadia and lines implying their sexual relationship had to be cut before the film received even a limited official imprimatur.)[23] Valia's intervals with Maksim last longer, but still end in separation.

The censors perceived Valia's attitude towards work as 'mechanically dutiful, rather than enthusiastic'.[24] Maksim – restless, rootless and undependable – chooses to be out in the field because he loathes paper work and office politics more than he loves Valia. Vladimir Vysotskii, who plays Maksim, was already suspect in his real-life role as a poet-bard, both because his 'raucous' voice differed 'so starkly from the velvety and hollow sounds of mass song crooners' and because his songs broke taboos about sex, violence, the army, criminal life and official hypocrisy.[25] In Vysotskii's performance Maksim emerges as an utterly appealing character quite indifferent to 'socially responsible' behaviour.

Above and beyond any particular 'sin', Muratova transgressed official bounds with her personal vision, her disregard for edifying precepts, her mosaic narrative, and her subtle characterization of Valia (whom she plays). 'This indisputably talented work', wrote chief editor I. Kokoreva, 'lacks a clear authorial concept. Having fashioned interesting images and situations, the film-maker fails to evaluate them clearly and from a Party-minded position. As a result the material can be interpreted in various ways.'[26] The reviewer for *Iskusstvo kino* agreed: 'You get the impression that the director, sitting at the editing table, just rearranged individual pieces of film without really justifying the rearrangement.'[27]

Marlen Khutsiev's *July Rain* elicited similar disgruntlement. Khutsiev's Moscow mirrors the southern city of *Brief Encounters*; both worlds have become unstable and frangible, their inhabitants full of inchoate longing. For *July Rain* German Lavrov filmed Moscow's broad avenues and streets in long dollying shots, much as Margarita Pilikhina had in *Ilich's Gate*, but keeps his camera much further away, observing with detachment streets clogged with traffic, people isolated in their locked cars or scurrying impatiently past one another in crowds.

Instead of the camaraderie and warmth that characterized *Gate*, where the camera seemed part of the world it filmed, Lavrov's camera remains aloof and

Forbidden Games

31. *July Rain*

slightly intimidating. Like a voyeuristic observer it stalks the heroine, Lena, as she hastens along the pavement, and she glances back over her shoulder several times. In one lengthy sequence limousines pull up to the French embassy, depositing ambassadorial guests at a reception to honour de Gaulle's visit to Moscow. The camera stands on the opposite side of the street amid a group of ordinary citizens, surveying the comings and goings of distinguished guests. They are so divorced from the world across the street that they might as well be staring at exotic animals in a zoo.

Khutsiev's characters are Moscow's intellectual elite. Lena, at twenty-seven a senior engineer at a printing plant, supervises the publication of a richly illustrated volume on Renaissance art. (The opening sequence, when the camera tracks her through the streets, cuts from the 'faceless multitudes' to the highly individualized faces painted by Raphael and Leonardo.) Her lover, Volodia, and their friends are affluent professionals who dress modishly and live in comfort, taking for granted the luxuries that in 1967 in Moscow signified status as well as income: stereo systems, imported recordings of up-to-date music, cars. If they worry about money it is in 'western' terms; one man discourages Volodia from pursuing a particular branch of research as insufficiently lucrative.

Their prosperity and prestige fail to satisfy them. At their gatherings the camera visually isolates individuals within the surrounding sea of people. When friends persuade Alik, played by poet-bard Iurii Vizbor, to pick up his guitar and sing, the guests listen languidly, passively. They trade repartee rather than conversation, and prize quick wit over sincerity. They don't touch when they dance, whether in joyless line-dancing or – in the 'old' dances that are back in fashion – at arm's length. Khutsiev ironically refers us to the poetry reading in *Ilich's Gate*: the party guests are the same people, barely half a dozen years older, yet they have lost their passion and eager involvement, the sizzling excitement of the audience at the Polytechnic. What they once found important has become meaningless, almost vulgar.

July Rain offers no public conflict to contextualize the characters' personal and internal dramas and desires, and intimate relationships are strained and crepuscular. Lena and her mother love each other, but they share neither information nor emotions. When they redecorate, a bookshelf splits the screen vertically, the physical barrier suggesting the separation between Lena, scrubbing the floor on one side, and her mother on the other. At the wake after Lena's father's death, mother and daughter do not touch each other; each grieves alone.

Lena reveals herself only to Zhenia, the young stranger who casually lent her his jacket for protection from the July shower. She welcomes Zhenia's periodic phone calls and their long, searching conversations. The phone wire is fragile, Zhenia's voice at times inaudible. Inter-city operators interrupt the calls, lack of privacy forces Lena into the lavatory with the phone. Yet their closeness is genuine, and more meaningful than her relationship with Volodia.

When Volodia finally proposes marriage, self-mockingly offering to drop to bended knee, visual signs proclaim the couple's estrangement. The stationary camera calmly records from a middle distance, while Lena and Volodia stand facing forwards in front of a wall, as if in a police line-up; their folded arms protect their bodies. Neither looks at the other, both seem to be speaking to the camera, and when Lena admits Volodia's good qualities, she itemizes them as a series of negatives: he doesn't drink, he doesn't chase women. She turns him down.

Like *Wings* and *Brief Encounters*, *July Rain* concludes ambiguously, with images of bemedalled veterans embracing outside the Bolshoi Theatre on Victory Day, followed immediately by shots of young people and children – faces frequently used by film-makers to suggest hope and anticipation. Here they express wariness and mistrust. If they are looking into the future, they don't much like what they see. Friendly critics characterized *July Rain* as Khutsiev's attempt to convey the atmosphere of a society 'in search of an ideal'. They knew, though, that the gilded world of *July Rain*, with its 'anguish, insignificance, the vanities of people who too often exchange apartments, faces, women's hearts, where noise replaces gaiety and conversation skims over what is important',[28] actually exposed the very notion of the Ideal as illusory.[29]

The censors disliked Khutsiev's bleak vision, his deviant individuals who, with their 'pitiful passions and flabby languor', egregiously misrepresented Soviet intellectual circles. An open letter to Khutsiev published in *Sovetskaia kultura* in August 1967 charged him with forfeiting 'conceptual clarity' [*ideino otchetlivaia forma*] and failing to create an 'edifying parable'.[30]

Tolerance for any kind of nonconformity was ebbing swiftly. Everyone in the film industry, in the arts, in intellectual life, in science and scholarship felt it. Twenty years later, Lev Anninskii looked back on a little-noticed defence of *July Rain* he published in 1967 and glossed its cautious, compromising tone:

> I could neither explain to myself nor believe in the inevitable and oppressive fate looming for this picture, and in general for the kind of art close to me, and for my whole generation. I could not and would not acknowledge it. So I went around in circles trying to keep up my courage and hide my fear, I tried as hard as I could to be cheerful, but fear crept in.[31]

18. Farewell, My Lovely

Developments sadly justified Anninskii's fear. The Party's noose tightened. Despite the production, and even the release, of several good films in 1966 and 1967, the cultural environment was growing increasingly hostile towards personal vision, and increasingly fearful of originality and innovation.

Typically, the more distinctive a film, the more trouble it encountered; officialdom regarded the 'auteur' with deep disquiet. Kulidzhanov had hinted as much at the First Congress of the Union of Cinematographers, back in 1965:

> It may seem strange to insist at a cinema congress that film is an art ... No one directly denies this, but in practice, because of its mass nature and its unparalleled accessibility, it is often regarded as either entertainment or as a carrier of ideas, precepts and examples, as a means of disseminating these ideas, norms and paradigms ... The aesthetic nature of film, its poetry, the particularities of its language are not considered, which gives rise to the illusion that it's easy to judge films, anyone can do it. As a result, political, ideological or moral evaluations of a film are artificially separated from aesthetic analysis.[1]

Certainly Aleksei Romanov, who became chair of Goskino in 1963 after having been deputy chair of the Central Committee's Department of Propaganda and Agitation, and who held the post until 1972, felt no obligation to consider film aesthetics. His report on the state of the film industry in 1967 complimented Party organizations for making use of the 'best Soviet films' in their 'ideological work during the anniversary year'. The Union, studios, and Goskino had permitted errant film-makers undeserved latitude. Yet the 'crooked mirror' they held up to Soviet life undermined the chief purpose of Soviet films and of Soviet art generally: 'the political enlightenment and aesthetic education of the people', in accordance with 'the interests of communist construction and the Soviet nation'.[2]

A year later the situation had deteriorated, and Romanov employed exclusively ideological terms:

Forbidden Games

In an intensifying ideological struggle it is especially important for those active in literature and art to oppose forcefully any manifestation of bourgeois ideology, to propagandize communist ideals and the advantages of socialism, to analyse and unearth every sort of petty bourgeois and revisionist tendency. The question of film quality is, therefore, a question of how the supervisory bodies in the film industry and the leadership of the Union implement their responsibilities, how they work with and educate those who create art.

Romanov castigated film-makers who, by 'de-heroizing' reality, 'violated the essence' of Soviet life, those who distorted the early period of the Second World War by creating 'false legends about weak leadership ... an endless chain of encirclements and defeats for our troops', and those who relied on 'plainly formalistic, even rococo [*shtukaturskie*] features' entirely alien to the traditions of Soviet cinema.[3]

Romanov's language and tone patently signalled the disappearance of official tolerance for film-makers who wished to push at the boundaries of the permissible. Intensified censorship restricted the scope of Soviet cinema and deformed its natural development. Concepts never became scripts, scripts never became films. Completed films lost chunks of footage to re-editing before they opened in theatres, if they opened at all. Progression from one film to the next was truncated. Experimental work, rarely successful with audiences but vital for film-makers, was proscribed. By 1968, with these new policies firmly in place, even the best and most original films followed channels cut by their predecessors. Individuals who tried to chart radical new routes paid heavy prices for their independence and creativity. Their ideas, their scripts, their movies and in some cases their careers fell victim to the pervasive chill. As Mikhail Kalik later commented, the guillotine had resumed its operations.[4] The thaw did not die a natural death, but, after a dozen years, it was finally over.

Had cinema – as an industry, an entertainment medium and an art form – changed in those years? Most certainly it had. The industry had fully recovered from the moribund condition to which it had been degraded in the late Stalin years. In 1953 the central studios functioned at minimal levels and few of the republican studios functioned at all; in 1967 fifteen thriving republican studios produced fifty-seven full-length feature films, and Mosfilm, Lenfilm and Gorky made over seventy. The number of documentaries, juvenile films and television films had grown proportionately, as had film publications. *Iskusstvo kino* still occupied pride of place among 'serious' cinephiles, but Soiuzinformkino, the national centre for information about movies, published a monthly illustrated brochure about new films, *Moviegoer's Companion* [Sputnik kinozritelia] for general audiences, as well as *New Films* [Novye fil'my], a guide for industry professionals, and a guide to children's movies.

The State Committee for Motion Pictures (Goskino), directly subordinate to the Council of Ministers, had expanded in tandem with the industry, acquiring authority and privileges as it grew out of its original administrative headquarters in the centre of Moscow to occupy sites all over the city. Its constituent units included the script-editorial board (GSRK, itself composed of 'thematic' groups), and departments in charge of feature films, film distribution, advertising and international relations. The Central Committee of the Party, in particular its culture department, routinely vetted ideological matters.

After many years, Ivan Pyrev's dream, the Union of Cinematographers, had become an officially recognized entity in 1965 and quickly assumed a central position in the industry, with a branch in each city that housed a film studio. The union represented several thousand directors, scriptwriters, actors and actresses, camera operators, set designers, composers, editors and film critics, each selected on the basis of recommendations and work assessment. Membership in the Cinematographers' Union, like membership in the Unions of Writers, Artists and Composers, conferred practical as well as professional advantages: access to better medical care and vacation resorts, housing, loans. The union's virtual monopoly on the production and sale of movie souvenirs, such as posters and postcards, ensured a steady source of funding.

By 1967 the industry produced a large number of films for mass audiences, many of them made for television. Official reprehensions notwithstanding, such popular movies formed a distinct body of work including films of every genre. The profusion of science fiction and adventure films, thrillers, melodramas and comedies, with or without an appropriate ideological gloss, clearly differed from experimental or innovative films for small audiences.[5]

Thematically, cinema had left far behind the pomposity and spurious social unity and contentment of the late Stalinist movies. After two decades of insistence on the primacy of public life, the thaw and its movies had re-legitimized the private lives and emotions of individuals, even within highly ideologized political contexts, such as the civil war and the Second World War. The screen reflected the thaw's 'feminization' of Soviet life, with its (often bathetic) insistence on the absolute value of sincerity and its identification of authenticity with family life and romantic love.

The thaw did not denote rejection of all aspects of Stalinist society. Rather, it signified a cleansing of the excrescences grafted by Stalinism on to a legacy of utopianism. The ideal of the collective held sway for some time, as did revolutionary idealism, minus revolutionary clichés and with a new penetration of the revolutionary hero's psychology.[6] The cult of labour initially replaced the cult of personality, as the heroism of ordinary men and women superseded the heroism of the leader, until by the mid-1960s the very concept of heroism could no longer be imagined without some kind of cinematic questioning, stylization, irony or distance. Thus from the 'ordinary' heroes of the mid-1950s, directors found their way to the folkloric heroes of the late 1950s, to the

Forbidden Games

children of the early 1960s, and to the parodic, non-heroic and anti-heroic protagonists of 1966 and 1967.

Following the Twenty-second Party Congress, film-makers sought adequate and appropriate aesthetic means to probe the painful moral issues it raised, and to express the alienation, anxiety and discontent of their compatriots. They challenged the logocentricity so characteristic of earlier Soviet films, spurning it entirely or recasting it as parody; they defied the rigidity of generic boundaries to create richly unpredictable hybrids. Audiences avid for truthful representations of reality both encouraged and embraced film-makers eager to tell the truth about their society as they saw it – hence the simultaneous rise of hyper-realistic and lyric cinema.

A dozen years is a short time. But the dozen years between 1955 and 1967 substantially modified Soviet society. They witnessed the commencement, efflorescence and destruction of the phenomenon of 'the thaw', every stage and aspect of which Soviet cinema documented and stimulated, shaped and reflected. The movies made then were products of thaw metamorphoses, and generated transformations in turn. Each influenced the other, each benefited, in a symbiotic relationship of major significance for both. During the Brezhnev era, cinema, like society, resisted innovation and dynamism; it preferred equilibrium to instability, and security to the risks and rewards of creativity. When the thaw ended, so – for better or worse – did its cinema.

Notes

Abbreviations

IK: *Iskusstvo kino* (Film Art)
RGALI: Russkii gosudarstvennyi arkhiv literatury i iskusstva (Russian State Archive of Literature and Art)

1. The Big Sleep: Introduction

1. George Counts and Nucia Lodge, *The Country of the Blind* (Boston: 1949), 125–9, 144–50. *A Great Life* and *Ivan the Terrible*, Pt II were both released in 1958 to relatively little reaction.

2. Peter Kenez, *Cinema and Soviet Society 1917–1953* (Cambridge: 1992), 216.

3. Ibid., 210.

4. For a summary of this period see Abraham Rothberg, *The Heirs of Stalin: Dissidence and the Soviet Regime, 1953–1970* (Ithaca, NY: 1972), 3–5 and 12–14.

5. RGALI Fond 2453, op. 3, d. 10.

6. 'It is the scenario which gives the director material whose ideological quality determines the political correctness and artistic convincingness of the film,' wrote *Sovetskoe kino* in 1933; cited by Kenez 141. See Vladimir Mikhailov, 'Stalinskaia model' upravleniia kinematografom', *Kino: Politika i liudi (30–e gody)*, ed. Lilia Mamatova (Moscow: 1995), 9–25.

7. RGALI Fond 2453, op. 3, d. 10.

8. 'Iz analiticheskoi spravki ministerstva kul'tury SSSR v TsK KPSS', *Istoriia sovetskoi politicheskoi tsenzury: dokumenty i kommentarii*, ed., T. M. Goriaeva (Moscow: 1997), 116–18.

9. According to Val Golovskoy, a former Soviet film journalist, Communist Party members were clearly identified as such; KGB agents were not. Val S. Golovskoy with John Rimberg, *Behind the Soviet Screen: The Motion-Picture Industry in the USSR 1972–1982* (Ann Arbor, MI: 1986), 26.

10. 'Za dal'neishii rost, za razvitie vsekh zhanrov kinoiskusstva!', *IK* 1 (1954): 3, 9.

11. I. Morozov, 'A v zhizni – slozhnee i iarche', *IK* 1 (1954): 11.

12. K. Slavin, 'V poiskakh novogo', *IK* 4 (1954): 63.

13. 'Khronika: Obsuzhdenie novykh stsenariev'. *IK* 7 (1954): 121–2.

14. Kenez, writing about the 1920s, comments that the Bolsheviks wanted films 'that could be used for propaganda purposes, would be artistically satisfactory, and would attract an audience' (82). So did their successors.

15. 'Rezko uvelichit' vypusk novykh fil'mov', *IK* 8 (1954): 3.

16. 'Za rastsvet kinodramaturgii!' *IK* 9 (1954): 6–7.

17. Josephine Woll, *Invented Truth: Soviet Reality and the Literary Imagination of Iurii Trifonov* (Durham, NC: 1991), 103.

18. Eldar Riazanov gratefully recalled Pyrev's support for his debut film, *Carnival Night*, in the face of strong opposition. See 'Neistovyi', in *Ivan Pyr'ev: v zhizni i na ekrane*, ed. G. B. Mar'iamov (Moscow: 1994), esp. 149–55.

19. 'Khronika', *IK* 7 (1955): 103.

20. Cited by Abraham Brumberg in 'Iconoclasm in Moscow – a Commentary', *Russia Under Khrushchev*, ed. A. Brumberg (New York: 1962), 72.

21. Future human-rights activist Ludmilla Alexeyeva, then in her late twenties, describes a fairly typical experience. She heard the text at a Party meeting at the Institute of Economics and Statistics in Moscow. 'I cannot say that I was shocked by the revelations. They simply validated views I had held since 1953. But I was amazed to hear such admissions from the Communist Party leader.' She and a friend, a former prosecutor, spent hours drinking and trading confidences in conversations that 'would have been unthinkable a few weeks earlier. Now, suddenly, they had become normal, commonplace, and necessary.' Ludmilla Alexeyeva and Paul Goldberg, *The Thaw Generation: Coming of Age in the Post-Stalin Era* (Boston: 1990), 76–9.

22. Irina Shilova, ... *I moe kino* (Moscow: 1993), 11.

23. Vitalii Troianovskii identifies the components of this 'peculiar hybrid' as sincere love for 'the holy socialist ideal' and the reflexes of the apostate, who wished to 'perfect his former collectivist faith in order to make it a guarantor of individual freedom'. 'Chelovek ottepeli', *Kinematograf ottepeli* (Moscow: 1996), 7.

24. Evgenii Evtushenko, 'Stantsiia Zima', *Oktiabr'* 10 (1956).

25. Harry Willetts, 'The "Literary Opposition"', *Russia Under Khrushchev*, 364–5.

26. See Louis Harris Cohen, *The Cultural-Political Traditions and Developments of the Soviet Cinema from 1917 to 1972* (Arno Press Cinema Program: 1973), 253–4.

27. I. Rachuk, 'Khudozhestvennaia kinematografiia v 1956 godu', *IK* 1 (1956): 8–11. Rachuk was then the assistant director of the Ministry of Film Production.

28. Alex Inkeles, 'Soviet Nationality Policy in Perspective', *Russia Under Khrushchev*, 310.

29. S. Mukhamedov, 'Tashkentskaia kinostudiia', *IK* 4 (1956): 91.

30. V. Stoliar, 'Belarus'fil'm', *IK* 4 (1956): 90.

31. 'Uvelichenie proizvodstva fil'mov – vazhnaia gosudarstvennaia zadacha', *IK* 2 (1956): 4.

32. 'Istochnik vdokhnoveniia,' *IK* 3 (1956): 5.

33. Lev Anninskii, *Shestidesiatniki i my* (Moscow: 1991), 27.

2. The Fallen Idol

1. Cited by Denise J. Youngblood, *Movies for the Masses: Popular Cinema and Soviet Society in the 1920s* (Cambridge: 1992), 75.

2. 'Obsuzhdenie novykh stsenarii', *IK* 7 (1954): 123.

3. See Katerina Clark, *The Soviet Novel: History as Ritual* (Chicago: 1981), and Peter Kenez, *Cinema and Soviet Society 1917–1953* (Cambridge: 1992), 158–9.

4. Rostislav Iurenev, 'Ne legkii put'', *IK* 1 (1956): 43–4.

5. 'Obsuzhdenie novykh stsenarii', 122–3.

6. Iosif Kheifits, 'Rezhisserskie zapisi', *IK* 1 (1966): 55.

7. Vitalii Troianovskii, 'Chelovek ottepeli', *Kinematograf ottepeli* (Moscow: 1996), 15–16.

8. Irina Shilova, ... *I moe kino* (Moscow: 1993), 16.

9. Iu. Lukin, 'Zhurbiny ... kotorye ivanovy i ne ivanovy', *IK* 1 (1955): 44–5.

10. Troianovskii, 16.

11. Kheifits, 55, 58.

12. Troianovskii, 51.

13. 'Tematicheskii plan proizvodstva khudozhestvennykh fil'mov', *IK* 8 (1955): 4.

14. 'O chem dumaet zritel' (obzor chitatel'skikh pisem)', *IK* 9 (1955): 92.

15. Kenez, 213–14.

16. Richard Stites, *Russian Popular Culture: Entertainment and Society since 1900* (Cambridge: 1992), 125.

17. G. Kremlev, 'Bez dogm v teorii, bez shtampov v tvorchestve', *IK* 12 (1954): 64.

18. G. Aleksandrov, 'Traditsiia klassikov i kinokomediia', *IK* 1 (1955): 33.

19. A. Bazhenova, 'Glavnaia zadacha: obraz nashego sovremennika', *IK* 5 (1955): 3.

20. I. Chekin, 'Otvetstvennost' khudozhnika', *IK* 7 (1955): 7.

21. Kalashnikov's comments are quoted in 'Khronika', *IK* 7 (1955): 100.

22. Bazhenova, 3–10 *passim*; and Chekin, 7–8. The same phrases appear in a dozen other articles from 1955.

23. 'Tematicheskii plan proizvodstva khudozhestvennykh fil'mov', *IK* 8 (1955): 4–5.

24. Semen Freilikh, 'Tema i talant', *IK* 6 (1955): 51–3.

25. Lev Anninskii, *Shestidesiatniki i my* (Moscow: 1991), 11–12.

26. Rostislav Iurenev, 'Khlopoty o kritike', *Kinematograf ottepeli*, 223.

27. A. Karaganov, 'Siuzhet – istoriia kharaktera', *IK* 10 (1955): 10. He rebuts I. Vinokurov, 'Puti sozdaniia obraza polozhitel'nogo geroia', *IK* 8 (1955): 17–34. See also N. Gromov, 'Nash sovremennik', *IK* 12 (1955).

28. 'Kinozriteli o khudozhestvennom masterstve', *IK* 3 (1956): 81–2.

29. 'Nenuzhnaia zashchita ot kritiki: replika "literaturu"' *IK* 12 (1955): 35.

30. Recent scholarship has shown the Pavlik Morozov story to be a near-total fabrication. See Iurii Druzhinikov, *Voznesenie Pavlika Morozova* (London: 1988); tr. *Informer 001: The Myth of Pavlik Morozov* (New Brunswick, NJ: 1997).

31. Troianovskii, 22.

32. Among Ershov's literary/cinematic prototypes are the blind, paralysed Pavel Korchagin, protagonist of Ostrovskii's *How the Steel was Tempered*, and the legless pilot-hero of Boris Polevoi's 1946 *The Story of a Real Man*.

33. M. Iof'ev, 'Obrazy trebuiut siuzhetov', *IK* 2 (1956): 55–6.

34. 'Kinozriteli o khudozhestvennom masterstve', 83.

35. A. Dement'ev, 'Vernye poiski', *IK* 4 (1956): 3. To cite just one statistic in re the actual situation: in 1953, 13 per cent of the kolkhozes in Tadzhikistan, which received substantial monetary support from the regime, paid their farmers no cash wages for their labour; 28 per cent paid one ruble per labour day. Seweryn Bialer, 'But Some are More Equal than Others', *Russia Under Khrushchev*, ed. A. Brumberg (New York: 1962), 43.

36. Shilova, 25.

37. Movies of every genre featured hidden or disguised enemies; the screen continually warned of wolves in sheep's clothing, sometimes within the family itself. Troianovskii, 6–7.

38. Troianovskii, 24–5.

39. Dement'ev, 6.

40. Shilova recalls her revulsion at that chest: such abundance, while she and her friends had barely a skirt between them (27).

3. Beat the Devil

1. Ia. Vostrikov, 'Ob odnom retsidive formalizma', *IK* 8 (1955): 63–4.
2. Report by G. Britikov, Gorky Studio's director, sent to V. N. Surin, then deputy Minister of Culture. RGALI Fond 2468, op. 1, d. 4: 45–9.
3. Stanislav Rostotskii, 'Khronika', *IK* 5 (1956): 115.
4. RGALI Fond 2468, d. 4: 93.
5. Irina Shilova, ... *I moe kino* (Moscow: 1993), 40.
6. Vladimir Makanin, *Left Behind* [Otstavshii], tr. Nadezhda Peterson, *Glasnost: An Anthology of Russian Literature Under Gorbachev*, ed. Helena Goscilo and Byron Lindsey (Ann Arbor: 1990), 209–10.
7. V. Razumnyi, 'Illiustrativnost' – vrag iskusstva', *IK* 5 (1956): 9.
8. V. Ognev, 'O sovremennosti', *IK* 7 (1956): 10.
9. Iu. Khaniutin, 'Reshaet khudozhnik', *IK* 7 (1956): 22.
10. N. Gromov, 'Zhivye primety nashikh dnei', *IK* 6 (1956): 12.
11. In late 1953 *Komsomol'skaia pravda* urged Soviet writers to write thrillers because 'they instil in the young a love for the heroic calling of a Soviet intelligence officer'. Cited by Maurice Friedberg, *A Decade of Euphoria: Western Literature in Post-Stalin Russia, 1954–64* (Bloomington, IN: 1977), 105.
12. Ognev, 17–18.
13. Ibid., 14.
14. Semen Freilikh, 'Pravo na tragediiu', *IK* 12 (1956): 25.
15. T. Trifonova, 'Protiv stilisticheskogo raznoboia', *IK* 9 (1956): 9.
16. Ognev, 18.
17. Lev Anninskii, *Shestidesiatniki i my* (Moscow: 1991), 15.
18. When Gorky Studio discussed the script in July 1955, participants disagreed about the portrayal of Lenin. Boris Barnet praised the accuracy of Lenin's language and intonation, while Sergei Gerasimov felt that the characterization was too superficial, that the 'human' element was inadequate. RGALI Fond 2468, op. 2, d. 155.
19. Anninskii, 13.
20. Cited by Anninskii, 17.
21. *Komsomol'skaia pravda*, 7 February 1957. The newspaper asked for reader responses and published both positive and negative ones.
22. Anninskii, 18.
23. Rufus Mathewson, *The Positive Hero in Russian Literature*, 2nd edn (Stanford: 1975), 248. Mathewson's comment refers to the novel but applies equally to the film.
24. Vitalii Troianovskii, 'Chelovekottapeli', *Kinematograf ottepeli* (Moscow: 1996), 34.
25. Protazanov 'ends the picture with a visual question mark: is this her victory as a Bolshevik or her defeat as a person? (Protazanov's answer seems to be the latter.)' Denise J. Youngblood, *Movies for the Masses* (Cambridge: 1992), 114.
26. G. Chukhrai, 'Lichnost'', *Ivan Pyr'ev: v zhizni i na ekrane*, ed. G. B. Mar'iamov (Moscow: 1994), 130–1.
27. Vladimir Naumov, '"Obryvki" i "konchiki" vospominanii', *Ivan Pyr'ev: v zhizni i na ekrane*, 173.
28. 'Although *The Forty-first* was generally quite well received ... there were some disquieting notes that portended problems soon to come. "Arsen", one of the most

censorious of the new breed of "hard-line" critics, labelled it a "socially primitive" and "decadent" example of the "Western adventure" picture – all the more "dangerous" because it was so well done.' Youngblood, 114.

29. After the completed film was screened to an appreciative audience, Pyrev showed Chukhrai a letter he had received from Koltunov. Angry at the way the rough cut of the film diverged from his scenario, Koltunov denounced Chukhrai in politically fraught terms: 'I want to inform you,' he wrote to Pyrev, 'that I will not put my honourable name on this dirty White Guardist concoction.' Chukhrai, 132–3.

30. Freilikh, 18.

31. The titles of typical reviews appearing in both national and local papers included 'A Film about Revolutionary Duty', 'Revolutionary Duty Triumphs', 'A Film about Courage and Duty', 'A Film about Courage' and 'The Heroism of the Revolution'. Anninskii, 21.

32. In *Turkmenskaia iskra*, 8 January 1956. Cited by Anninskii, 22.

33. Freilikh, 24.

34. Anninskii later contrasted Protazanov's 'purely informative' shots of the desert with Urusevskii's visual poetry. In Chukhrai's film 'the sand becomes a lyric theme, the object of admiration ... clean, pinkish, curling into waves of dunes' (24).

35. Troianovskii, 31.

4. Modern Times

1. V. Frolov, 'Na ekrane – tragediia Shekspira', *IK* 5 (1956): 16.

2. Andrei Shemiakin, 'Dialog s literaturoi', *Kinematograf ottepeli*, ed. Vitalii Troianovskii (Moscow: 1996), 138.

3. Leonid Agranovich, 'Bez strakhuiushchei setki', *Ivan Pyr'ev: v zhizni i na ekrane*, ed. G. B. Mar'iamov (Moscow: 1994), 197–9.

4. One contemporary critic felt that the film should have emphasized Nadia's culpability in bearing a child who has no father. S. Rozen, 'Fil'm ponravilsia ... ', *IK* 1 (1957): 118.

5. Vitalii Troianovskii, 'Chelovek ottepeli', *Kinematograf ottepeli*, 53.

6. 'V Ministerstve kul'tury SSSR', *IK* 7 (1956): 110, 112.

7. 'Zasedanie khudsoveta Mosfil'ma s aktivom kinodramaturgov', *IK* 10 (1956): 115.

8. Lev Anninskii, *Shestidesiatniki i my* (Moscow: 1991), 27.

9. Jay Leyda, *Kino: A History of the Russian and Soviet Film* (Princeton: 1960), 129.

10. Miron Chernenko, *Marlen Khutsiev: tvorcheskii portret* (Moscow: 1988), 6.

11. Maia Turovskaia, 'Marlen Khutsiev', *Molodye rezhissery sovetskogo kino: sbornik statei*, ed. N. R. Mervol'f (Leningrad–Moscow: 1962), 179.

12. Chernenko, 6.

13. Still in use, they are nicknamed *khrushchoby*, a pun on *trushchoby*, slums.

14. Turovskaia, 179–80. Later critics such as Anninskii, Chernenko and Troianovskii acknowledge Turovskaia's seminal interpretation.

15. Anninskii, 30.

16. Turovskaia, 179, 181.

17. Turovskaia, 187–8; and Troianovskii, 28. Turovskaia sees this sequence as psychologically and stylistically alien to the film. More orthodox critics interpreted the montage as an apotheosis of labour; they, like Tania, were transfixed by what they saw.

18. Troianovskii, 30.

19. N. Basin, 'Mnogotochie', *Sovetskii ekran* 17 (1988): 16.

20. Troianovskii, 29.

21. Turovskaia, 185.

22. Irina Shilova, ... *I moe kino* (Moscow: 1993), 37.

23. G. Groshev and V. Leonov, 'Vtoroi festival' kinokartin Mosfil'ma', *IK* 9 (1956): 114.

24. Denise J. Youngblood, *Movies for the Masses: Popular Cinema and Soviet Society in the 1920s* (Cambridge: 1992), 73.

25. Abram Tertz, *On Socialist Realism* (New York: 1960), 75.

26. On *estrada* culture, see Richard Stites, *Russian Popular Culture: Entertainment and Society since 1900* (Cambridge: 1992), 16–22 and 49–53.

27. Youngblood, 74–6, 128–38.

28. Stites, 88–92.

29. Peter Kenez, *Cinema and Soviet Society 1917–1953* (Cambridge: 1992), 212–14.

30. Grigorii Aleksandrov, 'Traditsiia klassikov i kinokomediia', *IK* 1 (1955): 33–5 *passim*.

31. I. Kalashnikov, 'Khronika', *IK* 7 (1955): 100.

32. 'V Soiuze pisatelei SSSR: Obsuzhdenie plana Mosfil'ma,' *IK* 10 (1956): 114.

33. 'Avtorskaia zaiavka', 12 September 1955, RGALI Fond 2453, op. 3, d. 564: 1.

34. 'Avtorskaia zaiavka', 2–10 *passim*.

35. Eldar Riazanov, 'Neistovyi', *Ivan Pyr'ev: vzhizni i na ekrane*, 150–2.

36. RGALI Fond 2453, op. 3, d. 561: 7.

37. Troianovskii, 54.

38. G. Kremlev, 'Protiv ogurtsovykh', *IK* 3 (1957): 99. Kremlev is citing a comment made by Boris Shumiatskii, Soviet film czar in the 1930s, on *Jolly Fellows*. English excerpts from *A Cinema for the Millions* [Kinematografia millionov, 1935] appear in *The Film Factory: Russian and Soviet Cinema Documents, 1896–1939*, ed. Richard Taylor and Ian Christie (Cambridge, MA: 1988).

39. Neia Zorkaia, *The Illustrated History of Soviet Cinema* (New York: 1991), 207.

40. T. Trifonova, 'Protiv stilisticheskogo raznoboia', *IK* 9 (1956): 5.

41. Klimentii Mints, 'Poiski novogo v kinokomedii', *IK* 3 (1957): 2.

42. Aleksandr Zarkhi, *O samom glavnom: zametki kinorezhissera* (Moscow: 1964), 18–19.

43. Zarkhi, 45.

5. The Rules of the Game: Introduction

1. For detailed discussions of these reforms, see Alec Nove, *An Economic History of the USSR 1917–1991* (London and New York: 1992), 351–69.

2. 'Razgovor o kinokritike, o zhurnale', *IK* 1 (1957): 3.

3. Sergei Iutkevich, 'Dorogu talantam!: studiia molodykh', *IK* 1 (1957): 89.

4. 'Delo chesti kollektiv studii', *IK* 4 (1957): 14.

5. 'Nachalo s"emok kartiny, "Kommunist"', *IK* 3 (1957): 125.

6. Irina Shilova, ... *I moe kino* (Moscow: 1993), 46.

7. Harry Willetts, 'The "Literary Opposition"', *Russia Under Khrushchev*, ed. A. Brumberg (New York: 1962), 371.

8. Ilia Erenburg, 'Uroki Stendali', *Inostrannaia literatura* 6 (1957); English tr. in Ilya Ehrenburg, *Chekhov, Stendhal, and Other Essays* (London: 1962).

9. The worst attacks appeared in *Literaturnaia gazeta*, 22 August 1957, and *Znamia* 10 (1957). See Joshua Rubenstein, *Tangled Loyalties: The Life and Times of Ilya Ehrenburg* (New York: 1996), 302–7.

10. Andrei Shemiakin, 'Dialog s literaturoi, ili opasnye sviazi', *Kinematograf ottepeli*, ed. Vitalii Troianovskii (Moscow: 1996), 135.

11. Ibid., 144.

12. For the specific role of cinema, see I. Bol'shakov, *Sovetskoe kinoiskusstvo v gody Velikoi Otechestvennoi Voiny* (Moscow: 1950); and Peter Kenez, 'Black and White: The War on Film', *Culture and Entertainment in Wartime Russia*, ed. Richard Stites (Bloomington, IN: 1995).

13. Musya Glants, 'The Images of War in Painting', *World War 2 and the Soviet People*, ed. John and Carol Garrard (London: 1993), 109.

14. Ibid., 110–12.

15. Nina Tumarkin, *The Living and the Dead: The Rise and Fall of the Cult of World War II in Russia* (New York: 1994), 103–4.

16. Neia Zorkaia, *The Illustrated History of Soviet Cinema* (New York: 1991), 199.

17. Shilova, 54.

18. Nikita Gribachev, 'Oblik zhizni', *IK* 5 (1957): 53–4.

19. Aleksandr Shtein, 'Razgovor s druz'iami', *IK* 3 (1959): 7–8.

20. V. Kolodiazhnaia, 'Geroi prikliuchencheskogo fil'ma', *IK* 3 (1958); Viktor Orlov, 'Geroi deistvuiushchii, geroi mysliashchii', *IK* 9 (1958); Iu. Khaniutin, 'Esli smotret' podriad', *IK* 9 (1959).

6. The Best Years of Our Lives

1. RGALI Fond 2468, op. 2, d. 190: 16.

2. RGALI Fond 2468, op. 2, d. 190: 23–43 *passim*.

3. RGALI Fond 2468, op. 2, d. 190: 73, 83.

4. Irina Shilova, ... *I moe kino* (Moscow: 1993), 43. Matvei prefigures Vasilii Shukshin's prose and film heroes, men whose inability to conform suggests creativity and individuality as well as their yearning for an ill-defined and incompletely understood 'freedom' [*volia*].

5. RGALI Fond 2453, op. 3, d. 303: 7, 9.

6. RGALI Fond 2453, op. 3, d. 303: 30, 25.

7. Aleksandr Zarkhi, *O samom glavnom: zametki kinorezhissera* (Moscow: 1964), 23, 41.

8. The loyal band of Reds consists of a woman, a doctor, an actor and the Bolshevik hero. Heavily outnumbered by the faceless enemy, the Reds race their wagon across the vast treeless landscape, the girl snatching up the reins after the driver is killed. During the chase, as the Whites pursue on horseback, one expects to hear Indian war whoops and see arrows flying.

9. Iu. Khaniutin, 'Tragediia, kotoraia ne rasskazana', *IK* 9 (1956): 19–20.

10. The screen did not represent the special victimization of Jews, however, until Aleksandr Askoldov's *The Commissar* [Komissar, 1967, rel. 1988]. For the 'history' of *The Commissar*, see V. I. Fomin, *Polka* (Moscow: 1992), 46–76.

11. For decades Jack London was widely printed in Russia; Soviet readers regularly chose him as one of their favourite writers. M. Friedberg, *A Decade of Euphoria* (Bloomington, IN: 1977), 71–4 and 122–3.

12. Many Russians considered Tchaikovsky synonymous with Russian culture. Shostakovich described the Germans' near-destruction of Tchaikovsky's home in Klin in November 1941 as an attempt by 'the Nazi barbarians ... to destroy the whole of Slavonic culture'. Cited by Boris Schwarz, *Music and Musical Life in Soviet Russia 1917–1970* (London: 1972), 176.

13. Lev Anninskii, *Shestidesiatniki i my* (Moscow: 1991), 10.

14. Tat'iana Samoilova, interview, 'Eto bylo moe ... ', *Kinovedcheskie zapiski* 17 (1993): 47.

15. Neia Zorkaia, *The Illustrated History of Soviet Cinema* (New York: 1991), 212.

16. Richard Stites, *Russian Popular Culture: Entertainment and Society since 1900* (Cambridge: 1992), 101.

17. Vitalii Troianovskii, 'Chelovek ottepeli', *Kinematograf ottepeli*, ed. V. Troianovskii (Moscow: 1996), 50.

18. Irina Shilova, 'Pobeda i porazhenie', *Kinovedcheskie zapiski* 17 (1993): 48.

19. Anninskii, 37.

20. Shilova, 'Pobeda i porazhenie', 48.

21. Samoilova, 40.

22. Shilova, 'Pobeda i porazhenie', 48–9.

23. See Anninskii, 33–43; and Vitalii Troianovskii, '*Letiat zhuravli* tret' veka spustia', *Kinovedcheskie zapiski* 17 (1993): 49–56. On Samoilova, see Maia Turovskaia's essay in *Aktery sovetskogo kino* (Moscow: 1966); on Urusevskii's camerawork, see Maia Merkel', *Ugol zreniia* (Moscow: 1980). Aleksei Batalov reminisces about the filming of *Cranes* in *Sud'ba i remeslo* (Moscow: 1984), 116–36.

24. Troianovskii, '*Letiat zhuravli* tret' veka spustia', 49.

25. RGALI Fond 2453, op. 3, d. 617: 68.

26. RGALI Fond 2453, op. 3, d. 617: 41–3. When Mosfilm discussed the script on 17 June 1956 this scene was not mentioned; presumably it had already been cut. See RGALI Fond 2453, op. 3, d. 619.

27. RGALI, Fond 2453, d. 620.

28. R. Iurenev, 'Vernost'', *IK* 12 (1957): 10.

29. Zarkhi, 10.

30. Maia Turovskaia, '"Da" i "Net"', *IK* 12 (1957): 15–17 *passim*.

31. R. Messer, 'Molodye o molodykh', *Molodye rezhissery sovetskogo kino: sbornik statei*, ed. N. R. Mervol'f (Leningrad–Moscow: 1962), 21.

32. I. Shneiderman, 'V poiskakh stilia', *Molodye rezhissery sovetskogo kino*, 219–22 *passim*.

33. Dmitry and Vladimir Shlapentokh, *Soviet Cinematography 1918–1991* (New York: 1993), 138.

34. Shneiderman (222) and Messer (22) both cite Serezha's speech as the credo of Soviet youth, 'a living ideal they wish to emulate'. Two years later, however, it was deemed abstract and ahistorical. A man can discover bauxite and oil 'but if he takes a neutral stance toward the life and death issues of his country', he forfeits the sympathy of audiences. F. Khodzhaev, 'My ishchem geroia', *IK* 1 (1959): 59.

35. Shneiderman, 216.

36. RGALI, Fond 2468, op. 2, d. 208: 15, 23, 31. The last speaker admitted being moved by the 'farewell' scene and Veronika's return to her bombed-out apartment, but attributed their power to their artlessness [*bez lukavstva*] rather than to their art.

37. RGALI, Fond 2468, op. 2, d. 208: 36–7.

38. S. Ginzburg, 'Bez vneshnykh effektov', in 'Dom, v kotorom ia zhivu: Obsuzhdenie fil'ma', *IK* 2 (1958): 91.

7. Great Expectations

1. Several films made for the fiftieth anniversary of the Revolution, including Askoldov's *Commissar*, Shepitko's *Motherland of Electricity* [Rodina elektrichestva] and Smirnov's

Angel [Angel], portrayed the civil war in an manner unacceptable to the censors, and they were shelved.

2. Gabrilovich wrote the script in response to a government decree calling for works devoted to the forthcoming anniversary, after Pyrev showed Gabrilovich and Iulii Raizman an article on the first years of the Shaturskii Electrification Plant. 'Suddenly I realized that just because the film had to be about the Civil War period, it didn't have to be about war.' Cited by A. Zorkii in 'E. Gabrilovich – 73', *Kinopanorama: Sovetskoe kino segodnia,* ed. V. I. Fomin (Moscow: 1975), 226.

3. RGALI Fond 2453, op. 3, d. 568: 39, 5.

4. RGALI Fond 2453, op. 3, d. 570.

5. See Sheila Och, *Lenin im sowjetischen Spielfilm,* Studien zum Theater, Film und Fernsehen 17 (Frankfurt: 1992) for an account of film portrayals of Lenin.

6. E. Gabrilovich, 'Rasskaz o Lenine', *IK* 10 (1957): 81.

7. Neia Zorkaia, 'Sem'ia geroev', *IK* 1 (1958): 39.

8. One critic worried that Lenin's lapse of memory reflected badly on him; viewers might wonder how Lenin could forget such a man. RGALI Fond 2453, op. 3, d. 569: 24a. To allay such fears Raizman shot another version of the scene, with Lenin's memory intact, but test audiences disliked it, and the original scene was restored. See Iulii Raizman, 'Sdelannoe i zadumannoe', *IK* 11 (1962): 73.

9. Vitalii Troianovskii, 'Chelovek ottepeli', *Kinematograf ottepeli* (Moscow: 1996), 34.

10. RGALI Fond 2453, op. 3, d. 569: 10–11, 2.

11. RGALI Fond 2453, op. 3, d. 569: 24a, 5, 3.

12. Ia. Varshavskii, 'Za chto boretsia fil'm?' *IK* 4 (1958).

13. Gubanov reverses the motivation of Korchagin by sacrificing himself for the sake of life, while Korchagin lives for the sake of self-sacrifice, his existence unimaginable outside extreme heroic circumstances. Troianovskii, 39.

14. L. Pogozheva, 'Iz dnevnika kritika', *IK* 6 (1959): 85.

15. D. Pisarevskii, 'Vtoraia zhizn' literaturnogo obraza', abridged transcript of discussion held at the Academy of Sciences, *IK* 6 (1959): 88.

16. A. Zis', 'Protiv revizionizma v estetike', *IK* 9 (1958): 136.

17. A. Speshnev, 'Tvorchestvo kinodramaturga i sovremennost'', *IK* 2 (1959): 36.

18. F. Khodzhaev, 'My ishchem geroia', *IK* 1 (1959): 58.

19. See, for instance, 'Vsiu silu kinoiskusstva – delu stroitel'stva kommunizma!', *IK* 3 (1959), esp. 24–5, and Rostislav Iurenev's comments, 'Vtoraia zhizn' literaturnogo obraza', 94. Neia Zorkaia defended, cautiously, all three beleaguered films in 'O iasnosti tseli', *IK* 4 (1959).

20. Grigorii Kozintsev wrote in his diary on 2 September 1959: 'A code of rules has appeared: rain cannot fall ("lighten the gloom"), "rude words" may not be used – that is, words that are not rude but that people use in their everyday speech ... proper behaviour must be spelled out, preferably at a meeting. Otherwise the result is "chaotic", "rambling", "confused".' 'Iz rabochikh tetradei. 1958–1969 gody', *IK* 8 (1989): 96–7.

21. Sergei Gerasimov, 'Razmyshleniia o molodykh', *IK* 2 (1960): 22. Gerasimov also chaired the Ministry of Culture discussion; his remarks on *Someone Else's Children* appear in 'Poddel'noe i podlinnoe', *IK* 5 (1960): 18–19.

22. Miron Chernenko, *Marlen Khutsiev: Tvorcheskii portret* (Moscow: 1988), 9.

23. Marlen Khutsiev, 'Ia nikogda ne delal polemichnykh fil'mov', *Kinematograf ottepeli*, 195.

24. Cited by Chernenko, 10.

25. Zorkaia, 'O iasnosti tseli', 39.

26. Maia Turovskaia, 'Kharakter i vremia', *IK* 4 (1959): 24.

27. Viktor Nekrasov, 'Slova "velikie" i "prostye"', *IK* 5 (1959): 58.

28. Ia. Varshavskii, 'Nado razobrat'sia', *IK* 5 (1959): 62–3.

29. A. Karaganov, 'Geroi nashikh dnei', *IK* 7 (1959): 42.

30. Aleksandr Dovzhenko, 'Poema o more', *IK* 1 (1957): 29. Dovzhenko's candid portrayal of the destruction of village life anticipates later 'Village Prose' literature, especially Valentin Rasputin's fiction. For example, when someone justifies flooding the village in the name of 'historical necessity', a character angrily retorts: 'I've heard it a hundred times! ... I don't say that we don't need the sea ... I've worked for it too. But I'm upset, you understand? Can't you respect my pain? ... I'm not just a collection of molecules of enthusiasm! I'm a man!' (44).

31. *Domashniaia sinemateka*, ed. Sergei Zemlianukhin and Miroslava Segida (Moscow: 1996), 497.

32. Ia. Varshavskii, 'Potrebnost' molodoi dushi', *IK* 10 (1960): 31. He cites a studio administrator who accused *Ballad of a Soldier* of 'pathology' because Shura cries out in alarm when – thinking herself alone in the box car – she spies Alesha. 'Why did she cry out? It wasn't a fascist soldier she saw, after all' (31–2).

33. I. Shneiderman, 'Ballada o soldate', *Molodye rezhissery sovetskogo kino: sbornik statei*, ed. N. R. Mervol'f (Leningrad–Moscow: 1962), 108–9.

34. S. Rostotskii, 'Ot imeni pokolenii', *IK* 1 (1960): 66–7.

35. E. Vorob'ev, 'Ia vam zhit' zaveshchaiu', *IK* 1 (1960): 70.

36. Zakhar Agranenko, 'S liubov'iu k geroiu-rovesniku', and Nina Ignat'eva, 'Èto nuzhno liudiam', *IK* 1 (1960).

37. Cited by Lev Anninskii, *Shestidesiatniki i my* (Moscow: 1991), 46. The film took first prize at the 1960 Minsk festival of Soviet films, and Chukhrai and his co-author Valentin Ezhov won Lenin Prizes in 1961. *Ballad* won Grand Prizes at 1960 Czech, San Francisco and Polish festivals, and awards in London, Milan, Mexico, Tehran and Athens.

38. Maia Turovskaia, 'Ballada o soldate', *Novyi mir* 4 (1961): 250.

39. Valerii Fomin, *Vse kraski siuzheta* (Moscow: 1971), 65–6.

40. Fomin, 70.

41. Anninskii, 49.

8. The Grand Illusion: Introduction

1. See, for instance, Vsevolod Kochetov's *Regional Secretary* [Sekretar' obkoma] and Natan Rybak's *A Time of Hopes and Achievements* [Pora nadezhd i svershenii], both novels published in 1961.

2. Cited by Max Hayward, 'The Struggle Goes On', *Russia Under Khrushchev*, (New York: 1962), 378–9, 385.

3. Extracts from Ehrenburg's letters to Vladimir Lebedev, Khrushchev's adviser, as well as to Khrushchev himself, appear in Joshua Rubenstein, *Tangled Loyalties: The Life and Times of Ilya Ehrenburg* (New York: 1996), 336–43 and 349–51.

4. Merle Fainsod, 'The Twenty-second Party Congress', *Russia Under Khrushchev*, 130–2 *passim*.

5. Cited by Fainsod, 136.

6. Ibid., 127.

7. Starikov buttressed his argument with selective quotation from Ehrenburg's work, which enraged Ehrenburg. When the frightened editors of *Literaturnaia gazeta* declined

to publish Ehrenburg's angry rebuttal, he explained to chief ideologue Mikhail Suslov that western journalists were pressing him for a reaction to the Evtushenko affair. He would prefer 'to express his views in the Soviet press rather than in a European journal that would exploit his position for "anti-Soviet" purposes. Suslov gave in.' Rubenstein, 319.

8. Cited by Max Hayward, *Writers in Russia 1917–1978* (London: 1983), 113–14.

9. Abraham Rothberg, *The Heirs of Stalin* (Ithaca, NY: 1972), 50.

10. The story of *Ivan Denisovich*'s publication has been told many times, most thoroughly by Michael Scammell, *Solzhenitsyn: A Biography* (New York: 1984), 410–45.

11. Viktor Nekrasov, *Both Sides of the Ocean*, tr. Elias Kulukundis (London: 1964), 58–9.

12. Boris Schwarz, *Music and Musical Life in Soviet Russia 1917–1970* (London: 1972), 367, 369–71.

13. Cited by Priscilla Johnson, 'The Politics of Soviet Culture', *Khrushchev and the Arts: The Politics of Soviet Culture, 1962–1964*, ed. Priscilla Johnson and Leopold Labedz (Cambridge, MA: 1965), 3.

14. 'As anyone who trailed him on visits to Western exhibitions is aware, Khrushchev appeared genuinely to detest modern art, as distinct from functional architecture. Thus, those who instigated his visit to the Manezh no doubt counted on an outburst of profanity and were ready to use it for their own ends.' Johnson, 9.

15. Mikhail Romm, *Ustnye rasskazy* (Moscow: 1991), 132–3. See also Vasilii Aksenov, 'Kak Nikita possorilsia s pisateliami', *Argumenty i fakty* 45 (November 1991). Romm describes a surreal atmosphere in which tension and suppressed hysteria occasionally exploded in nervous laughter (134–50).

16. Ehrenburg's theory of high-level acquiescence in the purges particularly infuriated the Kremlin. Khrushchev echoed Ilichev: 'The question arises whether the leading cadres of the party knew about, let us say, the arrests of people in that period. Yes, they did. But did they know that absolutely innocent people were arrested? No, they did not. They believed in Stalin and could not even imagine that repression could be used against honest people devoted to our cause.' Cited by Rubenstein, 355.

17. Schwarz, 368.

18. Evgenii Margolit, 'Dialog pokolenii', *Kinematograf ottepeli*, ed. V. Troianovskii (Moscow: 1996), 120. Margolit also speculates that they envied the younger men their war experience.

19. V. Surin, 'Spravedlivo!' *IK* 5 (1963): 1.

20. 'Èto kasaetsia kazhdogo', *IK* 4 (1963): 1.

21. Tat'iana Koniukhova, 'Glavnoe – chelovek', and G. Miasnikov, 'Vperedi – uvlekatel'naia rabota', *IK* 6 (1963): 4 and 6. Similar pieces appear in virtually every issue between April 1963 and April 1964.

22. Rolan Bykov, 'Zhivoi, real'nyi', *IK* 5 (1963): 13.

23. A. Groshev, 'Fil'my i kinokritika: po stranitsam zhurnala *Iskusstvo kino*', *Kommunist* 3 (1963): 86–7. 'Tvorit' dlia naroda – vysshaia tsel' khudozhnika' appeared in *Kommunist* 1 (1963).

24. 'O reaktsionnykh kontseptsiakh sovremennoi burzhuaznoi èstetiki kino', *IK* 8 (1963).

25. Vera Shitova, 'Deviat' fil'mov odnogo goda', *IK* 11 (1962).

26. Excerpted in 'Sluzhit' narodu!', *IK* 2 (1964): 5–12.

27. Cited by Johnson, 50.

28. Johnson, 223, 228.

29. V. Frolov, 'Sasha Zelenin i ego druz'ia', *IK* 4 (1963): 97. Frolov may have been

trying to protect the film, and Aksenov, after the harsh attacks on Aksenov at the March meeting.

30. Afanasii Salynskii, 'Printsipial'naia udacha iskusstva', *IK* 7 (1963): 25–6.

31. Larisa Kriachko, 'Kogda "poisk' – vsego lish" psevdonim banal'nosti', *IK* 8 (1963): 14.

9. Children of Paradise

1. Lev Anninskii, *Shestidesiatniki i my* (Moscow: 1991), 61.

2. Cited by Vitalii Troianovskii, 'Chelovek ottepeli', *Kinematograf ottepeli* (Moscow: 1996), 63.

3. 'Kak khorosho, chto nash Gagarin/ Ne Armianin i ne Tatarin,/ Ne zhid, ne Chukchi, ne Uzbek/ A nash sovetskii chelovek.' (Thanks to Samuel Kassow.)

4. Evgenii Vorob'ev, 'Zemliak v kosmose', *IK* 6 (1961): 5.

5. G. Plisetskii, 'Otkrytie mira', *Molodye rezhissery sovetskogo kino: sbornik statei*, ed. N. R. Mervol'f (Leningrad–Moscow: 1962), 314.

6. M. Kuznetsov, 'Zhil-byl mal'chik', *IK* 7 (1960): 28.

7. Irina Shilova, … *I moe kino* (Moscow: 1993), 60.

8. Plisetskii, 321.

9. 'Colour, Soviet "reality", Soviet rhetoric and sentimentality would all be banished from the later films, the last three never to return.' Julian Graffy, 'Tarkovsky: The Weight of the World', *Sight and Sound* (January 1997): 20.

10. Shveitser had problems with censorship more than once. His film of Vladimir Tendriakov's *The Tight Knot* [Tugoi uzel', 1957] was blocked because it portrayed the entire power structure, with the exception of one ordinary Party member, as cowardly and compromised. 'We thought that if people, especially communists, were honest and brave and didn't think only of themselves, then everything would be fine. We were demolished.' Mikhail Shveitser, 'Ottepel' otkryla liudiam, chto mozhno byt' luchshe', *Kinematograf ottepeli*, ed. V. Troianovskii, 181–2. He was forced to make major changes before the film opened under the title *Sasha Begins Life* [Sasha vstupaet v zhizn']; a restored print of the original version was released in 1988. See N. Miloserdova, 'Mikhail Shveitser: Kak zatiagivalsia tugoi uzel'', *Sovetskii ekran* 18 (1988): 16.

11. Semen Lungin, 'Schastlivaia èpokha stsenarnogo sochinitel'stva', *Kinematograf ottepeli*, 186. He adds, 'They [Party officials] were afraid to show normal people, afraid of historical personalities, afraid of human particularity. They thought they knew exactly what revolutionaries were like and how they behaved.'

12. Rosalind Marsh, *Soviet Fiction Since Stalin: Science, Politics and Literature* (London: 1986), 239–40.

13. Critics of Tendriakov's novella considered the priest insufficiently negative, and 'scientific atheism' inadequately represented. Marsh, 244.

14. L. Gurov, 'Beloe i chernoe', *IK* 1 (1961): 95.

15. Lungin, 187.

16. Anninskii, 72.

17. N. Ignat'eva, 'Liudi i vremia', *IK* 7 (1961): 37. Her comments were echoed by Tat'iana Bachelis: 'Did people really think that way? They did. Was it like that? It was.' 'Real'nost' schast'ia', *IK* 8 (1961): 77.

18. Vasilii Aksenov, *Kollegi*, *Sobranie sochinenii* (Moscow: 1994), 1: 17. The Russian text is deliberately colloquial, rejecting 'fine words' by example as well as precept. In the introduction to this volume, Aksenov calls his novel 'conformist', as indeed its

resolution demonstrates. The character who was initially put off by the debased language of idealism comes to revise his views: 'Fine words don't scare us. We see things clearly. We will purify those words' (180).

19. Shilova, 70.
20. Cited by Anninskii, 62.
21. '"Tiazhko, tovarishchi!" Obsuzhdenie fil'ma *Mir vkhodiashchemu*', *IK* 5 (1990): 21.
22. Ibid., 21–2.
23. Vladimir Naumov, interview on Soviet television in the early 1990s, before *Peace to Him Who Enters* was broadcast.
24. M. Kvasnetskaia, 'V dekorativnom obramlenii', *IK* 1 (1960): 83.
25. Marsh, 197.
26. Lenina Ivanova, 'Gumanizm ili sentimental'nost'', *Oktiabr'* 2 (1962): 186. She further rebukes irresponsible writers (implicitly, Aksenov) who fail to persuade young people of the need for 'fine words'.

10. Lost Horizon

1. Maia Turovskaia, 'Prozaicheskoe i poeticheskoe kino segodnia', *Novyi mir* 9 (1962): 239. V. Zhuravleva and G. Al'tov called *The Amphibious Man* a 'primitive adventure film' that attracted audiences 'above all because of the enormous hunger for science fiction films'. 'Ekran, otkrytyi v budushchee', *IK* 2 (1965): 65.

2. *The Man from Nowhere* was effectively shelved until 1988. Riazanov recalls that even before the film's release, *Sovetskaia kul'tura* (22 June 1961) published a 'letter from a viewer' (actually a prominent critic, Vladimir Shalunovskii, writing under a pseudonym) who claimed to have seen the film in Poltava (where it had not played), and to have found its 'senseless stunts' [*bessmyslennoe triukachestvo*] a crime against art. In Moscow the film ran for a few days. Chief ideologist Mikhail Suslov, who had seen and disliked it, spotted a poster for it outside the Khudozhestvennyi Theatre and closed it down. He criticized the film at the Twenty-second Party Congress, ironically asking where *The Man from Nowhere* had come from and how much government support had been wasted on it. Suslov's speech emboldened Shalunovskii to write a new piece, this time under his own name. See Eldar Riazanov, *Nepodvedennye itogi* (Moscow: 1995), 113–22.

3. Lev Anninskii, *Shestidesiatniki i my* (Moscow: 1991), 96.

4. Neia Zorkaia, *Portrety* (Moscow: 1966), 248. Rosalind Marsh suggests that while intellectuals had a genuine interest in the relationship between art and science, the 'physicists and lyricists' debate may also have been 'artificially sponsored, or at least encouraged, by the Party in order to create the semblance of intellectual ferment, and to divert attention from more controversial political issues such as the problems of "fathers and sons" and "Stalin's heirs"'. *Soviet Fiction Since Stalin: Science, Politics and Literature* (London: 1986), 215.

5. Marsh, 196.

6. The experiment ended thanks to a combination of jealousy within Mosfilm (none of the other directors had his own studio) and the negative response of then-Minister of Culture Mikhailov to a satire that came out of Romm's group, Gaidai's *Fiancé from the Other World* [Zhenikh s togo sveta, 1958]. Gaidai was forced to make substantial cuts in the film before Mikhailov would authorize its release. Daniil Khrabrovitskii, 'Deviat' dnei odnogo goda', *Moi rezhisser Romm*, ed. I. G. Germanova and N. B. Kuz'mina (Moscow: 1993), 239.

7. Mikhail Romm, 'Razmyshleniia u pod"ezda kinoteatra', *Besedy o kino* (Moscow: 1964), 309.

8. RGALI Fond 2453, op. 4, d. 1073.

9. Aleksei Batalov, 'Kak ia byl Gusevym', *Moi rezhisser Romm*, 259.

10. Irina Shilova, ... *I moe kino* (Moscow: 1993) 67–9.

11. RGALI Fond 2453, op. 4, d. 1008: 25.

12. RGALI Fond 2453, op. 4, d. 1008: 34.

13. Letter from V. Emelianov to Romanov, in the Council of Ministers, with a copy to Surin, director of Mosfilm. Undated, it refers to the third variant of the script, and was probably written in September 1960. RGALI Fond 2354, op. 4, d. 1048: 23.

14. RGALI Fond 2453, op. 4, d. 1016: 32.

15. RGALI Fond 2453, op. 4, d. 1016: 72–3. I do not know how Romm inflected his words, but his remark seems to me decidedly ambiguous.

16. S. Kapitsa, 'Dva prosmotra dvukh fil'mov', *Moi rezhisser Romm*, 285.

17. Rolan Bykov, 'Rommovtsy', *Moi rezhisser Romm*, ed. Germanova and Kuz'mina, 297.

18. Mark Zak, *Mikhail Romm i ego fil'my* (Moscow: 1988), 205–12 *passim*.

19. Khrabrovitskii, 257.

20. Anninskii points out that Romm chose many of the actors in the wedding scene (Nikulin, Kozakov, Evstigneev) from the Sovremennik Theatre, then considered the most 'intellectual' of theatres and the most representative of the younger generation (99).

21. Shilova, 71.

22. Cited by Anninskii, 95, from *Film* 44 (Warsaw) (1962).

23. Marsh suggests that the dedicated scientist hero stood in for the artist. 'Soviet writers were generally unwilling to depict an historian or a literary scholar, because many scholars in the humanities had been compromised by their servility to the party in Stalin's time. Only a scientist dealing with highly abstract concepts ... could be sufficiently independent of party control to serve as a satisfactory image of the honest writer, while at the same time appearing conventional enough to be accepted as a "positive hero" by editors and censors' (149).

24. Romm explained the subtext: 'When the old man asks, "Will you stay with me a while?" he's really asking, "Will you die soon? Will I see you again or did you come to say goodbye?" And Gusev's reply, "No, father [*batia*], I'm leaving tomorrow," is his farewell.' Cited by Zak from a tape of Romm's lecture at VGIK, 217.

25. Mikhail Romm, *Kogda fil'm okonchen* (Moscow: 1964), 130.

26. A. Macheret, *O poetike kinoiskusstva* (Moscow: 1981), 148.

27. Zorkaia, 253.

28. Anninskii lists the titles of various reviews: Zorkaia's 'Clever People', Pogozheva's 'Ninety Minutes of Thought', Gabrilovich's 'Toward a Cinematography of Ideas', Khaniutin's 'Drama of Ideas', etc. These brilliant characters 'affected the critics like radiation'; they found the film a jousting between 'knights of intellect ... a holiday of the mind' (94–5).

29. 'Pomoch' khoroshemu, pomeshat' plokhomu!' *IK* 3 (1962): 12.

30. L. Pogozheva, 'Poltora chasa razmyshlenii', *IK* 4 (1962): 7.

31. Valentin Liukov and Iurii Panov, 'Eto li gorizonty?' *Oktiabr'* 5 (1962): 184–5.

32. Liukov and Panov, 186.

33. P. Strokov, 'Pravda zhizni i pravdopodobie', *Oktiabr'* 11 (1962): 159.

34. 'Za rabotu, tovarishchi kinematografisty!' *IK* 1 (1962): 3–4.

35. 'Gorizont', *IK* 2 (1962): 103. Young people occasionally agreed with their elders:

Shilova recalled that many students were offended by Baklanov's depiction in *Horizon* of a young intellectual who goes to work on the Virgin Lands project and then regrets the waste of his talent. While life might indeed be like that, art had a responsibility to show something better (64–5).

36. Anninskii, 80.
37. Maia Turovskaia, 'Po tu storonu zhalosti', *IK* 4 (1962): 18.
38. Ibid., 21.
39. Teachers seeking a 'new way of communicating' with their students regarded the film more sympathetically. Anninskii cites L. Ivanova's 'A esli èto dazhe ne liubov'?', printed in *Uchitel'skaia gazeta* (79).
40. Anninskii, 83.
41. Shilova, 73–4.
42. Liukov and Panov, 182–3.

11. Kameradschaft

1. Vida T. Johnson and Graham Petrie provide a thorough bibliography in *The Films of Andrei Tarkovsky: A Visual Fugue* (Bloomington, IN: 1994).
2. Julian Graffy, 'Tarkovsky: The Weight of the World', *Sight and Sound* (January 1997): 20.
3. Neia Zorkaia, 'Nachalo', *Mir i fil'my Andreia Tarkovskogo* (Moscow: 1991), 29.
4. Graffy, 20.
5. Neia Zorkaia, 'Chernoe derevo u reki', *IK* 7 (1962): 103.
6. Maia Turovskaia, 'Prozaicheskoe i poèticheskoe kino segodnia', *Novyi mir* 9 (1962): 250.
7. Denise Youngblood, 'Post-Stalinist Cinema and the Myth of World War II: Tarkovskii's *Ivan's Childhood* (1962) and Klimov's *Come and See* (1985)', *Historical Journal of Film, Radio and Television* 14.4 (1994): 415.
8. Evgenii Margolit, 'Peizazh s geroem', *Kinematograf ottepeli*, ed. V. Troianovskii (Moscow: 1996), 110.
9. Zorkaia, 'Nachalo', 31.
10. See V. Fomin, *Vse kraski siuzheta* (Moscow: 1971), 72–6; and A. Nekhoroshev, *Techenie fil'ma: o kinematograficheskom siuzhete* (Moscow: 1975), 55–70 *passim*.
11. M. Stamboltsian, *Problemy kino i televideniia* 2 (Erevan: 1984), 171.
12. Margolit, 113.
13. Miron Chernenko, *Marlen Khutsiev: Tvorcheskii portret* (Moscow: 1988), 15.
14. Ibid., 13–14.
15. Ibid., 13.
16. RGALI Fond 2468, op. 2, d. 278: 2, 12, 25. A. Demenok brings together excerpts from several archival documents in '*Zastava Il'icha* – urok istorii', *IK* 6 (1988).
17. Demenok, 97–8.
18. Iurii Khaniutin, untitled afterword to *Mne dvadtsat' let*, *IK* 7 (1961): 96.
19. He had told the studio back in December 1960 that if plans to build an overpass in Samotechnaia Square materialized in the summer, he would film Sergei at work there. 'We have to fuse these two circumstances – his work and the city.' RGALI Fond 2468, op. 2, d. 278: 36.
20. Ezhov's comment at the December discussion of the script is indicative: 'If necessary,' he said, 'we'll go to Ekaterina Alekseevna and she will understand.' RGALI Fond 2468, op. 2, d. 278: 12.

Notes to Chapters 11 and 12

21. Marlen Khutsiev, interview, Tatiana Khlopliankina, *Zastava Il'icha: Sud'ba fil'ma* (Moscow: 1990), 31.

22. Khlopliankina, 36–7.

23. Mikhail Romm, *Ustnye rasskazy* (Moscow: 1991), 128.

24. Khutsiev described the opening sequence to his Gorky Studio colleagues: 'These stones remember that generation ... The image of the soldiers is even more important because one of them is Sergei's father, and he will be rendered not via memories [*on budet dan ne kinematograficheskim naplyvom, vo vospominaniakh*], but in absolutely realistic form.' RGALI Fond 2468, op. 2, d. 278: 35.

25. Khlopliankina, 46.

26. The dog analogy was first made by a fireman at a studio discussion of the film. Khlopliankina believes that Khrushchev's assault on *Ilich's Gate*, like his reaction to the Manège exhibit, was provoked and manipulated by conservatives, and that someone in the studio sent the remark to the Kremlin, where it was incorporated into Khrushchev's prepared speech (51–2).

27. Khrushchev's speech first appeared in *Pravda*, 10 March 1963. I have modified the translation in *Khrushchev and the Arts*, ed. Priscilla Johnson and Leopold Labedz (Cambridge, MA: 1965), 152–5 *passim*.

28. Romm, 134.

29. Viktor Nekrasov, *Both Sides of the Ocean*, tr. Elias Kulukundis (London: 1964), 124.

30. Johnson and Labedz, 177.

31. Ibid., 54.

32. *Sovetskaia Rossiia*, 16 March 1963.

33. Demenok, 109.

34. Ibid., 114.

35. Ibid., 103–6, 112–13 *passim*.

36. Khlopliankina, 60.

37. Ibid., 58–60 *passim*.

12. Meet John Doe

1. 'Diskussiia v Vil'pre', *IK* 5 (1962): 130, 133.

2. Mikhail Romm, 'Posleslovie k kartine', *IK* 11 (1962): 77.

3. Vera Shitova, 'Deviat' fil'mov odnogo goda', *IK* 11 (1962): 67–9 *passim*.

4. Ivan Pyr'ev, 'Tvorit' s narodom – dlia naroda', *IK* 2 (1963): 2.

5. Maia Merkel, 'Snimaet Vadim Iusov', *IK* 1 (1963).

6. 'Sekret vozdeistviia na zritelia', *IK* 1 (1963): 8, 15.

7. Val Golovskoy with John Rimberg, *Behind the Soviet Screen: The Motion-Picture Industry in the USSR 1972–1982* (Ann Arbor, MI: 1986), 50–1.

8. *Domashniaia sinemateka*, ed. Sergei Zemlianukhin and Miroslava Segida (Moscow: 1996), 304, 146, 450.

9. Vasilii Aksenov, *Zvezdnyi bilet*, *Sobranie sochinenii* v 4 (Moscow: 1994), 1: 183.

10. Aksenov, interview preceding screening of *My Younger Brother* on Russian television.

11. His occupation links him with Ernst Neizvestnyi, as does the criticism of his work: he is called a 'pygmy', one of the terms of abuse used by conservatives during the 1963 campaign. At first the film seems to defend Kolia, but then it turns on him for producing spurious art. As the film ends, a repentant Kolia is trying to start from scratch, this time ready to produce genuine art.

12. Rosalind Marsh notes that in the fiction of those years, opportunism often characterizes the 'middle' generation, while idealism links the 'grandfathers' and the 'sons'. *Soviet Fiction Since Stalin: Science, Politics and Literature* (London: 1986), 73–4.

13. In Georgii Danelia's *Path to the Mooring* [Put' k prichalu, 1962], a young sailor aboard a doomed ship treasures his Bible. His faith both forms and informs his goodness. Unlike the priest, however, who is fully flesh and blood, the boy is something of a *iurodivyi*, an otherwordly innocent and an artless instrument of the protagonist's moral regeneration.

14. Gerald Brooke, an Englishman who spent more than four years in Soviet prisons and labour camps (1965–69), recalls that although movies were often shown to inmates, *Everything Remains for People* was not, presumably because the priest was portrayed so sympathetically. Personal interview, 2 May 1997.

15. Rostislav Iurenev 'Odin den' iunykh', *IK* 4 (1964): 26. Ten years later Danelia recalled his annoyance at such criticism. L. Gurevich, 'Ego Velichestvo fil'm', *Panorama* (Moscow: 1975), 285–6.

16. Irina Shilova, ... *I moe kino* (Moscow: 1993), 98.

13. Strange Interlude: Introduction

1. Michael Scammell, *Solzhenitsyn: A Biography* (New York: 1984), 480–95 *passim*.

2. *Khrushchev and the Arts: The Politics of Soviet Culture, 1962–1964*, ed. Priscilla Johnson and Leopold Labedz (Cambridge, MA: 1965), 76.

3. 'Pervoe slovo zriteliu', *IK* 1 (1964): 2. See also the Central Committee's discussion of Mosfilm (*IK* 2), Pyrev's speeches (*IK* 2, 5), N. Balabanova's 'Udarnaia sila ideologicheskogo fronta' (*IK* 7), and many others.

4. V. G. Pashuto, 'Vozrozhdennyi Rublev', *IK* 5 (1964): 159.

5. Provincial critics responded less dogmatically, Kozintsev noted in his diary: 'Neither *Pravda* nor *Izvestia* has any influence on what people who live far from the centre think. Not one of the [local] articles corresponds to the criticism in the capitals' (dated May 1964). 'Iz rabochikh tetradei raznykh let', *IK* 8 (1992): 73.

6. A. Anikst, '*Gamlet* Grigoriia Kozintseva', *IK* 6 (1964): 13–14.

7. 'Iskusstvo geroicheskoi èpokhi', *IK* 8 (1964): I–IV.

8. 'O rabote kinostudii Mosfil'm', paraphrased in 'K novomu pod"emu sovetskogo kinoiskusstva', *IK* 8 (1964): 2.

9. V. Surin, 'Byt' trebovatel'nee k sebe!' *IK* 10 (1964): 31–6 *passim*.

10. William J. Tompson, *Khrushchev: A Political Life* (London: 1995), 267.

11. M. McCauley, *Khrushchev and the Development of Soviet Agriculture* (London: 1976), 94–6.

12. 'Harebrained scheming, half-baked ideas, hasty decisions and actions divorced from reality; bragging and bluster, a penchant for management by decree, a reluctance to consider the conclusions of science and practical experience – these are alien to the Party.' (*Pravda*, 17 October 1964.)

13. Cited by Boris Schwarz, *Music and Musical Life in Soviet Russia 1917–1970* (London: 1972), 440–1.

14. Ibid., 442–3.

15. Cited by Abraham Rothberg, *The Heirs of Stalin: Dissidence and the Soviet Regime, 1953–1970* (Ithaca, NY: 1972), 144–45, from *Pravda*, 27 August 1965.

16. Cited by Schwarz, 442, from *New York Times*, 10 September 1965.

17. Scammell, 522–7 *passim*.

18. V. Surin, 'Nuzhny bol'shie peremeny', *IK* 7 (1965): 13.
19. Lev Kulidzhanov, 'Vse v nashikh silakh', *IK* 7 (1965): 10.
20. Lev Anninskii, *Shestidesiatniki i my* (Moscow: 1991), 158.

14. Odd Man Out

1. *Novyi mir* 2 (1963). The character of a young woman journalist, played by Bella Akhmadulina, is based on the story 'Lelia Selezneva s fakul'teta zhurnalistiki', from *Sel'skie zhiteli*.
2. Iurii Tiurin, *Kinematograf Vasiliia Shukshina* (Moscow: 1984), 85.
3. Vasilii Shukshin, *Nravstvennost' est' Pravda* (Moscow: 1976), 263.
4. Irina Shilova, ... *I moe kino* (Moscow: 1993), 93.
5. Vladimir Korobov, *Vasilii Shukshin* (Moscow: 1988), 105.
6. E. Gromov, 'Poètika dobroty', *O Shukshine* (Moscow: 1979), 23.
7. Lev Anninskii, *Shestidesiatniki i my* (Moscow: 1991), 160.
8. According to Tiurin, this was the first time matchmaking was shown as part not of a historical film, but one with a modern timeframe (103).
9. Cited by Korobov, 98.
10. Ibid., 112.
11. Larisa Kriachko, 'Boi "za dobrotu"', *Oktiabr'* 3 (1965): 179–80. She bracketed the ideologically 'confused' *A Boy Like That* with the ideologically 'vacuous' *I Walk Around Moscow* and the ideologically 'inadequate' *I am Twenty*.
12. Vasilii Shukshin, 'Posleslovie k fil'mu *Zhivet takoi paren'*', *Voprosy samomu sebe* (Moscow: 1981), 112.
13. RGALI Fond 2453, op. 4, d. 1403: 21–3 *passim*.
14. Ian Christie, 'Unauthorised Persons Enter Here', *Monthly Film Bulletin* (London) (July 1987): 200.
15. Semen Lungin, 'Schastlivaia èpokha stsenarnogo sochinitel'stva', *Kinematograf ottepeli*, ed. V. Trioanovskii (Moscow: 1996), 188.
16. Christie, 200.
17. The designers carefully considered visual choices. RGALI Fond 2453, op. 4, d. 1405.
18. RGALI Fond 2453, op. 4, d. 1411: 62.
19. RGALI Fond 2453, op. 4, d. 1411: 34–6, 68.
20. Christie, 200.
21. Lungin, 188.
22. *Domashniaia sinemateka*, ed. Sergei Zemlianukhin and Miroslava Segida (Moscow: 1996), 124, 348, 303.
23. 'Predsedatel'', *IK* 12 (1964): 6.
24. 'At first they decided simply not to release the picture, then they chopped it up [*iskromsali*] and sent it around to [film] clubs, but on the day of the première, at the very time it was supposed to be shown, they blocked it. We were standing in front of viewers in the Rossiia theatre, and all over Moscow they were tearing down posters with Ulianov's face, demolishing billboards publicizing the film's release, destroying plywood stands and placards.' Iurii Nagibin, *Dnevnik* (Moscow: 1996), 188.
25. Anninskii, 173–4.
26. Children under sixteen were not admitted: 'the truth about the past – and perhaps not only about the past – is more frightening than erotic temptation. The truth is equated with pornography.' Nagibin, 188.

27. V. Kardin, *Dostoinstvo iskusstva: razdum'ia o teatre i kinematografe nashikh dnei* (Moscow: 1967), 239.
28. RGALI Fond 2453, op. 4, d. 648: 8–12 *passim*.
29. RGALI Fond 2453, op. 4, d. 638: 20, 25.
30. RGALI Fond 2453, op. 4, d. 631: 56.
31. RGALI Fond 2453, op. 4, d. 638: 52, 60.
32. RGALI Fond 2453, op. 4, d. 631: 12, 31.
33. RGALI Fond 2453, op. 4, d. 631: 47.
34. Anninskii, 170.
35. RGALI Fond 2453, op. 4, d. 633: 40, 45, 54.
36. RGALI Fond 2453, op. 4, d. 648: 26.
37. Anninskii, 171.
38. Shilova, 106–7.
39. A. Nekhoroshev, *Techenie fil'ma: o kinematograficheskom siuzhete* (Moscow: 1975), 76. See also E. Surkov, 'Tsena pravdy', *IK* 2 (1965): 18–23; V. Novikov, 'Khudozhestvennyi poisk', *Znamia* 12 (1965): 226–8; the polemic between Aleksandr Ianov ('Polozhitel'nyi geroi ili Don Kikhot?') and A. Karaganov ('Trubnikov snova pod ognem'), *Voprosy literatury* 8 (1966): 3–30.
40. Kardin, 251.
41. Ibid., 248.
42. *Kino i zritel': Opyt sotsiologicheskogo issledovaniia*, ed. L. N. Kogan (Moscow: 1968), 72–3.
43. Ibid., 254, 260–1.
44. Ibid., 257. The researchers continue: 'The character's stature, his active love for people and for life united him in viewers' minds with the heroes of distant eras: kolkhoz chairman Egor Trubnikov, our contemporary, and … Hamlet, Danish prince.'
45. Anninskii, 176.

15. The Last Laugh

1. Pavel Strokov, 'Mozhno bylo ozhidat' bol'shego'; Anatolii Grebnev, 'Muzyka zhizni', *Sovetskaia kul'tura*, 30 June 1965.
2. *Kino i zritel': Opyt sotsiologicheskogo issledovaniia*, ed. L. N. Kogan (Moscow: 1968), 186.
3. '*Mne dvadtsat' let*', *IK* 4 (1965): 27.
4. Ibid., 27, 36.
5. Ibid., 34.
6. Lev Kulidzhanov, 'Vse v nashikh silakh', *IK* 7 (1965): 7.
7. Sergei Paradzhanov, 'Vechnoe dvizhenie', *IK* 1 (1966): 60, 66.
8. Ibid., 65.
9. Ivan Dziuba, 'Den' poiska', *IK* 5 (1965): 79.
10. V. Turbin, 'Zhivoi ogon'', *Molodaia gvardiia* 2 (1965).
11. Ia. L'vov, 'Izuchaia sekrety uspekha', *IK* 2 (1965): 90.
12. See Denise J. Youngblood, *Movies for the Masses* (Cambridge: 1992), 24–8 and 155–7 for audience surveys in the 1920s.
13. Such applied research expanded in the 1970s and 1980s, at research institutes under the auspices of Goskino and the Department for Film Reproduction and Distribution. Val Golovskoy with John Rimberg, *Behind the Soviet Screen* (Ann Arbor, MI: 1986), 50–2.

14. Kogan (ed.), 111.

15. *Domashniaia sinemateka*, ed. Sergei Zemlianukhin and Miroslava Segida (Moscow: 1996), 61.

16. Kogan (ed.), 259–61.

17. Ibid., 261.

18. Ibid., 263, 260.

19. Sergei L'vov, 'Smeiat'sia, pravo, ne greshno … ', *IK* 10 (1965): 40.

20. El'dar Riazanov, *Nepodvedennye itogi* (Moscow: 1995), caption under photo, unpaginated.

21. Ibid., 100.

22. Ibid., 101.

23. Elem Klimov, 'Ia sam vybral svoi udel … ', *Kino i vlast'*, ed. V. Fomin (Moscow: 1996), 176.

24. Marcel Martin, *Le Cinéma Soviétique de Khrouchtchev à Gorbatchev* (Lausanne: 1993), 55.

25. Klimov, 177–8. The figure is Klimov's; according to Zemlianukhin and Segida, seventy-eight copies were made (348).

26. Of the seventeen citations in *Sovetskie khudozhestvennye fil'my: Annotirovannyi katalog* (Moscow: 1969), eleven are items that appeared while the film was in production. The handful dated after the film's opening come mainly from the provincial press (*Komsomolets Tadzhikistan*, Murmansk's *Poliarnaia pravda*). Given Danelia's earlier success with *Serezha* and *I Walk Around Moscow*, the silence is all the more telling.

27. V. Baskakov, 'Khoroshaia rabota', *Ekran 1967–1968* (Moscow: 1968), 74.

28. Maia Turovskaia and Iurii Khaniutin, 'Romm, kinokamera i my', *IK* 3 (1988): 89. (The essay was written in 1968.) Thoughtful viewers perceived the (unspoken) resemblances between Hitler's regime and Stalin's, but Lev Anninskii believes that Romm was constrained by internal as well as external censorship from identifying Stalinism as the mirror image of Nazism. *Shestidesiatniki i my* (Moscow: 1991), 187–8.

29. Turovskaia and Khaniutin, 90.

30. Anninskii, 177.

31. M. Zak, *Mikhail Romm i ego fil'my* (Moscow: 1988), 247.

32. Mikhail Romm, *Izbrannye proizvedeniia v 3–kh t.* (Moscow: 1981), 2: 304.

33. N. Abramov, 'Dialog o fil'me', *IK* 1 (1966): 23.

34. Lev Kulidzhanov, 'Doklad "Kommunisticheskoe stroitel'stvo i zadachi sovetskoi kinematografii"', *IK* 12 (1965): xx (supplement).

35. One fan of Smoktunovskii's Hamlet requested a publicity still because he wanted 'a portrait of Man'. 'S uchastiem zritelia', *IK* 6 (1965): 82–3.

36. Anatolii Solonitsyn as Andrei Rublev also typified this ideal of 'natural' acting; while *Rublev* was not released commercially until 1971, film cognoscenti saw it earlier.

37. Ia. Varshavskii, 'Ot pokoleniia k pokoleniiu', *IK* 6 (1965): 53.

38. Evgenii Margolit, *Sovetskoe kinoiskusstvo. Osnovnye ètapy stanovleniia i razvitiia* (Moscow: 1988), 77.

39. Anninskii, 212.

40. M. Dolinskii and S. Chertok, 'Metamorfozy', *Ekran 1967–68*, 45.

41. Irina Shilova, 'Cherno-beloe kino', *Kinovedcheskie zapiski* 32 (1996–97): 25, 29.

42. Martin, 64.

43. Cited by Valerii Fomin, 'Mezhdu poèziei i prozoi', *Kinopanorama: Sovetskoe kino segodnia* (Moscow: 1974), 111.

44. Mikhail Agranovich, 'Pobeda v kino byvaet tol'ko obshchei', *IK* 2 (1990): 82.

Rerberg significantly influenced Agranovich, Abuladze's cameraman on *Repentance*.
45. Natelli Lordkipanidze, 'Drugimi glazami', *IK* 12 (1965): 18.
46. Margolit, 82.

16. Forbidden Games: Introduction

1. Cited by B. Kisun'ko, 'Zhizn', otdannaia revoliutsii', *IK* 4 (1967): 27.
2. 'God 1967', *IK* 1 (1967): 2.
3. 'Festival' iubileinogo goda', *IK* 6 (1967): 2.
4. Vladimir Baskakov, 'Polemicheskie zametki', *IK* 9 (1967): 33.
5. *Domashniaia sinemateka*, ed. Sergei Zemlianukhin and Miroslava Segida (Moscow: 1996), 79.
6. Andrei Smirnov, 'My, deti porazheniia … ' *Kino i vlast'*, ed. V. Fomin (Moscow: 1996), 242–5 *passim*.
7. Valerii Fomin, 'Nikakoi epokhi kul'ta lichnosti ne bylo … ili Kak kino izbavliali ot kramol'noi temy', *IK* 1 (1989): 97. Reprinted in *Kino i vlast'*.
8. Ibid., 107.
9. Ibid., 98–9.
10. Ibid., 103.
11. Ibid., 103–7 *passim*.
12. Ibid., 108.
13. Ibid.
14. Lazar Lazarev, 'Nevynosimo trudno zhit' i rabotat'', *IK* 4 (1991): 99.
15. Zemlianukhin and Segida (eds), 27.
16. Valerii Fomin, 'Na bratskikh mogilakh ne staviat krestov … ', *IK* 1 (1990): 101–4 *passim*. Reprinted in *Kino i vlast'*.
17. After *Man Follows the Sun* Kalik made *So Long, Boys*, a charming and poignant depiction of the period immediately before the war as the 'coming of age' experience for three Odessa boys. According to Marcel Martin, *So Long, Boys* was held back for a year and a half after Khrushchev's removal from office. In 1966 Suslov decided to approve limited distribution, with hardly any publicity and absolutely no export. *Le Cinéma Soviétique de Khrouchtchev à Gorbatchev* (Lausanne: 1993), 56.
18. *Kino i vlast'*, 316. It also effectively ended Kalik's career within the Soviet Union. He emigrated to Israel in 1972.
19. Tat'iana Derevianko, 'Vernemsia v 1965–yi … ', *IK* 12 (1990): 57.
20. Derevianko, 61.
21. Martin, 50. Paradzhanov suffered personally as well as professionally. On 17 December 1973 he was arrested on a charge of homosexuality and served four years of a seven-year sentence.
22. Tatiana Vinokurova, 'Khozhdenie po mukam, Andreia Rubleva'', *IK* 10 (1989): 65.
23. Vida T. Johnson and Graham Petrie, *The Films of Andrei Tarkovsky* (Bloomington, IN: 1994), 81. See pp. 79–82 for a summary of the film's vicissitudes. The version distributed in the Soviet Union and in Paris in 1971 was substantially longer than the version released in the USA and Britain two years later (265).
24. Johnson and Petrie, 95.
25. Joseph Frank, *Dostoevsky: The Stir of Liberation, 1860–1865* (Princeton, NJ: 1986), 200–2 *passim*.
26. Valerii Fomin, *Polka* (Moscow: 1992), 17.

27. Andrei Shemiakin, 'Dialog s literaturoi, ili opasnye sviazi', *Kinematograf ottepeli*, ed. V. Troianovskii (Moscow: 1996), 146.
28. Fomin, *Polka*, 21–2.
29. See Stanislav Rassadin's thoughtful analysis, 'Zachem?', *Ekran 1966–1967* (Moscow: 1967).
30. Fomin, *Polka*, 24–5.
31. Shemiakin, 146.

17. To Have and Have Not

1. Evgenii Margolit, *Sovetskoe kinoisskusstvo. Osnovnye ètapy stanovleniia i razvitiia* (Moscow: 1988), 85.
2. Iurii Sokol, 'Vozvrashchenie', *Ekran 1967–1968* (Moscow: 1968), 51. For the *derevenshchiki*, the village represented 'deference, reverence, belief and habit', as well as a sense of kinship with the natural environment. See Kathleen Parthé, *Russian Village Prose: The Radiant Past* (Princeton, NJ: 1992), 6–12.
3. Lev Anninskii, *Shestidesiatniki i my* (Moscow: 1991), 156.
4. Valerii Fomin, *Kino i vlast'* (Moscow: 1996), 20.
5. Anninskii, 219.
6. Shukshin adapted these episodes from two stories he published in *Novyi mir* 11 (1965), 'Stepka' and 'Snake Venom' ['Zmeinii iad']. The third episode is based on 'Ignakha Arrived' ['Ignakha priekhal'].
7. Vasilii Shukshin, *Voprosy samomu sebe* (Moscow: 1981), 49–50.
8. Bykov continued this characterization as Efim Magazinik, the poor Jewish tinker who takes in the pregnant commander of Red Army unit in *The Commissar*.
9. Eldar Riazanov, *Nepodvedennye itogi* (Moscow: 1995), 87.
10. Ibid., 57.
11. Neia Zorkaia, 'Svoi fil'm', *IK* 9 (1966): 14.
12. Riazanov, 104.
13. Irina Shilova, … *I moe kino* (Moscow: 1993), 114. Shilova describes the mood among the intelligentsia in the mid-1960s: 'We slowly realized we were all [like Detochkin] on the other side of the law. Not because we had committed anti-state acts, but simply because we were continuing to live as we had in the late 1950s. As before, we read *samizdat* behind closed doors, in near-secrecy watched forbidden films shown only to friends … Culture took up residence underground' (115).
14. Riazanov, 104–6 *passim*.
15. Khrisanf Khersonskii, 'Èstetika v deistvii', *IK* 9 (1967): 79.
16. Shilova, 99.
17. Lynn Attwood (ed.), *Red Women on the Silver Screen* (London: 1993), 83.
18. Shepitko took the part of the character's cool, rational and critical alter-ego, standing off-camera and arguing with the actress. Inna Levshina, 'Ot epizodov *Kryl'i*', *IK* 11 (1966): 85.
19. Giovanni Buttafava, cited by Marcel Martin, *Le Cinéma Soviétique de Khrouchtchev à Gorbatchev* (Lausanne: 1993), 57.
20. *Domashniaia sinemateka*, ed. Sergei Zemlianukhin and Miroslava Segida (Moscow: 1996), 218; *Ekran 1966–1967*, 16.
21. Anninskii, 218.
22. Jane Taubman, 'The Cinema of Kira Muratova', *Russian Review* 52 (July 1993): 371.

23. Fomin, 19–20.

24. Anna Lawton, *Kinoglasnost: Soviet Cinema in Our Time* (Cambridge: 1992), 113.

25. Richard Stites, *Russian Popular Culture: Entertainment and Society since 1900* (Cambridge: 1992), 158.

26. Fomin, 55.

27. N. Kovarskii, 'Chelovek i vremia', *IK* 10 (1968): 56. Taubman notes that this was 'probably the only contemporary review of the film'; a planned defence by Leonid Gurevich, slated to follow Kovarskii's piece, did not appear (370).

28. Neia Zorkaia, 'Vokrug kartiny *Iul'skii dozhd*'', *IK* 2 (1968): 27, 33.

29. Evgenii Margolit, 'Peizazh s geroem', *Kinematograf ottepeli*, ed. V. Troianovskii (Moscow: 1996), 113.

30. Cited by Miron Chernenko, *Marlen Khutsiev: Tvorcheskii portret* (Moscow: 1988), 20. As he notes, the language typifies official criticism during this period.

31. Anninskii, 143.

18. Farewell, My Lovely

1. Lev Kulidzhanov, 'Doklad "Kommunisticheskoe stroitel'stvo i zadachi sovetskoi kinematografii"', *IK* 12 (1965): xx (supplement).

2. Aleksei Romanov, *Nravstvennyi ideal v sovetskom kinoiskusstve* (Moscow: 1971), 113–15.

3. Ibid., 117–22.

4. Cited by Marcel Martin, *Le Cinéma Soviétique de Khrouchtchev à Gorbatchev* (Lausanne: 1993), 63.

5. See the interesting discussion between Nina Tsyrkun and Aleksandr Shpagin after Shpagin organized a retrospective of such films for Russian television. 'Istoriia kino – zhivoi organizm', *IK* 2 (1998): 111–17.

6. In Aleksandr Timofeevskii's iconoclastic view, the intellectuals of the thaw destroyed Russia's potential for democracy by reviving the collectivist utopianism of the 1920s instead of cultivating the 'salon' dream of post-war Stalinism. 'Poslednie romantiki', *IK* 5 (1989): 62; tr., 'The Last Romantics', in *Russian Critics on the Cinema of Glasnost*, ed. Michael Brashinsky and Andrew Horton (Cambridge: 1994), 24–9.

Filmography

This filmography includes Soviet films that receive more than passing reference in the text. They are listed in alphabetical order of my English translation, followed by the Russian title, the name of the director(s) and the year of production, with major discrepancies of release date noted.

Adventures of a Dentist [Pokhozhdenie zubnogo vracha, 1965] Elem Klimov

Alien Kin [Chuzhaia rodnia, 1955] Mikhail Shveitser

The Amphibious Man [Chelovek-amfibiia, 1962] Gennadii Kazanskii and Vladimir Chebotarev

And Quiet Flows the Don [Tikhii Don, 1958] Sergei Gerasimov

And What If It's Love? [A esli èto liubov'?, 1962] Iulii Raizman

Andrei Rublev [1966, rel. 1971] Andrei Tarkovskii

Ballad of a Soldier [Ballada o soldate, 1959] Grigorii Chukhrai

The Big Family [Bol'shaia sem'ia, 1954] Iosif Kheifits

A Boy Like That [Zhivet takoi paren', 1964] Vasilii Shukshin

Brief Encounters [Korotkie vstrechi, 1967] Kira Muratova

Carnival Night [Karnaval'naia noch', 1956] Eldar Riazanov

Ch.P.: An Extraordinary Event [ChP: Chrezvychainoe proisshestvie, 1959] Viktor Ivchenko

The Chairman [Predsedatel', 1964] Aleksei Saltykov

Clear Skies [Chistoe nebo, 1961] Grigorii Chukhrai

Clouds over Borsk [Tuchi nad Borskom, 1960] Vasilii Ordynskii

Colleagues [Kollegi, 1962] Aleksei Sakharov

Come Back Tomorrow [Prikhodite zavtra, 1963] Evgenii Tashkov

The Communist [Kommunist, 1958] Iulii Raizman

The Cranes are Flying [Letiat zhuravli, 1957] Mikhail Kalatozov

Don Quixote [Don Kikhot, 1957] Grigorii Kozintsev

Everything Remains for People [Vse ostaetsia liudiam, 1964] Georgii Natanson

Faithful Friends [Vernye druz'ia, 1954] Mikhail Kalatozov

The Fate of a Man [Sud'ba cheloveka, 1959] Sergei Bondarchuk

The Fiery Miles [Ognennye versty, 1957] Samson Samsonov

The First Echelon [Pervyi eshelon, 1956] Mikhail Kalatozov

Filmography

The First Teacher [Pervyi uchitel', 1965] Andrei Mikhalkov-Konchalovskii

The Forty-first [Sorok-pervyi, 1956] Grigorii Chukhrai

The Frozen Sea [More studenoe, 1954] Iurii Egorov

Give Me the Complaint Book [Daite zhalobnuiu knigu, 1965] Eldar Riazanov

Grown-Up Children [Vzroslye deti, 1962] Villen Azarov

Hamlet [Gamlet, 1964] Grigorii Kozintsev

Heights [Vysota, 1957] Aleksandr Zarkhi

The House I Live in [Dom, v kotorom ia zhivu, 1957] Lev Kulidzhanov and Iakov Segel

Hussar Ballad [Gussarskaia ballada, 1964] Eldar Riazanov

I am Cuba [Ia – Kuba, 1964] Mikhail Kalatozov

I Walk Around Moscow [Ia shagaiu po Moskve, 1963] Georgii Danelia

Ilich's Gate [Zastava Il'icha, 1961; rel. 1965 as *I am Twenty* (Mne dvadtsat' let)] Marlen Khutsiev

Immortal Garrison [Bessmertnyi garnizon, 1956] Zakhar Agranenko

It Happened in Penkovo [Delo bylo v Pen'kove, 1957] Stanislav Rostotskii

Ivan's Childhood [Ivanovo detstvo, 1962] Andrei Tarkovskii

July Rain [Iiul'skii dozhd', 1967] Marlen Khutsiev

Land and People [Zemlia i liudi, 1955] Stanislav Rostotskii

Leaffall [Listopad, 1966] Otar Ioseliani

The Lesson of Life [Urok zhizni, 1955] Iulii Raizman

Liana [1955] Boris Barnet

The Living and the Dead [Zhivye i mertvye, 1964] Aleksandr Stolper

Man Follows the Sun [Chelovek idet za solntsem, 1961] Mikhail Kalik

The Man from Nowhere [Chelovek niotkuda, 1961] Eldar Riazanov

Midshipman Panin [Michman Panin, 1960] Mikhail Shveitser

The Miracle Worker [Chudotvornaia, 1960] Vladimir Skuibin

Murder on Dante Street [Ubiistvo na ulitse Dante, 1956] Mikhail Romm

My Dear Man [Dorogoi moi chelovek, 1958] Iosif Kheifits

My Younger Brother [Moi mladshii brat, 1962] Aleksandr Zarkhi

Nastasia Filippovna [1958] Ivan Pyrev

A Nasty Tale [Skvernyi anekdot, 1965] Aleksandr Alov and Vladimir Naumov

Nine Days of a Year [Deviat' dnei odnogo goda, 1962] Mikhail Romm

No One Wanted to Die [Nikto ne khotel umirat', 1966] Vitautas Zalakiavicius

Operation 'Y' and Shurik's Other Adventures [Operatsiia 'Y' i drugie prikliucheniia Shurika, 1965] Leonid Gaidai

Ordinary Fascism [Obyknovennyi fashizm, 1965] Mikhail Romm

Pavel Korchagin [1956] Aleksandr Alov and Vladimir Naumov

Peace to Him Who Enters [Mir vkhodiashchemu, 1961] Aleksandr Alov and Vladimir Naumov

A Person is Born [Chelovek rodilsia, 1956] Vasilii Ordynskii

Poem of the Sea [Poema o more, 1958] Iuliia Solntseva

The Prisoner of the Caucasus or the Further Adventures of Shurik [Kavkazkaia plennitsa, ili novye prikliucheniia Shurika 1966] Leonid Gaidai

Restless Youth [Trevozhnaia molodost', 1954] Aleksandr Alov and Vladimir Naumov

The Return of Vasilii Bortnikov [Vozvrashchenie Vasiliia Bortnikova, 1953] Vsevolod Pudovkin

The Rumiantsev Case [Delo Rumiantseva, 1955] Iosif Kheifits

Serezha [1960] Georgii Danelia and Igor Talankin

Shadows of Forgotten Ancestors [Teni zabytykh predkov, 1964] Sergei Paradzhanov

A Simple Story [Prostaia istoriia, 1960] Iurii Egorov

The Sky of Our Childhood [Nebo nashego detstva, 1967] Tolomush Okeev

Soldier Ivan Brovkin [Soldat Ivan Brovkin, 1955] Ivan Lukinskii

A Soldier's Father [Otets soldata, 1964] Revaz Chkheidze

Soldiers [Soldaty, 1956] Aleksandr Ivanov

Someone Else's Children [Chuzhie deti, 1958] Tengiz Abuladze

Someone's Ringing, Open the Door [Zvoniat, otkroite dver', 1965] Aleksandr Mitte

A Spring for the Thirsty [Rodnik dlia zhazhdushchikh, 1965, rel. 1988] Iurii Ilenko

Spring on Zarechnaia Street [Vesna na Zarechnoi ulitse, 1956] Marlen Khutsiev and Feliks Mironer

The Steamroller and the Violin [Katok i skripka, 1960] Andrei Tarkovskii

Stillness [Tishina, 1964] Iurii Bondarev

Tales of Lenin [Rasskazy o Lenine, 1958] Sergei Iutkevich

A Test of Faith [Ispytanie vernosti, 1954] Ivan Pyrev

They were the First [Oni byli pervymi, 1956] Iurii Egorov

Thirty-three [Tridtsat' tri, 1965] Georgii Danelia

Two Fedors [Dva Fedora, 1958] Marlen Khutsiev

The Ulianov Family [Sem'ia Ul'ianovykh, 1957] Valentin Nevzorov

An Unfinished Tale [Neokonchennaia povest', 1955] Fridrikh Ermler

The Unsent Letter [Neotpravlennoe pis'mo, 1959] Mikhail Kalatozov

Volunteers [Dobrovol'tsy, 1958] Iurii Egorov

Watch the Car [Beregis' avtomobilia, 1966] Eldar Riazanov

Welcome, or No Trespassing [Dobro pozhalovat', ili postoronnim vkhod vospreshchen, 1964] Elem Klimov

When the Trees were Big [Kogda derev'ia byli bol'shimi, 1962] Lev Kulidzhanov

Wind [Veter, 1958] Aleksandr Alov and Vladimir Naumov

Wings [Kryl'ia, 1966] Larisa Shepitko

Women [Zhenshchiny, 1965] Pavel Liubimov

Your Son and Brother [Vash syn i brat, 1965] Vasilii Shukshin

Bibliography

This bibliography does not aim to be comprehensive and does not attempt to reproduce endnote citations. It includes books and articles of particular interest for those who wish to pursue the subject further.

Books

Anninskii, Lev, *Shestidesiatniki i my* (Moscow: 1991)

Attwood, Lynn (ed.), *Red Women on the Silver Screen* (London: 1993)

Batalov, Aleksei, *Sud'ba i remeslo* (Moscow: 1984)

Chernenko, Miron, *Marlen Khutsiev: Tvorcheskii portret* (Moscow: 1988)

Cohen, Louis Harris, *The Cultural-Political Traditions and Developments of the Soviet Cinema from 1917 to 1972* (Arno Press Cinema Program: 1973)

Fomin, V., *Vse kraski siuzheta* (Moscow: 1971)

— *Kinopanorama: Sovetskoe kino segodnia* (Moscow: 1974)

— *Polka* (Moscow: 1992)

Fomin, V. (ed.), *Kino i vlast'* (Moscow: 1996)

Germanova, I. G. and N. B. Kuz'mina (eds), *Moi rezhisser Romm* (Moscow: 1993)

Golovskoy, Val S. (ed.), *Ekran 1966–1967* (Moscow: 1967)

Golovskoy, Val S. with John Rimberg, *Behind the Soviet Screen: The Motion-Picture Industry in the USSR 1972–1982* (Ann Arbor, MI: 1986)

Horton, Andrew and Michael Brashinsky, *The Zero Hour: Glasnost and Soviet Cinema in Transition* (Princeton, NJ: 1992)

Johnson, Priscilla and Leopold Labedz (eds), *Khrushchev and the Arts: The Politics of Soviet Culture, 1962–1964* (Cambridge, MA: 1965)

Johnson, Vida T. and Graham Petrie, *The Films of Andrei Tarkovsky: A Visual Fugue* (Bloomington, IN: 1994)

Kardin, V., *Dostoinstvo iskusstva: razdum'ia o teatre i kinematografe nashikh dnei* (Moscow: 1967)

Kenez, Peter, *Cinema and Soviet Society 1917–1953* (Cambridge: 1992)

Khlopliankina, Tatiana, *Zastava Il'icha: Sud'ba fil'ma* (Moscow: 1990)

Kino: èntsiklopedicheskii slovar' (Moscow: 1986)

Kogan, L. N. (ed.), *Kino i zritel': Opyt sotsiologicheskogo issledovaniia* (Moscow: 1968)

Korobov, Vladimir, *Vasilii Shukshin* (Moscow: 1988)

Lawton, Anna, *Kinoglasnost: Soviet Cinema in Our Time* (Cambridge: 1992)

Leyda, Jay, *Kino: A History of the Russian and Soviet Film* (Princeton, NJ: 1960)

Macheret, A., *O poetike kinoiskusstva* (Moscow: 1981)

Margolit, Evgenii, *Sovetskoe kinoiskusstvo. Osnovnye ètapy stanovleniia i razvitiia* (Moscow: 1988)

Mar'iamov, G. B. (ed.), *Ivan Pyr'ev: v zhizni i na èkrane* (Moscow: 1994)

Marsh, Rosalind, *Soviet Fiction Since Stalin: Science, Politics and Literature* (London: 1986)

Martin, Marcel, *Le Cinéma Soviétique de Khrouchtchev à Gorbatchev* (Lausanne: 1993)

Merkel', Maia, *Ugol zreniia* (Moscow: 1980)

Mervol'f, N. R. (ed.), *Molodye rezhissery sovetskogo kino: sbornik statei* (Leningrad–Moscow: 1962)

Nagibin, Iurii, *Dnevnik* (Moscow: 1996)

Nekhoroshev, A., *Techenie fil'ma: o kinematograficheskom siuzhete* (Moscow: 1975)

Nekrasov, Viktor, *Both Sides of the Ocean*, tr. Elias Kulukundis (London: 1964)

Och, Sheila, *Lenin im sowjetischen Spielfilm*, Studien zum Theater, Film und Fernsehen 17 (Frankfurt: 1992)

Poznanskaia, L. (ed.), *Ekran 1967–1968* (Moscow: 1968)

Riazanov, Eldar, *Nepodvedennye itogi* (Moscow: 1995)

Romanov, Aleksei, *Nravstvennyi ideal v sovetskom kinoiskusstve* (Moscow: 1971)

Romm, Mikhail, *Besedy o kino* (Moscow: 1964)

— *Kogda fil'm okonchen* (Moscow: 1964)

— *Izbrannye proizvedeniia v 3–kh t.* (Moscow: 1981)

— *Ustnye rasskazy* (Moscow: 1991)

Schwarz, Boris, *Music and Musical Life in Soviet Russia 1917–1970* (London: 1972)

Shilova, Irina, ... *I moe kino* (Moscow: 1993)

Shlapentokh, Dmitry and Vladimir, *Soviet Cinematography 1918–1991* (New York: 1993)

Shukshin, Vasilii, *Nravstvennost' est' Pravda* (Moscow: 1976)

— *Voprosy samomu sebe* (Moscow: 1981)

Sovetskie khudozhestvennye fil'my. Annotirovannyi katalog, vols 1–3 (Moscow: 1961); vol. 4 (Moscow: 1967); vol. 5 (Moscow: 1979)

Stamboltsian, M., *Problemy kino i televideniia* 2 (Erevan: 1984)

Stites, Richard, *Russian Popular Culture: Entertainment and Society since 1900* (Cambridge: 1992)

Tarkovsky, Andrey, *Sculpting in Time: Reflections on the Cinema*, tr. Kitty Hunter-Blair (London: 1986)

Tiurin, Iurii, *Kinematograf Vasiliia Shukshina* (Moscow: 1984)

Troianovskii, Vitalii (ed.), *Kinematograf ottepeli* (Moscow: 1996)

Youngblood, Denise J., *Movies for the Masses: Popular Cinema and Soviet Society in the 1920s* (Cambridge: 1992)

Zak, Mark, *Mikhail Romm i ego fil'my* (Moscow: 1988)

Zarkhi, Aleksandr, *O samom glavnom: zametki kinorezhissera* (Moscow: 1964)

Zemlianukhin, Sergei and Miroslava Segida (eds), *Domashniaia sinemateka* (Moscow: 1996)

Zorkaia, Neia, *Portrety* (Moscow: 1966)
— *The Illustrated History of Soviet Cinema* (New York: 1991)
— *Mir i fil'my Andreia Tarkovskogo* (Moscow: 1991)

Articles

This list excludes articles from *Iskusstvo kino* between 1953 and 1967, since the text makes use of virtually every issue published during that period. It includes articles in other periodicals and in *Iskusstvo kino* from other years.

Anninskii, Lev and Larisa Kriachko, 'Sut' poiska: kriticheskii dialog', *Oktiabr'* 8 (1962)

Demenok, A., '*Zastava Il'icha* – urok istorii', *IK* 6 (1988)

Derevianko, Tat'iana, 'Vernemsia v 1965–yi ... ', *IK* 12 (1990)

Fomin, Valerii, 'Nikakoi èpokhi kul'ta lichnosti ne bylo ... ili Kak kino izbavliali ot kramol'noi temy', *IK* 1 (1989)

— 'Na bratskikh mogilakh ne staviat krestov ... ' *IK* 1 (1990)

Ianov, Aleksandr, 'Polozhitel'nyi geroi ili Don Kikhot?', and A. Karaganov, 'Trubnikov snova pod ognem', *Voprosy literatury* 8 (1966)

Kozintsev, Grigorii, 'Iz rabochikh tetradei: 1958–1969 gody', *IK* 8 (1989)

— 'Iz rabochikh tetradei raznykh let', *IK* 8 (1992)

Kriachko, Larisa, 'Boi "za dobrotu"', *Oktiabr'* 3 (1965)

Lazarev, Lazar, 'Nevynosimo trudno zhit' i rabotat',' *IK* 4 (1991)

Liukov, Valentin and Iurii Panov, 'Èto li gorizonty?' *Oktiabr'* 5 (1962)

Novikov, V., 'Khudozhestvennyi poisk', *Znamia* 12 (1965)

Shilova, Irina, 'Pobeda i porazhenie,' *Kinovedcheskie zapiski* 17 (1993)

— 'Cherno-beloe kino', *Kinovedcheskie zapiski* 32 (1996–97)

Shrayer, Maxim, 'Why Are the Cranes Still Flying?', *Russian Review* 56 (July 1997)

Strokov, P., 'Pravda zhizni i pravdopodobie', *Oktiabr'* 11 (1962)

Taubman, Jane, 'The Cinema of Kira Muratova', *Russian Review* 52 (July 1993) '"Tiazhko, tovarishchi!" Obsuzhdenie fil'ma *Mir vkhodiashchemu*', *IK* 5 (1990)

Timofeevskii, Aleksandr, 'Poslednie romantiki', *IK* 5 (1989); tr. 'The Last Romantics', in *Russian Critics on the Cinema of Glasnost*, ed. Michael Brashinsky and Andrew Horton (Cambridge: 1994)

Troianovskii, Vitalii, '*Letiat zhuravli* tret' veka spustia', *Kinovedcheskie zapiski* 17 (1993)

Tsyrkun, Nina and Aleksandr Shpagin, 'Istoriia kino – zhivoi organizm', *IK* 2 (1998)

Turbin, V., 'Zhivoi ogon'', *Molodaia gvardiia* 2 (1965)

Turovskaia, Maia, 'Ballada o soldate', *Novyi mir* 4 (1961)

— 'Prozaicheskoe i poeticheskoe kino segodnia', *Novyi mir* 9 (1962)

Turovskaia, Maia and Iurii Khaniutin, 'Romm, kinokamera i my', *IK* 3 (1988)

Vinokurova, Tatiana, 'Khozhdenie po mukam ,Andreia Rubleva'', *IK* 10 (1989)

Youngblood, Denise, 'Post-Stalinist Cinema and the Myth of World War II: Tarkovskii's *Ivan's Childhood* (1962) and Klimov's *Come and See* (1985)', *Historical Journal of Film, Radio and Television* 14.4 (1994)

Index

Index

Index

Index